Thomas Baines, Edward Baines

Yorkshire, past and present

A history and a description of the three ridings of the great county of York, from

the earliest ages to the year 1870: Vol. II

Thomas Baines, Edward Baines

Yorkshire, past and present
A history and a description of the three ridings of the great county of York, from the earliest ages to the year 1870: Vol. II

ISBN/EAN: 9783337560539

Printed in Europe, USA, Canada, Australia, Japan

Cover: Foto ©ninafisch / pixelio.de

More available books at **www.hansebooks.com**

YORKSHIRE,

PAST AND PRESENT:

A HISTORY AND A DESCRIPTION OF

THE THREE RIDINGS OF THE GREAT COUNTY OF YORK,

FROM THE EARLIEST AGES TO THE YEAR 1870;

WITH AN ACCOUNT OF ITS

MANUFACTURES, COMMERCE, AND CIVIL AND MECHANICAL ENGINEERING.

By THOMAS BAINES,
AUTHOR OF "LANCASHIRE AND CHESHIRE, PAST AND PRESENT," ETC.

INCLUDING

AN ACCOUNT OF THE WOOLLEN TRADE OF YORKSHIRE,

By EDWARD BAINES, M.P.,
AUTHOR OF "THE HISTORY OF THE COTTON MANUFACTURE," ETC., ETC.

VOL. II.

WILLIAM MACKENZIE, 22 PATERNOSTER ROW, LONDON;
LEEDS, 27 PARK SQUARE; LIVERPOOL, 14 GREAT GEORGE STREET;
MANCHESTER, 65 DALE STREET; NEWCASTLE-ON-TYNE, 74 CLAYTON STREET.

YORKSHIRE:

PAST AND PRESENT.

CHAPTER I.

HISTORY OF THE PRINCIPAL CITIES AND TOWNS OF YORKSHIRE.

HAVING in the first volume of this work given a general description and history of the county of York, we now proceed to supply a more detailed account of its principal cities, boroughs, seaports, and towns. This we shall follow, in a subsequent division, by a history and description of the wapentakes, parishes, and townships of Yorkshire, thus completing our account of this extensive county. We commence our second volume with a history of the ancient and celebrated city of York, which was for so many ages the capital of Roman Britain, and is still one of the most interesting cities in the British dominions. We shall afterwards trace the history of the populous and flourishing manufacturing towns of Leeds, Bradford, Halifax, Huddersfield, Wakefield, and Dewsbury, the principal seats of the woollen manufacture, which has for so many ages formed the chief industry of Yorkshire. We shall also give an account of Sheffield and the populous Hallamshire district, which have so long held the first rank in the manufacture of cutlery, and at the present day have united to their ancient industries many great branches of business unknown in former times. In this portion of the work we shall likewise trace the history of the port and commerce of Hull, the great outlet of the commerce of Yorkshire, from early times to the present day; and also that of the other seaports of the county, including Scarborough, Whitby, Bridlington, and Middlesborough, the last of which has sprung into importance in the present generation, under the influence of a sudden and great development of mining industry and wealth. We commence with an account of the ancient city of York.

THE HISTORY OF THE CITY OF YORK.

Eboracum, or York, as the Capital of the Roman Province of Britain.—York, the Eboracum of the Romans, is one of the oldest cities in Britain, having a history, supported by written or printed evidences, extending over a period of upwards of 1700 years. Eboracum is first mentioned by name by Claudius Ptolemy, the Greek geographer of Alexandria, in his account of the geography of the ancient world, supposed to have been written between A.D. 138 and A.D. 161; but it is believed that the British Aberach or Everach was founded by the Britons previous to the Roman invasion, and that it was occupied and fortified as a stationary camp by Julius Agricola, about the year 79 of the Christian era. Ptolemy speaks of Eboracum as being in his time a Roman station, and the head-quarters of one of the three or four legions, which held Britain in subjection to the Roman empire. The legion thus spoken of, and which was permanently established at Eboracum, or York, was the Sixth Victorious Legion. This was sent into Britain by Hadrian, A.D. 117, and its head-quarters appear to have been chiefly at York for nearly 300 years, namely, from the reign of that emperor to the final retirement of the Roman armies from Britain, about the year 420 of the Christian era. But during a considerable portion of this time the Romans had another legion at York, namely, the Ninth, or Spanish legion, *Legio Nona Hispanica;* and for a small part of it also the Second Augustan Legion.* This concentration of troops is accounted for by the military necessities of the Roman dominion in Britain; for not only was Eboracum, or York, the capital of the Roman province of Britain, and the seat of the imperial government, but it was also situated near the border of what was then the most exposed frontier of the empire. The position of the Sixth Legion at York was much more liable to attack than that of the Twentieth Victorious Legion, whose head-quarters were at Deva, the present Chester, on the borders of what we now call North Wales; or than that of the Second Augustan Legion, whose head-quarters were long at Isca Silurum, afterwards known as Caer Leon, near the present Newport, on the borders of South Wales, districts which were soon thoroughly subdued by the Romans.

Eboracum is supposed to have been selected as the military capital of Britain by Julius Agricola, at the close of his second

* Eburacum, or York, under the Romans. By C. Wellbeloved, p. 12, 1842.

campaign in Britain, when many cities and states submitted to the Roman authority;* and it was, probably, of this amongst other military positions chosen by Agricola in Britain, that Tacitus the historian, and the son-in-law of that great commander, stated that they were selected with so much judgment and attention that none of the newly explored parts of Britain were left unguarded. For more than 1500 years Eboracum, or York, under various names, was the military bulwark of this part of Britain. There is no inscription which establishes the date at which the Roman walls of Eboracum were erected, but it is probable that they were built at the time when that city became the head-quarters of the Sixth Legion, in the reign of the Emperor Hadrian. This is rendered likely, not only by the fact of Hadrian's visit to Britain, but by the circumstance of that emperor having been the builder of many other great works, in the northern parts of Britain, including the Roman wall extending from sea to sea, and some of the principal military roads. The Roman walls of Eboracum included a quadrangular space of about 650 yards from east to west, and 550 yards from north to south, and the camp contained an area of nearly seventy acres.† The Roman fortification stood in an angle of land formed by the junction of the river Fosse with the river Ouse, in a position of considerable natural strength, and was easily defended, reinforced, and supplied with munitions of war, both by land and by water.‡

The name of Eboracum is supposed to be a Romanized form either of the British word Aberach, which is said to mean the "mound by the confluence," namely, that of the river Ouse with the Fosse; or of Everach, which means "the mound by the Ure," and implies that in former times the name of the Ure was given to what we now call the Ouse, at least as far down the stream as Eboracum, or York. But we are told by Ptolemy that the ancient name of the Humber was the Abus, a name evidently derived from the circumstance of its being the great receptacle of the almost innumerable streams which flow into it, and discharge their waters through its mouth into the sea. We have no means of knowing how far up the stream the Abus bore the name mentioned by Ptolemy; but it may perhaps have been almost as far as the estuaries and rivers of the Thames and Severn, which

---

* Eboracum. C. Wellbeloved p. 9.   † Eboracum. C. Wellbeloved, p. 53.
‡ Professor John Phillips' Yorkshire, p. 76.

seem to have been always known by the same name from the springs of the main stream, down to the point at which their collected waters fall into the sea. It is not improbable that this may also have been the case with the Abus, or at all events that the name may have extended up the stream, at least as far as the tideway reaches, which is to the immediate neighbourhood of the ancient Eboracum, the present city of York, if not to the junction of the Ure and the Swale, above that city. Supposing that to have been the case, the name of the ancient Aberach of the Britons, the Eboracum of the Romans, may have been derived from the Abus, and Aberach may have been the mound or fortification by the Abus. This seems to be at least as probable as that the name was derived from the junction of so small a stream as the Fosse with the river Ouse. The meaning of the latter word, Ouse, is supposed to be merely "the water," and to be derived from the British word Uisge, meaning "water;" and that is also the meaning of the word Eure, derived from a more ancient language than that of the Celts.[*] There seems, however, to be no doubt that the name of Eboracum was derived from the confluence of two or more of the streams of this well-watered district, though whether it was from the Abus, the stream into which all the rivers of Yorkshire, and most of those of the midland district, flow; from the river Eure, which joins the Ouse several miles above the city of York; or from the junction of the river Fosse with the Ouse at York—must remain somewhat doubtful. The Fosse clearly bears a Roman name, and owes that name to the circumstance of its having formed part of the fosse or trench around the city, at the time when Eboracum was a Roman fortress; but we have no means of knowing what was the Celtic name of the Fosse.

But leaving these ancient names, it may be useful to mention the advantages, for the purpose of inland navigation, of the streams, which, under various appellations, discharge their waters into the Abus, or Humber, either flowing under the walls of York or joining the same stream further down, with the lengths of their respective courses. The most important of these streams are the Ouse, which has a course of fifty-nine miles in length, and which above the city of York receives the Swale, seventy-one miles in length, the Eure, sixty-one miles, the Nidd, fifty-five miles, and

[*] See vol. i. p. 306 of this work.

the Wiske, twenty-five miles. Immediately opposite to York it receives the Fosse, seventeen miles in length. Below that city the Ouse receives the Wharfe, seventy-five miles in length; the Aire, eighty-seven miles; the Calder, forty-seven miles; the Don or Dun, sixty-eight miles; and the Derwent, seventy-two miles. In addition to these Yorkshire streams—all of which may have been used at certain seasons of the year, when moderately full of water, for the purpose of floating down the produce of the surrounding country, either to York, or into the tideway of the Humber and the Ouse, which has an easy communication at all times and seasons with York—that city also possessed, by means of the Ouse and the Humber, a regular and easy line of inland communication, by means of the great river Trent and its tributaries, as far as the present Lincoln, Nottingham, Derby, and even Leicester. The Romans, who dreaded the open sea, and especially the tides of the Atlantic, availed themselves eagerly of the safe, easy, and cheap resources of inland navigation; and the streams which we have mentioned afforded them the means of inland navigation between Eboracum and the central parts of Britain. Nearly the whole of the Roman commerce across Gaul was carried on by means of navigable rivers, extending from the Mediterranean to the British Channel, with only occasional portages from one stream to another; and there is no doubt that so sensible and practical a people as the Romans employed the inland navigation of Britain for similar purposes. Whether they were the original constructors of the short canal, only eight miles in length, which connected the city of Lincoln with the river Trent, and thus formed a line of water communication between the two great Roman stations of Eboracum and Lindum (York and Lincoln), as well as an uninterrupted line of inland navigation from Eboracum to what is now known as the southern part of the coast of Lincolnshire, is a matter of some uncertainty. But the name of the Fosse of Lincolnshire, like that of the Fosse of Yorkshire, is Roman, and the canal which bears that name, and seems to have given it to the adjoining Roman road, is so short as to be quite insignificant in comparison with canals that were formed by the Romans in Italy and in the north of Europe. We are told by Tacitus that one of the Roman commanders formed a scheme for uniting one of the tributaries of the Rhone with one of those of the Rhine, and of thus connecting the Mediterranean with the German Ocean, by an uninterrupted line of inland navigation; and we are also informed by the same writer that another of the Roman generals, Drusus, formed a canal (*fossa Drusi*) from the river Rhine into the Flevus, the present Zuyder Zee, through which the Roman fleet forced its way into the North Sea.*

The river Ouse was exactly such a stream as the Romans preferred in the choice of their seaports. The tides nearly exhaust themselves in reaching that part of the river Ouse on which Eboracum was built, seldom rising there to a greater height than five or six feet above the ordinary level of the fresh water. In this respect the position of Eboracum would be regarded by the Romans as much more favourable than that of Hull; the rise of the average tides at Naburn Lock on the Ouse, a few miles below the city of York, being about six feet four inches, whilst at Hull the average is sixteen feet three inches, and that of the highest tides twenty-six feet four inches.† Such tides as those that prevailed at the mouth of the Humber were quite unmanageable by the Romans, who were accustomed to run their vessels on shore in the winter months, and to load and discharge them on the beaches of rivers; and hence they built their seaports at points at which the tides had nearly exhausted their strength, as at London, Chester, York, and Gloucester. It has been said that a river is a moving road; but a tidal river is a road with the motive power applied both ways, first up and then down the stream, at intervals of a few hours. This circumstance long gave Eboracum an immense advantage, as a place of trade, over all the other towns in the interior, none of which possessed either navigable rivers or the strong motive power of the tides of the ocean, to bring vessels up the stream, or the advantage of great and durable lines of road extending in every direction.

Below the city of Eboracum the Romans had encampments, at Acaster Malbis and Acaster Selby, to protect the navigation of the Ouse. Eboracum was made the seat of a Roman colony, though it is not known by which of the emperors. The forming of a colony implied the settlement of a considerable number of Roman citizens, who received one-third of the land, at the place where the colony was established.‡ This was, no doubt, the case at Eboracum. The vale of York, in the middle of which the ancient Eboracum was built, contains a large portion of the best land in

---

* Tacitus Annal, 2. Cap. 8. † Vol. i. p. 209 of this work. ‡ Schmitz's History of Rome, p. 458.

Yorkshire, and was particularly well suited to become the seat of a flourishing agricultural colony. The rivers were full of fish; and the climate was, as it still is, amongst the healthiest in Britain. The country districts around the city were no doubt peopled by Roman colonists, and all the arts of life are very likely to have been as fully developed at York as in other provincial capitals. Alcuin speaks of Eboracum as a second Rome, the Palatium and Prætorium, that is, the seat of justice and of dominion, in Britain. He also describes it as a great emporium, and place of trade, by sea and land. For many ages it was the principal, if not the only place of trade in the north of Britain, and it was to this circumstance that it owed its early greatness, quite as much as to its military strength and importance. No port in Britain, except London, was better situated than Eboracum for the trade in copper, lead, corn, wool, hides, cattle, and slaves, the chief articles of export sought by the Romans. There were also manufactories of earthenware and probably of glass in the neighbourhood of York, and perhaps furnaces for the smelting of iron. A great forest, known as the Forest of Galtres, "the dwelling of the Gael or Celts," extended from the immediate neighbourhood of Eboracum northward, furnishing abundant supplies of fuel, and also game and skins, the products of the chase.

Amongst the Roman emperors who are known to have visited the city of York were Hadrian, who reigned from A.D. 117 to 138; Septimius Severus, A.D. 193 to 211; Caracalla, A.D. 211 to 217; Constantius, A.D. 305 to 306; and Constantine the Great, A.D. 306 to 337. The last of these was proclaimed emperor at Eboracum.

At the time of Hadrian's visit the Roman dominion in Britain had been considerably shaken by insurrections amongst the Brigantes, the Caledonians, and other powerful British tribes. In order to maintain the Roman authority, Hadrian constructed a very extensive system of fortresses and of military roads, extending through the greater part of Britain, especially through the northern provinces. Several of these roads, or branches connected with them, were united at the city of Eboracum, from which point they formed a safe and easy communication with the eastern and western shores of Britain, at the mouths of the Abus or Humber, and of the Ribble and the Dee; with both the extremities of that great military wall which Hadrian constructed across the northern part of the island, from the mouth of the river Tyne to the Solway Frith; and southward to London, the coast of Kent, Gaul, and Rome.

In the reign of Antoninus Pius, A.D. 138 to 161, the Brigantes again rose in insurrection, being supported by the Caledonians north of the Wall. The Brigantine insurgents were suppressed, after numerous battles, by Lollius Urbicus, who ultimately succeeded in restoring tranquillity in Britain, and fortified the upper isthmus from the Forth to the Clyde. But that position was not long retained by the Romans.

Not many years later the state of affairs in Britain had again become so dangerous, that the Emperor Septimius Severus found it necessary to cross over into Britain, A.D. 204, with his two sons Caracalla and Geta, for the purpose of re-establishing the shaken authority of Rome. He remained at Eboracum for a considerable time, and there collected a large Roman army, at the head of which he advanced into Caledonia, overrunning the more open and level portions of the country, on the southern and eastern coasts of Scotland, and compelling the Caledonians to retire into the rugged mountain ranges, forming the north-western angle of Britain. For a while the emperor, having overcome the enemy in the open field, supposed that all effectual resistance was vanquished, and at the end of the campaign he returned to Eboracum in triumph. But scarcely had he marched southward when the Caledonians issued from their concealments in the moors, glens, and forests, and soon after the arrival of Severus at York, he had the mortification to learn that the people of the whole of North Britain were again in arms. The emperor's health had suffered severely in this northern campaign, in which the Roman army sustained, as well as inflicted, enormous losses. His illness increased rapidly, and he died soon after at Eboracum, partly from the mortification of defeat, partly from disease, and breathing out murderous threats against the Caledonians, on whom he urged his two sons to wage a war of extermination. His sons almost immediately removed from Eboracum to Rome, to plot for the favour of the army, and to plan each other's destruction; and there it was that Geta, the better of the two, was murdered by the guards of Caracalla, his brother, almost in the presence of his mother. According to Spartian, the Emperor Severus, after his first campaign in Caledonia, greatly strengthened the rampart from sea to sea, originally erected by the

Emperor Hadrian; but it has been shown by the Rev. Mr. Hodgson, the historian of Northumberland, and by one of the most learned of the many able writers whom York has produced—the Rev. Charles Wellbeloved—that the most important parts of the Roman wall, if not the whole, were erected by the Emperor Hadrian, and that there is little authority for believing that Septimius Severus did anything to it, beyond repairing the injuries sustained after the departure of Hadrian from Britain.* A natural hill in the immediate neighbourhood of York still bears the name of Severs Ho, or the hill of Severus; and there was a tradition that the body of Septimius Severus was there consumed on the funeral pile. The ashes of the emperor are said to have been conveyed to Rome, in a porphyry or an alabaster vase, for interment, in an imperial sepulchre, by the Appian Way.

The Emperor Constantius Chlorus also died at York in A.D. 306. He had come over into Britain to suppress the insurrection of Carausius and Alectus, the former a naval chief of Menapian origin, the latter his minister, and afterwards his assassin. Constantius was succeeded by his much more celebrated son, Constantine the Great, A.D. 306 to 337, who first publicly proclaimed himself a believer in the Christian religion, and made Christianity the established religion of the Roman empire. It was long contended that Constantine was born at Eboracum, and that he was thus a native of Britain; and it was also asserted that his mother, the Empress Helena, was the daughter of a British chief or king; but modern investigations have destroyed the belief in both these traditions. There is no doubt that the Roman army first saluted Constantine as emperor at York, on the death of Constantius. About this time the Roman empire was divided into four præfectures, namely, those of Italy, Gaul, Illyria, and the East. Britain was included in the præfecture of Gaul, and was subdivided into three parts or principalities—namely, Britannia Prima, or the country in the south of Britain, the chief town being Londinum, or London; Britannia Secunda or the country of the west, of which Isca Colonia, or Silurum, afterwards known to the Britons as Caer Leon, was the capital; and Maxima, or Flavia Cæsariensis, the Roman dominion in the north of Britain, the capital of which, and of the whole province of Britain, was Eboracum or York.

* Eboracum. C. Wellbeloved, p. 10.

Constantine the Great died in the year 337, and though the Romans continued to hold sway in Britain for about seventy years after that event, their writers make few and scanty references to this island. The Sixth Legion remained in its old quarters at Eboracum until the final abandonment of Britain by the Roman armies. The Ninth Legion was also stationed at York, but it is supposed to have been early dissolved as a separate force, and incorporated with the sixth. The Second Legion, long transferred from Eboracum to Isca Silurum, had by this time been removed to Rutupiæ, or Richborough, in Kent, to guard the passage of the channel.*

The Roman coins found and preserved at York extend over a period of about 400 years, and form historical evidence of the presence of the Romans at Eboracum during the greater part of that period. The coins commence a few years previous to the invasion of Britain by the Romans, and continue to within a few years of their final retirement from this island. The first coins of the series are those of the Emperor Augustus, which we may date about thirty years previous to the Christian era, as that was the time when he was rendered secure in the possession of the imperial power, by his great victory over Antonius in the battle of Actium; and the coins found at York come down to the reign of the Emperor Gratianus, A.D. 383.† The coins discovered at York show very few gaps in this long period of time, and they would no doubt have been quite complete, if anything like the care now given to the preservation of Roman coins and antiquities found at York had been bestowed in former times. The following are the coins of Roman emperors given in the list furnished in Wellbeloved's "Eburacum," which include most of those in the collection made by Mr. Longwith of York, between the years 1700 and 1727, for his son, the Rev. Dr. Longwith of Petworth, Sussex.

The series commences with coins of Augustus, who was born B.C. 61, and who became unopposed emperor, B.C. 31. Next are the coins of the Emperor Tiberius, his successor, A.D. 14 to 37. These are succeeded by those of Caligula, A.D. 37-41, and by the coins of Claudius, A.D. 41-54, in which reign Britain was invaded by the Roman armies and partially conquered. Then come those of Nero, A.D. 54-68, in whose reign Britain was nearly lost to

* Appendix to Drake's Antiquities of York. † Notitia Imperii.

the Romans by the insurrection of Boadicea. Next come those of Galba, A.D. 68-9, and of Otho and Vitellius, both of whom reigned for a few months, A.D. 69. These are followed by Vespasian, A.D. 70-79, and it was in the last year of this emperor's reign that the Brigantes, the ancient inhabitants of Yorkshire, were conquered by Agricola, and that their capital city, Aberach or Eboracum, was captured by that commander, and made the capital of the Roman province of Britain. Coins have also been found at York of the Emperors Titus, 79-81; Domitian, 81-96; Nerva, 96-98; Trajan, 98-117; and of Hadrian, 117-134. The Sixth Legion was brought over into Britain in the first year of this emperor's reign, and it is probable that the Roman walls of Eboracum were built about this time. In the following reign, namely, that of Antoninus Pius, A.D. 138-161, there was a great insurrection of the Brigantes against the Romans, which, however, failed, as is shown, amongst other evidence, by the coins of that and many succeeding emperors found at York, including those of his immediate successor, Marcus Aurelius, A.D. 161-180; of Commodus, in whose reign the Roman legions in Britain were in full revolt against their commanders,* A.D. 180-192; and of Septimius Severus, A.D. 193-211. This emperor resided at Eboracum for three or four years, and there died. His coins, and those of a long series of his successors, have also been discovered at York, including those of his son Caracalla, A.D. 211-217, and his younger son Geta, who was murdered by his brother, A.D. 212; Elagabalus, A.D. 218-222; Alexander Severus, A.D. 222-235; Maximinus, A.D. 235-238; Gordianus III., A.D. 238-244; Philippus, 244-249, whose name is found on some of the Roman mile-stones in this part of Britain; Decius, A.D. 249-252; Gallus, A.D. 251-253; Valerianus, A.D. 253-260; Gallienus, A.D. 260-268; Postumius, A.D. 267; Tetricus, A.D. 267-274; Diocletian, A.D. 287-305; Maximianus, A.D. 286-305; Carausius, A.D. 288; and Alectus, A.D. 304. The two latter were altogether usurpers, being in open revolt against the recognized Roman emperors. They were vanquished and succeeded by Constantius Chlorus, who came over to Britain, and died at Eboracum, A.D. 305-306. Coins have also been found of the Emperor Constantine the Great, A.D. 306-337, whose name is inseparably connected with Eboracum, and of the Emperors Constans, A.D. 337-350; Magnentius, 353; Julian the Apostate, A.D.

* Schmitz's History of Rome, p. 509.

361-363; Valentinianus, A.D. 364-365; and Gratianus, A.D. 367-383. A fine coin of Honorius, the last Roman emperor who claimed to rule in Britain (A.D. 395-423), was also found in the neighbourhood of York, and was long used on the signet ring of the abbots of Selby.* Coins have also been found of several of the Roman empresses, including the Empress Helena, the wife of the Emperor Constantius, and mother of Constantine the Great, who though not of British birth was long believed to be so, and whose name is still preserved in the city of York and the neighbourhood, in the names of churches and fords of rivers, over which she was supposed to have a safety-giving influence.

The construction of the Roman walls of York was well described nearly 200 years ago by Dr. Martin Lister (one of the earliest members of the Royal Society, and a man equally distinguished by his classical learning and his love for science), in a paper addressed by him to that society. Speaking of the antiquities of this ancient city, in which he then resided, he says:—"Carefully viewing the antiquities of York, the dwelling of at least two of the Roman emperors, Severus and Constantius, I found a part of a wall yet standing which is undoubtedly of that time. It is the south wall of the Mint Yard, and consists of a multangular tower, which did lead to Bootham Bar, and part of a wall which ran the length of Coning, King Street, as he who shall attentively view it on both sides may discern.

"The outside to the river (Ouse) is faced with a very small squared stone of about four inches thick, and laid in levels like our modern brickwork. The length of the stones is not observed, but they are as they fell out in hewing. From the foundation twenty courses of these small squared stones are laid, and over them five courses of Roman brick. These bricks are placed, some lengthways, some endways, in the wall, and were called *lateres diatoni*; after these five courses of brick, other twenty-two courses of small square stones, as before described, are laid, which raise the wall some feet higher; and then five more courses of the same Roman bricks, beyond which the wall is imperfect and capped with modern building. In all this height there is not any casemate or loophole, but one entire and uniform wall, from which we may infer that this wall was built some courses higher, after the same order. The bricks were to be as "thoroughs," or, as it were, so many new found-

* Appendix to Drake's Antiquities of York, p. xii.

ations to that which was to be superstructed, and to bind the two sides firmly together, for the wall itself is only faced with small square stone, and the middle thereof filled with mortar and pebble.

"These bricks are about seventeen inches long, of our measure, about eleven inches broad, and two and a half thick. This, having caused several to be carefully measured, I give in round numbers, and we find them to agree very well with the Roman foot, which the learned antiquary Graves has left us, namely, of its being about half an inch less than ours. They seem to have shrunk in the baking more in the breadth than in the length, which is but reasonable, because of their easier yielding that way; and so, for the same reason, more in thickness, for we suppose them to have been designed in the mould of three Roman inches. This demonstrates Pliny's measure to be true. And indeed, all I have yet seen with us in England are of Pliny's measure, as at Leicester, in the Roman ruin there called the Jews' wall; and at Saint Alban's, as I remember; as well as with us at York.

"I shall only add this remark, that proportion and uniformity, even in the minutest parts of building, are to be plainly perceived, as this ruin of Roman workmanship shows. In our Gothic buildings there is a total neglect of measure and proportion of the courses, as though that was not very material to the beauty of the whole; whereas, indeed, in nature's works it is from the symmetry of the very grain whence arises much of the beauty."*

Since Dr. Martin Lister drew the attention of the public to these ancient walls, nearly 200 years ago, their course has been carefully traced, notwithstanding the immense masses of comparatively modern buildings with which they have been covered in many centuries. The walls have been very clearly traced on three sides, and are thus described in Wellbeloved's "Eburacum:"—"From the remains of three of the walls of Eburacum which have been discovered, we seem warranted in concluding that the Roman city was of a rectangular form of about 650 yards by about 550, inclosed by a wall and rampart mound of earth on the inner side of the wall, and perhaps a fosse without the wall, on the south-west side, extending from the multangular tower nearly to Jubbergate. The south-east wall crossing Feasegate, the new Market Street, Patrick Pool, then proceeding north-west of St. Andrew Gate, and terminating in or near Aldwark" (which means an ancient

* Drake's Antiquities of York, p. 59.

fortification in the Norse language); "the wall on the north-west extending from the multangular tower, by Bootham Bar, probably to the angle of the present city wall in the Deanery Garden. Of a fourth wall no remains are recorded to have been discovered, but it is highly probable that some exist in the rampart of the present city wall on the north-east, or that it was very nearly in the line of that wall. And if the interesting portion of the north-west wall discovered between the multangular tower and Bootham Bar, which has been so particularly described, may be considered as a specimen of the construction of the rest, we may conclude that there were four principal entrances corresponding with the four gates of a Polybian camp, four principal angular towers, and a series of minor towers or turrets, from twenty-four to thirty perhaps in number."

In addition to the Roman walls of York, and to a long series of Roman coins, extending over a period of about 400 years, the presence of these ancient lords of the world at Eboracum is shown by the remains of temples, altars, public baths, private houses, and an almost endless variety of objects connected with their public and private lives. Amongst objects connected with the religion of the Romans are the following:—An altar with an inscription, "To Jupiter, the best and greatest, and to all the friendly Household Gods and Goddesses, by Publius Ælius Marcianus, Præfect of a Cohort, on account of the preservation of the health of himself and his family;" an inscription on a large tablet, now deposited among the Roman remains in the museum of the Yorkshire Philosophical Society, from a temple dedicated to the holy god Serapis, erected from the foundation, most probably near the site where the tablet was discovered, by Claudius Hieronymianus, legate of the Sixth Victorious Legion; a group representing the rites performed in the worship of Mythras, an Eastern god, supposed to be identical with the sun, and connected with the worship of that glorious object; an altar to the Mother Goddesses, erected by a soldier of the Sixth Victorious Legion, in performance of a vow under which he had come; an altar dedicated to the Goddess Fortune, by Sosia Junonia, the daughter of Quintus Antonius Isauricus, of the Augustine Legion; another altar, supposed to have been erected at the time of the visit of Severus, with three figures upon it, which may perhaps represent the Emperor Severus and his two sons, Caracalla and Geta, associated with him in the empire. On one side of this altar three persons are represented sitting in a recess; on another side are two in a standing position; on the third side is one person in the same position; on the fourth side, which has been much injured, there are traces of an altar, and of a victim prepared for sacrifice. Another pedestal has been found inscribed to the Genius of Britain, and erected by Publius Nicomedes, a freedman of the Augusti, probably of Severus and his son Caracalla. Another votive tablet, to the Genius probably of Eboracum, is indefinitely dedicated to the genius of the place. There is also historical evidence of the existence at Eboracum, in the time of Septimius Severus, of a temple to Bellona—Spartian, in his life of that emperor, mentioning that he, on coming to the city after his campaign in Caledonia, desiring to offer sacrifice, was conducted first by a rustic soothsayer to the temple of Bellona, the goddess of war and was considered unfortunate in going to the palace followed by black victims. The position of the Prætorium, or imperial residence, is supposed to have been near the site of the present Bootham Bar, and the gate, lately discovered on the site of the present Bootham Bar, to have been the Prætorian gate. A large set of baths, extending over a very extensive area, has also been discovered near the river Ouse, outside of the walls of the Roman fortification. In these baths many of the tiles bear the inscription of the Sixth Victorious Legion, and others that of the Ninth or Spanish Legion, both of which were so long stationed in the ancient Eboracum. In addition to these remains of public buildings, some beautiful tesselated pavements, the remains of the floors of large public or private buildings, have also been discovered at York, together with immense quantities of ancient pottery, some articles of glass, and many personal ornaments. Amongst the most striking objects connected with the Roman garrison at York are some funereal monuments and inscriptions, recording the death and interment of officers, soldiers, and male and female attendants of the army. It was the custom of the Romans to bury their dead in tombs erected along the sides of their chief high roads. The road leading from Eboracum, first to Calcaria or Tadcaster, but ultimately to Mancunium and Deva in one direction, and to London, Gaul, and Rome, in another, would naturally be regarded as the principal road; and so numerous have been the sepulchral remains in that direction, that we are told it might not inappropriately be called the Street of the Tombs.* But there were other places of burial along the other great lines of Roman road leading out of Eboracum. Among the funereal inscriptions discovered on the sides of these roads some are of great interest. Amongst these is one on a sort of theca or chest, which was prepared for himself, while living, by Marcus Verecundus Diogenes, of Biturix Cubus (supposed to be the present Bourges in France), who had emigrated to Britain, and had become sexumvir of the colony of Eboracum, where he died. Another funereal inscription was erected to the memory of Aurelius Superius, centurion of the Sixth Legion, who lived thirty-eight years, four months, and thirteen days, and to whom Aurelia Censorina, his wife, set up this inscription, dedicated to the gods of the Shades. Another inscription is to Lucius Duccius Rufinus, son of Lucius, of the Voltinian tribe of Vienne, standard-bearer of the Ninth Legion, aged twenty-eight, who is said to be buried here. There is also a touching inscription to Simplicia Florentina, "a most innocent being," who lived ten months, and to whom Felicius Simplex, her father, of the Sixth Victorious Legion, dedicated this inscription. Another imperfect inscription bears the name of Minne or Minna, as that of the person to whom the monument had been erected, and the letters D.M. show that she also had passed to what was supposed to be the dominion of the Manes, the gods of the Shades. With this notice of the funereal inscriptions, and of the declining empire of Rome, we pass away from the curious and interesting history of Eboracum, or York, during the Roman period.

Eoforwic, or York, as the Capital of the Anglian Kings of Northumbria.—We next hear of York under the Anglian name of Eoforwic, as the capital of the Anglian kingdom of Northumbria, which extended from the banks of the Humber, as far north as the swords of the Angles and Saxons could cut a passage, into the ranks of the Celtic tribes. In the time of Bede, Northumbria is spoken of as extending to Abercorn on the river Forth; but this seems to have been an extreme, and probably a temporary northern limit, of the Anglian kingdom. The Anglian name of Eofor-wic either means the "Camp of Eofor"—a corruption of Ebor; or it means the "Camp of the Wild Boar," Wic being the Anglian name for a camp, and Eofor that of a wild boar. This fierce animal was honoured by the Angles, as sacred to their god of war.

* C. Wellbeloved's Eburacum, p. 99.

The Anglian history of York commences with Eadwine or Edwin, the first Christian king, for although we have the names of Ida, Ethelfrith, and one or two others of his pagan predecessors, we know nothing of them, in connection with the city of York, except that they conquered that city about fifty years after the retirement of the Romans from Britain, and that under their influence the Roman name of Eboracum, or possibly the British name of Abcrach, which is mentioned by Nennius, a very early British writer, as still in use, was changed to Eoforwic, and sometimes to Eoforwic-Castre, a curious mixture of Anglian and corrupted Latin.

It appears from an inscription on a coin of King Eadwine, that he was crowned at Eboracum, or Eoforwic, probably about the year 617, ten years previous to the arrival of Paulinus in Northumbria. The inscription on this coin is "Eadwin Rex A.," or Eadwin king of the Angles. On the reverse there is the name of the moneyer by whom the coin was struck, and the place at which it was minted. The name of the moneyer is Seeval, and the name of the place is On Eofor, from the city of Eoforwic, which already was the name given to Eboracum. The mint, which already existed at York, continued in existence for many hundred years, as is shown by a long succession of coins; and it was only in the reign of King William III. that the mint of York ceased to exist, being swallowed up by that of London, after having struck many hundred thousand coins, during many centuries.

We have no information as to the condition of the fortifications of York, either at the time when the Romans retired from Britain, about the year 420, or as to their state when the Celtic Britons were driven out of York by their Anglian conquerors, about 100 years later. There is no reason to believe that the more important military works erected by the Romans at York had then been destroyed, for they built with extreme solidity, and portions of their works are still in existence, after the lapse of 1500 to 1700 years. It was very difficult to destroy works so strong and solid as those of the Romans, in an age when the blasting power of gunpowder, or any stronger disintegrator than the pickaxe, was unknown; and in cases where there was no strong motive for destroying great lines of fortifications, they continued almost uninjured, for much longer periods of time than the 400 years which elapsed between the building of the Roman walls at York, and the conquest of that city by the Angles. The Roman walls at Chester, built in the same age, and of a less solid stone than that of the walls of York, are still in existence, and parts of the Roman work can be traced; and the original line of the Roman fortifications of Eboracum can still be ascertained.* Extensive walls and fortifications were afterwards constructed by the Angles, the Danes, and the Normans, and even so late as the great civil war, when new fortifications were formed at York, in advance of the ancient walls. Most of the names of the bars and gates of York are of Anglian, Danish, or Norman origin, though that of Walmgate is supposed to be derived from the Latin word *vallum*.

The Anglian Minster, or Cathedral Church of York. — The greatest work effected in the city of York by the Anglian kings was the building of the minster. The Angles were not indeed the builders of the minster in its present form, which justly ranks amongst the noblest structures in the north of Europe; but they were the planners and builders of successive churches, some of wood, and others of stone, which stood on the ground covered by the present fabric. Eoforwic, or York, was the See of the great Northumbrian archbishopric, which extended from the Humber almost to the Forth, and even over the Sodor or southern islands of the western seas, of which the Isle of Man forms the chief.† Whatever amount of architectural skill and royal liberality could be brought to bear upon the ecclesiastical buildings at York in this age, were certainly applied to them. Here also was formed a noble library, containing the works of Aristotle, Cicero, Virgil, Pliny, and of the Greek, Latin, and Anglian fathers of the church.‡ These, indeed, were subsequently destroyed in internal wars amongst the Angles themselves, or in the desperate efforts made in resisting the invading Danes and Normans. But York was for several centuries the intellectual as well as the military capital of Britain. We know that it was visited by the Venerable Bede, whose works, dedicated to King Coelwolf, were copied and published there, and that it was the birth-place, and for many years the home of Alcuin, the tutor and librarian of the Emperor Charlemagne, as well as of Archbishops Egbert and Albert, the founders of the library of York, which was the first great library formed in Britain.

There is very little historical evidence as to the condition

---

* See plan of Roman walls of York at commencement of Wellbeloved's Eburacum.
† See vol. i. of this work, p. 401.   ‡ See Alcuin's account of this library, vol. i. p. 405 of this work.

of the Christian church at Eboracum or Aberach (as the Britons called it), in the ages which elapsed between the establishment of Christianity in Britain, and the other provinces of the Roman empire, by Constantine the Great, and the conquest of this part of Britain by the pagan Angles, the worshippers of Thor and Woden, about the year 500 of the Christian era. Three British bishops are mentioned whose names and sees were— Eborius, bishop of Eboracum, Restitutus, bishop of London, and Adelfius, bishop of Isca (Silurum), or Caer Leon. It is the opinion of Lappenberg, that there was an archbishopric of York in those ages, and that the last British archbishop of York was expelled by the pagan Angles about the year 500, and took refuge in Gaul, amongst the Christian inhabitants of Brittany.

Nearly one hundred years after the conquest of this part of Britain by the pagan Angles and Saxons, Christianity was again introduced by Augustine the monk, who was sent into Britain for that purpose by Pope Gregory I. At that time there were only two well established kingdoms in Britain, under the dominion of the Angles and the Saxons. The first was the kingdom of Kent, governed by the Saxon king Ethelbert, and the second the kingdom of Northumbria, governed by Eadwine, one of the descendants of Ina, the first Anglian conqueror of the country extending from the Humber to the Tweed. Under the teaching of Augustine, Christianity was adopted by Ethelbert and the greater part of his subjects, the inhabitants of the Saxon kingdom of Kent; and a few years after, on the marriage of Ethelburga, the daughter of Ethelbert, to Eadwine, king of Northumbria, Augustine, seeing a favourable opportunity for the introduction of Christianity into that country, sent Paulinus, one of the most learned and devoted of his bishops, into Northumbria, in the train of Ethelburga, in order that he might introduce Christianity among the Anglian population of that kingdom. Canterbury, the capital city of the kingdom of Kent, became the seat and residence of Augustine, the first archbishop of Canterbury and of Kent; and York, or Eboracum, became the residence of Paulinus, the first archbishop of Northumbria. Kent and Northumbria were at that time independent kingdoms, and Pope Gregory made their dioceses equal in dignity.[*]

Eadwine, the first Christian king of Northumbria, was baptized

[*] See Pope Gregory's letter, vol. i. p 400 of this work.

at York on Easter Day, April the 12th, A.D. 627, by Paulinus, in a small oratory or chapel built of timber, and standing on part of the ground on which the minster of York now stands. Eadwine soon afterwards began to build a large church, or minster, constructed of stone, in the immediate neighbourhood of the original church of wood, which he intended to inclose within the walls of the enlarged church. But Eadwine did not live to see the completion of this second minster; for scarcely were the walls raised when his kingdom was invaded by Penda, the pagan chief of Mercia, by whom his army was defeated, in a great battle fought at Hatfield, near Doncaster, in the year 633. After that battle, in which Eadwine himself was slain, the city of York was captured by the pagan Mercians, supported by an auxiliary force of Christian Britons, whom the arrogant claims of Augustine had induced to become the allies of the pagan people of Mercia, rather than of the Christians of Northumbria. York was taken by the united forces of the pagans and Britons; the minster was in a great measure destroyed; and Paulinus was compelled to take to flight, and to seek refuge in the Christian kingdom of Kent, taking with him Ethelburga, the daughter of the king of Kent, and the widow of Eadwine. He was there received with great kindness, and appointed bishop of Rochester, which dignity he held until the time of his death, about fourteen years afterwards. A few of the Christian inhabitants of York appear to have kept together, under the instruction of James the deacon, one of the followers of Paulinus, and the head of King Eadwine was afterwards recovered and buried within the walls of the minster of York, of which he was the founder.

About the year 635 the Christians were again triumphant in Northumbria, under the command of Oswald, king and martyr, the son of Ethelfrith. He succeeded in expelling both the Mercians and the Britons. Oswald is numbered amongst the founders of the minster of York, and no doubt was so in intention, if not in fact; but he was slain soon after in another great battle with the pagan armies of Penda. Although something may have been done towards the restoration or the completion of the minster of York by him, and probably also by his brother and successor, Oswy, who finally expelled the pagans from Northumbria, and who founded twelve churches, or minsters, in different parts of Northumbria, the cathedral of York still remained in a very unfinished and, indeed, ruinous condition. About this time extensive lands were settled on the Cathedral Church of York by Ulphus, a Christian sub-regulus of Deira, the southern part of Northumbria. The horn of Ulphus, given with the lands, is still amongst the curiosities of the minster.

The dilapidated condition in which the minster at York was found by Archbishop Wilfrid, so late as the year 669, is minutely described by an ancient chronicler, who states that the timbers of the roof were rotten, the walls decayed, and the windows without glass; that the interior of the building was exposed to the injuries of the weather, and that the birds of the air were the undisturbed inhabitants of the ruined edifice. No sooner, however, had Archbishop Wilfrid obtained the control, than he commenced an effectual repair of the minster. He strengthened the walls, renewed the woodwork of the roof, covered it with lead, protected the windows with glass, whitewashed the walls, and rendered the minster in every respect fit for the services of religion.

The founders of the minster of York, in Anglian times, are mentioned in an inscription drawn up by that accomplished scholar, the Rev. T. Gale, dean of York, which is affixed in the minster. Four persons of Anglian race are dignified with the name of founders of this magnificent building; the first, the date of whose movement in favour of that object is fixed A.D. 627, is Eadwine, king of Northumbria, the first founder; next, in the year 632, is Oswald, king of Northumbria, the second founder; third, in the year 669, is Wilfrid, archbishop of York or Northumbria, the third founder; and fourth, in the year 762, is Albert, archbishop of York, the fourth founder of the minster, and the first builder of the library, which was connected with the minster in Anglian times.

In the introduction to the "Fabric Rolls of York Minster," published by the Surtees Society, in the year 1858, the learned editor of that work states "that the annals of the minster may be said to date from the year 627, when Eadwine, the Saxon king of Northumbria, was baptized in that city by Paulinus. That ceremony took place in a church of wood, which, at the suggestion of Paulinus, the monarch ordered to be surrounded with a basilica of stone, of a square form. Fifty years, however, had not elapsed before the new church began to stand in need of repair. It had been constructed, in all probability, in a hasty and imperfect manner; and when Wilfrid ascended the chair of Paulinus in 669, he found the windows unprotected, and the roof unable to keep out the rain. To remedy these defects was his chief endeavour: the windows, which had formerly been filled with linen or boards, pierced with holes, he now glazed; he covered the roof with lead, and purified and furnished anew the interior of the church."*

The first minster of York, of which Kings Eadwine and Oswald and Archbishop Wilfrid were the founders, was built under extraordinary difficulties. Both these kings were killed in sanguinary battles with the pagans, from the country south of the Humber, within a few years after their commencement of this great work; and in the interval between the reigns of Eadwine and Oswald the pagans had possession of York, and raged with extraordinary fury against the Christian adherents of those kings. After the death of Eadwine every thing that was valuable and movable was removed from the minster, and conveyed by Paulinus, and the widow of King Eadwine, to Canterbury, where they both took refuge, and where Paulinus accepted the bishopric of Rochester from the king of Kent; which position he held to the time of his death. The progress of the building of the minster at York must have been very slow under these circumstances, even if the works were not destroyed by the pagan invaders. Nor would it be very rapid under Archbishop Wilfrid, who very soon became involved in a violent contest for supremacy with King Egfrid, which ended in the expulsion of the archbishop from his diocese. Still, in the midst of all these wars and commotions, the first minster was ultimately finished, and the two kings, Eadwine and Oswald, and Archbishop Wilfrid, divide amongst them the honour of having been the first, second, and third founders of York minster.

Little mention is made of the cathedral or minster of York from the time when Egbert's library was presented to it, to the year 741, in which year it suffered severely from fire. Archbishops Egbert and Albert, the latter a learned native of York, who was promoted to the see in the year 767, took the minster down entirely, in consequence of the damage done to it by the fire. The latter prelate, with Eanbald, who succeeded him, and the learned Alcuin, rebuilt the cathedral in the finest style of Saxon architecture. Archbishop Albert lived to finish the restored building, but died ten days after its consecration, on the 8th of November, 781. This

---

* The Fabric Rolls of York Minster, with an Appendix of Illustrative Documents. The Surtees Society Publications, vol. xxxv. 1859.

structure is described by Alcuin as being of considerable height, supported by columns and arches covered by a vaulted roof, and provided with large windows. It had porticoes and galleries, and thirty altars adorned with various ornaments. The library which Egbert had founded was greatly augmented by Archbishop Albert, who added to it a valuable collection of books (MSS.) which he had purchased during his travels abroad in his younger days.

With regard to the second Anglian minster built at York, the learned editor of the "Fabric Rolls of York Minster" observes:— " In the year 741, according to Roger Hoveden, there was a fire at York in which a monasterium was destroyed. Now, as the cathedral was in old times frequently called the monasterium or minster, I cannot but think that the chronicler intended to refer to that building. He was probably a Yorkshireman by birth, and he therefore applies to the cathedral the name which was usually assigned to it. Hoveden is in general an accurate historian, and I see no reason in this instance to question his authority. Now if this disastrous fire actually occurred, we must expect to find some record of the restoration of the temple which it destroyed. Accordingly we have a statement made by Alcuin, who was an eye-witness and aider of the work, that Archbishop Albert, who came to the see in 767, did actually erect a most magnificent basilica. Professor Willis is of opinion that this basilica is not the minster, but some other church either in York or in the diocese. From this opinion, however, I must be permitted to dissent. If the monasterium destroyed was actually the minster, as I believe it to be, it is hardly conceivable that its restoration should be unrecorded, or that the archbishop should erect another splendid edifice while his cathedral was in ruins. Again, there is no church beyond the walls of the city of York which can possibly be identified with the basilica described by Alcuin; and within the city itself, which was then small, it is scarcely possible that there should exist at that early period, and at the same time, a cathedral church and a gorgeous basilica, in which there were no less than thirty altars. But there is a statement on the table of the benefactors to (founders of) the minster, which goes far to prove that these two buildings were identical; Albert is there placed among the five founders or builders of the cathedral. Would his name stand there if the basilica which he undoubtedly erected were, not the minster, but some other church, either in York or elsewhere in the diocese? It is my impression, therefore, that Archbishop Albert was actually the builder of that church, which was in existence at the Norman conquest. Of its shape and extent there is nothing now known. Among the fragments of early masonry which have been disclosed in the crypt, there are one or two which have in all probability belonged to Albert's church; but there is nothing whatever in the fabric of the present minster to connect it with the Saxon times, except, perhaps, a mutilated image of the Virgin, which is imbedded in the eastern wall of the presbytery."

Little is known of the history of the Anglian city of Eoforwic, or York, from the time when the minster was rebuilt by Archbishop Albert, to the time when the city was taken by the Danes in the year 867, which ended in the destruction of the Anglian kingdom of Northumbria, of which that city was the capital. A few extracts from the "Anglo-Saxon Chronicle," and from the "History" of Symeon of Durham, contain all that is recorded of the city of York in that dark and disturbed period of the history of the Anglian race. The following passages, in which York is mentioned, show how little there was of peace and order in that age. Symeon of Durham's "History of the Kings of the Angles and Danes" commences with the year 732, and it is to him that we are indebted for the chief part of the little information that we possess as to this period.

A.D. 741. This year the monastery (or minster) in the city of York was burnt.[*]

A.D. 758. Oswolf was slain by his servants at Machil Wagntone (supposed to be Market Weighton between York and Beverley).[†]

A.D. 774. Alrid, king of Northumbria, was driven from his kingdom at York.

A.D. 790. Ethelred, having returned from exile, was again seized by Osrid and taken to the city of York, where he was made a monk.[‡]

A.D. 791. Elfwald was carried off from the city of York, and afterwards killed.

A.D. 795. Eanbald I., archbishop of York, consecrated Eudwulf, king of Northumbria.[||]

A.D. 796. Eanbald II., archbishop of York, received the Pallium.[§]

A.D. 796. Eardulf, recalled from exile, was made king, and was consecrated at York in the church of St. Peter at the altar of the blessed Apostle Paul, where the Anglian race first received the grace of baptism.[**]

A.D. 867. In this year, the nineteenth year of (the life of) Alfred (the Great), the army of the pagan Danes marched from the country of the East Angles to the city of York, which is situated on the north bank of the river Humber. In that year a violent discord raged among the Northumbrians, so that all who loved contention and strife found it in those days. Osbryght, the lawful king of Northumbria, had been expelled, and a certain tyrant Ælla had been made king; but the pagan invaders entering the kingdom, by divine counsel on the best part of the people, that discord was appeased. Therefore, the Kings

[*] Symeon of Durham, vol. i. p. 18. Surtees Society, vol. i. p. 51.
[†] Ibid. p. 21. [‡] Ibid. p. 30. [||] Ibid. p. 49. [§] Anglo-Saxon Chronicle. [**] Symeon of Durham, p. 24.

Osbryght and Ælla having united their forces, with their joint armies marched to the city of York. On their approach the multitude from the Danish fleet took flight, whose fear being seen by the Christians rendered them more resolute. The battle was fought very fiercely on both sides, and both the Anglian kings were killed. Those who escaped made peace with the Danes.*

In other words, the Angles of Northumbria were completely vanquished; their rival kings were both slain; and those who escaped or survived submitted to the authority of the Danes, who from that time became kings and rulers over the ancient city of Eoforwic, and over the Anglian kingdom of Northumbria.

Jorvic, or York, under the Danish Kings and Earls of Northumbria.—The Danes who stormed and conquered York in the year 867, changed the name of the city from Eoforwic to Jorvic. Vic in the Norse language means "a port," or harbour, and Jor is either the Danish name for the river Ure, or Yore, or it is a corruption of the first part of Eoforwic, the Anglian name. Under the Danes York became the military capital of the Danelagh, or the portion of England subject to the Danish law and dominion, which extended over Northumbria and East Anglia.

We are informed by Symeon of Durham that, after the overthrow of the two Anglian kings Osbert and Ælla, the Danes established their authority over York, *super Eboracum*, but that an interregnum or, in plain English, anarchy, prevailed in that city and the surrounding country, from the year 867 to the year 875. In that year, as we are told on the same authority, the Danes, under their chief Halfdene, overran the kingdom of Northumbria, and established themselves as rulers there, dividing and cultivating the soil. The reign of Halfdene, the first Danish king, commenced in the year 875, and ended in the year 882. He was succeeded by Guthrum, the Danish king conquered by Alfred the Great, and with whom Alfred divided the kingdom of England.

This Guthrum consented to be baptized, as one of the conditions of peace, and King Alfred acted as his sponsor at the font, giving him the fine name of Athelstane, or Ethelstane, meaning the noble stone or rock. Guthrum, or Athelstane, reigned at York from 882 to 890. One of the ancient gates of the city, known to the present time as Goodram Gate, was probably named after this celebrated Danish king. There has also been found a coin struck in the reign of this king, at York, and bearing the name which he received at his baptism from King Alfred. This coin, which was formerly in the

* Symeon of Durham, p. 48.

museum of Ralph Thoresby, at Leeds, bore the following inscription:—On the obverse were the words "Æthelstan Rex," and on the reverse the name of the moneyer who struck the coin, which name was Abertee, and the place of coinage, which was On Eo.; that is, at Eoforwic, or York.*

Under this king his new capital of Yorvic, or York, enjoyed a few years of peace, for we are informed that Guthrum, or Athelstane, maintained peace with Alfred to the time of his own death, which took place, according to Symeon of Durham, in the year 890. In the events of that year Symeon mentions that Guthrum, king of the Northumbrians, died. He, as above stated, was baptized; King Alfred acting as his sponsor, and giving him the name of Ethelstane. †

After the death of Guthrum the Northumbrian Danes again plunged into war with Alfred the Great, and from that time to the Norman conquest the city of York, as well as the kingdom of Northumbria, was the scene of many furious conflicts between the rival races of the Angles, the Anglo-Saxons (as the followers of the victorious West Saxon kings called themselves), and the Danes. Thus we are told that in the year 919 the Danish King Ingold conquered York.‡ In 927, as we are informed by the "Anglo-Saxon Chronicle," Guthfrith (not Guthrum), king of Northumbria, was expelled by king Athelstane, the grandson of Alfred the Great. This King Athelstane, in the year 937, captured York from the Danes, and overran the whole of the north of England, defeating Olaf, king of the Danes, and Constantine, king of Scotland, in a great battle fought at Brunanburh. After this victory Athelstane took the title of king of the whole of Britain, as appears, among other evidence, from coins of that king struck at York soon after this great victory. These coins, one of which was formerly in Thoresby's Museum at Leeds, had on the obverse this inscription:— "Ethelstan Rex to. Brit. (totius Britanniæ.)" On the reverse the inscription was "Regnald Mo. Eoforwic—Regnald, the moneyer, York."§ There were other coins of the same king, on most of which he was described as king of the whole of Britain, struck at the mints of Leicester, Chester, Derby and Winchester, as well as in London and at York.

* Catalogue of Coins, &c., in the Museum Thoresbyanum, vol. ii.; Whitaker's Loidis and Elmete, p. 56 of Catalogue; also Appendix to Drake's Antiquities of York.
† Symeon of Durham, p. 62. ‡ Ibid. p. 63.
§ Whitaker's Loidis and Elmete; Catalogue of the Thoresby Museum, vol. ii. p. 57.

But after the death of Athelstane and the murder of his successor, the Danes recovered possession of the city of York. Symeon of Durham, in his account of the events of the year 939, says "Ethelstan the king died : in this year Onlaf (a Danish chief) first came to York, which he took. Peace was afterwards made, and the boundary of each kingdom was fixed at Watlinga Street (Watling Street, the line of the old Roman road running across England, from the neighbourhood of London, either to Chester or Manchester). Edmund, the son of Althelstane, had the southern side; Onlaf, the northern.* But in the year 952 there were no longer any kings of Northumbria, for from that time the province was administered by earls,"† some of Danish and others of Anglian race. In the year 1013 the Danes again landed in great strength under King Sweyn, and subdued the greater part of England. He died at York :—"Suanus the Tyrant, suffering great torments, ended his life by a miserable death, and was buried at York."‡ He was succeeded by his son Canute the Great.

The last great series of events witnessed at York previous to the Norman conquest, which reduced Dane, Angle, and Saxon to equal subjection, was that of the desperate battles between King Harold of England and King Harald of Norway, the latter aided by Earl Tostig, at Fulford, on one side of York, and Stamford Bridge on the other. A full account of these battles will be found in the first volume of this work. All that it is necessary to add here is, that the ancient city of Jorvic or Yorwic, to which we may henceforth give its more familiar name of York, was almost ruined, either by the battles, or in the repeated sieges to which they led. Previous to those events York was a city containing about 1600 burgage houses, and a population of at least 10,000 inhabitants; which was a greater population than then existed in any other English city, with the exception of London. In the course of these battles and sieges, and in the still more desperate sieges of York by the Normans under William the Conqueror, which followed the battle of Hastings, the city was pretty nearly reduced to a heap of ruins; and in one of the sieges, in which an attempt was made to expel the Normans, it was set on fire by the Norman garrison, to prevent an attack on their position, and the Anglian minster was burnt to the ground, along with the library and many hundred houses, churches, and other buildings.

* Symeon of Durham, p. 65.   † Ibid. p. 66.   ‡ Ibid p 79.

York at the time of the Domesday Survey.—The Record of the Domesday Survey gives us the first full and detailed account of the city of York, and shows its condition, both as it had been previous to the Norman conquest, A.D. 1066, in the reign of Edward the Confessor, and as it was twenty years subsequent to the battle of Hastings, A.D. 1084-86. It appears from this account that previous to the Norman conquest, York was a city containing 1418 inhabited houses belonging to the king, and 189 belonging to the archbishop. According to the usual proportion between houses and their inhabitants, which is about five persons to each house, this would give a population of at least 10,000 persons, exclusive of the Norman garrison in the towers and castles, and of the multitudes of strangers who attended the markets and fairs, at which nearly all the business of the country was in those ages carried on. At that time there was no other city or borough in England, except London, and possibly Winchester, Gloucester, and Lincoln, that contained anything like so large a population as York. The other towns of Yorkshire, if there were then any places in that county that deserved the name of towns, were all of them very small; Leeds, the largest of them, did not contain more than from 200 to 300 inhabitants, and we have no account of Hull. At that time a population of 10,000 persons formed a first-rate city, and such was the position of York for some hundred years preceding the Norman conquest, and for at least 400 years after. During the latter period it advanced considerably in population and wealth, increasing to at least 20,000 inhabitants; and, until the commencement of the eighteenth century, it was not merely the capital and bulwark in war, but also the largest commercial and trading city, in the north of England.

The immediate result of the Norman conquest, and of the long and numerous battles and disastrous sieges by which it was both preceded and followed, appears to have been to cause the destruction or flight of a large portion of the Anglian and Danish inhabitants of the city of York. This was followed by the transfer of the principal mansions of the city, and of most of the burgages, to Norman barons, knights, and military followers of the Conqueror, who formed a permanent garrison there. Immediately after the Norman conquest, two great castles were built by the Conqueror on opposite sides of the Ouse, so placed as to command the navigation of the river, and so constructed as to give the Norman residents and garrisons two strong citadels, within which they might retire, if assailed by an insurrection within the city, or by an enemy from without. The latter was a matter of great importance at a time when the Danes and Norwegians had the command of the sea, as well as of the great estuary of the Humber, and when their attacks were made, not only by land, but by water, up to the walls of the city of York.

The following is the account given of the city of York (*civitas Eboracum*) in the Domesday Records:—

"In the city of York (*Eboraco civitate*) in the time of King Edward the Confessor, besides the ward of the archbishop, there were six wards [seyre], one of which was destroyed when the [Norman] castles were built. In five wards there were 1418 inhabited mansions. The archbishop of York has yet a third part of one of these wards. In these wards no one but a burgess was entitled to any customs, except Merlesuain,* in one house, which is below the castle; except the canons of York wherever they reside; and except four judges, to whom the king granted this privilege by his writ, and that for their lives. But the archbishop was entitled to all customary payments in his ward. Of all the abovementioned mansions there are now [at the time of the Domesday Survey] in the king's possession [William the Conqueror], 391 inhabited houses, great and small, paying custom or rent; 400 uninhabited houses which do not yield customary payments, but some only 1d. rent; 540 mansions so uninhabitable that they pay nothing at all. Freuchmen or Normans, *Francigenæ*, hold 145 houses—making altogether, 1476.

"Saint Cuthbert [that is, the church of Durham], has one mansion, which he always had, as many say, quit of custom; but the burgesses say that it was not quit in the time of King Edward, unless as to one of the burgages, and for this he had his own toll and that of the canons. Besides this the bishop of Durham has from the king's gift the church of All Saints and what belonged to it, and all the land of Uctred [earl of Northumberland], and the land of Ernuin, which Hugo the sheriff quit claimed to Walcherus, bishop of Durham, by the king's writ. And the burgesses who rent it say that they hold it under the king.

"THE EARL OF MORTON [one of the most powerful of the Norman followers of William the Conqueror], has there [at York] fourteen mansions, and two stalls in the butchery, and the church of Saint Crux. Osbern, the son of Baso, had these and whatever belonged to them granted to him; they had been the mansions of Conulfus the priest, one; Morulfus, one; Sterrus, one; Esnarrus, one; Gamel, with four drenghs [a Danish name for military followers or soldiers], one; Archil, five; Levingus, the priest, two; Turfin, one; Ligulfus, one.

"Nigel de Moneville has one house of a certain monier. Nigel Frossart has two houses of Modera, and holds them under the king; Waldin usurped two houses of Ketel the priest for one house of Sterre. Hamelin has one house in the City Ditch; and Waldiu one house of Eunifulus, and another of Alwin. Richard de Surdetal has two houses of Turchil and Ranechil. Nigel Frossart usurped two houses, but said that he had restored them to the bishop of Constance [the chief justiciary of England].

"William de Percy has fourteen mansions of these men, Dernulphus, Gamelbar, Sort, Egbert, Selecolf, Algrim, Norman, Dunstan, Odolphus, Weleret, Ulchel, Godolaut, Sonnate, Osbert, and the church of Saint Mary. Of Earl Hugh the same William [de Percy] has two mansions, of two bailiffs of Earl Harold [King Harold]. But the burgesses say one of them had not been the earl's, but the other had been forfeited to him. The church of Saint Cuthbert the same William also claims of Earl Hugo, and seven small houses, extending

* Merlesuain, the son of Thurkyl, a Danish earl.

fifty feet in width, besides one house of a certain person, named Uctred. The burgesses declare that William de Percy included one house within the castle, after he had returned from Scotland. William himself denies that he had the land of this Uctred; but he affirms that the house was laid to the castle by Hugo the sheriff, the first year after its destruction (Anno 1070).

"Hugo, son of Baldric, has four houses of Adulphus, Hedned, Torchil, and Gospatric, and twenty-nine small mansions, and the church of St. Andrew, which he bought.

"Robert Malet (son of William Malet, the high-sheriff of Yorkshire) has nine houses of these men, namely, Tumme, Grim, Grinchetel, Ernne, Elsi, and another Erune, Glunier, Hulden, Ravenchel. Ernise de Buron [Byron] has four houses of Grim, Alwin, Gospatric, and the church of St. Martin; two of these mansions pay 14s.

"Gilbert Maminot has three houses of Meurdoc. Beranger de Todenai has two houses of Gamel [Carle] and Alwin, and eight houses at rent; a moiety of these are in the city Ditch.

"Osbert de Archis has two houses of Brun the priest, and his mother, and twelve houses at a rent, and two houses of the bishop of Constance.

"Odo Balistarius [the slinger, or cross-bowman] has three houses of Forne and Orme, and one of Elaf at a rent, and one church.

"Richard, son of Erfast, has three houses of Alchmont and Gospatric and Bernulf, and the church of Holy Trinity. Hubert de Montcanisi has one house of Bundus.

"Landric, the carpenter, has ten houses and a half, which the sheriff made over to him.

"In the time of King Edward the value of the city of York to the king was £53 a year [equal to £795 of modern money]; now it is £100 [£1500 of modern money] by weight [in weighed money].

"In the time of King Edward there were in the archbishop's ward 189 inhabited houses paying rent. At present there are 100 inhabited, great and small, besides the archbishop's palace and the canons' houses. The archbishop has as much [that is, the same rights] in his ward, as the king in his wards (scyris).

"Within the guild of the city there are four score and four carucates of land, and every one of them taxed as one house of the city, and they, with the citizens, did the three works for the king [Burgbote, Brigbote, and Expeditio: performed the three duties, together called Trinoda Necessitas].

"Of these the archbishop has six carucates, which three ploughs may till. These compose the farm belonging to his palace. This was not improved and let for rent in the time of King Edward, but here and there cultivated by the burgesses; it is the same now. On this land the King's pool destroyed two mills of the value of 20s., and overflowed one carucate of arable, meadow, and garden ground. Valued in King Edward's time, at 16s.; now, 3s.

"In Osboldvic there are six carucates of land belonging to the canons of York, where there may be three ploughs. The canons have now there two plough lands and a half, and six villeins, and three bordars, or peasants, having two carucates and a half; likewise, in Morton, the canons have four carucates of land, where there may be two ploughs, but it is waste; these two vills are one mile in breadth, and one in length. In Stockton there are six carucates, where there may be three ploughs; they are waste. Of these, three belong to the canons, and three to Earl Alan [the earl of Richmond]. These are half a mile in length, and half a mile in breadth. In these neither meadow nor wood.

"In Sabura there are three carucates, where there may be one plough and a half, but waste. Rudolphus Pugenel holds it. The canons say that they had it in the time of King Edward.

"In Hewarde, Orme had one manor of six carucates of land, where there may be three ploughs. Hugo, son of Baldric, has now one vassal and one plough, value in King Edward's time, 10s.; now, 5s. In the same ville Waltheof had one manor of three carucates of land; Richard now has it of the earl of Morton; value in King Edward's time 10s.; now, 10s. 8d. This vill is one mile long and half a mile broad.

"In Fulford, Morcar [Earl] had one manor of ten carucates of land; Earl Alan now has it;

there may be five ploughs. There are now in the demesne two ploughs, and six villeins have two ploughs there. It is in length one mile, and in breadth half a mile ; value in King Edward's time 20s., now 10s. In the circuit of the city Torfin had one carucate of land, and Torchil two carucates ; these two ploughs may till. In Clifton there are eighteen carucates of land subject to the tax, or geld ; these nine ploughs may till ; it is now waste ; value in King Edward's time, 20s. Of these, Morcar [Earl] had nine carucates of land and a half to be taxed, which five ploughs may till. Earl Alan has now there two ploughs, and two villeins, and four bordars, with one plough. In it are fifty acres of meadow ; of these, twenty-nine belong to St. Peter, and the rest to the earl. Besides these the archbishop has eight acres of meadow. This manor in King Edward's time was worth 20s.; the same now. The canons have eight carucates and a half ; they are waste.

"In Rawcliffe there are three carucates of land to be taxed, which two ploughs may till ; of these Saxford, the deacon, had two carucates with a hall (now Saint Peter, and the value 10s.), and Torbar had (now the king) one carucate with a hall, and the value 5s. ; now both are waste. There are three acres of meadow there. In the whole, half a mile long and as much broad.

"In Overton there are to be taxed five carucates of land, which two ploughs and a half may till ; Morcar had a hall there. Earl Alan has now there one plough and five villeins, and three bordars with three ploughs, and thirty acres of meadow and wood pasture, one mile long and two furlongs broad. In the whole, one mile in length and half a mile in breadth ; value in King Edward's time, and now, 20s.

"In Skelton there are nine carucates of land to be taxed, which four ploughs may till ; of these Saint Peter had three carucates in King Edward's time, of the value of 6s. ; it is now waste. Torbar held two carucates of this land, with a hall and six oxgangs. Now one farmer (*unus censorius*) has it under the king; there are two ploughs and six villeins ; value in King Edward's time 6s., now 8s.

"Two carucates and six oxgangs of the same land, belonging to Overton. Earl Alan has there one vassal with one plough. In the whole, half a mile in length and half a mile in breadth.

"In Morton there are to be taxed three carucates of land, which one plough may till. Archil held this land, and the value was 10s.; it is now waste.

"In Wichitun there is to be taxed one carucate of land, which one plough may till. Saxford the deacon held it, now Saint Peter has it ; it was and is waste. There is a copse wood there ; the whole length half a mile, and the breadth the same.

"These [persons] had sac, soc, toll, theam, and all customs, in the time of King Edward the Confessor, Earl Harold, Merlesuan, Vifenise, Turgod [the Lageman, Lawyer, or Judge], Tochi, son of Outi ; Edwin and Morcar [earls], upon the land of Ingold only ; Gamel, son of Osbert, upon Cottingham only ; Copoi upon Coxwold only ; and Cnut, or Canute. Of those, whoever forfeited made satisfaction to no one but to the king and the earl.

"The earl had no right whatever in the church manors, neither the king in the manors of the earl ; except what relates to spiritualities, which belonged to the archbishop in all the land of Saint Peter at York, Saint John (of Beverley), Saint Wilfrid (of Ripon), and Saint Cuthbert (of Durham), and the Holy Trinity. The king likewise hath not had any custom there, neither the earl, nor any other.

"The King has three ways by land [high roads] and a fourth way by water. On these all forfeitures for offences committed (such as assault or highway robbery), belong to the king and the earl, which soever way they go ; either through the land of the king, or of the archbishop, or of the earl.

"The king's peace, given under his hand and seal, if it shall have been broken, satisfaction is to be made to the king only, by twelve hundreds; every hundred, £8.

"Peace given by the earl, by whomsoever broken, satisfaction is to be made by six hundreds ; every hundred, £8

"If any one shall have been exiled according to law, no one but the king shall pardon him. But if an earl or sheriff shall have exiled any one from the county, they themselves may recall him and pardon him, if they will.

"Those thanes, who shall have more than six manors, pay relief of lands to the king only. The relief is £8.

"But if any thane shall have had only six manors, or fewer, three marks of silver shall be paid to the sheriff for the relief.

"But the burgesses, citizens of York, do not pay any relief."

Such was the city of York, the capital of Yorkshire and of the North, at the time when the Domesday Survey was made; that is, in the years 1084–86, twenty years after the Norman conquest. It is clear that it had passed through many and great changes. In the long and obstinate sieges to which it had been exposed, in which a large portion of the inhabitants had either been destroyed or driven from the city, the Anglian and Danish inhabitants, at least of the upper class, seem to have been superseded by chosen warriors of Norman blood. The result of this had been to bring together, within or around the city of York, a large and powerful class of noblemen and gentlemen of the conquering race, who along with the archbishop (who was an accomplished Norman gentleman and scholar), the canons of the cathedral, and the representatives of the great churches of Beverley, Ripon, and Durham, formed the aristocracy of the city and neighbourhood. For many subsequent ages the principal noblemen and gentlemen of the county had mansions in the city of York, or in the immediate neighbourhood; and as the country became more settled, York became, in the north of England, what London was in the south; that is, the favourite resort of the nobility, the gentry, and clergy of the surrounding country. The Anglian and Danish inhabitants, though for some years depressed by the Norman ascendancy, gradually recovered by industry and commerce what their forefathers had lost in war. York, like all other cities in England, having once been subdued by the Normans, was freed, by their complete military and naval organization, from all danger of being successfully attacked by any foreign enemy. Subsequent to its complete conquest by the Normans that was a misfortune that never happened to the city of York; for though frequently assailed, in the numerous civil wars during the period which followed the Norman conquest, it was never successfully attacked by any foreign force, and never even seriously threatened, except, on one occasion, by the victorious armies of Robert Bruce.

Although little is known in detail of the progress of York during the two hundred years that followed the Norman conquest, that progress appears to have been very considerable. No better proof of this can be adduced than the fact that the Jews, who were at that time the only great capitalists of Europe, sought and obtained permission to settle there. It was only in large and flourishing cities that these enterprising capitalists settled; and the picture drawn by Sir Walter Scott of the wealth and the intelligence of "Isaac of York" is probably no exaggeration, either of their wealth or of their mental superiority. They were in communication with the Jews in every part of Europe, and were able to bring together abundance of capital, according to the wants of the time, wherever it could be employed with advantage. According to the custom of that, and of long succeeding ages, they had a Jewry, or a separate quarter of their own, where they lived, and kept themselves and the Christians free from the pollution which, at that time, was supposed to attend on the friendly social intercourse of Jews and Christians. The street in York still known as Jubbergate is supposed to have been the Jew Burg, or residence of the original Jews of York. Unfortunately, their wealth excited envy, and they became the victims of intense and cruel persecution, which did not cease to rage against them until they had been driven not only from York, but from London and all other English cities, and from England itself, first by popular fury and fanaticism, and afterwards by an unjust and impolitic law of the reign of King Edward I.

The circumstances which preceded and attended the expulsion of the Jews from York form a painful chapter in the history of religious persecution. Their wealth excited envy; and the debts owing to them by many of the Christian population, to whom the Jews had lent money at rates of interest proportioned to the badness of the security, caused them to have many enemies. In addition to this, the ordinary fanaticism of that age was aggravated by the excitement produced by the Crusades. Under these circumstances it was easy to arouse the popular fury, and a hermit noted for his fanatical zeal led the attack, which commenced on the 16th March, 1190, by an assault on the house of Benet, the chief Jew of York, whose house was plundered and his wife and children slain. After this commencement of the massacre, the Jews, 500 in number, and including many women and children, fled to the castle, and succeeded in obtaining refuge in that strong fortress, where after many days' resistance they were overpowered, and the greater part of them murdered by the fanatical populace. Their debtors effectually cleared off their obligations, by burning all the documents given in security for their debts, in the nave of the cathedral. King Richard I., who was at that time abroad, commanded that the most signal punishments should be inflicted on the murderers of the Jews, and a court of inquiry was held in the city of York. Too many, however, were implicated in the crime for any to be convicted, and though heavy fines were inflicted on the richer citizens, none of the murderers were punished in proportion to their guilt. This destruction of the richest capitalists of the city must have had a very mischievous effect on the trade and commerce of York, of which they were the mainspring. For a time the Jews were permitted to return, but few would be disposed to avail themselves of that dangerous privilege; and a few years later the whole of the Jews were banished from England by King Edward I., to the great injury of the trade of the country, which at that time stood greatly in need both of their capital and of their commercial intelligence.

The Early Municipal and Mercantile Charters of York. — The municipal and commercial charters granted to the citizens of York by the Norman kings, commence with the reign of King Henry I., the youngest son of William the Conqueror. These charters are probably merely confirmations of much older charters, granted by the Danish and Anglian kings of York, and possibly even of rights enjoyed under the Roman emperors. Every Roman city of any rank or dignity possessed important civic rights, and a good many of the privileges enjoyed by the most ancient cities of Europe may be traced to the Romans. Most, however, of the rights existing in the older English cities were known by Anglian, Saxon, or Danish titles, and originated in those times.

We have no copy either of the charters granted by Henry I. or Henry II., or of that of Richard I., to the citizens of York; but these charters are very distinctly referred to in the charters of King John, and of his son Henry III., and they probably included the greater part, if not the whole, of the valuable rights and franchises contained in the two latter charters. The charter of King John is entitled a confirmation of the charters of the citizens of York, and is as follows in substance:—"John, by the grace of God, king of England, &c. Know that we have conceded [or confirmed] to our citizens of York, all their liberties, laws, and customs, and that more particularly we have confirmed to them their Guild Merchant, and their Hanses in England and Normandy, with freedom from lastage [or tounnage] through the coasts of the seas, as fully, or more so, than they ever enjoyed them in the time of King Henry, the ancestor of our father. And we will and firmly command that they shall have and hold the same liberties and customs, with all liberties pertaining to their said Guild Merchant and Hanse, as well and peacefully, as fully and quietly, and if possible, more fully and more quietly, than they had and held them in the time of the aforesaid King Henry our father, as is reasonably shown by the charter of our aforesaid father, and by the charter of our brother, King Richard I. Also, Know that we have conceded, and by our present charter confirmed to all our citizens of York, freedom from toll, lastage, wreck, pontage, passage, and trespass, and from all customs, throughout the whole of England, Normandy, Aquitaine, Anjou, Pictou, and through all the ports and coasts of the sea of England, Normandy, Aquitaine, Anjou, and Pictou. Wherefore we will and firmly ordain that they shall hence be quit from these charges, and we forbid that any one should disturb them in these matters, under a forfeiture of £10 [£150], as is shown and commanded in the charter of our above brother, King Richard: the Witnesses being Galfridus Plantagenet, archbishop of York, Gaufridus the son of Peter, earl of Essex, and others. Given by the hand of S. Welles, archdeacon, and of John de Gray, at York, on the 25th March, in the first year of our reign" (1199–1200).*

It must not be supposed that King John granted all these freedoms and exemptions to his citizens of York, without obtaining a handsome equivalent. In return for this charter they agreed to pay to the king, yearly, the sum of £160 of the money of that time, which was equal in value, in the money of the present time, to somewhat more than £2000 a year, or fifteen times as much as the nominal value of money in the reign of King John. This arrangement continued in force for nearly two hundred years; that is, until the reign of King Richard II., who not only confirmed this and all other charters, but also agreed that the sum of £100, equal to £1500 a year, out of the rent

* Drake's Antiquities of York, p. 203.

above stated, should be applied by the lord mayor and citizens, to the repairing and the maintaining of the bridges within the city of York. All the rights which King John had confirmed to the citizens of York, were again confirmed to them by his son and successor, King Henry III., in more numerous words, and with some additions to the rights conceded. A curious and characteristic addition to the rights granted to the citizens of York in Henry III.'s charter, was that it provided that their dogs should no longer be subject to the disagreeable operation of expeditation, or the cutting off of the front claw or joint. This was done under the old Forest laws, lest the dogs should hunt and pull down the king's deer, and other royal animals of chase. As the limits of the ancient forest of Galtrees, which must have been full of game of all sorts, came within one mile of the walls of York, it would no doubt be a great advantage, both to the citizens and to their dogs, to be free from this disagreeable process. This same charter also granted to the citizens a much more important privilege; namely, that no vicecomes, or high sheriff, and no bailiff except their own, should intermit or interfere with any citizen of York, within the liberties of that city, in any matter connected with their former rights. The witnesses of this agreement were Guydo de Lezingnan, and William de Velentia, who are described as the brothers of the king (being his brothers-in-law); John Maunsell, præpositus of Beverley, and the king's favourite secretary; Master William de Kilkenny, the archdeacon of the convent; Bertram de Criol, Gilbert de Segrave, Roger de Thurkelby, Edward de Weston, Bartholomew Pethey, Johan Suband, Nicholas Mauro, Ranulf de Bukepuz, Johan de Geres, and others. This de St. charter was signed at Westminster, on the 26th February. Amongst other rights it gave the citizens the right of seizing their debtors, and of defending themselves by appeal to the oaths of thirty-six of their fellow citizens, except in cases of pleas of the crown. *

Subsequent to the reign of Henry III., the citizens of York obtained many other charters from the crown, of which the following are amongst the most important—Charters, 5th Edward II., 1311-12; 10th Edward II., 1316-17; 1st Edward III., 1327-28; 2nd Richard II., 1378-79; 15th Richard II., 1391-92; 19th Richard II., 1395-96; 1st Henry IV., 1400; 2nd Henry V., 1414-15; with many other charters, coming almost to modern

* Drake's Antiquities of York, p. 204.

times, and relating to all manner of subjects. The general effect of these charters was to confer on the citizens of York all the municipal and commercial rights enjoyed by the citizens of any other city in England, and even to give them certain rights, with regard to foreigners (as all non-citizens were called), which were neither for their own advantage, nor for that of the community at large. Thus, for instance, they obtained the power of passing such bye-laws as the following: "That no person or persons who are common sellers of woollen cloth, or linen cloth, or of any other manner of wares, at that time after this present proclamation, shall put to sale any of their cloth or wares to any stranger or strangers within this city (which is commonly called foreign bought and foreign sold), against the ancient grants, statutes, and ordinances of this city, except in the Thursday market of the said city, when they may put up their said cloth for sale without any penalty or contradiction in that behalf." *

Notwithstanding occasional mistakes, like the above, as to the best method of obtaining the greatest amount of trade from the non-citizens of York (which included all the rest of the world), York continued to be by far the most flourishing place of trade in the north of England, at least down to the time of the Tudor kings. The first severe competition to which the ancient capital of the north was exposed, was that which it experienced from the enterprising merchants and shipowners of Hull. This competition began to be considerable, even before the reign of King John. This is clearly shown by comparing the amounts paid by Hull and York to a tax of one fifteenth, called a quinzieme, raised in the 6th year of King John, 1205. It was chiefly a tax on goods and merchandise, and to that the citizens of York paid only £175, whilst the burgesses of Hull paid £344. At the same time a considerable trade had sprung up at Grimsby, Hedon, Ravenspurn, Barton, Selby, and other places, on the Humber. This began to withdraw from York a portion of the trade and commerce which it possessed exclusively in earlier times, Hull taking the lion's share.

The Norman and the English Restorations and Reconstructions of York Minster.—We hear little of the minster of York from the Anglian times until the wars and sieges of the Norman conquest. In the year 1069 the Northumbrians or Angles, aided by the Danes, attempted to overthrow the power of the Norman con-

* Drake's Eboracum.

queror, and to seize upon York. The garrison, in defending their position, set fire to several houses in the city, and a brisk wind blowing towards these houses, carried the flames to the cathedral, which, together with its valuable library, was burnt to the ground. William the Conqueror soon afterwards made Thomas, a canon of Bayeux in Normandy who was his chaplain and treasurer, archbishop of York, and to him restored the revenues of the see, in the year 1070. This Norman archbishop was one of the most accomplished men of his time, having travelled through Germany and Spain, and being acquainted not only with classical literature, but with the literature of the Saracens or Moors, who were at that time far in advance of the Christians in every branch of learning. By the exertions of Archbishop Thomas the ruined cathedral soon rose again, larger and more beautiful than before.

The learned editor of the "Fabric Rolls of York Minster" says that "Archbishop Thomas' church is supposed to have consisted of nave, aisles, and transepts, the aisles and transepts ending probably in apses. There was a central tower of magnificent proportions, and probably there were two towers at the west end of the church. The choir erected by Archbishop Thomas, judging from the remains of it in the crypt, must have been of a very substantial character."* It is on account of this entire rebuilding of the minster, and of his having come forward at a period of extraordinary depression and desolation to save this ancient and noble fabric from utter ruin, that Thomas, the first of the Norman archbishops of York, has obtained the title of one of the founders of the minster. He is one of the five to whom that honourable title is given in Dean Gale's inscription, the five being, Kings Eadwine and Oswald, Archbishops Wilfrid and Albert, in the Anglian period; and last, but by no means least, Thomas, the first Norman archbishop of York.

No alteration was made in Archbishop Thomas' church till the year 1172, when Archbishop Roger began to build a new choir. This is said to have been rendered necessary by a fire which occurred in 1137; but the editor of the "Fabric Rolls" says that there are some grave reasons for doubting the fact, and that it is quite enough to suppose that Archbishop Roger, a new and active prelate, found the old choir to be inconveniently small, and on that account began to reconstruct it. "The cathedral was now a complete specimen of the Norman style of architecture; but a new

* The Fabric Rolls of York Minster, published by the Surtees Society: preface by the Editor, Rev. James Raine.

style came into favour with the new century, and soon extended to the Norman minster of York. The innovator was that munificent prelate, Archbishop Walter Grey. To him the church at York was indebted for the south transept, with its noble and graceful proportions. This work was probably completed by the year 1240, and its erection was immediately followed by the building of the north transept, which, according to Stubbs,* was reared at the sole expense of John Romanus, the treasurer of the minster. That officer is also said to have rebuilt the southern tower; as, however, there are still traces in it of Norman masonry, it is probable that Romanus merely refaced it, putting in at the same time new windows, to make it harmonize with the recently erected transepts.

"The credit of commencing that glorious work, the rebuilding of the nave, is given to another John the Roman, who was archbishop of York. He was the son of the treasurer who had done so much to renovate the church, and he inherited the taste and energy of his sire. The first stone of the new nave was laid by the archbishop in the year 1291. The erecting of a building so vast and so magnificent as the present nave, was no ordinary undertaking. The chapter of York, however, were resolved to complete what they had begun, and they were most generously assisted by others. In 1296 they imposed upon their prebends and dignitaries a tax of two-sevenths; in 1298 the chapter sent their sub-chanter, Roger de Mar, to the court at Rome, and he was there directed to secure the permission of the pope for the imposition of a tenth and a third upon the non-resident members of the chapter. The archbishop, John Romanus, laid the foundation stone of the nave, and in all probability contributed largely to the fabric fund. Archbishop Corbridge granted an indulgence of forty days on behalf of the same work. His successor, William Greenfield, made a similar concession, and gave, amongst other donations, the munificent sum of 500 marks, equal to £5000 of modern money, to the church. Archbishop Melton, who succeeded Greenfield, was a most generous benefactor to the minster. He issued more than one brief on behalf of the fabric, and gave 500 marks to further the progress of the works. In 1338 they were far enough advanced to allow several of the windows to be glazed, and in that year the great west window was filled with glass, at the expense of Archbishop Melton, who gave 100 marks for that purpose. In the year 1345

* Lives of the Archbishops of York.

the stonework of the nave was complete, but that of a ceiling of wood was still wanting. This defect was not supplied till the year 1355, when the munificence of Archbishop Thoresby enabled the chapter to complete their magnificent nave.

"Simultaneous with the nave proceeded the building of the chapter-house. As it is built in the flowing decorated style of architecture, it could scarcely have been completed before the middle of the fourteenth century. On the parapet of that building appear several bears, which it may fairly be presumed are the device of Francis Fitz-Urse, who became treasurer of the minster in 1337. It may therefore be inferred that Fitz-Urse took a considerable part in the erection of the chapter-house.

"The restoration and reconstruction of the choir was undertaken by Archbishop Thoresby, to whom we are indebted for the conception and the commencement of that glorious work. The foundation stone was laid in 1361, but at least thirty years elapsed before the whole was completed. From this archbishop the chapter received the most munificent aid. He gave up to them his manor-house at Sherburn, and his purse was always open for that object. It was Thoresby who roofed the new nave, and he was, so to speak, the builder of the choir. His successors, Scrope and Bowet, nobly followed his example, and numberless other instances might be given, in which the archbishops of York have evinced their care for their metropolitan church.

"There were also many other benefactors, less noted indeed in position, but hardly less distinguished in their liberality. The famous bishop, Walter Skirlaw, was a large contributor towards the renovation of the lantern; Haxey may be called the builder of the library; and to Dean Andrew the church was indebted, amongst other things, for the battlements of the choir. Indeed, so widely diffused was the spirit of sacrifice and the wish to decorate one of the noblest of God's temples, that there were few wills in which there was no bequest to the fabric. The canons, especially, were lavish in their testamentary gifts. To the family of Scrope the minster was under the greatest obligations. Nor must we forget two other houses, Percy and Vavasor, which strove with each other in their endeavours to beautify God's house."[*] The restoration and renovation of York minster was perfected and completed during the

---

[*] The Fabric Rolls of York Minster, from the Publications of the Surtees Society; preface by the Editor, p. 24.

reigns of the Plantagenet kings, and forms one of the most glorious works of that age.

Parliaments and Political Negotiations at York.—York was the scene of all manner of public events connected with the political relations of England and Scotland during the times of the Plantagenet, the Tudor, and the Stuart kings. In the year 1160, Kings Henry II. of England and Malcolm of Scotland met at York, to arrange the terms of peace between the two countries. In the year 1174 Henry II. also held a meeting at York, with King William of Scotland, after the latter had been taken prisoner in an incursion into England, and had been ransomed on very severe conditions. In the year 1200 King John had a meeting with William of Scotland at York, at which it was arranged that Richard and Henry, the sons of King John, should in the space of nine years marry Margaret and Isabel, the daughters of William of Scotland. In the reign of Henry III., in the year 1220, Alexander the king of the Scots agreed to marry Johanna, a sister of King Henry III., and the marriage was afterwards celebrated at York.

The wars between England and Scotland, during the reigns of the three Edwards, induced them to make York their capital, sometimes for long periods of time, and frequently to hold their courts and Parliaments there. In the year 1298, King Edward I. summoned one of the earliest Parliaments to meet at York, in which the commons of the realm were represented, and in which the king, besides confirming Magna Charta and the great Charter of the Forests, engaged not to raise taxes without the consent of the representatives of the freeholders and burgesses of the kingdom. Another Parliament was held at York by Edward I., in the year 1299, and from that time to the close of his reign he spent much of his time in this northern capital of England, from which he could carry on his schemes of conquest against Scotland more successfully. For three or four years the courts of King's Bench and Exchequer met at York, and not in London, in order that they might be nearer to the king's person; and it was not until the year 1306 that they were removed back to London, it being then supposed that Scotland was effectually conquered. In the following year all Scotland was again in arms, and Edward I. died at Burgh-upon-Sands leading his last attack against that country.

In the next reign, King Edward II. fled to York after the

defeat of his army at Bannockburn, and there he called together a great council and Parliament to consult as to what should be done to restore the shattered fortunes of the kingdom. In the same year the national records and the judges of the King's Bench were again removed from London to York, when they had a very narrow escape of being captured by Randolph, earl of Murray, one of Robert Bruce's ablest commanders, who advanced to the very gates of York, and was very near taking them, along with Queen Isabel, in that city. The archbishop of York of that day, hoping to rival the great deeds of Archbishop Thurstan, whose high spirit and skilful management had greatly contributed to the success of the English army at the battle of the Standard, fought in the reign of King Stephen, succeeded in bringing together an army at Myton-upon-Swale, about eleven miles from York, in the year 1320. There a great battle was fought, in which Nicholas Fleming, the lord mayor of York, who had headed the citizens, was slain with many of the citizens, and with so many of his clerical supporters, as to give to the battle the names of the White Battle, and of the Chapter of Myton.

In the following year, Thomas, earl of Lancaster, rose in insurrection against King Edward II. in the neighbourhood of York, but was defeated at Boroughbridge. Some of his principal supporters, including Lord Neville, Lord Clifford, and Lord Mowbray, were executed at York, while the earl of Lancaster himself was beheaded at his own castle of Pontefract. In the following year another powerful Scottish army marched into Yorkshire, and surprised Edward II. at Byland Abbey, about fourteen miles from York. John, earl of Richmond, was taken prisoner, and the king himself narrowly escaped, the swiftness of his horse enabling him to reach the city of York.

After the death of Edward II. his youthful, but most warlike son, Edward III., assembled the whole military force of his kingdom at the city of York, supported by a formidable body of mercenaries from Hainault and Brabant. These foreign forces were excessively turbulent and licentious, and conducted themselves with so much violence towards the citizens of York, that they were compelled to give them battle. This they did with so much spirit as to restore peace within the city, and to enable the youthful king to lead his army against the Scots. It was some time, however, before he could find the enemy; and fearing that the Scots might surprise the city in his absence, he addressed a strong precept to the lord mayor and bailiffs of the city of York, commanding them to restore and strengthen the walls, ditches, and towers, and to put the city in a state of complete defence. The following is the order:—

TO THE MAYOR AND BAILIFFS OF YORK.

"The King to his well beloved the mayor and bailiffs of his city of York, greeting. Since the Scots, our enemies and rebels, have thought fit to enter our kingdom in hostile manner near Carlisle, with all their power, as we are certainly informed; and to kill, burn, destroy, and inflict other mischiefs so far as they are able; we have drawn out our army, in order, by God's assistance, to restrain their malice, and to that end turn our steps towards that country and those enemies.

"We—considering that our aforesaid city of York, especially whilst Isabel, queen of England, our most dear mother, and our brother and sisters abide in the same, ought to be more safely kept and guarded, lest any sudden danger from the enemy's approach should happen to the said city, or fear or danger to our mother, brother, and sisters, which God avert, for want of sufficient munitions and guard—we strictly command and charge you, upon your faith and allegiance, and on [pain of] the forfeiture of everything that you can forfeit to us, immediately, on sight of these presents, without excuse or delay to inspect and overlook all your walls, ditches, and towers, and the ammunition proper for the defence of the said city, taking with you such of our faithful servants as shall be chosen for this purpose, and taking such order for its defence that no danger may happen to the city, by neglect of such safeguards.

"And we by these presents give you full power and authority to distrain and compel all and singular owners of houses, or fees, in the said city, or merchants or strangers inhabiting the same, by the seizure of their bodies or goods, to be aiding towards the security of the walls, bulwarks, or towers, and as you in your discretion shall think fit, to ordain for the making other useful and necessary works about it, punishing all those that are found to contradict or rebel against this order, by imprisonment or what other methods you think fit. Study therefore to use such diligence in the execution of the premises, that we may find it in the effect of your works, and that we may have no occasion from your negligence, should danger happen, to take severe notice of you."

"By the King.

"Dated at Durham, July 15th, A.D. 1327."

The danger thus feared soon passed away, and in a short time the armies of Edward III. became too formidable to be successfully attacked by Robert Bruce's feeble successor. But Edward and his court remained at York, and there the youthful king was married on the 24th January, 1328, to the beautiful Princess Philippa, the youngest daughter of William, count of Hainault and

Holland, and of his wife, Jane de Valois, of the royal house of France. The marriage was celebrated in York Minster, Archbishop Melton, and Hotham, bishop of Ely, performing the ceremony. Never was there a happier marriage, and on this occasion "there was nothing," says Froissart, "but jousts and tournaments in the daytime, maskings, revels, interludes, with songs and dances, in the evenings, along with continual feasting for three weeks together."

Nearly twenty years later Queen Philippa, who had first appeared as a bride at York, came in a very different capacity to that city. In the year 1347 her husband, Edward III., and her son the Black Prince, being engaged in a great war in France, David Bruce, king of Scotland, led a formidable army into England, with which he endeavoured to advance to the walls of York. Philippa was then in York, and in the absence of her husband and son, collected all the forces of the northern counties, which advanced to Neville's Cross, near Durham, where they encountered, defeated, and captured the greater part of the Scottish army, including David Bruce, the Scottish king. In that warlike age the archbishop of York, William de la Zouche, commanded the second corps of the English army at the battle of Neville's Cross, and behaved very gallantly in the fight. "After the battle," says Drake, "the victorious queen returned to York with great joy and triumph, where soon after King David was delivered to her, by Sir John Copeland who took him prisoner, with much ceremony. The queen stayed at York till she had seen it strongly fortified, and then leaving the Lords Percy and Neville to the governance of the north, she returned to London, carrying her royal prisoner along with her, to present him to the king."*

In the year 1389, the youthful King Richard II., the son of the Black Prince, who had many excellent qualities, in spite of his sad misfortunes and miserable end, visited the city of York. According to Knighton, the object of his visit was to accommodate some differences which had arisen betwixt the archbishop, the dean and chapter, and the mayor and commonalty of the city. The affair was settled to the great satisfaction of the citizens, and it was on this occasion that King Richard II. took his sword from his side, and gave it to be borne before William de Selby, as the first lord mayor of York.†

* Drake's Eboracum, p. 105.   † Ibid. p. 106.

The Progress of the Trade and Commerce of York under the Plantagenet Kings.—Speaking of the city of York in the ages immediately following the Norman conquest, William of Malmesbury describes it as a large and metropolitan city, still bearing marks of Roman elegance, divided into two parts by the river Ouse, which receives on its bosom the ships of Germany and Hibernia. At that time the principal ports of Ireland were in the hands of the Northmen, who carried on an extensive trade, not only with Norway, but as far west as Iceland and Greenland, at the same time that the Germans traded with every part of the Baltic. We learn from the charter of King John that the citizens of York had a Hanse in that age, and no doubt traded with all the ports of the Hanse towns, which then held in their hands the greater part of the trade of northern Europe. The Merchants' Hall at York, "a fine old spacious building," says Drake, "stands near the point at which the Ouse and the Foss unite. The company of merchants trading there was long known as the Old Hanse Company. In the reign of Edward III., the great staple or monopoly in the trade of wool was established at York, from which port the chief trade in that article was carried on with the manufacturing districts of Flanders and Brabant. In that reign also, successful attempts were made by the king to induce many of the Flemish manufacturers to settle in England, and we have the names of the Flemings who established themselves at York, and who no doubt gave a strong impulse to a great branch of manufacture for which this part of England was so well adapted. They were William and Hanikin, or little John, weavers of Brabant. York, Beverley, and Ripon, seem to have been the places in which the woollen manufacture first flourished in the time of the Plantagenet kings; but about the time of the accession of the House of Tudor, the woollen manufacture began to flourish in all parts of the West Riding, and by the close of the seventeenth century the immense advantages afforded by a boundless supply of water-power and of coal, gradually transferred the woollen manufacture from the central and eastern divisions of Yorkshire, to the rising towns and villages of the West Riding." *

The trade flourished in York down to the time of the Tudor kings and queens. In order to promote the prosperity of the city of Calais, which was then an English fortress, Edward III. established the staple or monopoly of importing English wool

* Drake's Eboracum, pp. 41, 57.

into that place, and gave to a few seaport towns and cities of
England the exclusive right of exporting English wool to that
great depot, from which it was afterwards sent to the manufacturing towns of Flanders and the Low Countries. The merchants
of York had a considerable share in this staple, and were many of
them members of this corporation. Thus in the year 1442, John
Thrush, a great merchant who dwelt in Hungate, York, is styled
"mayor of the staple of Calais," and also treasurer. In the year
1449, William Holbeck, mayor of York, is spoken of as a merchant
of that staple. And in the year 1460 Sir Richard York, who was
sheriff of the city for that year, and was one of the guests at
Archbishop Neville's great feast, is called "mayor of the staple of
Calais," though he was sheriff of the city of York at the same time.
That the woollen manufacture also existed extensively at York in
the same ages, appears from the fact that the weavers of York paid
a very considerable yearly rent for their farm or privileges. The
weavers and dyers of York are mentioned in the Close Rolls as
early as the 2nd Henry III., 1217, and in the reign of Edward III.
a number of Flemish weavers, as we have seen, were encouraged by
the king to settle at York. This manufacture continued to flourish
in that city, at least down to the reign of King Henry VIII., at
which time the city of York is mentioned in the preamble of an Act
of Parliament in the following terms:—"Whereas the city of York,
being one of the ancientest and greatest cities within the realm of
England, before this time hath been maintained and upholden by
divers and sundry handicrafts then used, and most principally by
making and weaving of coverlets and coverings for beds, and thereby
a great number of the inhabitants and people of the said city and
suburbs thereof, and other places within the county of York, have
been daily set on work, in spinning, dycing, carding, and weaving
of the said coverlets." The Act then proceeded to give the citizens
of York full power for the sole making and vending of the said
articles. But there are some things too strong even for an Act of
Parliament, and trading competition is one of these. Drake, writing
in 1736, observes, "This Act continues still in force." He adds,
"But though this branch of trade must have been, and would be
still, very beneficial, I do not believe that there is one coverlet
wrought in the city of York in a twelvemonth, at this day." *

The City of York during the Wars of York and Lancaster.—Few

* Drake's Eboracum, p. 230.

English cities passed through more numerous and violent changes of fortune during the wars of York and Lancaster, than the ancient city of York. The citizens, as we have seen, had received the strongest marks of favour from King Richard II., whose deposition by Henry Bolingbroke, afterwards King Henry IV., was the first of a series of sanguinary revolutions, which lasted, with a few short intervals of uncertain repose, from the commencement to the close of the fifteenth century. From the beginning of these commotions the citizens of York were involved in them, partly owing to the great influence of the noble houses of Neville, Percy, and Scrope, with whom they were closely connected, and still more from the circumstance that the archbishopric of York was then held by Richard Scrope, a man of the highest talents and character, who returned the many favours which he and his family had received from the elder branches of the Plantagenet family, the descendants of the Black Prince, and of the houses of Clarence and York, by unbounded zeal and devotion. As we have seen, even his high rank in the church could not save Archbishop Scrope from being tried, convicted, and executed, for his known devotion to the house of Mortimer; and almost all the other members of the Scrope family shared the same fate, being put to death, on one pretence or another, by the triumphant house of Lancaster. We have already mentioned the circumstances under which Archbishop Scrope was convicted and beheaded, and it will be seen from the following royal order that the citizens of York, for a time at least, forfeited their municipal rights, for the same offence which cost the archbishop of York his life :—

TO SIR JOHN STANLEY, KNIGHT, AND ROGER LEECHE.

"The king to his chosen and faithful servants, John Stanley and Roger Leeche, greeting.

"Know ye that for certain special causes, intimately concerning us and the state of our kingdom of England, we do assign you, together or separately, our city of York, together with all and singular liberties, franchises, and privileges, to the citizens of the said city, by our progenitors or predecessors, sometimes kings of England, or ourself before this time, granted and confirmed, to take and seize into your hands; and the said city thus taken and seized, till further orders from us in our name, to keep and govern.

"Witness the king, at his castle of Pountefreyte, the 3rd day of June, A.D. 1405, in the sixth year of his reign."

In a short time, however, the rights of the citizens were restored, though the city continued strongly opposed to the house of Lancaster.

In the year 1408, Percy, earl of Northumberland, the father of Harry Hotspur and the friend of Archbishop Scrope, collected an army at Bramham Moor, near York, which force was defeated by Sir Thomas Rokesby, the high sheriff of Yorkshire. After that battle King Henry IV. came to York, where "what he had left undone before was now completed, in the executions and confiscations of the property of such citizens as were supposed to be hostile to his claims." In the next reign, and in the year 1412, King Henry V. having determined to lead an army into France, in order to strike terror into the enemies of the house of Lancaster, seized, condemned, and executed for high treason, on very slight grounds, Thomas, Lord Scrope of Masham, the lord treasurer of England, who was a well known adherent of the houses of York and Mortimer. Lord Scrope was executed at Southampton, but his head was struck off and was sent to York, with a royal order that it should be placed on the top of Micklegate Bar. At the same time the lord mayor of York received a mandate from King Henry V., ordering him to seize and confiscate the estate and effects of Lord Scrope. The earl of Cambridge, Richard Plantagenet (the son of one duke of York, and the father of another), who had married the heiress of the house of Mortimer, was beheaded at the same time with Lord Scrope.

For a time these acts of cruelty terrified the adherents of the house of York into submission; but, in the year 1460, Henry VI. having become imbecile, Richard, duke of York, caused himself to be declared lawful heir to the crown. He never, however, succeeded in wearing the crown, having been defeated by the army of Margaret of Anjou at the battle of Wakefield, and his head having been cut off and sent to York, where it was crowned with paper, and placed on the top of Micklegate Bar, with its face to the city, that, as Shakspeare makes the haughty Queen Margaret say, "York may overlook the town of York." Short, however, was the triumph of the house of Lancaster; for in a few weeks after the Lancastrian army was totally defeated by Edward IV., the son and heir of the above Richard, duke of York; and after that battle the head of Richard was taken down, and the heads of Courtney, earl of Devon, and several other Lancastrian chiefs, were exposed in its place. From that time the house of York retained the crown until the death of Richard III. on Bosworth-field, and the citizens of York received numerous marks of confidence and affection from that branch of the royal house. In the month of September, 1478, King Edward IV. made a progress into the north, accompanied by the whole of the nobility, gentry, and authorities of the northern counties. Amongst others he was met by John Farriby, then lord mayor of York, who rode out, accompanied by many of the richest citizens, as far as Went Bridge, almost on the southern border of the county, to meet the king, and escorted him to Pontefract. In a week after Edward visited the city of York, where he was received with great rejoicings, and presented with a handsome sum of money by the citizens.

Richard, duke of Gloucester, and brother of King Edward IV., was at York when the king died, in April, 1483, and there he had a solemn funeral requiem performed in the minster, for the repose of his brother's soul. There also he commenced those dark intrigues, which ended in the murder of his nephews in the Tower, and in the ultimate usurpation of the crown by himself. Believing himself to be much stronger in the north than in the south, he removed from London to York, after he had usurped the crown, and there he went through the ceremony of a public coronation. In the hope of gaining the favour of the citizens and clergy of York, Richard III. had determined to make splendid endowments in York minster.

The editor of the Fabric Rolls, in recording the events of the year 1485, says:—

"In the beginning of his reign, Richard III. gave orders for the establishment of a college of a hundred chaplains in the church at York. It seems to have been his object to found a grand college at York on a large scale. Policy, as well as affection, would induce Richard to win the regard of that people. He was at York in great state in 1483, going to the minster in all the pomp of royalty. At a solemn banquet in the city, which took place shortly afterwards, the king's youthful son was created Prince of Wales. It was probably on one of these occasions that the college of the hundred chaplains was ordered to be established."

The editor of the Fabric Rolls adds, speaking of Richard III., "that he also gave to the minster a very precious cross, and that to the vicars choral he was a benefactor and a patron, prevailing on the chapter to advance them to their original number." He further says, "that the piety of Richard III. won the favour of the clergy, and that it was a dark day for the north when its sun set upon the field of Bosworth." We conclude from this passage that the writer does not believe that Richard III. was the murderer of his brother's children and the usurper of their throne, but in this he differs from most of the historians of England.*

Testamenta Eboracensia.—A flood of light is thrown on the ownership of property and the occupations of men of all classes of society in the Plantagenet and Tudor times—from the greatest noblemen and church dignitaries of the county, to the smaller landowners, the merchants, the tradesmen, and even the artizans in the city of York, the port of Hull, and the various towns and boroughs of Yorkshire—by the wills registered at York, of which several volumes have been published by the Surtees Society.

In introducing the will of Richard Russell, citizen and merchant of the city of York, the editor very justly observes that "the will of this great merchant, made in the year 1435 (during the time of the Plantagenets), gives us a fair and at the same time a very favourable picture of the wealth of York, the metropolitan city of the north at that time." He further observes "that commerce, which has since enriched the towns of Leeds, Bradford, Halifax, and Sheffield, at that time of comparatively little importance, was then seated at York, Beverley, and Hull; and at no place perhaps was it in a more thriving state than in York. Few ancient cities could at this time show a larger number of companies and guilds for the advancement of trade, and in few cities was there a closer union between commerce and religion. York in the olden days was rich beyond description in churches and in religious and charitable institutions, for which she was principally indebted to the piety and munificence of her merchants. The testator (Richard Russell), citizen and merchant, who appears to have taken a high place among the merchant princes of the city, was brought up in his youth in the monastery at Durham, and the legacy which he leaves to it in his will shows that he still remembered the place of his nativity. From one or two notices in his will, we may infer that his wealth was derived from the sale of wool, and he was probably connected with that great company of merchants who formed the staple at Calais, and who were so intimately connected with the city of York. In 1412 he was one of the sheriffs for the city, and in the years 1421 and 1430 he was elected to the office of mayor. He lived in Hungate, and was buried in the church of Saint John in that street." †

* Fabric Rolls of York Minster, p. 87.
† Testamenta Eboracensia, vol. ii. The Surtees Society's Publications, vol. xxx.

In the wills executed at York we find those of men of every rank and occupation. Amongst them are those of archbishops, bishops, treasurers of the minster, clergymen of the numerous churches of the city, citizens of York of every occupation, including merchants, mercers, drapers, grocers, advocates, goldsmiths, valets, tailors, shipowners, painters, coopers, bakers, fishermen, buckler-makers, parchment-makers, engravers, bowers, potters, barbers, anchor-smiths, proctors, domestic servants, scholars, builders, tapestry-makers, masons, scheremen, saucemakers, woolmen, coverlet-makers, and many others; armigers, or gentlemen entitled to bear arms, being younger sons of county families living at York as a pleasant residence. Several ladies, also, are mentioned.

Most of the clerical and legal wills, and also most of the wills drawn up at York, where members of the learned professions always abounded, are written in the Latin language. Most of the wills of the great nobles and county families are still written in Norman French; and a good many, drawn up at Hull, Leeds, and other country towns, and some in York and in the country districts, are in very fair English, and show that the language had begun to take its present form.

York under the House of Tudor.—The city of York was greatly disturbed at the beginning of the reign of Henry VII. The first disturbance arose from the pretended claims to the throne of Lambert Simnel, who passed himself off as the earl of Warwick and the son of George Plantagenet, duke of Clarence, the brother of Edward IV. and Richard III. This impostor, who was supported by the earl of Lincoln, the earl of Kildare, Lord Lovel, and an army of Burgundians supplied by the duchess of Burgundy, the sister of Edward IV., landed on the coast of Lancashire, and marched across Yorkshire into Lincolnshire, where he was finally encountered and defeated by the army of Henry VII. at Stoke-on-Trent, near Newark. After this insurrection several of the principal insurgents were taken prisoners, and were gibbeted in the city of York. Another insurrection of a more local kind took place in the year 1489, arising out of an attempt of Henry VII. to impose an obnoxious tax, to carry on an unpopular war with Brittany. In this insurrection the earl of Northumberland was attacked, and slain with many of his servants. The insurgents were afterwards headed by Sir John Egremond, whom Lord Bacon calls a factious person, and by John a'Chambre, who is described as a fellow of mean extraction. Their forces, however, were soon defeated by Thomas Howard, earl of Surrey, who took the leaders prisoners, and had them executed at York, Chambre being hung on a gallows of more than usual height. After peace had been restored, Henry VII. visited the city of York. Its tranquillity was not seriously disturbed during the rest of his reign, so that on the occasion of the marriage of the Princess Margaret, Henry's eldest daughter, to James IV. king of Scotland, she was received with great rejoicings at York, on her journey northward, making her entrance into the city with 500 lords, ladies, and gentlemen.

The Battle of Flodden.—The marriage of the Princess Margaret, the sister of Henry VIII., with James IV. of Scotland, did not insure peace between the two countries. In the year 1513, King Henry having led his forces into France, James IV. seized the opportunity of marching into England at the head of a numerous and well-appointed army. This was encountered by an English army equally numerous and well-appointed, and more skilfully commanded by the earl of Surrey, in the memorable battle of Flodden Field. On that occasion the citizens of York raised 500 men, whom they sent to battle under the command of Sir John Mandeville. The old ballad of Flodden Field, in describing the gathering of the English army says:—

> "Next went Sir Ninian Markinfil,
> In armour coat of cunning work;
> And next went Sir John Mandeville,
> With him the citizens of York."

In this battle, James IV., king of Scotland, Henry's brother-in-law, was slain. His body was conveyed to York, and there exposed to public view till Henry's return from France, when it was presented to him at Richmond, near London.

The Walls of York under the Tudors.—We have a good account of the walls of York, as they existed in the time of the Tudor sovereigns, in Leland's "Itinerary," published in the reign of King Henry VIII. In describing the city of York he says that it "standeth on the west and east banks of the river Ouse," running through it, but that the part that lies on the east side of the river is twice as great, in building, as the other. The course of the wall from the Ouse, on the east part of the city of York, was as follows at that time:—First, there was a great tower, with a chain of iron to cast over the Ouse, and stop the navigation in time of war. Then there was another tower, and so the wall ran on to Bootham Gate. From Bootham Gate to Goodram Gate, of Bar, there were ten towers. Thence there were four towers to Laythorpe, a postern gate, and so by the space of a two flight shotts (arrow shots), "the blind and deep water of Fosse coming out of the forest of Galtres, defendeth this part of the city without walls." Then to Walmgate were three towers; and thence to Fisher Gate, "stopped up since the commons of York burnt it, in the reign of King Henry VII." Thence to the bank of Fosse there were three towers, and in the three a postern; and thence over Fosse, by a bridge, to the castle.

The west part of the city Leland describes as being thus inclosed. First a turret, and so the wall running over the side of the dungeon of the castle, on the west side of Ouse, right against the opposite castle, on the east bank. The plat of that castle, he says, "is now called Old Baile, and the area and ditches of it do manifestly appear." Betwixt the beginning of the first part of this west wall and Micklegate, were nine towers; and betwixt Micklegate and the bank of the river Ouse, eleven towers. At the eleventh tower was a postern gate, and the tower was right against the east tower (at the castle), to draw over the chain on the river Ouse, betwixt them.[*]

Such was the state of the walls of York in the year 1538, when Leland's "Itinerary" was written by command of Henry VIII. The walls were then quite complete, except at Fisher Gate, where some injury had been done by the populace, in a riot that took place in the reign of Henry VII. There were four principal gates or bars for entrance into the city, and five posterns or smaller gates. The four gates or bars were Micklegate Bar on the south-west, Bootham Bar on the north-west, Monk Bar on the north-east, and Walmgate Bar on the south-east. The five posterns were those of the North Street, the Skelder-gate, the Castle-gate, the Fisher-gate, and the Laythorpe posterns. To these were afterwards added the Lendal Postern, and long after, in Drake's time, the postern leading to the Long Walk.

The connection between the streets of the city and the suburbs, as well as between the different parts of the fortifications, was kept up by means of five bridges, which were as follows, down to the beginning of the present century:—Ouse Bridge, five arches, one of seventy feet; Foss Bridge, two; Laythorpe Bridge, five arches;

[*] Leland's Itinerary, vol. i.

Monk Bridge, three arches; and Castle Bridge, one arch. The whole circumference of the walls of York was two miles and nearly three quarters, the distances between the different works being, from the Red Tower to Walmgate Bar, sixty perches; thence to Fisher-gate Postern, ninety-nine perches; thence to Castle-gate Postern, fifty-eight; thence to Skelder-gate Postern, thirty-four; thence to Micklegate Bar, 136 perches; thence to North Street Postern, 140 perches; thence to Bootham Bar, eighty-six; thence to Monk Bar, 116; thence to Laythorpe Postern, sixty-six; and thence back to the Red Tower, eighty perches; making a total of 875 perches, or two miles, four furlongs, and ninety-six yards.*

Influence of the Reformation in the City of York.—Looking merely at the material interests of the city of York, it cannot be doubted that it lost many sources of prosperity by the Reformation. York was the ecclesiastical capital of the north of England, the see of a wealthy and powerful archbishopric possessing almost regal power, the seat of numerous wealthy religious houses, the head of upwards of forty parish churches, and the scene of almost innumerable charities and religious endowments. At the time when the Reformation took place there were upwards of forty chantries in York minster, all of which had their endowments, as well as numerous monasteries, hospitals, and other chantries. They were all either given away by the king, too often to undeserving favourites, or were frittered away on objects of no public importance. There were at that time the means of forming a university in the city, which might have taken rank even with the universities of Cambridge and Oxford. No doubt the church had become far too rich in that age; but there were objects connected with learning and charity, on which its excessive resources might have been expended with great national and local advantage.

At this time, according to a list of parishes given in Drake's Eboracum, York contained, besides the stately minster with its numerous chantries (every one of which had an endowment sufficient to maintain one or two, if not more priests, to perform masses for the dead), forty-one parish churches, seventeen chapels, sixteen hospitals, and nine religious houses, including the magnificent abbey of Saint Mary without Bootham Bar. "It cannot be denied," says Drake, "that after the dissolution of the religious houses by King Henry VIII., with the chantries, chapels, hospitals, and other houses for the sustenance of

* Drake's Eboracum, p. 261.

the poor, this famous and then flourishing city received a terrible shock, by the tearing up of those foundations. No sooner was the mandate given here, but down fell the monasteries, the hospitals, chapels, and priories in this city, the materials and revenues of all being converted to secular uses."*

The following were the churches and religious houses of York previous to the Reformation, with their value when it can be ascertained. This value was originally fifteen times as great as that of money of the present time; it afterwards fell to about ten times that value, owing to depreciation of the coinage. In the reign of Henry VIII., about forty years after the commencement of the influx of gold and silver caused by the discovery of America, it was still at least five times as much as it is at present. At that time, as Leland tells us, "a right honest or very respectable" man could dine (at Wakefield) for 2*d*; a quarter of wheat was sold for 10*s*. or 12*s*., and wages were about 6*d*. a day.

CHAPELS BEFORE THE DISSOLUTION, TEMP. HENRY VIII., IN THE CITY AND SUBURBS OF YORK.

1. St. Anne's, at Foss Bridge; 2. St. Anne's, at Horse Fair; 3. St. Trinity in the Bedern; 4. St. Christopher; 5. St. Christopher, at the Guildhall; 6. St. Catherine's, in Haverlane; 7. Bishop's Chapel, in the Fields, near Clementhorpe; 8. St. George's Chapel, betwixt Foss and Ouse; 9. St. James', without Micklegate; 10. St. Mary's Chapel, in St. Mary's Abbey; 11. St. Mary's Chapel, at the Whitefriars; 12. St Mary's Chapel, in St. Mary's Gate; 13. St. Mary Magdalene, near Burton-Stone; 14. St. Stephen, in the Minster; 15. St. Sepulchre, near the Minster; 16. St. Trinity's Chapel, at the Merchant's Hall; 17. St. William's Chapel, on Ouse Bridge.

"These chapels," says Drake, "being all chantry chapels, fell at the Reformation, and are all extinct, except two; one belonging to the Vicars Choral, in the Bedern, and the chapel at Merchant's Hall, still kept up by that company."†

HOSPITALS AT YORK BEFORE THE REFORMATION.

1. The hospital of Our Lady, Horse Fair; 2. The hospital of St. John and Our Lady, in Fossgate; 3. The hospital of St. Leonard, now the Mint Yard, says Drake; 4. The hospital of St. Anthony, in Peaseholm; 5. The hospital of St. Nicholas, without Walmgate; 6. The hospital of St. Thomas, without Micklegate Bar; 7. The hospital belonging to the Merchant's Hall; 8. The hospital of St. Catherine, beside St. Nicholas Church; 9. The hospital, or Maison Dieu, of the Shoemakers, near Walmgate Bar; 10. The hospital, or Maison Dieu, on Ouse Bridge; 11. The hospital, or Maison Dieu, at the Tailors' Bridge; 12. The Spital of St. Loy, at Monkbridge End; 13. The Spital of St. Catherine, without Micklegate Bar; 14. The Spital of —— in Fishergate, beside St. Helen's; 15. The house of St. Anthony, in Peaseholm; 16. The house of St. Anthony, in Gelygate.‡

* Drake's Eboracum, p. 263.   † Drake's Eboracum, p. 235.   ‡ Ibid. p. 236.

According to Roger Dodsworth there were forty-four chantries in the Cathedral church at York; but Torre mentions the names of more than sixty chantries, besides forty-six obits, "though probably some of their stipends may have failed previous to the Reformation." It appears by a catalogue of all the chantries within this cathedral, as they were certified into the Court of Augmentations in the 37th year of Henry VIII., that there were above forty altars erected in different parts of it. The following is the list of the chantries and the altars as given by Roger Dodsworth:—

CHANTRIES IN THE MINSTER OF YORK PREVIOUS TO THE REFORMATION, A.D. 1536, WITH THEIR ENDOWMENTS.

	Yearly Value. £ s. d.		Yearly Value. £ s. d.
1. The Chantry at the altar of the Holy Innocents,	5 13 4	24. The Chantry of Jesus and Our Lady,	6 13 4
2. A Chantry of a different foundation,	5 13 4	25, 26. Two Chantries at the altar of St. Stephen,	13 6 0
3. Another, at the same altar,	3 6 5	27, 28. Two Chantries at the altar of Holy Cross,	6 13 4
4. A Chantry at the altar of St. Saviour, in the loft on the south side of the minster,	16 16 10	29, 30. Two Chantries at the altar of St. Agatha Scolace,	4 8 2
5. The Chantry of St. Friswith, on the same side,	17 0 0	31. Another Chantry, at the altar of St. Lawrence,	3 6 8
6. The Chantry at the altar of St. Cuthbert,	12 0 0	32. The Chantry at the altar of St. James, Minor,	3 6 8
7, 8. Two Chantries at the altar of Allhallows,	36 8 0	33. The Chantry at the altar of St. Paulinus and Cedda (Archbishops of York),	3 6 8
9. The Chantry of St. Mary Magdalene,	3 1 0	34. The Chantry of St. Gregory,	3 6 8
10. The Chantry of St. Saviour and St. Ann,	10 7 4	35. The Chantry of St. Edmond, king and martyr,	3 6 0
11. The Chantry of St. John the Evangelist,	6 13 4	36. The Chantry at the Altar of St. John the Evangelist,	4 13 0
12. The Chantry of St. Agatha, Scolace, and Lucia,	8 0 0	37. The Chantry at the Altar of St. John of Beverley (A. of York),	3 6 8
13. The Chantry of St. Ann and St. Anthony,	6 13 4	38. Another Chantry at the Altar of the Innocents,	3 6 8
14. The Chantry of St. Lawrence,	3 1 4	39. Another Chantry at the Altar of St. Nicholas,	3 13 0
15. The Chantry of St. William (Archbishop of York),	8 9 6	40. The Chantry at the Altar of St. Blaise, the patron saint of the wool combers,	3 18 4
16. The Chantry of St. Nicholas,	2 13 4	41. Another to the same Saint, of a different foundation,	3 6 8
17. The Chantry of St. Thomas the Apostle,	2 4 0	42. The Chantry at the Altar of the Holy Trinity, and the Cross,	5 13 4
18. The Chantry of St. Michael,	10 13 4	43. A second Chantry at the Altar of St. Gregory,	3 6 8
19. The Chantry of St. Christopher,	2 2 0	44. A Chantry at the Altar of St. Thomas à Becket,*	4 2 8
20. The Chantry of Our Lady,	8 19 0		
21. " "	5 8 0		
22. The Chantry of St. Andrew,	4 13 4		
23. The Chantry of St. Wilfrid (Archbishop of York),	6 13 4		

* Drake's Eboracum, p. 520.

PAST AND PRESENT. 57

We find another list of these chantries in the Fabric Rolls of York Minster, published by the Surtees Society. The following is a list of the parish churches in York in the reign of Henry V.

A GENERAL LIST OF ALL THE PARISH CHURCHES IN THE CITY AND SUBURBS OF YORK, IN THE TIME OF KING HENRY V., WITH THEIR YEARLY VALUE.

1. Allhallows, in the Pavement, £9; 2. Allhallows, near Fisher Gate, £1; 3. Allhallows, in North Street, £8; 4. Allhallows, in Peasholm or Peaceholm, £3; 5. St. Andrews, £3 6s. 8d.; 6. St. Clement's, in Fossgate, £1; 7. St. Cuthbert's, in Peasholm, £2; 8. St. Crux, or Holy Cross, £9; 9. Christ Church, or St. Trinity, £8; 10. St. Dyonis, £7; 11. St. Helens, on the Wall, £2; 12. St. Helens, out of Fishergate, £1; 13. St. Helens, in Stonegate, £6; 14. St. Edward, £1 6s. 8d.; 15. St. Gregory's, £2; 16. St. Giles, —; 17. St. George, at Bean-hills, £4; 18. St. George, in Fishergate, —; 19. St. John de la Pyke, £4; 20. St. John, in Hungate, £1; 21. St. John Evangelist, at Ousebridge End, £8; 22. St. Lawrence, £9; 23. St. Mary, without Laythorp Postern, £2; 24. St. Mary, Bishop Hill, £10; 25. St. Mary, Bishop Hill, junior, £6; 26. St. Mary, in Castle Gate, £6; 27. St. Margaret's, £7; 28. St. Martin, in Micklegate, £6; 29. St. Martin, in Conyng Street, £10; 30. St. Maurice, £2; 31. St. Michael de Belfrey, £12; 32. St. Michael, in Spurrier Gate, £10; 33. St. Nicholas, by Micklegate Bar, £6; 34. St. Nicholas, without Walm Gate, £5; 35. St. Olave, in Mary Gate, £24; 36. St. Peter, in the Willows, £1; 37. St. Peter, the Little, £7; 38. St. Saviour, £8; 39. St. Sampson, £8; 40. St. Trinity, Gothram Gate, £4 13s. 4d.; 41. St. Wilfred's, Blake Street, £5. To these parish churches Drake adds the Church of St. Benedict, in Patrick Pool; St. Stephen, a church mentioned in Dugdale's "Monasticon," vol. i. p. 385; St. Bridget, mentioned in the "Monasticon," vol. i. p. 564, and said to be in "Mucclegata;" and St. Michael extra Walmgate, mentioned by Mr. Torre.

These parish churches were not abolished, indeed most of them still exist; but several of the smaller and poorer were consolidated with others in the reign of Queen Elizabeth.

RELICS FORMERLY PRESERVED AT THE MINSTER AT YORK.

We find in the Fabric Rolls of York Minster a list of the relics preserved there previous to the Reformation. The list occurs on a fly-leaf of the MS. copy of the Gospels in the office of the dean and chapter; and in the opinion of the editor of the Fabric Rolls the handwriting is that of the middle of the thirteenth century. The list shows that Archbishop Roger was the donor of many of the relics, and that he arranged and dedicated others. It also appears that Archbishop Roger brought many of the relics from Rome—*de domo domini Papæ*. Others were collected by St. William, archbishop of York, Archbishop Thurstan, and others.

"The list commences very solemnly, with the words, *In nomine Domini, Amen*, and then proceeds to state that these are the relics preserved in the church of Saint Peter at York, stating very particularly where they were placed. Some of them were within a great cross which stood beyond the pulpit at the entrance to the choir, which cross Roger, the archbishop, had caused to be prepared, and had afterwards dedicated. Others were in another cross which stood behind the great altar, which the same Roger, archbishop of York, had caused to be prepared, and had afterwards dedicated. Others were in a great bier behind the high altar, some in a white pix, others in a green pix, and others in a red pix. Others were in a bier behind the altar in a cross made of the gold which Roger the archbishop gave for the redemption of the king [Richard I.], from the treasures of the church, and which was afterwards redeemed by the chapter. Others were in another bier covered with gold plates. One of these relics was shown as a bone of Saint Peter the apostle, which the venerable Roger, archbishop of York, had brought *de domo domini*. In another case, covered with gold leaf, were a number of relics which were described as having been brought by Archbishop Roger, *de domo domini Papæ*.

The relics thus carefully preserved amounted to some hundreds in number, of which the following were the most remarkable:—Relics of the holy apostles Peter, Paul, and Matthew; of Saint Luke the Evangelist; a joint of the finger of Saint John the Baptist; a stone from the sepulchre of our Lord; a tooth of Saint Stephen the protomartyr; a tooth of Saint Bridget the virgin; a stone from the rock on which St. John the Baptist sat; a portion of the manna which rained down from heaven on the people of Israel; a stone from the sepulchre of our Lord Jesus Christ; an arm of Saint Sebastian; part of the robes of the holy apostles Simon and Jude; two teeth of Saint Paulinus, archbishop of York, and other bones of the same; a stone on which the Lord Jesus sat when he fasted in the wilderness; the stone on which the angel sat; relics of Saint Dunstan the archbishop, and of Saint Cedda the archbishop; more of the manna which was rained from heaven; relics of Saint Cuthbert the bishop; others from the sepulchre of Saint Oswald, king of Northumbria; part of the cross of our Lord; the vest of Saint Mary the virgin; the angelic clothing of Saint Agnes the virgin; one of the bones of the apostle Peter, which the venerable Roger, archbishop of York, brought from the home of his master; also relics brought by Saint William (of York), and Archbishops Henry and Thurstan, of the bones of the apostles Simon and Jude; some of the blood of St. Stephen the protomartyr; a finger of Saint Dionisius; the cross on which Saint Andrew was crucified; bones of Saint Lazarus and his sister Martha; bones of Saint Matthew the apostle; part of the rock of the sepulchre of our Lord; bones of Saint John the Baptist; one of the bones of Saint Paul the apostle, *in quadam ampulla cristolina;* vestments of the apostles Peter and Paul; the chin and rib of a certain saint, whose name could not be known on account of the antiquity of the writing; one of the sandals of Saint Peter the apostle, which Archbishop Roger brought *de domo domini Papæ;* the rod of Aaron; relics from Mount Sinai; from the sepulchre of our Lord; from the sepulchre of Lazarus; a stone from the River Jordan; part of the cross of our Lord; and relics from the body of Saint Helena. There were a multitude of other relics preserved and shown in the Minster, but these will probably be considered quite sufficient.[*]

The Pilgrimage of Grace.—The insurrection in Yorkshire and the northern counties, called the Pilgrimage of Grace, only brought

[*] The Surtees Society's Publications, vol. 35, A.D. 1858. The Fabric Rolls of York Minster, pp. 150-153.

destruction on its leaders, and on all who were engaged in it; although the city of York and the fortress of Hull, the two strongest places in the north of England, fell into the hands of Robert Aske of Aughton, Lord D'Arcy, Sir Robert Constable, and other leaders of the 40,000 men who joined in the pilgrimage, before any effectual steps could be taken to stop their progress southward. This, however, was at last done by the floods of the river Don, aided by a small army of 5000 men, under the command of the duke of Norfolk. Having no military leaders of any skill, and no support from the rest of the kingdom, the insurgents were at length induced to lay down their arms by promises of mercy, which were very badly kept. Aske, the leader of the insurrection, was hung, and suspended from a tower, probably Clifford's, at York; the abbots of Fountains, Jervaux, and Rivaulx, and the prior of Bridlington, were executed at Tyburn; Sir Robert Constable was hanged in chains over Beverley Gate, at Hull; Lord D'Arcy was beheaded at Tower Hill; and many persons of inferior rank were hung in different places. After all resistance had been completely subdued, Henry VIII. visited the city of York and other places in the north of England, and was everywhere received with homage and liberal presents. On his entry into Yorkshire he was welcomed by 200 gentlemen, attended by 4000 yeomen and servants, who, through Sir Robert Bowes, made their humble submission, and presented the king with a sum of £900, equal in value to at least £5000 of modern money. On Barnsdale the king was met by Dr. Lee, the archbishop of York, who had been a prisoner in the hands of the insurgents, and by upwards of 300 of his clergy, who joined in making another present of £600 to the king. Thence he proceeded to the city of York, where he was received with great state by the lord mayor, who presented him with £100. The mayors of Newcastle and Hull came to meet the king, and made him presents of similar sums.

The Council of the North established at York.—The Council of the North was established at York by King Henry VIII., on this visit to the northern part of his dominions. This council became a sort of northern parliament, and continued in existence down to the breaking out of the great civil war in the reign of Charles I., when that monarch destroyed the council, by bringing it into direct conflict with a large portion of his own people, and with the Parliament of England, sitting at Westminster. While it lasted the Council of the North was a body of considerable importance, being always presided over by a nobleman of the highest standing; having a powerful control in the northern counties; and an able body of lawyers to advise it in its proceedings. The first president was Thomas Howard, duke of Norfolk. It had the power to hear and determine all causes on the north side of the Trent. In the year in which this formidable court was founded, Sir John Neville, knight, and ten other persons, were taken in rebellion or resistance to the will of the king, and were executed at York.

The Rising of the North.—The city of York had the good fortune to escape any serious danger in the second great rising of the Roman Catholics of Yorkshire, in the reign of Queen Elizabeth, known as the "Rising of the North." At that time York was garrisoned by 5000 of the queen's soldiers, under the command of the earl of Sussex. The objects of the insurrection, which was headed by the two great northern earls, Thomas Percy, earl of Northumberland, and Charles Neville, earl of Westmoreland, were to restore the Roman Catholic religion, to dethrone Queen Elizabeth, and to place Mary Queen of Scots on the throne of England. The insurrection broke out in the neighbourhood of Barnard Castle, and the insurgents advanced to the neighbourhood of York; but finding that they could make no impression on that city, they retired northward, the two leaders escaping into Scotland, and a great slaughter being made among their followers. Amongst the persons executed at York were Simon Digby of Askew, John Fulthorp of Iselbeck, Robert Pennyman of Stokesby, and Thomas Bishop, jun., of Pocklington, who were hung, beheaded, and quartered on Knavesmire, near York, and their heads set up on the four principal gates of the city. Three years later Thomas, earl of Northumberland, who had returned from the Continent to Scotland, was given up by the earl of Morton, regent of Scotland, to Lord Hunsdon, governor of Berwick. He was speedily conducted as a prisoner to York, and beheaded on a scaffold erected for that purpose on the Pavement of that city. It is said that as many as 800 persons were put to death for their share in this insurrection, which was the last attempt to restore the Roman Catholic religion by force in this kingdom.

Camden's Description of York.—The best description of the city of York in Tudor times is contained in Camden's "Britannia." That great topographer visited York in the reign of Queen Elizabeth, and wrote an admirable account, both of its antiquities and of its state and condition at the time of his visit. We have already given the substance of the information collected by Camden, as to the antiquities of York. With regard to the city in his own times, he says that "York is the second city in England, the first in this part of the island, and is a great strength and ornament to the north. It is," he says, "pleasant, large, and strong, adorned with fine buildings, both public and private; populous, rich, &c. The river Ure, which now takes the name of the Ouse, runs gently from north to south quite through the city, and divides it into two parts, which are joined by a noble stone bridge. The west part of the city is no less populous, lies in a square form, inclosed partly by stately walls and partly by the river, and has but one way to it, namely, by Micklegate Bar. The east part is larger, where the buildings stand thick and the streets are narrow, is shaped like a lentil, and strongly walled. On the south-east it is defended by the Fosse or ditch, very deep and muddy, which runs by covered ways into the very heart of the city, and, gliding close by the castle walls, a little further down falls into the Ouse."*

The Corporation of York.—The city of York was governed for many ages by a corporation, which in many respects greatly resembled the corporation of London. The ancient municipal government of the city of York, like the government of the kingdom of Great Britain, had its three estates; namely, the lord mayor as sovereign, the aldermen and body of twenty-four as a house of Lords, and the common council, which was a representative body, corresponding in some degree to the House of Commons. This was the original constitution of the municipal governments of London and York, and of most of the old cities of the kingdom; and if the Stewart kings had not very unwisely destroyed the popular element by establishing town councils appointed by the Crown and self-elected in all future times, this form of local government would probably have continued to exist in the older cities and boroughs of the kingdom, and the corporations of the newer boroughs would have been formed on a somewhat similar principle. The general form of the local government of the city of York down to the Municipal Reform Bill was as follows—a lord mayor, a recorder, two city counsel, a number of aldermen, generally amounting to ten or twelve, from whom the lord mayor was elected; two sheriffs for the city of York, a town

* Camden's Britannia.

clerk, the gentlemen who had served the office of sheriff for the city, six chamberlains, and a numerous body of common councilmen elected by the citizens in the four wards of Walmgate Ward, Monk Ward, Bootham Ward, and Micklegate Ward. There were also coroners for the city and ainsty, and for the liberty of St. Peter's, a jurisdiction specially connected with the archbishopric.

The residence of the lord mayor of York in more modern times was the mansion-house, a stately edifice built in the year 1756, and standing at the north end of Coney, more correctly, Conyng Street, on the site of the ancient chapel of the guild of St. Christopher.

The guild-hall is situated behind the mansion-house, and was built in the year 1446. In this fine Gothic hall, ninety-six feet in length by forty-three feet in width, the assizes for the city of York are held. The elections for members of Parliament were also held here. Here also the lord mayor, and at least one other city magistrate, held daily sittings for the administration of justice.

The council chamber of the city formerly stood on Ouse Bridge, and when the old bridge was taken down in 1810 new council chambers were built. The inner room and the lower house, namely, the common council, held their deliberations in one of them, while the upper house, consisting of the lord mayor, the recorder, the city council, the aldermen, the sheriffs, and the gentlemen of the twenty-four, assembled in the upper chamber.*

Trades at York in the Time of James I.—We find about this time an account of the several trades carried on in the city of York in the year 1623, with the statement of what sum every trade paid yearly to the city, for the repair of their Moot-hall, or place of public meeting, called St. Anthony's Guild. The payments are small, but the number of trades is still considerable, though at this time both the commerce and the manufactures of York are spoken of in public documents as being in a declining state, chiefly owing to the bad state of the navigation of the river Ouse. To this must also be added the rapid increase of commerce at Hull, and of manufactures in the rising towns of the West Riding. The following is a list of the trades of York of this time, with an account of their yearly payments to the upholding of their place of meeting:—Merchants and mercers, 5s.; drapers, 4s.; goldsmiths, 2s.; dyers, 1s.; haberdashers, 1s.; vintners, 2s.; saddlers,

* Gazetteer and Directory of Yorkshire, 1823.

2s.; bakers, 3s.; butchers, 4s.; wax chandlers, 8d.; mariners, 8d.; brasiers, 1s.; barbers, 8d.; embroiderers, 4d.; girdlers, 1s. 4d.; blacksmiths, 8d.; pannier-men, 1s. 4d.; bricklayers, 1s. 4d.; parchment makers, 2s.; linen weavers, 1s. 2d.; pinners, 6d.; curriers, 8d.; cobblers, 1s.; silk weavers, 1s. 4d.; tallow chandlers, 8d.; tanners, 4s.; cordwainers, 2s.; carpenters, 1s.; bladesmiths, 2s.; pewterers, 1s. 8d.; glovers, 1s. 6d.; armourers, 1s.; inn-holders, 4s.; millers, 3s. 4d.; coopers, 1s. 4d.; skinners, 1s. 6d.; glaziers, 1s.; shearmen, 6d.; spurriers, 6d.; locksmiths, 4s.; cooks, 1s.; painters, 8d.; founders, 1s.; coverlet weavers, 1s. 8d.; ropers, 1s.; porters, 1s.; labourers, 8d.; musicians, 1s. Such were the trades of York about the time when the Stewarts began to reign.*

The Siege and Blockade of York in the Great Civil War.—The last great military event in the history of York was the defence of that city by William Cavendish, marquis of Newcastle, the commander of the royal armies of Yorkshire and the north of England, in the great civil war in the year 1644; and the siege and blockade of the city by the united armies of Fairfax, Cromwell, and their Scotch auxiliaries. So great was the importance attached to the possession of the city of York by Charles I., that he sent an army of upwards of 10,000 men to its relief, under the command of his nephew Prince Rupert, with written instructions to fight a great battle, if it should be necessary, rather than allow York to be taken by the parliamentary army. Although Prince Rupert was accused of having exceeded his orders by fighting a battle without any necessity on Marston Moor, after he had compelled the parliamentary generals to raise the siege of York, it cannot be doubted that his instructions were not merely to occupy, but to hold the city of York permanently, and that he was justified by them in fighting a battle for that object, if he was of opinion that he could not hold the city without doing so. But his military judgment was weak; and he was in no respect qualified to decide so important and difficult a question.

Until the advance of the Scottish army into Yorkshire, in the month of April, 1644, the royalist party had no difficulty in holding the city of York, which was still the strongest fortress in England, and was secure against everything except famine, caused by a long blockade. The city was already occupied by a royalist garrison, strong in numbers, though incapable of keeping the field against

* Drake's Eboracum, p. 224.

the three great armies that were assembling around the city. The marquis of Newcastle arrived at York, April 19, 1644, bringing with him an army of about 6000 men. He was supported by two able officers, General King, soon afterwards made a peer, by the title of Lord Eythin, and Sir Thomas Glenham. The poet laureate, Sir William Davenant, was also there, to command the Ordnance, and to celebrate Newcastle's victories.

A few days after the arrival of the marquis of Newcastle at York, he found himself surrounded by three parliamentary armies. The first of these was the Scottish army of about 20,000 men, under the slow but veteran soldier, the earl of Leven, supported by a gallant body of officers and soldiers, many of them trained in the wars of the great Gustavus. The Scottish part of the line of blockade of York extended round Micklegate Ward, from the Ouse below Poppleton, to the same river above Bishopthorpe, each wing resting on a bridge of boats, by which communication was kept up with the other besieging corps.

The army of the Associated Counties, commanded by the earl of Manchester, with Oliver Cromwell as his commander of the horse, extended from the Ouse along the Manor House wall and St. Mary's Tower, to Bootham Bar, and thence by Monk Bar to the Fosse. The Yorkshire forces, under the Fairfaxes, took the line from the Ouse by Fishergate Postern and Walmgate Bar to the Red Tower, while their horse watched the two bridges over the Fosse.

But though the city and fortress were thus completely inclosed, the strength of the works was so great, and the advantage which the royalists had, in being able to move their troops from one point to another by inner lines and well protected bridges, was so important, that very little impression was made on the works, which had been much strengthened by the king's generals before the war began. Heavy guns had been planted round the walls, and on the bars or gates, and two out-lying forts had been constructed, one beyond Micklegate Bar, and the other in Bishop's Fields, which were garrisoned and armed. Clifford's Tower had been in ruins since 1642, but the earl of Cumberland had caused it to be repaired, and a deep moat was dug round it, with a drawbridge, and a platform was fixed upon it for guns. Two demi-culverins and a saker were placed on this platform, and Clifford's Tower was well defended by Sir Francis Cobbe.

The siege operations commenced June 3, and a heavy fire was opened on the besiegers from Clifford's Tower, and from the walls, before they could get their guns into position. On the 5th June, Lord Fairfax completed a battery on a hill by the side of the road to Heslington, on which he planted five guns, which fired all the afternoon on Walmgate Bar. The Scots assaulted and took the forts outside Micklegate Bar, and Manchester's troops captured the houses outside Bootham Bar, thus occupying the greater part of the suburbs. Seeing this, the garrison sallied out, and set the whole of the suburbs on fire, on the evening of the 6th of June; thus depriving the besiegers of all cover, but at the same time inflicting great injury on the inhabitants.

On the 8th of June the marquis of Newcastle received news that Prince Rupert was advancing to his assistance through Lancashire; but this news did not stop the operations of the besieging army, though it gave greatly increased confidence to the besieged. The most important operation of the besiegers was the blowing up of St. Mary's Tower, on the 16th June. This was done by General Crawford, a headstrong Scottish officer, without any orders or any proper arrangement of supports, on Trinity Sunday. In this attack the parliamentary forces were repulsed with the loss of many men killed, sixty wounded, and upwards of 200 prisoners. What was even worse, St. Mary's Tower was entirely destroyed, with the precious stores of historical and antiquarian information of which it had long been the receptacle. Happily, the antiquary Roger Dodsworth had been employed for many years by Sir Thomas Fairfax in making copies of these records, and the laborious task was just completed before the siege of York commenced. These copies are still preserved, and may be consulted in the Bodleian Library at Oxford. We are informed by the author of the "Life of the Great Lord Fairfax," that he also offered rewards to any soldier who rescued a document from amongst the rubbish, and that in that way a great number were saved, which his uncle, Charles Fairfax, took charge of a few months afterwards. Charles Fairfax and Roger Dodsworth themselves searched diligently for other documents, and amongst the ruins they recovered the Rhyming Charter of King Athelstan to St. John of Beverley. A Mr. Thompson, of whom nothing else is known, but whose name deserves to be preserved, also collected thirty bundles of papers from amongst the rubbish.*

* A Life of the Great Lord Fairfax; by Clements R. Markham, F.S.A.: London, 1870, p. 148.

But these operations and the negotiations commenced to gain time, were effectually put an end to on the 30th June, by the news that Prince Rupert was marching with 20,000 men to raise the siege of York, and that he was that night at Boroughbridge, only twelve miles distant. On hearing this important news the parliamentary generals immediately raised the siege, and retired to Marston Moor, the nearest open ground available for fighting a great battle. Prince Rupert entered York, July 1, with about 9000 horse and 8000 foot, and at once took the command of the whole of the royal forces, thus superseding the marquis of Newcastle, who had commanded the northern army from the commencement of the war, and who was allowed to be a good general, "for an amateur."

We have already described the leading events, and mentioned the well-known result of the battle of Marston Moor—the last and the most decisive of many battles fought for the possession of the city of York. After the complete overthrow of the royal army, it fled to York the same night in utter confusion; and there it was effectually dissolved, by a violent and irreparable quarrel between the marquis of Newcastle and Prince Rupert. The result of this quarrel was that the marquis of Newcastle set out for Scarborough, early on the morning of the 3rd July, where he embarked for Hamburg, accompanied by several of the leading royalists of the north; while Prince Rupert, having entirely ruined the king's affairs in the north, left the city of York to its fate, and marched into Lancashire, afterwards conducting his defeated army to the headquarters of the king, in the midland counties.

On the day after the battle, the gallant Sir Thomas Glenham, though deserted by both Rupert and Newcastle, got together about 1000 men, with whom he made some show of resistance. But real resistance had become hopeless, and a few days afterwards Sir Thomas Glenham offered to capitulate. The commissioners appointed to arrange the articles of surrender were Sir Adam Hepburn on the part of the Scots, Sir William Constable for the Fairfaxes, and Colonel Montague for Lord Manchester. Sir Thomas Glenham, as he deserved, obtained most honourable terms. He was to deliver up the city with the forts, Clifford's Tower, and all munitions of war, on the 15th; he and his garrison were to march out with all the honours of war, and to be safely conveyed to the nearest royalist garrison; no officer or soldier was to be stopped or plundered on the march; the citizens were to retain all their privileges, and no soldiers were to be quartered within the walls. On Thursday, July 16, Sir Thomas Glenham, with Sir Henry Slingsby and about 1000 men, marched out of York. The besiegers were drawn up in line on both sides of the road, extending for a mile from Micklegate Bar. As soon as the royalists were clear of the city, the three allied generals went to the minster, where a psalm was sung, and thanksgiving offered by Lord Leven's chaplain. No cathedral in England suffered less from the civil war than York minster, and the immunity was due to the unceasing watchfulness of Sir Thomas Fairfax, to whom Yorkshire owes a debt of gratitude for his thoughtful care of her proudest monument.*

The capture of the city of York by the parliamentary forces was followed very shortly by the appointment of Sir Thomas Fairfax to the command of the newly organized army of the Parliament. Very soon after Fairfax's appointment, Oliver Cromwell was named as his lieutenant; and after the whole kingdom had been overrun, and the royalists had been everywhere subdued, there commenced those discussions between the independent and republican party, headed by Cromwell, and the monarchical and presbyterian party, headed by Sir Thomas Fairfax, which soon ended in a complete rupture between the moderate and the extreme supporters of Parliament. In this contest the general feeling of the city and county of York seems to have been with Fairfax and the presbyterian party; but Cromwell had also a considerable number of supporters both in the city and the county, and until his death this party had the upper hand. At the beginning of the year 1649 the city of York was deprived of its parliamentary garrison, with the exception of that of Clifford's Tower, of which the lord mayor of York was appointed governor. This office he held under a vote of Parliament, of 26th February, by which it was resolved that Clifford's Tower should be kept as a garrison, with three score foot in it.†

In the year 1650, the Scottish Presbyterians having advanced into Lancashire with a formidable army, Cromwell was despatched to drive them back; Sir Thomas Fairfax having refused to take the command. As we are informed, "On the 5th July, 1650, Cromwell came to York, on an expedition into Scotland, at which time all the artillery of the tower (Clifford's) was discharged. The next day he dined with the lord mayor, and on the following

* Markham's Life of Fairfax, p. 181. † Drake, vol. i. p 192, and vol. ii. p. 204.

set forward to Scotland. In compliment to Cromwell, and to show their zeal for the cause, the magistrates then thought fit to take down the king's arms at Micklegate and Bootham Bars, through both of which he must needs pass in his journey, and put up the Commonwealth's arms in their stead."*

After the death of Cromwell York was the scene of most active negotiations between Lord Fairfax and General Monk, which ended in the restoration of Charles II., in the year 1660. These negotiations were in progress between Fairfax and Monk before the latter left Scotland with his army. On arriving at York he found the support of Fairfax so strong, and the position of the royal cause so good, that he was disposed to proclaim the king there. But Fairfax was altogether opposed to the taking of so important a step without the consent of Parliament, and General Monk concealed his intentions until his arrival in London. The plan was at length carried out with the assent of Parliament, and on the 11th of May, 1660, Charles II. was proclaimed with great solemnity, at York, as king of England. On that day the lord mayor, aldermen, and council, on horseback and in their richest habits, led the procession of the city and the county; next followed the chamberlains and common councilmen, on foot and in their gowns; these were attended by more than 1000 citizens under arms; and the procession was closed by a body of country gentlemen nearly 300 strong, with Lord Fairfax at their head, who rode with their swords drawn, and their hats upon the points of their swords. Charles II. was then proclaimed king at the usual places of the city; the bells rang, and the cannon in Clifford's Tower fired salutes. At night the city was brilliantly illuminated, and the proclamation of the king was everywhere received with demonstrations of joy. On the 29th of the same month of May, the restored king made his public entrance into London.†

But the restoration of the house of Stewart was of very short duration, and in the year 1688, the citizens and the county of York led the way in the final expulsion of that incurable dynasty. In 1684 Charles II. and his advisers deprived the corporation of York, and those of many other towns and cities, of their charters; and, immediately after the accession of James II. to the throne, that ill-advised monarch, amongst other unpopular acts, placed a garrison of soldiers in Clifford's Tower, which commanded

* Allen, vol. i. p. 174. † Ibid. p. 176.

the city, under Sir John Reresby. Shortly before this event, in the year 1679, religious dissensions running very high, and the bill of exclusion (to deprive James, duke of York, of his right to the succession of the throne, as an avowed and zealous Roman Catholic) having been brought forward, the duke, judging it expedient to retire from court, went to Edinburgh, and in his way passed through York. The sheriffs of the city met him at Tadcaster Bridge and accompanied him into the city, but the lord mayor and aldermen neglected or refused to do so. This being represented to the king as an insult, a reprimand, signed by the secretary of State, was forwarded to the lord mayor. This reprimand was followed in January, 1684, by a writ of *quo warranto*, by which the members of the corporation were commanded to show how they came "to usurp to themselves" several liberties, many of which they had enjoyed from the time of the Norman kings. Their charter was also demanded for perusal, and detained by the king and his ministers. In the same year the notorious Judge Jefferies attended at York, as one of the judges of assize, and informed the lord mayor and corporation that the king expected to have the government of the city at his own disposal. He further informed the citizens that it was the pleasure of the king that they should apply for a new charter, in which he would reserve to himself the nomination and approbation of the magistrates and persons in office in the city. The death of Charles II. put an end to these arbitrary proceedings. When James II. succeeded to the throne in February, 1684, he agreed, on the petition of the citizens, to restore their charter; but the final order for the restoration does not seem to have been issued till November, 1688, when the Prince of Orange had sailed for England.

It was in the year 1684 that Clifford's Tower was set fire to, and reduced to ruins. An old manuscript diary of those times gives the following account of this event:—"About ten o'clock on the night of Saint George's day, April 23rd, 1684, happened a most dreadful fire within the tower called Clifford's Tower, which consumed to ashes all the interior thereof, leaving standing only the outshell of the walls of the tower, without other harm to the city save one man slain by the fall of a piece of timber, blown up by the force of the flames, or rather by some powder therein. It was generally thought a wilful act, the soldiers not suffering the citizens to enter until it was too late; and what made it more suspicious was, that the gunner had got out all his goods before it was discovered." That this tower was intentionally destroyed is very probable, not only from the escape of the soldiers, but also from the fact of the placing of a garrison within the tower being highly offensive to the citizens, who regarded it as the first step towards the establishment of military power amongst them.*

Seizing of the City of York at the Revolution of 1688.—The seizing of the city of York was one of the first steps taken by Thomas Osborne, then earl of Danby and afterwards duke of Leeds, and the friends of William, prince of Orange, towards the overthrow of King James II. at the Revolution of 1688. Before the landing of the Prince of Orange at Torbay, in Devonshire, a number of his friends met in the north and midland districts, to organize a rising in Yorkshire and Nottinghamshire. This meeting was held at a small country inn, on the borders of Yorkshire and Derbyshire, the three most important persons present being Thomas Osborne, then earl of Danby, William Cavendish, earl of Devonshire, and John Darcy, the heir of the earl of Holderness. There it was arranged that the earl of Danby should seize upon the city of York, with the support of the adherents of the Prince of Orange in that city and county; and that as soon as that city was in his hands, the earl of Devonshire should proclaim the prince king at Nottingham, and raise the midland counties against James II. The movement at York, which went far towards deciding the fate of the kingdom, is thus described by Sir John Reresby, the governor of the city, who refused to join the movement, but did nothing effectual to prevent it:—"Rumours were now daily spread that William, prince of Orange, was preparing to land in this country, and, according to some of these reports, at the mouth of the Humber, with a considerable army, and as the champion of the Protestant religion. The deputy-lieutenants of the county [of York], ten in number, held a consultation, and Sir Henry Goodrick proposed a meeting of the gentry and freeholders of the county, for the purpose of preparing and signing a declaration of attachment to the king in this season of danger; and also for considering what course would be most advisable for preserving the public peace. This proposal was agreed to, and the meeting was summoned to assemble at York on Thursday, the 19th September, 1688." The result of the meeting, however, was very different from what was expected, and

* Allan, vol. ii. p. 205.

served to show that James II. had not a single friend left in Yorkshire, who could be relied upon to stand by him in this desperate emergency. Sir John Reresby, the governor, thus describes the events of that day:—

"Now came the day of meeting," says Sir John, "a fatal one I think. I would not go to them at the Common Hall, which was the place appointed; nor, indeed, was I very well able, by reason of some bruises I had received by my horse falling under me. But I heard that in the midst of about a hundred gentlemen who met, Sir Henry Goodrick delivered himself to this effect— That there had been great endeavours made by government of late years to bring popery into the kingdom, and by many devices to set at naught the laws of the land; that there could be no proper redress of the many grievances we laboured under but by a free Parliament; that now was the only time to prefer a petition of that sort; and that they could not imitate a better pattern than had been set before them by several lords, spiritual and temporal.

"There were those who differed with him in opinion, and would have had some expressions in the paper moderated and amended; and observed that, at the same time that they petitioned, as they designed, it would be but their duty to assure his Majesty, that they would stand firmly by him in the midst of the danger which threatened both him and his kingdom, at the hazard of their lives and fortunes; but this was overruled. When therefore the draft was completed according to the mind of Sir Henry Goodrick and his friends, though several disliked and went away, they proceeded to sign it; but before a third man could subscribe it, in came one Mr. Tankard with a useful story that the papists were risen, and that they had actually fired upon the militia troops.

"Alarmed at this the gentlemen ran out, and those that were privy to the design betook them to their horses, which were conveniently at hand for their purpose. Lord Danby, meanwhile, in his lodgings, waited for the false alarm, and mounted with his son, with Lord Lumley, Lord Horton, Lord Willoughby, and others, who together with their servants formed a body of horse consisting of 100 in number, well mounted and well accoutred.

"These rode up to the four militia troops drawn out on another account, and cried out, 'A Free Parliament, the Protestant Religion, and no Popery.' The captains of those troops were Lord Fairfax, Sir Thomas Gower, Captain Robinson, and Captain Tankard, who being admitted to the secret the night before, and being prompt and ready enough in their nature for any action of the kind, immediately cried out the same, and led their troops over to them.

"In the first place they went to the main-guard of the standing company, which, the number not exceeding twenty, they surprised before I [Sir John Reresby, the governor] had the least notice or even jealousy of what was even in agitation; not thinking it possible that men of such quality and such estates could give way to their discontent, however great and just it might be, to the degree of engaging themselves in an attempt so desperate, and so contrary to the laws they boasted, and the religion they professed."

The earl of Danby, and the adherents of the Prince of Orange, endeavoured to persuade Sir John Reresby to join them, urging that they were in arms for the Protestant religion and for the freedom of England, which James had nearly subverted, but which his son-in-law, the Prince of Orange, had landed to restore. But having failed to persuade the governor to join them, he and his inferior officers were taken prisoners; though he was allowed to remain on parole, on pledging his honour that he would not remove from his own house in York. The guard-house, magazine, and stores, with the whole of the fortress, were afterwards seized by the earl of Danby and the militia; who were joined on the following day by a company of foot soldiers that had been raised for the support of the king in the neighbourhood, and also by a company of grenadiers who were on their march from the north. This military force was zealously supported by the lord mayor and the citizens, the chief magistrate having called a meeting of these, and urged them to join in support of the Revolution and the Protestant religion. On the 14th December, 1688, the Prince of Orange was openly recognized as the head of the government, and in the course of the month of February following, on the 17th day of the month, William, prince of Orange, and the Princess Mary his wife, the eldest daughter of James II., were proclaimed king and queen of England in the usual manner, and at the accustomed places in that city, in the presence of many thousands of spectators. In the course of the following winter a large body of Danish soldiers in the service of England, amounting to 5000 foot and 1000 horse, were quartered in York and the adjoining villages, on their way to join the army of William III. in the north of Ireland.*

The military history of York, extending from the age of the Romans to modern times, ends with the successful rising of the citizens and of the militia of Yorkshire in support of the principles of the Revolution in 1688. The last movement was not the less important for having been bloodless. It was so because it was unopposed, and it was unopposed because the English people had become all but unanimous as to the principles on which they were determined to be governed. They steadily supported those principles at the time of the Jacobite insurrections of 1715 and 1745, in which the citizens and authorities of York showed their readiness again to take arms if needful, in defence of the principles by which they had so resolutely held at the Revolution of 1688.

Defoe's Account of York in 1727.—Daniel Defoe visited York many times in his frequent journeys between London and Scotland, and in the course of his extensive wanderings over every part of Yorkshire, as well as the other counties of England. His description of York was published in the year 1727, the 1st year of George II., and represents the condition of that ancient city during the greater part of the eighteenth century. Defoe made York the birthplace of his most famous hero, Robinson Crusoe, whom he describes as the son of a Hull merchant, who had made a fortune in that busy seaport, and had retired to York, to spend his latter days in peace. This was a very frequent practice; for, as Defoe says in describing York at this time, it was a pleasant and beautiful city, and not the less beautiful because the lines and fortifications constructed in the great civil war had been demolished, without, however, destroying the ancient walls which connected it with former times. The general aspect was one of peace and prosperity, and even the destruction of the fortifications had a secret pleasantness, as he says, "from the contemplation of the public tranquillity that outshines all the beauty of advanced bastions, batteries, cavaliers, and all the hard-named works of the engineers about the city." He describes York as having risen again, and seems to have been particularly struck with the bridge across the river Ouse, which, he says, was vastly strong, and consisted chiefly of one large arch seventy feet in diameter. It was at that time the largest arch in England, and only inferior amongst arches and bridges to the Rialto

* Drake's Eboracum.

at Venice. At that time, he observes, there was no trade at York, except such as depended on the confluence of gentry; but there was abundance of good company, many families unconnected with trade and commerce living there for the sake of the pleasant company and the cheap living. At that time the chief articles imported into York were wines from France and Portugal, and timber from Norway. They also brought their coals from Newcastle and Sunderland, though they could have had them, by the Aire and Calder Navigation which had then been opened about twenty years, from Wakefield, Leeds, and other places on the Yorkshire coal-field. The city was full of large and handsome houses, sufficient, in Defoe's opinion, to receive the King, Lords, and Commons, as they had done when they entertained King Charles I. with his whole court, and with the assembly of peers, besides a vast confluence of gentry from all parts, and the greater part of the royal army.*

Drake's Eboracum.—About ten years after the publication of Defoe's account of York, in 1727, a very much fuller account of that city was published by Francis Drake, a gentleman long resident there, under the title of "Eboracum: or the History and Antiquities of York." The author had taken considerable pains to collect materials for such a work, besides having had the advantage of access to immense collections of extracts, relating to the archbishopric, the county, and the city, made by Roger Dodsworth (1644); by Sir Thomas Widdrington, one of the recorders of the city (1660); by Christopher Hildyard, recorder of Headon, and steward of St. Mary's at York; by John Torre, Esq. (1690), who spent his whole life in collecting materials relating to the city and county of York; by Roger Gale (1720), a man of great antiquarian learning; as well as in the published works of Camden, the chief of topographers, whose history of the city of York is one of the most valuable and interesting chapters in his description of England. In addition to these sources Drake had access to numerous records belonging to the Corporation of York, and to other valuable sources of information. But he seems to have been on unfriendly terms with the archbishop of his day, and with some of the clergy; and though he ultimately obtained the assistance of Dr. Longwith and some other excellent scholars, in the latter part of his work, he did not secure it until he had

---

* Defoe's Tour of a Gentleman through the whole Island of Great Britain, 1727, vol. iii. p. 165.

published, or printed off, some of the old stories of Geoffrey of Monmouth, and other writers respecting York, which are not now considered to belong to authentic history, and which, even in the reign of Queen Elizabeth, the learned Camden had passed by with a smile of contempt. Notwithstanding this defect, and an occasional want of good taste, the work of Drake contains a very extensive, though not well arranged, collection of historical materials, especially from the time of the Norman conquest to the revolution of 1688. Since that time several other works, some of great merit, have been published respecting this ancient city, its numerous antiquities, and its unrivalled minster.

In Drake's own time the ancient commerce and manufactures of York had been transferred to Hull, Leeds, and other manufacturing towns, but it was still one of the pleasantest cities in England. Speaking of York in 1737, he says:—"What has been and is the chief support of the city at present, is the resort to and residence of several country gentlemen with their families in it. These have found by experience that living at York is so much cheaper than London, that it is even less expensive than living at their own houses in the country; the great variety of provisions with which our markets abound, makes it very easy to furnish out an elegant table at a moderate rate. And it is true yet, what Fuller said of us in his time, that an ordinary at York would make a feast in London. Besides, our city is very well qualified for the education of their children, especially females, in all the necessary accomplishments belonging to that sex. The diversions which have been of late years set on foot, and are now briskly carried on every winter in the city, are another great inducement to bring company to it. About twenty years ago a weekly assembly was begun here, when gentlemen and ladies met every Monday night, to dance, play at cards, and amuse themselves with these and other innocent diversions of the place. It was first set up at the manor, was several years kept in Lord Irwin's house in the Minster Yard, and is now continued in the room built on purpose for it in the New Buildings. Two or three years ago a music assembly was begun in York, and is continued every Friday night, in the same room, when a set of choice hands and voices are procured to divert the company each winter. To these are added a company of stage-players, who by subscription act twice a week, and are allowed to be the best strollers in the kingdom.

"Twice in the year the assizes, or general gaol delivery for the city and county of York, are held here. On which occasion, besides the men of business, did formerly resort a great number of our northern gentry, to partake of the diversions that were usually set up in the city for that time. Of late years this is altered; and the grand meeting of the nobility and gentry of the north and other parts of England, is now at York, in or about the month of August, drawn thither by the hopes of being agreeably entertained for a week in horse racing, balls, assemblies, &c."

Modern York.—The progress of the city of York in population was slow, from the time of the accession of the House of Hanover to the throne to the commencement of the reign of King William IV., when the introduction of the railway system into this part of England gave fresh occupation to the capital and enterprise of the more wealthy and enterprising inhabitants of this ancient city, in constructing works even on a grander scale than that on which the engineers of Rome and Greece had constructed their lines of road from York to all other parts of Britain seventeen to eighteen hundred years ago. The natural lines of water communication were not merely retained, but improved, during the last century; and so far as the Ouse and the Foss, which unite at York, could be made more available for the purposes of inland trade, that was effected by rendering the river Ouse and its chief tributary the Ure navigable up to Boroughbridge and to Ripon, nearly to the entrance of Wensley Dale. The river Foss, though only seventeen miles in length, was also rendered navigable from the city of York, through the greater part of its course. A much bolder scheme for the improvement of the lower part of the navigation of the river Ouse, was proposed, near the beginning of the eighteenth century, by his grace the duke of Bolton, of the House of Paulett, whose principal residence was at Bolton Castle, in Wensley Dale. According to the description of this plan given by Drake, the duke of Bolton proposed to construct works for the improvement of the Ouse, from the point where it joins the Humber up to the city of York, by cutting a new and artificial course for the river, which was to have been less than half the length of the existing channel, but possessed of a much greater depth of water. Had the proposed work been carried out successfully, it would almost, if not altogether, have rivalled some of the earlier works constructed by Brindley and the duke of Bridgewater, in Lancashire, about the middle of the same century. But the duke of Bolton, though a man of considerable talents, was somewhat eccentric in his character and temper, and failed to induce any one to join him in this great undertaking. Hence the improvements made in the river Ouse were on a smaller scale, and did not give a greater depth of water in the neighbourhood of York than five or six feet, which is only about the fourth part of the depth of water at Hull, and not more than one-half the depth of water at Selby. Thus commerce passed away from the city of York, although the great improvements effected in the Ure, the Foss, the Derwent, the Aire, the Calder, and the Don, all of which flow into the Ouse or the Humber, gave the citizens of York greater advantages than they had ever before possessed of obtaining supplies of coal and other articles, whether produced in the county, or imported from abroad. York has thus always retained a considerable portion of inland trade, though from its distance from the coal-fields of Yorkshire, it has not been able to derive many of those advantages which the steam-engine, in its various applications, has given to the towns of the West Riding and to the port of Hull. But, as already mentioned, during the last thirty years the application of steam power to the purposes of locomotion on railways, has again had the effect of rendering the city of York a connecting point on a large scale between the north and the south, and the east and the west. The position of the city with reference to London, Edinburgh, Leeds, Manchester, Hull, and Liverpool, and the thickly peopled districts of which they are the capitals, as well as to England generally, must always make it an important place in the system of internal communications of Great Britain. The position of York was originally so well chosen in the centre of Britain, that the lapse of nearly two thousand years has failed to deprive it of many of its advantages.

Previous to this transition, York owed its chief advantages to its position and rank as the capital of the largest English county. Here it was that civil and criminal justice was administered twice a year, to all the inhabitants of the county of York, many of whom had, indeed, to travel fifty or sixty miles to the seat of justice. The archbishopric of York extended, as it still does, over a much wider district than the county, and the minster at York was the cathedral church of a province always increasing in population and wealth, and connected by many interesting ties with the whole of the north of England. In addition to this, York being situated in a fertile and healthy country, and always possessing much agreeable society, has ever been a favourite residence for families unconnected with trade, and seeking a pleasant place of abode. Coaches began to run from York to London and to Hull in the reign of Charles II., and when Drake published his "History of York," in the year 1736, there were in that city forty-two gentlemen's coaches, twenty-two hackney coaches, and twenty-two hackney chairs, or sedans, in full use."*

The Yorkshire Philosophical Society, and its Grounds and Museum.—During the last forty years the high reputation which the city of York acquired in ancient times, as a seat of learning and intelligence, has been well maintained. York has ever been, and never more than at present, a favourite seat of the delightful science of archæology; in no other city has the science of geology been more actively or successfully cultivated; and the museum of the Yorkshire Philosophical Society, opened on the 2nd February, 1830, is amongst the most prosperous in the kingdom. The singularly interesting grounds in which the museum stands, occupy one half of the ancient close of the Benedictine Abbey of Saint Mary, with a small portion of the old moat of the city walls, and of the inclosure within which the hospital of St. Leonard formerly stood. In this museum are collected an immense number of remains of antiquity; and there also is a very large assemblage of geological specimens. The former owe much to the late Rev. Charles Wellbeloved, assisted by the Rev. J. Kenrick. The geological collection is equally indebted to the persevering labours and the extensive discoveries of Professor John Phillips.

Amongst the recently discovered treasures of ancient times stored in this museum, are remains of an inscription as ancient even as the reign of the Emperor Trajan, which once adorned a great building erected at Eboracum in the year A.D. 108, in the seventh consulship of that emperor. These serve to show that the antiquity of the buildings and walls of Roman York is even greater than was supposed, namely, than the time of the Emperor Hadrian's visit to Britain, about the year 120 of the Christian era.

The Ancient and Modern Libraries of York.—Almost from the earliest Christian times of the Anglian monarchy of Northumbria,

* Drake, 241.

York was the seat of an extensive and valuable library, described in the first volume of this work. This noble collection of books, after being the delight of English scholars for several generations, seems to have been utterly destroyed, in the numerous sieges and the destructive fires to which York was exposed, in the wars with the Danes and the Normans. But when something like internal tranquillity was restored, another library was formed at York, in connection with the minster. This library has continued in existence ever since, and now contains upwards of 8000 works of reference, including many rare and valuable manuscripts. Good modern libraries were established at York at the beginning of the present century.

York Minster at the Present Time.—In the earlier part of this chapter we have very carefully traced the history of York minster from the time of King Eadwine of Northumbria (627), whom Dean Gale justly describes as the first founder of the minster, down to modern times; and in a subsequent summary of the principal dates of the history of York we shall show the progress of the fabric through its many stages, along with other remarkable events. No other cathedrals in England possess so many historical associations, except those of Canterbury and Westminster Abbey, the latter of which, however, only dates from the time of Edward the Confessor (1065-66); and in point of massiveness and grandeur, and of beauty combined with strength, it would be difficult to find anywhere in Europe a building producing so strong an impression as York minster. The beauty as well as the grandeur of this minster has been celebrated throughout Europe for many hundred years. Æneas Silvius, who was afterwards Pope Pius II., and who passed through York about the year 1450, even then described the church of York as worthy to be noted throughout the world for its vastness and beauty, and spoke of the chapter-house as a beautiful light chapel, whose glass walls rose between slender clustered columns. The best general exterior view of the minster is from the walls of York. One of the finest interior views, next to that seen on entering, as is usual, by the south transept, is that obtained by advancing from the west entrance about half-way up the nave, from which point the great tower arches and part of the windows of the lantern may be seen to advantage, as well as the long, high roofs of the nave and the choir, and the upper portion of the grand east window. The general impression made by the interior is that of grandeur displayed in harmonious proportions.

In 1863 the vast nave was fitted for congregational purposes, with movable benches, choir seats, and an organ, and was lighted with gas. The minster thus lighted is singularly beautiful. There are many fine monuments in York minster; but in this respect it cannot compare with Westminster Abbey. Amongst the best are those of several of the most eminent archbishops of York. Some members of the Ingram family, who delighted in York as a residence, are interred here. Here also rest the remains of Charles Howard, earl of Carlisle, interred 1684; Sir Henry Belassis, 1630; and Sir George Savile, who died 1784, after having represented the county of York in Parliament for twenty-five years. The last monument was erected by public subscription, to a man well deserving the honour.

A building like York minster, constructed through so many ages, must have many styles of architecture. The inner wall of the crypt presents a specimen of the Saxon style. Some remains of Norman architecture are found at the west end of the crypt. The late Norman exists in its eastern portion; the early English in the north and south transepts; the decorated in the nave and chapter house; the early perpendicular in the lady chapel and presbyteria; the perpendicular in the choir, and the late perpendicular in the central and two western towers. The stone of which the minster is built is magnesian limestone, from quarries near Tadcaster, from the Huddleston quarries near Sherburn, and from Stapleton, near Pontefract. Considerable sums are yearly expended in maintaining and repairing the building.* In the height of its roofs, which are $99\frac{1}{2}$ feet in the nave, and 102 feet in the choir, York minster exceeds every other English cathedral. The breadth of the nave is $104\frac{1}{4}$ feet, with its aisles. The breadth of the choir is ninety-nine and a half feet. The window at the eastern end contains a complete wall of beautiful coloured glass. It is one of the largest and finest windows in the world.

Modern Fires in the Minster at York.—This magnificent building has suffered twice in modern times from dangerous conflagrations, one of them the act of a dangerous lunatic, Jonathan Martin, who concealed himself in the building, and set fire to the choir, on the 2nd of February, 1829. His madness was so evident,

---
* Murray's Handbook of Yorkshire, p. 22.

that when put upon his trial on Monday, March 31, 1829, he was found Not Guilty, though he was confined in a lunatic asylum, to the time of his death in the year 1838, to prevent further mischief. A public meeting for the restoration of the building was held at the Concert Room, York, on the 5th March, the then earl of Harewood in the chair, when it was determined that every thing should be restored as much as possible to its original form. This was done at an expense of about £65,000, and the whole completed before the year 1831.* Another fire, accidental in its origin, if anything ought to be considered accidental that arises from the absence of the utmost precaution, occurred in the year 1840; did injury which it required £25,000 to repair; and again endangered a magnificent fabric, and remains of ancient genius, skill, and historical fame, which no amount of wealth could restore. While we write, the cathedral of Canterbury, almost the only building in England that can rival York minster, has narrowly escaped destruction, from what are also called accidental causes. It is only just to give the following note from the Rev. Mr. Raine's notes on the Fabric Rolls of York minster, as to the spirit in which this noble building is regarded and kept. The editor of the Fabric Rolls observes, that "in old times there were but few vacant spaces around our cathedrals. Commerce and traffic of every description were carried on at their very doors, as we may still see on the Continent. So it was at York. A range of tenements, extending from the west end of Belfrey's Church to the corner of Petergate, was removed within the last thirty years. The burial ground of the same church, which was adjacent to the minster, was frequently used for fairs and other festivities, nor was the inside of the cathedral itself free from gross neglect and profanation. There is more respect and consideration shown at the present day to our cathedrals, than was ever paid to them during the middle ages."

The Churches of York.—The churches in York are cast into the shade by the minster; but many are of interesting architecture, and like the cathedral are rich in windows of stained glass. The most remarkable of these churches are All Saints (Pavement), St. Helen's (Stonegate), St. Martin's (Coney Street), St. Mary's (Castlegate), All Saints (North Street), St. Martin-cum-Gregory (Micklegate), St. Michael-le-Belfrey (near the minster), Holy Trinity (Goodram-

* Allan's History of Yorkshire, vol. ii. p. 71.

gate), and St. Denis and St. Margaret's, both in Walmgate. There were forty-five churches in York before the Reformation; at the present time the number is still nearly thirty.

York Castle is situated near the junction of the Ouse with the Fosse, on the south-east margin of the city. All that now remains of the old castle, built most probably during the reigns of the first three Edwards, is the ruin of the keep called Clifford's Tower. This marks the site of one of the original fortresses built by William the Conqueror. The other is supposed to have been on the Baile Mound, on the opposite side of the river Ouse. To write the history of this castle, and its successor the Edwardian fortress, would be to re-write a great part of the history of the city of York.

The first printer of a newspaper in York was Grace White, the widow of Mr. John White, printer, and the first weekly number was issued on Monday, February 23, 1718. It was called "*The York Mercury*, or a general view of the affairs of Europe, but more particularly of Great Britain, with useful observations on trade." The price of the paper was 1½*d.*, and its dimensions seven inches by five inches and a half, small quarto, twelve pages. The papers now published in York are the *York Herald*, *Yorkshire Gazette*, *Yorkshire Chronicle*, and *Yorkshire Telegraph*, the two former published at 2*d.*, and the two latter at 1*d.* each.

The present Ouse Bridge, the successor of many ancient bridges across this fine river, one of which had the largest central arch in Europe, except the Rialto at Venice, was opened in the year 1820, in the second lord mayoralty of Mr. Alderman Peacock, who laid the foundation stone in 1810.

Lendal Bridge, which was erected according to a design of Mr. Page, of London, was opened in January, 1863. It crosses the river Ouse by a single Tudor arch of iron, the width of the span being 175 feet 2 inches. There is a clear height of 25 feet from the summer level of the river to the centre of the arch. The bridge has a footpath on each side 8 feet 3 inches in width, and the carriage way measures across 21 feet 4 inches, making the total internal width of the structure 37 feet 10 inches. The iron work is formed of six massive ribs let into the masonry of the abutments, and these ribs are supported to some extent by stone springers, which are carried down into the foundations. The carriage way is placed across the ribs, and consists of strong corrugated iron plates, thickly coated with asphalte to prevent corrosion. Upon these plates rests a bed of concrete, in which is fixed a paving of Mount-Sorrel granite, to make the road durable, the whole being covered with gravel. The footpaths are laid with smooth and broad flagging, obtained from the Hopton Wood quarries. The parapet on each side of the bridge is handsome. Its base has a plain surface of iron, and is surmounted by a neat coping. The beauty of the parapet lies in its central portion, which consists in a continuous series of quatrefoils, eighteen inches in diameter. In the middle of these quatrefoils are fixed shields with the arms of England, of the archiepiscopal see of York, and also of the white rose of York. No less than about 380 tons of iron were used in the building of the bridge; and the cost, including the approaches, amounted in round numbers to £35,000. The approaches to the minster from Lendal Bridge have been very much improved.

Railway.—The Great Northern Railway is worthy of the cities which it connects, and from which it extends. The present station, which was erected in 1841, is situated in Tanner Row; but a new station, estimated to cost £200,000, is in course of construction (1872). It is situated outside the walls, and lies between the entrance to the present station and the bridge by which the Scarborough line crosses the river. It is to have what is called an island platform, and will be a through instead of a terminal station, like the old one. There is to be a magnificent hotel connected with it, fronting the river.

St. Mary's Abbey, York.—Whilst so many noble edifices have totally disappeared, St. Mary's Abbey, for many ages one of the greatest glories of York, and still great in ruin, remains a monument of departed splendour. Happily these noble ruins have passed into the hands of the Yorkshire Philosophical Society, an association capable of appreciating their value, and certain to preserve them from every injury except the silent action of time.

The Hospitals, Asylums, and Schools of York.—The city of York contains the remains of almost innumerable hospitals, founded in different ages and for different objects. Amongst these are the hospital of St. Anthony, Agar's, Barton's, the Spital or hospital of St. Catherine, Coltons, Ingram's, St. Leonard's, the Spital of St. Loy, the Maison Dieu in Whitefriars' Lane, Mason's Hospital, Middleton's, St. Thomas', Trinity, the hospital of Sir Robert Watter, the Alms Houses of the Cordwainers, Winterskelf Hospital, Lady Hewley's Charity, Wilson's Hospital, the County Hospital, the Dispensary and the Lunatic Asylum, the Free Grammar School, &c.

Conclusion of History of City of York.—We conclude this account of the ancient and most interesting city of York, with the following extract as to Yorkshire and its time-honoured capital, from the Introduction to the Census of England, &c., for the year 1871.

"The country of the Brigantes was specially affected by the Romans; Agricola, it is said, founded York, which became the *Altera Roma* of his countrymen, and was famous once for its shipping and commerce, now deserted to points near the coast. It was Deira, the Deerland of the Saxons. Here the Northmen fought William I. and were conquered; the country was devastated, but soon recovered its station in English history. The battle of the Standard; the battle where the houses of York and Lancaster, on a Palm Sunday, fought out their great strife, and left on the fields of Towton thousands of slain; and Marston Moor, in the last English Civil War—finally attest the importance of this great battle-field of the kingdom. On the Derwent too, Harold had expended part of his forces in resisting the onslaught of the fleet of Northmen on the east side of the kingdom, while the more formidable foe arrived on the southern side, to strike the main blow at the heart of his dominions."

The population of the parliamentary city of York, according to the census of 1871, is 50,761, which is probably as large as it has been since the time of the Romans.

DATES OF THE PRINCIPAL EVENTS CONNECTED WITH THE HISTORY OF THE CITY OF YORK.

First Century of the Christian Era.—27 B.C. to A.D. 41.—Coins struck in the reigns of the Emperors Augustus, Tiberius, and Caligula, found at York, probably brought by the first Roman army.—"Yorkshire: Past and Present," Vol. ii. p. 78.

44.—The Roman Emperor Claudius sends an army to invade Britain.—Vol. i. p. 281.

79.—The Brigantes, whose capital was Eboracum or York, conquered by Agricola.—Vol. i. p. 282.

Second Century.—108.—Tablet found at York, in the year 1854, with inscription, stating that the work to which it belonged (probably a gateway in the walls of York), was erected by the Ninth Legion, by order of the Emperor Trajan, he being saluted Imperator the sixth time, corresponding to A.D. 108.—Vol. ii. p. 78.

120.—The Emperor Hadrian in Britain and founds many great works.—Vol. i. p. 317.

130.—Eboracum the head-quarters of the Sixth Roman Legion, vol. i. p. 321; and the capital of the Roman province of Britain.—Vol. i. p. 333.

Third Century.—211.—The Emperor Septimius Severus visits and dies at Eboracum.—Vol. i. p. 334–349.

Fourth Century.—304.—The Emperor Constantius Chlorus visits and dies at Eboracum.—Vol. i. p. 335.

306.—Constantine the Great proclaimed emperor at Eboracum.—Vol. i. p. 335.

Fifth Century.—420.—The Romans retire from Britain.—Vol. i. pp. 351–52.

Sixth Century.—547.—Ida, the first king of the Northumbrian Angles, lands on the north-east coast of Britain, and a few years later captures Eboracum, called by the Angles and Saxons, Eoforwic.—Vol. i. pp. 354, 391.

Seventh Century.—615 to 627.—Eadwine, the first Christian king of Northumbria, reigns, and coins money at Eoforwic, or York.—Vol. ii. p. 17.

627.—Eadwine, king of the Northumbrians, first founder of York minster.—Vol. i. p. 367. Vol. ii. p. 20.

632.—Oswald, king of Northumbria, second founder.—Vol. i. p. 370. Vol. ii. p. 20.

639.—Aldhelm, bishop of Sherburn, born this year, studied the Roman law, in the School of Law at York.

666.—Wilfrid, archbishop of York, third founder of the minster.—Vol. i. p. 377. Vol. ii. p. 21.

Eight Century.—731.—Bede's account of the archbishopric of Northumbria or York.—Vol. i. p. 379.

762.—Albert, archbishop of York, fourth founder of York minster, and first founder of the library of York.—Vol. ii. pp. 22, 23

766.—Athelstane, or Guthrum, Danish king of Northumbria, reigns and has a mint at York, called Jorvik by the Danes.—Vol. ii. p. 25.

Ninth Century.—804.—Alcuin describes the School of Roman Law as still existing at York.—Vol. i. p. 335.

Tenth Century.—901.—Yorvik much frequented by Danish merchants, and said to have had 30,000 inhabitants.

939.—Athelstane the Great, the grandson of Alfred the Great, captures York, and coins money there. After his death Olaf, the Dane, recovers York.—Vol. ii. p. 27.

Eleventh Century.—1079.—York besieged by the Normans and Danes. Two castles built there by William the Conqueror.—Vol. ii. p. 28.

1068, 3rd William the Conqueror.—Thomas of Bayeux first Norman archbishop of York, rebuilder, and described by Dean Gale as fifth founder, of York Minster.—Vol. ii. p. 38.

1084 to 1086.—At Domesday Survey nearly 2000 burgages at York.—Vol. ii. p. 29.

Thirteenth Century.—1200, 1st King John.—The king grants charters to citizens of York, and confirms previous charters of Henry I. and II.—Vol. ii. p. 34.

1200, 1st King John, to 1227, 11th Henry III.—Walter Gray, archbishop of York, commences the reconstruction of York minster.—Vol. ii. p. 39.

1216.—The register of the archbishops of York dates from this year, in the archbishopric of Walter Gray.

1250, 35th Henry III.—John Romanus, or the Roman, treasurer of York minster, builds the northern part of the choir and the bell tower, and refaces the southern tower.—Vol. ii. p. 39.

Fourteenth Century.—1327—Walls of York rebuilt and strengthened by order of King Edward III.—Vol. ii. p. 43.

1329—King Edward III. and Philippa of Hainault, married in York minster.—Vol. ii. p. 43.

1361, 44th Edward III.—First stone of easternmost part of the minster, laid by Archbishop Thoresby.—Vol. ii. p. 40.

1370, 44th Edward III.—Walter Skirlaw, prebendary of Fenton, afterwards bishop of Durham, builds the bell tower.—Vol. ii. p. 40.

1394—King Richard II. visits York, and makes Walter de Selby, then mayor, with all his successors, lords mayor of York.—Vol. ii. p. 44.

Fifteenth Century.—1461—Edward IV. crowned king of England at York, after battle of Towton Field, with royal cap, called Abacot.—Vol. ii. p. 48.

1466–67, 6th Edward IV.—College of S. William of York founded.

1472, 12th Edward IV.—"The interior of the minster being thoroughly finished, the minster consecrated on the 3rd of July, 1472."—Fabric Rolls.

1475, 15th Edward IV.—The central tower finished about this time.—Fabric Rolls.

1479, 19th Edward IV.—A payment made this year to John the Girdler for one zone of velvet, for the great horn of Ulphus.

1483.—Coronation of Richard III. and of his queen in York minster.—Vol. ii. p. 49.

Sixteenth Century.—1544, 35th Henry VIII.—The last Fabric Roll before the Reformation.

Seventeenth Century.—1640–1644.—Roger Dodsworth completes his collection of documents at York.—Vol. ii. p. 65.

1642–43—Charles I. assembles Peers and an army at York, to resist the Parliament.—Vol. ii. p. 63.

1644.—The Civil War. York besieged, and taken by Fairfax, Cromwell, and Leven, after the battle of Marston Moor.—Vol. ii. p. 67.

1688.—Rising of Thomas Osborne, earl of Danby, afterwards duke of Leeds, and of the citizens and militia at York, against James II.—Vol. ii. p. 72

1691.—Torre, the antiquary, commenced his collection at York.—Vol. ii. p. 74.

Eighteenth Century.—1727.—Daniel Defoe visits and describes the city of York.—Vol. ii. p. 73.

1736.—Francis Drake publishes his "Eboracum, or History and Antiquities of York."—Vol. ii. p. 74.

Nineteenth Century.—1829—Fire in the minster caused by an incendiary. Building restored, chiefly by contributions of the people of Yorkshire, at a cost of £65,000.—Vol. ii. pp. 80, 81.

1840—Fire in minster from negligence of workmen. Building restored, chiefly by the people of Yorkshire, at a cost of £25,000.—Vol. ii. p. 81.

1871.—Population of York, 1871, 50,761.—Vol. ii. p. 84.

SUCCESSION OF THE ARCHBISHOPS OF YORK.

627- 633 Paulinus, retired, buried at Rochester.
(See vacant above ten years.)
664- 669 Chadd, abbot of Lastingham, buried at Lichfield.
669- 678 Wilfrid I., retired.
678- 686 Bosa, retired.
686- 691 Wilfrid restored, deposed about 691, buried at Ripon.
691- 705 Bosa restored, buried at York.
705- 718 St. John of Beverley, bishop of Hexham, buried at Beverley.
718- 732 Wilfrid II., retired.
732- 766 Egbert, buried at York.
766- 782 Albert, buried at York.
782- 796 Eanbald I., buried at York.
796- 812 Eanbald II.
812- 831 Wulfsy.
837- 854 Wigmund.
854- 895 Wulfere.
895- 928 Ethelbald.
928- 930 Redewald or Lotheward.
931- 956 Wulstan I., buried at Oundle.
956- 972 Oskytel, bishop of Dorchester, buried at Bedford.
972 Ethelwold, resigned.
972- 992 Oswald, held the see of Worcester *in commendam*, buried there.
992-1002 Adulph, abbot of Peterborough, buried there.
1002-1023 Wulstan II., held Worcester *in commendam*, buried at Ely.
1023-1050 Alfrick Puttoc, provost of Winchester, buried at Peterborough.
1050-1060 Kinsius, chaplain to Edward the Confessor, buried at Peterborough.
1060-1069 Alfred, bishop of Worcester, buried at York.
1070-1100 Thomas I., treasurer of Bayeux, buried at York.
1101-1108 Gerard, bishop of Hereford, buried at York.
1108-1114 Thomas II., bishop-elect of London, buried at York.
1114-1140 Thurstan, canon of St. Paul's, buried at Pontefract.
1143-1147 William Fitzherbert, or St. William, treasurer of York, deposed.
1147-1153 Henry Murdoc, abbot of Fountains, buried at York.
1153-1154 St. William restored, buried at York, canonized by Nicholas III.
1154-1181 Roger de Pont l'Evêque, archdeacon of Canterbury, buried at York.
1191-1207 Geoffrey Plantagenet, bishop of Lincoln, retired in 1207.
(See vacant nine years.)
1216-1255 Walter de Gray, bishop of Worcester, buried at York.
1256-1258 Sewal de Bovill, dean of York, buried at York.
1258-1265 Godfrey de Ludham, dean of York, buried at York.
1266-1279 Walter Giffard, bishop of Bath and Wells, buried at York.
1279-1285 William de Wickwaine, chancellor of York, buried at Pontigny.
1286-1297 John Romanus, the Roman, precentor of Lincoln, buried at York.
1297-1299 Henry de Newark, dean of York, buried at York.
1300-1304 Thomas de Corbridge, canon of York, buried at Southwell.

1304-1315	William de Greenfield, dean of Chichester, buried at York.
1317-1340	William de Melton, provost of Beverley, buried at York.
1342-1352	William la Zouche, dean of York, buried at York.
1352-1373	John de Thoresby, bishop of Worcester, buried at York.
1374	Alexander Neville, prebendary of York, buried at Louvaine.
1388	Thomas Arundell, bishop of Ely, translated to Canterbury.
1396	Robert Waldby, bishop of Chichester, buried in Westminster Abbey.
1398	Richard Scroope, bishop of Lichfield, buried at York.
1407	Henry Bowett, bishop of Bath and Wells, buried at York.
1426	John Kempe, bishop of London, cardinal and lord chancellor, translated to Canterbury.
1452	William Booth, bishop of Lichfield, buried at Southwell.
1464	George Neville, bishop of Exeter, lord chancellor, buried at York.
1476	Lawrence Booth, bishop of Durham, buried at Southwell.
1480	Thomas Rotherham, bishop of Lincoln, buried at York.
1501	Thomas Savage, bishop of London, buried at York.
1508	Christopher Bainbrigge, bishop of Durham, buried at Rome.
1514	Thomas Wolsey, bishop of Lincoln, cardinal, buried at Leicester.
1531	Edward Lee, prebendary of York, buried at York.
1544-1553	Robert Holgate, bishop of Llandaff, deprived, buried at Hemsworth.
1555-1558	Nicholas Heath, bishop of Worcester, president of Wales, lord chancellor, deprived, buried at Cobham, Surrey.
1570	(1561, Lawton) Thomas Young, bishop of St. David's, first Protestant archbishop of York, buried at York.
1570	Edmund Grindall, bishop of London, translated to Canterbury.
1576	Edwin Sandys, bishop of London, buried at Southwell.
1589	John Piers, bishop of Salisbury, buried at York.
1595	Matthew Hutton, bishop of Durham, buried at York.
1606	Tobias Matthew, bishop of Durham, buried at York.
1628	George Mountaigne, bishop of Durham, buried at Cawood.
1629	Samuel Harsnet, bishop of Norwich, buried at Chigwell.
1632	Richard Neile, bishop of Winchester, buried at York.
1642	John Williams, bishop of Lincoln, buried at Llandeglay.
	(See vacant ten years.)
1660	Accepted Frewen, bishop of Lichfield, buried at York.
1664	Richard Storne, bishop of Carlisle, buried at York.
1683	John Dolben, bishop of Rochester, buried at York.
1688	Thomas Lamplugh, bishop of Exeter, buried at York.
1691	John Sharp, dean of Canterbury, buried at York.
1714	Sir William Dawes, Bart., bishop of Chester, buried at St. Catherine's College, Cambridge.
1724	Lancellot Blackburne, bishop of Exeter, buried at St. Margaret's, Westminster.
1743	Thomas Herring, bishop of Bangor, translated to Canterbury.
1747	Matthew Hutton, bishop of Bangor, translated to Canterbury.
1757	John Gilbert, bishop of Salisbury.

PAST AND PRESENT.   89

1761	Hon. Robert Hay Drummond, bishop of Salisbury, buried at Bishopthorpe.
1777	William Markham, bishop of Chester, buried at Westminster Abbey.
1808	Hon. Edward Venables Vernon Harcourt, bishop of Carlisle, buried at Stanton Harcourt, county Oxford.
1848	Thomas Musgrave, bishop of Hereford, buried in Kensal Green.
1860	Charles Thomas Longley, bishop of Durham, translated to Canterbury, buried at Addington.
1863	William Thomson, bishop of Gloucester and Bristol.

Diocese of York.—The county of York is divided into two dioceses. The see of Ripon, created in 1836, embraces Richmondshire, Craven, and part of the old deaneries of Pontefract and Doncaster. The diocese of York comprises the whole of the East Riding, and the eastern portion of the North and West Ridings. Its extent is 2,261,493 acres; there are 603 benefices in it, divided into thirty rural deaneries, and three archdeaconries.

MEMBERS OF PARLIAMENT FOR THE CITY OF YORK, SINCE 1831.

Date.	Candidates.	Elected.
1831	Samuel Adlam Bayntun, Esq.; the Hon. Thomas Dundas,	Samuel Adlam Bayntun. Hon. Thomas Dundas.
1832	Hon. E. R. Petre; S. A. Bayntun, Esq.; John Henry Lowther, Esq.; Hon. T. Dundas,	Hon. E. R. Petre. Samuel Adlam Bayntun.
1833	Hon. T. Dundas; John Henry Lowther, Esq.; vice Bayntum, deceased,	Hon. Thomas Dundas.
1835	John Henry Lowther, Esq.; Hon. John C. Dundas; C. F. Barclay, Esq.,	John Henry Lowther. Hon. John C. Dundas.
1837	John Henry Lowther, Esq.; Hon. J. Dundas; D. F. Atcherley, Esq.,	John Henry Lowther. Hon. J. Dundas.
1841	John Henry Lowther, Esq.; Henry Redhead Yorke, Esq.; D. F. Atcherley, Esq.,	John Henry Lowther. Henry Redhead Yorke.
1847	Henry Redhead Yorke, Esq.; John George Smyth, Esq.,	Henry Redhead Yorke. John George Smyth.
1848	W. M. E. Milner, Esq.; Henry Vincent, Esq.; Serjeant Wilkins. To supply the vacancy occasioned by the death of H. R. Yorke, Esq.,	W. M. E. Milner.
1852	J. G. Smyth, Esq.; W. M. E. Milner, Esq.; H. Vincent, Esq.; George Leeman, Esq., retired from the contest.	John George Smyth. W. M. E. Milner.
1857	J. P. Brown-Westhead, Esq.; John George Smyth, Esq.; M. Lewin, Esq.,	J. P. Brown-Westhead. John George Smyth.
1859	J. P. Brown-Westhead, Esq.; John George Smyth, Esq.; A. H. Layard, Esq.,	J. P. Brown-Westhead. John George Smyth.
1865	James Lowther, Esq.; Joshua P. Brown-Westhead, Esq.; George Leeman, Esq.,	James Lowther. George Leeman.
1868	James Lowther, Esq.; Joshua Proctor Brown-Westhead, Esq.; John Hall Gladstone, Esq.,	James Lowther. J. P. Brown-Westhead.
1871	George Leeman, Esq. To supply the vacancy occasioned by the resignation of J. P. Brown Westhead,	George Leeman.

LORD MAYORS AND SHERIFFS OF YORK SINCE THE PASSING OF THE MUNICIPAL REFORM ACT.

Served.	Lord Mayors.	Sheriffs.
1835	Thomas Wood Wilson (elected under the old regime),	Seth Agar and W. Scawin.
1836	Sir John Simpson, Knight,	John Roper.
1837	James Meek,	William Lockwood.
1838	George Hudson,	William Matterson.
1839	George Hudson (second time),	Edmund H. Roper.
1840	Sir William Stephenson Clark, Knight,	William North.
1841	Robert Cattle (paid fine),	John Walker.
1842	William Matterson,	Robert Tonge Horsley.
1843	Joseph Buckle,	Richard Nicholson.
1844	Joseph Buckle (second time), (J. Swann, J. Barber (2nd time), W. Scawin (paid fine)	James Chadwick.
1845	William Gray,	Henry Bellerby
1846	William Richardson,	George Jennings
1847	G. Hudson (3rd time), Sir J. Simpson (2nd), paid fine,	George T. Andrews.
1848	James Richardson,	Benjamin Dodsworth.
1849	James Meek (second time),	Richard Evers.
1850	George H. Seymour,	William Hotham.
1851	James Meek (third time),	Edward Day.
1852	Henry Cooper,	George Wilson.
1853	Richard Evers,	William Hudson.
1854	George Leeman,	William C. Anderson.
1855	George Wilson (William Hudson paid fine),	George P. Bainbridge.
1856	James Meek, jun.,	Richard Hey.
1857	Edward Richard Adersonn,	Richard Welch Hollon.
1858	John Wood (Joseph Rowntree paid fine),	Robert Farrer.
1859	William Dalla Husband,	J. B. Atkinson.
1860	Richard Evers (second time),	George Oldfield.
1861	George Leeman (second time),	Thomas Cabry.
1862	William Fox Clarke,	Edward Wade.
1863	William Fox Clarke (second time),	Francis Carr.
1864	Richard Welch Hollon,	Ralph Weatherley.
1865	Edwin Wade,	Edwin Thompson.
1866	James Meek (second time),	Thomas Sanderson.
1867	James Meek (third time),	Edward Smallwood.
1868	Ralph Weatherley,	James Day.
1869	Alfred Ely Hargrove,	Henry Steward.
1870	John Colburn,	Joseph Terry.
1871	George Leeman (third time),	Lancelot Foster.
1872	William Walker,	William Varey.
1873	Henry Steward,	Edward Rooke.

CHAPTER II.

THE HISTORY OF THE BOROUGH OF LEEDS.

HAVING traced the history of the ancient city of York, the capital of this county, from the British and Roman period to modern times, we next proceed to give an account of the other large towns of Yorkshire, which have come into existence, or grown up into wealth and influence, during that long period. We commence this part of our work with an account of the manufacturing towns of the West Riding, the chief seats of the woollen and worsted manufactures of England, and shall afterwards trace the rise of the other large Yorkshire towns, which owe their growth and prosperity to different sources of national industry and wealth.

The parliamentary and municipal borough of Leeds, the largest and most populous town in Yorkshire, containing upwards of a quarter of a million of inhabitants, is one of the oldest places in the north of England, having a history, founded on written or printed evidences, extending over a period of upwards of 1200 years. Thoresby, Gale, and other Yorkshire antiquaries suppose, that Leeds stands on the site of the ancient Roman or British town of Loid or Caer Loid Coit—the city of Loid in the Forest, mentioned by Nennius, one of the earliest British writers, in a list which he gives of cities or fortresses erected by the Romans in Britain.[*] This, if established, would carry back its existence at least 100 or 200 years further, and connect it with the Roman and British periods. Leeds, then Loid or Loidis, is mentioned by the Venerable Bede, and by Alfred the Great, his illustrious translator, as the capital of a small British kingdom, about the year 616; and afterwards more fully, in their accounts of the events of the year 655 of the Christian era, as the chief place of a district of the same name, in the Anglian kingdom of Northumbria. At that time the Angles and Saxons had few towns, except such as had been built by the Romans or

---

[*] Ducatus Leodiensis, or the Topography of the Town and Parish of Leeds, &c., by Ralph Thoresby, F.R.S., 1715. The second edition, with notes and additions by Thomas Dunham Whitaker, LL.D., F.R.S., vicar of Whalley. Leeds (1816).

the Britons; they being, themselves, chiefly accustomed to dwell in small villages or lone-built houses: and the mere fact of the existence of a town, of sufficient magnitude to give its name to even a small kingdom, at so early a period as that mentioned by Bede, in itself creates a presumption that the town so named was founded either by the Britons or the Romans. The close resemblance of the name of the Roman or British town of Loid, spoken of by Nennius, to that of the Anglian town of Loidis, or Leeds, mentioned by Bede, renders it still more probable that they were one and the same place. The position also corresponds, for at that time, and for many succeeding ages, the greater part of what now forms the West Riding of Yorkshire, and of the adjoining counties, was covered with extensive forests, stretching from the banks of the rivers Aire and Calder as far south as the river Trent, and covering the strong clay soils of the coal-field of Yorkshire, Nottingham, and Derby. The old British word Coit, "a wood" or forest, was long retained in the name of Coit or Cad Beeston, which originally meant Beeston in the Forest; and the remains of ironworkings, believed to have been those of the Romans, have been found within the borough of Leeds.

On these grounds, as well as on account of the course and intersection of the Roman roads from Eboracum to Ribodunum, and from Legiolium to Olicana, which can be very clearly traced in the neighbourhood of Leeds, it has been supposed that the Romans had at least a summer station within the limits of the present town of Leeds, and that there was a Roman ford and passage across the river Aire, situated near the point at which it is now crossed by the old bridge of Leeds. In this district, which is intersected by so many rivers and large brooks, all of them much flooded after heavy rains, several of the towns seem to have derived their origin, and some of them their names, from the fords on which they stood; as, Bradford and Castleford. The main line of the chief street of Leeds, now Briggate, from its elevation and its comparative freedom from floods, must have afforded safe access to the ancient ford of the Aire, for travellers in their journeys north and south, even when other parts of the banks of the river were inaccessible.

The ancient town of Leeds, whenever built, seems to have stood between the ford which formerly crossed the river, near the site of the old bridge, and the point at which the stream of the Adel or Sheepscar beck enters the river Aire, from the north. Such, as we have already shown, were the favourite military positions of the Romans, at or near the junction or confluence of two streams, which together formed the sides of a natural fortification, easily completed by running a trench and wall from one to the other. This was the position of York at the junction of the Ouse and the Foss; of London, near that of the Thames and the Lea; of Mancunium, or Manchester, at the point of union of the Irwell, the Medlock, and the Irk; and of ancient Leeds, at the junction of Adel beck with the river Aire. The parish church of Leeds, erected in Anglian times, stood in this angle, perhaps on the ground originally occupied by the fortifications and the houses of the Britons and the Romans. Near this point there were in Thoresby's time (1657 to 1724) the remains of an ancient camp, either of Roman or Anglian origin, known by the name of Wallflat. The first part of this name he supposed to have been derived from the Roman word *vallum*. Of this ancient camp Thoresby says:—" Upon the ascent of the hill (called Quarry Hill) are the *vestigia*, or outlines, of a very large camp; the trenches, considering its nearness to the town, and the interposition of so many ages, are very deep. But whether it was a Roman or a Saxon camp I dare not positively assert, though from the single *vallum*, and the conveniency of the water (which the Romans always made sure of) at the foot of the hill, I suppose the former. At the head of this very beck, near Adel Mills, is a Roman camp, very entire to this day (1714); it being upon the moor, four miles distant from the town. Somewhat of the word *vallum* is yet retained in the name Wallflat, for, as the learned Mr. Sumner shows, the Romans pronounced the letter *v* as we pronounce the *w*, and Casaubon particularly notices this in *vallum*; the termination flat signifies area, a plot of ground, *area belli*, 'battle ground.'" On this subject Dr. Whitaker, writing about the year 1816, observes:—" From the name, which evidently points at a Roman fortification, and from the site, on the turning brow of a smaller elevation and near a rivulet" (and, he might have added, a wide river), " I have no doubt that Thoresby's conjecture was right. I have carefully examined the ground, but though the central part remains, the lines of the trenches are almost wholly occupied by buildings."*

* Thoresby's Ducatus Leodiensis. Whitaker's Edition.

But whatever may have been the works constructed by the Romans and the Britons in the neighbourhood of Leeds, our chief knowledge respecting the earlier history of the town belongs to the Anglian times; is derived from the first Anglian historian, the Venerable Bede; and relates to the events of the seventh century of the Christian era. At that time our Anglian ancestors, who had subdued the Britons in the plains, though not in the hills, adopted the Christian religion, under the teaching of Paulinus the first archbishop of Northumbria or York, whose diocese extended from the river Humber to the river Forth, and included nearly the whole of the north of England, and much of the southern part of Scotland. We have already described generally, in the first volume of this work, the various events that arose out of the adoption of the Christian religion by the people of Northumbria, and more especially the sanguinary wars, which the first three Christian kings of Northumbria, Eadwine, Oswald, and Oswy, had to wage with Penda, the fierce champion of the pagan race, whose dominions stretched southward from the Humber, and included the central districts of England, forming the middle Anglian kingdom of Mercia. In his third invasion, in the year 655, the formidable army of Penda advanced into the district of Leodis or Leeds, as it is named by Bede, supported by the forces of thirty other pagan chiefs; and it was in this district that the Christian king, Oswy of Northumbria, whose capital was York, gained that decisive victory which secured the complete triumph of the Christian religion in England, during the Anglian and Saxon times.

There has been some discussion amongst local antiquaries as to the precise position of this memorable battle. According to the Venerable Bede it was fought in the district of Leeds (Leodis), on the banks of a flooded stream, in whose waters a large portion of the pagan army perished, after its defeat by the Angles under King Oswy. It has been supposed by Thoresby, and other writers, that the scene of the actual battle was Winmoor, or Whinmoor, a few miles to the north-east of the town of Leeds, and that the fugitives of the pagan army, after the defeat of their king, were swallowed up and drowned, in attempting to cross the river Aire, at Swillington, and the Calder and other Yorkshire streams further to the south. Bede states that at that time the rivers were flooded from heavy rains, and that more of the fugitives perished by the floods than by the sword. So far as the language of Bede enables us to fix the position of this great battle, it took place at Winweyd, which may be either the original name of the place at which it was fought, or may be a name derived from the Anglian words Win-weyd, which mean the field or meadow of battle or of victory, in the Anglian language. If the latter is the meaning of the word, it may apply to any position or place; but the actual scene of the battlefield is very likely to have been on the high grounds, between the river Aire and the river Wharfe, of which the present Winmoor or Whinmoor forms a part. This is connected with the great Roman road, a few miles east, which ran through Yorkshire from south to north, and was the usual line of advance taken by invading armies. A Roman road, still distinct enough to be marked on the Ordnance Map, leads from the river Aire, at Swillington, to this, as well as to another line of Roman road running from Eboracum to Olicana, or Ilkley, in Wharfedale. It lies between York and Leeds, which were the two principal towns of the kingdom of Northumbria, and is at no great distance from a country mansion, or royal residence, which the kings of Northumbria erected in the district of Leodis, or Leeds, after a more ancient royal residence, standing in the neighbourhood of Campodunum, or Doncaster, had been destroyed by Penda and his hordes, subsequent to their victory over Eadwine, the first Christian king of Northumbria. Camden believed that the meaning of the word Winweyd was "the field of victory," and in support of that opinion quoted the authority of Ortelius, the geographer, who states that the Germans, from whom the Angles were descended, gave the name of Winfield, or the field of victory, to the battlefield in Westphalia, on which the Roman legions under Varus were defeated and destroyed, by Arminius or Herman, the great hero of the Germans.* On the other hand, it has been supposed that Winmoor, or Whinmoor, was so named from the circumstance of its being overgrown with gorse, known locally as whins. This may be so, though at that time all the moors of Yorkshire must have been covered with whins, so that the name would then be no distinction. It is much more probable, as suggested by Camden and Ortelius, that the Winweyd mentioned by Bede was named from the fact of its having been the site of that great victory. The position of Winmoor is naturally strong, its approaches being covered by the deep and (then)

* Camden's Britannia—Brigantes.

swollen stream of the river Aire, lying along the line of the Roman road from York to the neighbourhood of Leeds, on high ground, and having in its rear (on the north of the Wharfe) a steep and hilly country, affording many strong defensive positions, even if the first had been carried by the invaders. The position was so well chosen as to render victory highly probable, and defeat totally ruinous to the invading army.

Probable as it is that the Britons and the Romans occupied the site of the older part of Leeds as a military position, and with a view to the passage over the river Aire, there is every reason to believe, from the great preponderance of Anglian or Teutonic names of places, both in the town of Leeds and the neighbouring villages, that the Angles or early English were at least the restorers and second founders of the town, as they were the ancestors of the race who have so long occupied this part of England. They probably reclaimed it from the state of wildness into which it had again fallen during the period of upwards of 200 years, which were consumed in the wars between the Romanized Britons and the Germanic tribes who invaded Britain after the retirement of the Roman armies. Agriculture being the earliest and most necessary of the arts, and being all but impracticable without fixed limits and boundaries, both to public and to private lands, new names and limits were given by the Angles to the townships, the parishes, the marks, and the larger divisions of territory which they settled. These names have been transmitted from generation to generation, down to the present time, and still serve to show that the Anglian or Teutonic race were the dividers of the land into its present limits, and the chief founders and organizers of the earlier forms of industry and cultivation in this part of England.

The Anglian names of places in England, as we have already shown, are principally derived from a few natural and simple distinctions and features, which can be easily traced to their origin. The chief Anglian terminations of the names of places are ley or lea, meaning a field, and ton or town, which originally also meant an inclosure. Of the eleven townships included in the present parish of Leeds, the names of six terminate with the Anglian word ley, or "field," namely, Armley, Bramley, Farnley, Headingley-cum-Burley, and Wortley. Three of them end in ton or town, which is an Anglian termination; namely, Beeston, Chapel-Allerton, and Potternewton. Woodhouse is also a name of Anglian origin. The three remaining names are Hunslet, Holbeck, and Leeds. Leeds is either derived from the British name Loid, or from the Anglian word leod, "the people," or "the populous place." The name Leod is also found slightly altered in Ludgate, or the people's gate, at London, and in Ledbury, or the people's borough, in Herefordshire, and is a very appropriate name for a populous town. Courts-leet were originally leod, or people's courts, and belong to a very early period of English history. Hunslet, according to Thoresby, is an Anglian name, meaning the hounds' or dogs' kennel, though we have some doubts as to the correctness of this derivation, and suspect that the name is derived from the Anglo-Saxon and Norse words hund and slot, meaning the camp of the hundred, as Hunmanby means the town of the hundred. Holbeck is probably a Norse or Scandinavian, rather than an Anglian name. The Angles occasionally used the word beck to describe a stream, although their usual name for a small stream was burn, as in Fairburn, and Sherburn. There is, however, a great preponderance of Anglian names in the townships forming the parish of Leeds, although there still remain a sufficient number of Norse or Scandinavian names, within the town and parish, to prove that the Danes long held a powerful position in this district.

The Danes captured the city of York in the year 867, and a few years later occupied and tilled the land of Yorkshire, and other parts of the kingdom of Northumbria. We find their names in the fertile valleys of the West Riding, though not often in the wilder or more barren parts. It was chiefly along rivers and navigable streams that they formed their settlements.

Amongst the most characteristic of the Norse or Scandinavian names found in the parish of Leeds are those of Holbeck, Burmantofts, Osmondthorp, Knowstrop, and Kirkstall. Toft is "a small field;" thorp, or trop, "a country house and estate;" and staller, "a station." The name of kirk, given to the church and to one of the older streets of Leeds, is also of Scandinavian origin. The church seems to have been known by the Scandinavian name of kirk from early times, and gave its name to Kirkgate, the street in which it stands. The use of the word gate, as applied to a street, also affords strong evidence of Scandinavian influence and residence. Street and lane are the principal Anglian names of what we still call streets and lanes;

but gata, or gate, is the old Danish or Scandinavian name. This we find at Leeds in Kirkgate, Briggate, Swinegate or Sweyngate, Mabgate, and Lidgate (mentioned by Thoresby), all very old streets. The original name of Briggate seems to have been Broadgate, and the present word Briggate dates from the time of the building of the bridge, in or before the reign of Edward III.* Two of the oldest names of streets in Leeds are Buhr Lane or Borough Lane, a purely Anglian name, strangely metamorphosed into Boar Lane, or even in some cases into Bore Lane, and Swinegate. Another ancient name is Call Lane, which is probably derived from calsey, the paved road formed in the middle of it. This name comes originally from the Latin word *calx*, "a flint." It is the root of the English word causeway, as well as of the French *chaussée*, and may have been brought into England by the Normans, and not by the Romans.

Almost the only historical name among the older streets of Leeds is Sweyngate, corrupted into Swinegate, which was probably named from King Sweyn, the father of Canute the Great, and his predecessor in the power if not in the title of king of England. The name of this famous chief, who all but conquered England, and left it an easy prey to Canute, is found, in Yorkshire and Lincolnshire, in many places. York was for many years the chief place in his English dominions, and there he died and was buried. The memory of his powerful fleets and armies is preserved in numerous harbours and headlands of Yorkshire and Lincolnshire, as in Swine, Swinefleet, and Swinehead. The word sweyn means a "youth," generally a royal youth. Boar Lane and Swinegate serve, however, to keep each other in countenance.

At the time of the Norman conquest Leeds was a vill or small town, containing a few hundred inhabitants, but it was already the most populous and flourishing place in this district. In the great survey of England, known as Domesday, made in the reign of William the Conqueror (1084-86), the Leeds of that day, and the other manors and vills, now included in the borough, are thus described:—

LEEDS AT THE DOMESDAY SURVEY, A.D. 1084-86.

The following is a Survey of such of the townships in the borough of Leeds as are recorded in Domesday Book:—

* Thoresby's Ducatus Leodiensis.

Armley.—In Ristone and Ermelai, Morcar [or Morfar] and Archil had six carucates of land to be taxed, where there may be three ploughs. Ligulf now has it of Ilbert [de Laci], and there are eight villeines there with three ploughs. Meadow, six acres. Wood pasture, half a mile long, and four quarentens broad. Value in King Edward [the Confessor's] time, twenty shillings; now ten shillings.

Beeston.—In Bestone, Turstan and Morfar had six carucates of land to be taxed, where there may be four ploughs. Ilbert [de Laci] now has it, and it is waste. Value in King Edward's time, forty shillings. Wood pasture, half a mile long and half broad.

Bramley.—In Brameleia, Archil had four carucates of land to be taxed, there may be two ploughs there. Ilbert now has it, and it is waste. Wood pasture, half a mile long and half broad. Value in King Edward's time, forty shillings.

Chapel-Allerton.—In Alreton, Glenner had six carucates of land to be taxed, where there may be three ploughs. Ilbert now has it, and it is waste. Value in King Edward's time, forty shillings. Wood pasture, one mile long and half broad.

Farnley.—Not recorded.

Headingley-cum-Burley.—In Hedingleia, seven carucates of land to be taxed. Land to three ploughs and a half. Two thanes held it for two manors. There are there two villeines, with one plough. It has been valued at forty shillings; now four pounds.

Holbeck.—Not mentioned, but is supposed to have been included with Leeds.

Hunslet.—In Hunslet, six carucates of land to be taxed, where there may be three ploughs. The soke [or lordship] is in Bestone. There are eight villeines there, having three ploughs, and six acres of meadow. Wood pasture, five quarentens long and four broad.

Leeds.—In Ledes, ten carucates of land and six oxgangs to be taxed Land to six ploughs. Seven thanes held it in the time of King Edward [the Confessor] for seven manors. Twenty-seven villeines, and four sokemen, and four bordars, have now there fourteen ploughs. There is a priest and a church, and a mill of four shillings, and ten acres of meadow. It has been valued at six pounds; now seven pounds.

Seacroft—Part of. (Coldcotes.) In Coldecotes, two carucates.

Temple-Newsam—Part of. (Osmondthorpe.) In Ossethorpe, four carucates.

Potternewton.—Not recorded.

Wortley.—Not recorded.*

It appears from the above statement that the land of Leeds was held in the time of King Edward the Confessor by seven thanes or gentlemen, for seven manors, in each of which the thane

* Extract from the Rev. William Bawdwen's translation of Domesday Book relating to Yorkshire, in Wardell's Municipal History of Leeds. Appendix, p 8.

held his land under the Crown. The number of small farmers or bondagers, engaged in the cultivation of the soil, was twenty-seven, and in addition to these there were four sokemen, or tenants under the jurisdiction of the lord, and four bordars, or inhabitants of bords or cottages. There was also a priest and a church; and there was a mill, no doubt with millers to work and manage it. There were also ten acres of meadow land, which was very valuable at a time when natural hay-grass was the only kind of fodder available for the support of cattle in the winter months. What is remarkable is that the value of the property in Leeds had increased from six pounds to seven pounds between the reign of Edward the Confessor, and the time when the Domesday Survey was made, near the close of the reign of William the Conqueror. How the town of Leeds had escaped, in the political storms of that period, from the desolation which had fallen on so large a portion of the county of York, does not appear; but from some cause or other the value of the property of Leeds had advanced from six pounds in the money of that time to seven pounds—or supposing the currency of that age to have been worth fifteen times as much as the present value (as computed by T. Duffus Hardy), from about £90 to about £115.* Probably William the Norman was a harder landlord than Edward the Confessor, who spent his life in hunting and hawking, and in building magnificent churches. This gives from forty-five to fifty heads of families in the Leeds township; and assuming the numbers to have been half as large in the other townships, some of which were waste, while the others were cultivated, this would give seventy to eighty families, or from 400 to 500 men, women, and children, for the population of the district included in the borough of Leeds, and now containing upwards of a quarter of a million of inhabitants. Dr. Whitaker estimates the number of the population at 270. In Edward the Confessor's time the population of the whole parish may probably have amounted to 800, 900, or even 1000 persons.

The Domesday Survey mentions a mill as existing at Leeds before the Norman conquest, and Thoresby supposes that the villani, mentioned in Domesday, held their lands in Leeds on condition of upholding the dam which supplied that mill with water-power from the river Aire. The following is his account of the ancient mill and mill dam of Leeds:—

* Introduction to Close Rolls.

Bondman Dam.—"Of the dams upon the river Aire, in this part of the manor of Leeds, Bondman Dam ought especially to be mentioned, to excite our gratitude for abolishing the old bond law that related to *terra nativa*, whereby not only the lands and services, but the bodies of the natives and their children after them, were absolutely at the disposal of the lord, and were sold or given away by them at their arbitrary pleasure, till it was afterwards enacted, 'that no buying or selling be used hereafter, in England, of men as of cattle.' But to be a little more particular, however, the copyholds chargeable with the repairs of this, which to this day (1715) is called the Bondman's Dam, I take to be as ancient as the Conquest, if not before; and that they are the same with those that in Domesday Book were in the possession of the twenty-seven villeins. 'Ilbert de Laci,' we are told in Domesday, 'had in Leeds ten carucates of land, &c. *Ibi nunc* 27 *villani*,' says that ancient record. And it is very observable that after more than 600 years time, twenty-seven of them are expressed by name in a duchy bill, exhibited by Gerv. Neville, Esq., as liable by their tenure to repair the said dam. Now the bondmen were of two sorts in those ages. First, villeins in gross, who without any determined tenure of land were at the arbitrary pleasure of their lords, and receiving their wages and maintenance at the discretion of the lord, were no better than absolute slaves; both themselves and their children, with whatever they had, being alienable at their pleasure. Thus," says Thoresby, "in the noble pedigree of the Gascoignes, curiously engrossed on sixteen large skins of parchment, and communicated to me by the courteous John Gascoigne of Parlington, Esq., it appears by an engrossed deed, that William, the son of John de Heaton, had sold unto Adam, the son of Benedict de Mirfeld, for a certain sum of money, William, the son of Roger Faber, of Potterheaton, "formerly my native or serf, with his descendants, born or to be born, and with all his chattels, moveable or immoveable." The other sort were of a superior degree, having some cottage and land assigned to them, for which they were obliged to perform some stated offices, as these here to the repair of Bondman Dam, in compensation whereof they and their successors, in that tenure, were hopper-free; that is, had the privilege of having their corn ground immediately on the emptying of the hopper, though there be never so many attending whose corn was brought to the mill before theirs. Yet even these villeins regardants, were conveyed as an appurtenance of the manor to every new lord, and had not power so much as to fell a tree in their gardens without the lord's leave. That their persons were conveyed along with their lands is evident, from the charter of Alice Lacy to Margaret Kirton, her damsell (damicille mee), or young lady, to whom she gave all the nativi of the said lands, with that toft of land that belongs to Radulf Brown, together with his body, his descendants, and his chattels, with the like of George of Saxton, with both body and land, &c.*

By the grant of William the Conqueror, Leeds became a portion of the vast estates of Ilbert de Laci, one of the most powerful of the Norman warriors, whose possessions extended from Pontefract Castle, in the south of Yorkshire, as far north and west as Clitheroe Castle, on the borders of the Ribble, in Lancashire. By him this portion of his large estates was subinfeuded to Ralph Paganel, a Norman baron, whose family name is still found in the name of the village of Pannal, near Knaresborough; and in Newport Pagnal, in Buckinghamshire, where the Paganels had another estate. They were the lords of Leeds for many ages, and it was by one of them that the earliest charter was granted to the burgesses of Leeds. They were the owners, amongst other property or rights, of the patronage of the parish church; and so early as the year 1089, Ralph Paganel, who was the high-sheriff of Yorkshire, granted the advowson of the church of Leeds to the Priory of the Holy Trinity at York, which he had built and endowed. The original church of Leeds existed previous to the Norman conquest, probably from the time when King Oswy of Northumberland defeated the pagan armies of Penda on the banks of the river Aire, and founded twelve religious houses or minsters, in celebration of his victory, and of his escape from destruction. But it seems to have been more than once re-built, the church mentioned in the Domesday Survey not being the old parish church, which was pulled down in the year 1838, to give place to a much handsomer building, but a still earlier fabric.

Soon after the Conquest, the Paganels built a castle at Leeds, to which an extensive park was attached. The memory of this park is preserved in the names of Park Place, Park Row, Park Square, and Park Lane, all of which were built on lands originally belonging

* Thoresby's Ducatus; vol. ii p 95 of Whitaker's Loidis and Elmete.

to the ancient park. No traces now remain of the ancient castle, but the line of the trench was discovered in 1836, on the banks of the river Aire, near the base of the rising ground long known by the name of Mill Hill. The King's Mills, as they were afterwards called, stood somewhat lower down the stream, but drew their supplies of water-power from the stream flowing through the *stagnum* or mill pond, which also served as a trench for the castle. The castle of Leeds passed in succession from the Paganel family to the Gaunts, the De Albinis, and to the earls of Chester; from them in a few years, back to the De Lacys, earls of Lincoln; from them to the Plantagenets, earls, and afterwards dukes, of Lancaster; and finally to the Crown, in the person of Henry of Bolingbroke, duke of Lancaster, afterwards king of England by the title of Henry IV.

It is stated that the castle of Leeds, in Yorkshire, was one of the places in which Richard II. was confined, after he had been dethroned by the aspiring Bolingbroke, and before he was removed to the neighbouring castle of Pontefract, where he was soon afterwards cruelly murdered; but this cannot be correct, if it be true, as believed by Thoresby, that Leeds Bridge was built in the reign of Edward III., the grand-father of Richard, with stone taken from the castle of Leeds. But this is quite uncertain.

Amongst the most important owners of property in the town and neighbourhood of Leeds, in ancient times, were the Knights Templars, the members of the great military order formed for the recovery of the temple and city of Jerusalem from the Saracens, in the days of the Crusades. The first and most important grant in Yorkshire to this warlike order was that made by William de Villiers, of the manor of Newsham, near Leeds, confirmed by the superior lord, Robert de Laci, the founder of Kirkstall Abbey.* The Templars built themselves a preceptory on their estate at Newsham, on the east side of the town, which house was thenceforward called after them, Temple Newsham. Their possessions extended to the town of Leeds, where a curious memorial of their power and privileges existed down to modern times. All their property, and that of their tenants, was free from the soke or feudal superiority of the ancient lords of the manor, and, amongst other feudal duties, from the obligation to grind their corn at the lord's or the king's mills, at which other inhabitants of the town of

* Thoresby's Ducatus Leodiensis.

Leeds were compelled to grind. The houses built on the lands of the Templars had in front of them large iron crosses. This denoted their freedom from this obligation, which was only abolished as to the inhabitants generally a few years ago, by the purchase of the right for a large sum of money. Timble Bridge, a corruption of Temple Bridge, is supposed to have been named after the Knights Templars, having been built on a stream crossing the road from the preceptory at Temple Newsham to the town of Leeds.

As already stated, Maurice Paganel, who lived in the reign of King John, granted a charter to his burgage tenants at Leeds, in the year 1207-8, the 9th John, by which they became entitled to the enjoyment of all the liberties and immunities usually granted in those ages, by kings and great lords, to the occupiers of burgage lands on their estates, but more especially to the rights which Roger de Laci, the chief lord, had granted to his burgesses of Pontefract. Tenancy in burgage was one of the freest and most secure kinds of occupancy existing in those times. In this charter it was provided that the burgesses were to be free, which was the most important of privileges, at a time when serfdom existed in most of the rural districts; when both male and female slaves were still sold in the public markets; and when there was little security for personal freedom, even in towns, unless that of the burgesses was guaranteed by a written charter, and by local officers empowered to enforce it. The charter of Maurice Paganel to the burgesses of Leeds further provided, that every burgess should have half an acre of land around his house, on payment to the lord of a burgage rent of sixteen pence, 1$s.$ 4$d.$, year for ever, which sum being equal to nearly 30$s.$ an acre of modern money, was a very good rent according to the payments of those times. These burgage lands the tenants were free to sell to any one who might wish to purchase them, reserving the lord's rights, and the buyer and seller each paying one penny fine to the lord. It was further provided that the purchaser of a toft, or part of a toft held in burgage, should himself be free, and have all the rights of a burgess. The chief officer of the town, known as the prætor or mayor, was appointed yearly by the lord, and collected his rents and tolls. The office was usually let to the person, being a burgess of the town, who was willing to pay the highest sum for it. This charter also created a local court of justice, and freed the burgesses from the obligation to appear in any other courts, except at the county assizes, in pleas of the crown, that is, for murder and other atrocious crimes. Although these charters were very defective, they still afforded a considerable amount of freedom and security to the inhabitants of the boroughs which possessed them, in comparison with the general population of the kingdom; and out of them grew, in course of ages, that system of local and municipal government, which forms one of the most solid foundations of English freedom, and has, by teaching the people of England the art of local government, prepared them for that of national. None of the boroughs of the kingdom possessed the right of returning members to Parliament in the reign of King John; but the parliamentary system was introduced in the reign of his son, Henry III., by Simon de Montfort and the English barons, and was completely established, with a fair representation both of counties and boroughs, in the reign of Edward I., the son and successor of Henry III. But the borough of Leeds was not one of the Yorkshire boroughs which was summoned to return members to Parliament even in the time of Edward I., or his immediate successors; and though Leeds was represented by Captain Adam Baynes, under the Commonwealth, the borough did not obtain the right of returning members to Parliament until the reign of King William IV. Subsequent to the granting of the oldest charter of Leeds, by Maurice de Paganel, the manor of Leeds returned to the chief lords, the De Lacys, earls of Lincoln. The following is the charter of Maurice Paganel to his burgesses of Leeds, which we copy from that valuable work, Mr. James Wardell's "Municipal History of Leeds:"—

CHARTER OF MAURICE PAGANEL TO THE BURGESSES OF LEEDS (TRANSLATION), 9TH KING JOHN, 11TH NOVEMBER, 1208.

The Grants and Immunities of the Burgesses of Leeds.—"Know all men, present and future, that I, Maurice Paganel, have given and granted, and by this present charter have confirmed to my burgesses of Leeds, and their heirs, liberty and free burgage, and their tofts [or homesteads], and with each such toft half an acre of arable land, to hold of me and my heirs in fee and by inheritance, freely, peaceably, and honourably, to pay to me and [my] heirs, for each such toft and half acre, sixteen pence at Pentecost, and [the feast of] St. Martin. I have also granted [given and confirmed] to my aforesaid burgesses and their heirs, the same freedom and laws as the burgesses of Roger de Laci of Pontefract enjoy, which [are] these:—Any burgess may give or sell his land to whom he will, except for [anything set apart for] religion, [a monastery or other religious house], saving the lord's superiority; and by the charter of the covenant he shall render the land into the hand of the prætor, and shall give one penny on account of toll, and the prætor shall render the [same] land to the purchaser [as] from the bounty of the lord, secure from every one, and the purchaser shall pay one penny. Whosoever shall purchase any part of any such toft, and be seized as aforesaid, is as free as if he had purchased the whole toft. If any one have more houses than one in his toft, and have let them to any one, he shall be free to sell and purchase all kinds of merchandise; but he who shall dwell in the chief house [the landlord] shall give four pence to the prætor every year, and [be as] free as a burgess may be. Whoever has committed an offence within the aforesaid borough, wherever he be attached, he shall abide by the judgment of the court: but the aforesaid burgesses shall not [be compelled to] go out of their borough for any plea or for any complaint, save only for the pleasure of the crown [or perhaps the pleas of the crown].

"When the prætor shall account for the rent to the lord of the borough at Pentecost, the lord shall remove him and put in his place whomsoever he shall think proper; but the burgesses shall be more eligible, if only they be willing to give as much [as] others [who are not burgesses]. Whoever has impleaded any one for any offence before the prætor unjustly or without ground, and has committed an offence against him within the peace; and he [the other] shall deny the charge, and the unreasonable offence, and [being within the] peace, and whatever he has said against him, he hath given a good answer. Whoever shall not deny the charge or the unreasonable offence, and shall not be blameless as to any of these things, shall be judged at the mercy of the prætor, and by payment of the penalty shall regain his competency as a witness. Whosoever shall begin expressly to deny [his own previous] words in his reply, and shall not have expressly denied [them] all, shall lose his cause, and on payment of the forfeiture regain his competency as a witness. An offence of a burgess shall be decided by twelve lawful men, chosen for this purpose. If the prætor think proper to condemn any one, no burgess shall pay a fine for the first offence; but for the second, except he be able to extenuate the offence, [by paying] one half [of the adjudged penalty]. Any burgess may pledge himself, unless he have been impleaded by the crown of our lord the king, or have [previously] omitted to fulfil his pledge.

"If any one in the service of the prætor have accused a burgess, he, the burgess, shall not answer without [his accuser producing] a witness. If any burgess have been impleaded for a breach of peace, for shedding of blood, or for striking, and deny the same, he shall clear himself by the oath of seven compurgators; if [the offence be] not for shedding of blood, by three; if any burgess be impleaded by another burgess for the same, he shall clear himself by twelve. Every burgess is bound to answer to another without a witness, but not to one [living] beyond the limits [of the borough], except for an apparent fact, or for the debt of a burgess, unless he have been appeased by [receiving] an equivalent. If one living beyond [the borough] have accepted an oath from a burgess, he shall incur the heaviest forfeiture. If one living beyond [the borough] owe a debt to any burgess, it shall be lawful for him any day in the week, except on festivals, to distrain upon his goods, without leave of the prætor. If any burgess have received a distress upon his goods, he shall be adjudged to free the same on the first day at his own cost; otherwise, if he be unwilling to do so, the distress shall be allowed to proceed. He who has left unpaid the lord's toll, shall forfeit after this manner: for a farthing, five shillings and one farthing; for a half-penny, ten shillings and one half-penny; for three farthings, fifteen shillings and three farthings; for a penny, twenty shillings and one penny. [It is lawful for any one to erect on his land what shops he may think proper, to make up the lord's rent]. Whoever shall deny or allow any [other] thing than that for which he has been impleaded, he shall continue liable to the penalty. It shall be lawful for all burgesses to convey grain by land or by water, wheresoever they may think proper, and all other merchandise, without toll or other bar, unless they are forbidden by the lord or his bailiffs. They [the purchasers of any of our lands], shall not be held to be answerable to any one, as to [the title of] any of our tenements, of which we have been seized, or which we have held for a whole year and a whole day, without claim. If any one be cited in our pleas during the time that he be elsewhere on his own business, he shall be blameless for that day if [he] answer [to the charge] as soon as he returns. If any burgess be impleaded of larceny from another, we will judge him in our borough, with the help of the lord's servant, he making one compurgation for the first offence, with thirty-six compurgators. If he be impleaded a second time, he shall either purge himself by combat or by water. No woman shall pay toll in our borough who is to be sold for slavery.

"Moreover I have given and granted to the said burgesses of Leeds, and their heirs, a release from all toll and custom throughout the whole of my lands belonging to the borough of Leeds. But the burgesses aforesaid shall continue to bake in my oven as they have been accustomed.

"And when our lord the king shall demand aid of the cities of England, my burgesses of Leeds aforesaid shall give unto my lord the king reasonable assistance.

"And that this my gift and grant may remain ratified and uninfringed to posterity, I have affixed my seal to the above-mentioned charter. [These men being] witnesses. Adam de Reinvile, Ivone de Lindesenses, Wilmot de Stapleton, Adam de Beiston, Hugo de Swillington, William Pictaviculus, [also] Radulph de Leeds, who wrote this charter and many other charters. Given at Leeds on the morning of Saint Martin, in the ninth year of the coronation of King John.*

"Such," says Dr. Whitaker, "are the contents of this curious and valuable charter, which holds up a lively picture of municipal jurisprudence in the borough of Leeds in the beginning of the thirteenth century. On reflecting upon the representation which it contains, the following observations present themselves. It

* Wardell's Municipal History of Leeds: Appendix.

is evident that in the interval of about 120 years (between the Domesday Survey and the date of this charter in the 9th of King John), Leeds must have become a considerable town. This, I think, is implied by the grant of so small a portion of arable land as half an acre to every toft,* for the homesteads of houses containing curtileges (inclosures), gardens, offices, and all the necessary accommodations of a family; but such at the date of this charter had been the increase of the population, that some of these had been subdivided, and several dwelling-houses had been erected on the site of one original toft. This implies want of space and increasing population, its cause. But what was the principle of this increase? and what the occupations of this increasing people? For the first it was evidently the protection of a castle, and the security (besides their numerous immunities) which in times of turbulence and rapine was enjoyed by burgesses. With respect to the second they exported grain and other commodities (*alia mercimonia*), and what is very singular, exported them by water as well as by land, so that the Aire must even then have been navigable. This is an interesting discovery; but the produce of the half acre afforded no grain for exportation: the burgesses therefore must have rented corn and perhaps grazing farms, out of which wool, hides, tallow, &c., the *alia mercimonia* of this charter, might be conveyed down the Aire, and the first of these commodities for exportation to Flanders, whence by a very unprofitable commerce, which the enlightened patriotism of Edward III. afterwards extinguished, they received their own raw article in manufactured clothing."†

Dr. Whitaker's views of political economy, as expressed in the latter part of the last sentence, have become somewhat antiquated since the year 1816, when this paragraph was written; which is not to be wondered at, seeing that much the greater part of the wool and other raw materials, now manufactured at Leeds and other places, is imported from foreign countries to be worked up there, and is sent back to those countries in a manufactured state. This is, in fact, the great trade of England at the present time, and a similar exchange of commodities was no doubt a good and profitable trade, at the time when Yorkshire wool was sent from Leeds to Flanders to be manufactured into cloth, which cloth was afterwards sold and used in England. As to

---

* Toft is a Norse or Danish word, meaning a small field, as in Burmantofts.
† Dr. Whitaker's History of Leeds, in Loidis and Elmete, vol. L p. 11.

what Dr. Whitaker says of the river Aire having been navigable in the reign of King John, it is probable that it was so for very small vessels, and under favourable circumstances, for there must always have been seasons when there was abundance of water in the Aire, even when it was not flooded. But it was not made navigable for vessels of any considerable size until the reigns of William III. and Queen Anne (1697-1709). One of the most remarkable paragraphs in the above charter is that which provides that women should not pay custom in the borough of Leeds, when sold into slavery. This shows clearly that not merely serfdom, but personal slavery of the very worst kind, continued to exist in England down to the reign of King John, and that no more was then thought of the sale of women—and, no doubt, men and children—than of the sale of cattle.

The common oven, *commune furnum*, with a soke annexed, which was at Kirkgate-end, continued several centuries after this time, but was ultimately abolished, probably when it became unprofitable to maintain it. "Another and very oppressive remnant of feudal dependence," says Dr. Whitaker, "yet remains in the king's mills," at which all the inhabitants of Leeds were compelled to grind their corn. This happily has also ceased to exist.

The connection of the Paganels with the borough of Leeds ceased, either in the latter years of the reign of King John or at the beginning of the reign of his son and successor, Henry III. We find that about that time the manor and borough of Leeds had become a part of the immense estates of Ranulph de Blondeville, the great earl of Chester, who held it to the time of his death. He was succeeded by his nephew, John the Scot, so named from his connection with the royal family of Scotland, who only held the earldom of Chester for two or three years, when he died, not leaving any issue. On his death, King Henry III. conferred the earldom of Chester and the principality of Wales on his own eldest son Edward, afterwards King Edward I.; but he divided a large portion of the estates of Ranulph de Blondeville amongst his four sisters and co-heirs. From one of them the estates passed to John de Laci, the first earl of Lincoln of that family, and already the chief lord. In the year 1251, 35th Henry III., Edmund de Laci, the second earl of Lincoln of that house, obtained a charter of free warren, giving him the right of hawking, and of hunting all animals of warren in his demesne lands of Pontefract, Rowel (Rothwell), Leedes, Berwick, Secroft, Bradford, Alemanbury, Windlesford (Woodlesford), Oltone, Carltone, Lofthous, Slateburne, Castleford, Methley, Grinlington, Swillington, Farnlegh, and Backshelf, in the county of York. In the year 1311, the 4th Edward II., Alice, widow of the above-mentioned Edmund de Laci, had assigned to her for her dowry the manors of Leedes, Rodwell, Burwick, Sladeburn, Grinleton, Bradford, &c. Alicia de Laci, the only daughter and heiress of Henry de Laci, the last earl of Lincoln of that family, married Thomas, earl of Lancaster, the nephew of King Henry III. By this marriage the manor of Leeds, with the other great possessions of the De Laci family, became united to the earldom of Lancaster, and ultimately passed to the duchy of Lancaster and to the crown, in the person of Henry of Bolingbroke, duke of Lancaster, afterwards Henry IV. From this period the manor and borough of Leeds were vested in the crown, till after the decease of Anne of Denmark, queen of King James I. of England, a part of whose jointure it was. After that it was sold into private hands.*

The River Aire.—"Where the bridge is now was of old," says Thoresby, "the ferry over the broad Aire, that *celeberrimum et præstantissimum fluvium*, as it is called in the survey made of the manor of Leeds, when it was part of the jointure of Queen Anne, consort of King James I." Dr. Whitaker says that "The bridge and chapel, as appeared by their foundation stones, 8th August, 1760, seem to have been built both together in or before King Edward III.'s time;" but recent examinations render it almost certain that part of it was built in Norman times. The bridge was enlarged for double carriages in 1730, and further enlarged in 1760.† Thoresby says the bridge was strong and robust, made of large square stones. On the west side of the bridge were stone stairs, built in the year 1583, with stone taken from Kirkstall Abbey. This appears from the churchwardens' accounts of that year. The labourers' wages paid for this work were at the rate of 6*d.* per day; which, allowing for the difference in the value of money, would still be 2*s.* 6*d.* or 3*s.* a day of our present money, if not more.‡

Chantry at Leeds Bridge.—In early times there was at Leeds Bridge a chantry, dedicated to Saint Mary the Virgin. This is shown

---

* Thoresby's Ducatus.   † Thoresby's Ducatus, second edition, (Whitaker's) vol. ii. p 77.
‡ Thoresby's Ducatus, vol. ii. p. 77.

by a deed, dated 5th of June, 1376. About 1515 this chantry owned three burgages, ten houses and cottages, and land called Saint Mary's Ings or Meadows, in Leeds; then valued at £4 6s. 8d. a year, equal to at least £40 to £50 of modern money.

The Earliest Notices of the Woollen Manufacture of Leeds.— The woollen manufacture is mentioned in the Pipe Roll, or high sheriff's account, as existing at Leeds in the reign of Henry III., in the year 1272. In the reign of King Edward III. we obtain positive evidence of the existence of a mill for the fulling of woollen cloth at Leeds. This appears by a record which sets forth that in the 47th Edward III., 1373, the fulling mills of Leeds were granted to Thomas Burgers:—"In the manor of Leeds. A fulling mill constructed in the water running from the King's Dam without the town, near the castle there, with nine acres of land, through the middle of which the aforesaid water runs. Granted to Thomas Burgers and his heirs, at 33s. 4d. per annum."* This deed not merely shows that there were fulling mills at Leeds in the reign of Edward III., but it also shows the existence of the castle at that time; and that the fulling mills were turned by a stream of water, originally derived from the river Aire, which encircled the castle, and served to fill its trench, before flowing down to the king's corn mills and the fulling mill.

We have scarcely any notices of the progress of Leeds during the next century, which may perhaps be accounted for by the wars and commotions that raged during the greater part of the fifteenth century. During that period the manor of Leeds belonged to the kings, first of the house of Lancaster, afterwards of the house of York, and ultimately to those of the house of Tudor. But there is reason to believe that the castle of Leeds, which, if still in existence, might have brought the contending armies into this part of Yorkshire, had been destroyed before the war began. Hence, in the conflicts between the adherents of the houses of York and Lancaster, though they approached as near to Leeds, on one side, as Wakefield (where the strong castle of Sandal became a great rallying point for the house of York), and the field of Towton on the other, where the house of Lancaster was totally defeated, they do not appear to have come to the neighbourhood of Leeds. Still the tumult and uncertainty which everywhere prevailed throughout the county must have interfered with the progress of industry in those times.

* Wardell's Municipal History of Leeds, p. 14.

When Leland visited Leeds in the reign of King Henry VIII., about the year 1536, he found that it was already a place of some trade. He says of Leeds, or as he spells it Leides:—

"Leidis, two miles lower than Crystal [Kirkstall] Abbey on the Ayre river, is a pretty market, having a parish church reasonably well builded, and is as large as Bradford, but not as quick [active] as it. The town standeth most by clothing."* Camden wrote his account of Great Britain about the year 1590, the 33rd of Elizabeth. He speaks of Leeds as a town which had been rendered wealthy by the woollen manufacture, but says nothing more of it, except what relates to its ancient history. The whole passage, however, relating to Leeds is worth giving, and is as follows:—
"When the Aire river has passed through Craven, it spreads itself widely over more fertile fields, and at length visits Leedes, in the Saxon language named Loydes, a town rendered wealthy by the woollen manufacture, where Oswy of Northumbria defeated Penda of Mercia; and with great advantage to both nations, as Bede observes, for he both freed his own nation from the hostile devastation of the Pagans, and converted the race of the Mercians to the Christian faith. The place in which the battle took place is called Winwid-field by historians, which name, I suspect, was given to it on account of the victory; as the place in Westphalia where Quintilius Varus with his legions was routed, in the German language, is called Winfield, or the field of victory, as has been observed by the most learned, and to me most warm friend, Abraham Ortelius." We have already referred to this passage, which derives a double interest from the greatness of the event which it describes, and from the learning and sagacity of the accomplished topographer by whom it is recorded.†

A few years previous to the visit of Camden to this part of England, in the year 1574, the 16th of Queen Elizabeth, we begin to obtain some light as to the population of the parish of Leeds, from the registers of the parish church; and as no proper census of the population was taken either at Leeds or anywhere else in England, until the commencement of the present century, this is the only certain information we can obtain as to the progress of the population to the close of the eighteenth century. The following figures show the number of persons who were baptized, married, and buried in the parish church and the chapels

* Leland's Itinerary.   † Camden's Britannia, Brigantes or Yorkshire, p. 560; edition, 1590.

of Leeds, yearly, at intervals from 1574, the 17th of Queen Elizabeth, to 1731, the 5th of King George II. The dates and numbers are as follows:—

Years.	Baptized.	Married.	Buried.
1574	133	32	78
1630	384	78	403
1666	329	89	382
1731	638	181	533

"So that in 157 years, from 1574 to 1731," says Dr. Whitaker, "the parish of Leeds (including the chapels) increased in baptisms, 505; in marriages, 149; and in burials, 455. At the first of these periods, allowing the parish to have been extremely healthy, it is difficult to conceive the whole population to have exceeded 4000 souls; the decrease in baptisms and burials between 1630 and 1666 is to be accounted for by the civil war, which swept off great numbers of males, and by the plague, which destroyed many more of both sexes; yet, in the meantime, the marriages increased, evidently because the young people born since the plague, which happened twenty-three years before, were beginning to intermarry."[*]
In addition to the causes which affected population from the year 1630 we may add, that about that time the emigration of the English race to North America commenced, and caused a considerable drain of the adult population, which was much felt at a time when the population of England was increasing very slowly, and did not amount to the fifth part of what it is at present.

At the time of the Reformation, about the year 1538, the presentation to the parish church of Leeds was transferred from the hands of one of the religious houses to a number of the principal parishioners. The church of Leeds, however, acquired by the Paganels in the very short interval between the date of the Domesday Survey (1084-86) and the year 1089, was given by Ralph Paganel, who was for a time vicecomes or high sheriff of Yorkshire, to his new foundation, the priory of the Holy Trinity of York. It was afterwards made subordinate to the house of Saint Martin of Marmoutier in France, with which the Paganels were probably connected previous to the Norman conquest. This grant transfers the church of Leeds (Leddis), and whatever pertains to it, and the tithes of the hall (*aula*), which Dr. Whitaker supposes to mean those of the

* Whitaker's History of Leeds, vol. i. p. 25.

demesne lands of the manor, together with half a carucate of land which the same Reginald de Paganel held, to the priory. Under this arrangement the prior and monks, by a private bargain with the presentee, assigned to him one-third of the tithes and altarage, reserving the other two-thirds to themselves.*

The above arrangement was naturally very unsatisfactory to the parishioners, and also to the archbishops of York; and successive appropriations were made by Thomas, Roger, and Geoffrey Plantagenet, successive archbishops of York, for the support of the parish church of Leeds, from the tithes and altarage of the living. All these continued to give great dissatisfaction, till at length Walter Gray, a decisive and resolute metropolitan, put an end to the dispute by ordaining a vicarage in the parish church of Leeds. The next transaction relating to this church, after the ordination of the vicarage by Walter Gray, is a release from Alice de Laci, widow of Edmund earl of Lincoln, to the prior and convent of the Holy Trinity at York, of the advowson of the church of Leeds. At the time of the Reformation, A.D. 1538, this priory of the Holy Trinity at York was dissolved by Henry VIII. On this occasion, as appears from a MS. return in the Augmentation Office, dated October 1, 30th Henry VIII., the patronage of the vicarage of Leeds had been assigned by that king to his new-erected cathedral church of Christ Church, in Oxford, together with a pension of £10, payable annually by the vicar of Leeds for the time being, and heretofore paid to the said prior and convent.†

For some reason not explained, King Henry VIII., who did pretty much as he liked in these and other matters, granted the advowson of the parish church of St. Peter, in Leeds, to Thomas Culpepper, Esq., on the 15th of March, in the year 1538, the 30th of his reign. The advowson thus granted by Henry VIII. was sold by Alexander Culpepper, son of the purchaser, to Roland Cowick, of London, Gent., who in the 5th Elizabeth disposed of it to Thomas Preston, of London, draper; and he, in the 11th of the same reign, sold it to Edmund Darnby, of London, haberdasher.‡

In the reign of Queen Elizabeth a portion of the parishioners opposed these grants and sales as illegal, when the case was brought before the famous Lord Bacon, then lord keeper. The result of

---

* Whitaker's History of Leeds, vol. i. p. 14. † Ibid. vol. i. p. 15. Thoresby's Ducatus Leodiensis.

‡ Whitaker's History of Leeds, vol. i. p 17.

these proceedings was that Lord Bacon decided that Birkhead, who had obtained the living under the grant of King Henry VIII., with his co-feoffees, should assign over the inheritance and fee simple of the said advowson to Sir John Savile, of Howley Hall, and others, for the benefit of the parishioners and their successors. This was the Sir John Savile who was afterwards created first Lord Savile, of Howley, and also the first alderman of Leeds, under the charter granted by Charles I. to that borough. The other trustees were Sir Philip Carey, Kt., Sir Arthur Ingram, Kt., Christopher Danby, Esq., Robert Savile, Gent., Seth Skelton, Gent., William Boynton, Gent., Richard Sykes, Matthew Cooper, Ralph Cooke, William Kaye, William Marshall, John Lambert, Thomas Pendey, John Sykes, John Watson, Peter Jackson, John Smith, William Pulleyne, Roger Oddey, George Hargreaves, Walter Laycock, John Jefferson, and William Scoles—in all, twenty-five.* These trustees confirmed Alexander Cooke as vicar, "as a man most fitted to the said place, and collated thereto at the request of the best and most religiously affected of the parishioners." Dr. Whitaker doubts the strict legality of this decision; but it seems to have met the justice of the case, and to have been generally acceptable to the parishioners.

Five clergymen in the neighbourhood were appointed as assistants or advisers to the assignees and patrons, on the next avoidance of the vicarage. These were Dr. John Favour, vicar of Halifax; Mr. William Lister, vicar of Wakefield; Mr. Robert Moore, rector of Guiseley; Mr. William Pullyane, rector of Ripley; and Mr. William Stock, rector of Kirk-Heaton—all memorable in their generation for learning and piety, and probably recommended to the lord keeper, by Mathews, archbishop of York, on that account.†

The following is an official return of the value of the tithes of the whole of the parish of Leeds, at the time of the Reformation, 1536. Supposing this to represent the real value of the tenth part of the produce of the parish, we must take the total produce at £480. But at that time money was at least four times as valuable as it is now, the ordinary price of a quarter of wheat being ten to twelve shillings. In money of the present time, the value of the produce of the parish of Leeds would be at least £2000 a year, in the reign of Henry VIII.

* Whitaker's History of Leeds, vol. i. p. 27. † Ibid. vol i p. 28.

TITHES OF THE PARISH OF LEEDS, IN THE YEAR 1538, THE 30TH HENRY VIII.

	£	s.	D.
Armley, Ricote Grange (in Armley), Wethergrange (Wither) Chapeltown, Moortown, Bramley, Gledhowe, and Allerton Grange, in the tenure of the Abbot and Convent of Kirkstall,	10	11	8
Burley, Headingley, Bargrange, and Moor Grange,	3	6	8
Leeds, Woodhouse, and two closes called Lekys,	3	6	8
Kirkbeston and Cottingley,	3	6	8
Knowesthorpe,	3	6	8
Potter Newton,	3	0	0
Wyrteley,	1	13	4
Skelton 12s., Armley Hall 20s., Gipton 20s.,	2	12	0
Colcotes 20s., Osmondthorpe 13s. 4d.,	1	13	4
Hunslite and Woodhouse (Hill),	4	13	4
Cad (Coit) Beston 10s., two Farnleys £2 10s.,	3	0	0
Northhall and two Sheepcars,	2	10	0
Tithe Hay within Leeds parish,	3	0	0
Holbeck 15s., Leeds Water Mills £1 6s. 8d.,	2	1	8
Total,	£48	2	0

Sale of the King's Mills at Leeds.—On the 29th of May, 1609, the seventh James I., that improvident king, or his more improvident ministers, sold a large portion of the royal mills and other properties to Edward Ferrers of London, mercer, and Francis Phelips of London, gentleman, their heirs and assigns for small sums. The property sold at Leeds was thus described:—" Also all that fulling mill of Leedes, in our said county of York, lying and being within the lordship of Leedes, with the whole soke and suit to the same mill belonging or appertaining, of the yearly rent of three pounds, eleven shillings, and eight pence. Also those our two corn mills of Leedes, under one roof within the lordship of Leedes aforesaid, with all houses, and all soke and suit to the said corn mills belonging or appertaining, within Leedes aforesaid, Leedes, Kirkgate, and Leedes-Main-Riding, in our said county of York, by a particular thereof of the yearly rent or value of thirteen pounds, eight shillings, and eight pence."[*]

The First Royal Charter of Leeds.—The first charter from the crown granted to the borough of Leeds was given by King Charles I., in the year 1626.

CHARTER OF INCORPORATION OF THE BOROUGH OF LEEDS (TRANSLATION), 2ND CHARLES I., 13TH JULY, 1626.

"The king to all to whom these presents shall come, greeting. Whereas our town of Leedes in our county of York is an ancient and populous town, and the inhabitants of the town and parish of Leedes aforesaid, for many years past have had, and skilfully exercised in the said town and parish, the art or mystery of making and working woollen cloths, commonly called in English "northern dozens," to their perpetual praise, and great increase of the revenue of the crown of England for the custom of the same cloths. And whereas we are informed by the humble petition of our beloved subjects, the clothiers and

[*] Appendix to Wardell's Municipal History of Leeds, p. 14.

inhabitants of the said town and parish of Leedes, that the cloths heretofore made in the said town and parish, have been sold and exported before other cloths of the country there, from their fit, good, and true workmanship and make; and that from the fame and estimation of the same cloths, divers clothiers of the same town and parish have begun to make and as yet endeavour to make deceptive cloths, and to dye the same with wood, called log wood, to the damage and prejudice of us, subversion of the clothiers of the town and parish aforesaid, and discredit of the inhabitants there, if immediate remedy for that purpose be not applied; and that divers other enormities and inconveniences for some time have sprung up, and do still increase, as well concerning the cloths aforesaid as the town and parish aforesaid, which in no way can be reformed without good rule, by our royal authority and power established."*

To put an end to these evils, real and imaginary, and to secure good government, the king proceeded by his charter to form the town and parish of Leeds into a municipal borough, and to vest the government thereof in an alderman, nine principal burgesses, and twenty assistants, under the corporate style of " The Alderman and Burgesses of the Borough of Leeds in the County of York." The king himself appointed the first alderman, in the person of Sir John Savile of Howley Hall, knight (afterwards created Baron Savile of Pontefract). He also appointed the first set of principal burgesses, namely, Ralph Hopton, Seth Skelton, John Harrison, John Hodgson, Samuel Casson, Richard Sykes, Robert Benson, Thomas Metcalf, and Joseph Hillery. His Majesty likewise appointed the first twenty assistants or common council men, whose names were Benjamin Wade, William Busfield, George Killingbecke, William Marshall, Ralph Cooke, Edward Killingbecke, Francis Jackson, Walter Haycocke, John Cooper, Henry Watkinson, Abraham Jenkinson, James Sykes, Robert Pease, George Dixon, Ralph Crofte, Peter Jackson, William Stable, John Jackson, Christopher Preston, and John Hargrave.

The original burgesses and assistants nominated by the king were appointed for life (or during what the law calls good behaviour); and they were also authorized to fill up all vacancies in their own numbers as they arose. Thus the rest of the burgesses were deprived of all power in the management of their own affairs. This is altogether opposed to the ancient free principles on which the corporations of London, York, and most other great cities were constituted.

The Part taken by Leeds in the Great Civil War.—Leeds Bradford, and Halifax, with the surrounding villages, engaged in the woollen trade, all took an active part in the great civil war, and formed the chief strength of the parliamentary party in the West Riding of Yorkshire. In April, 1642–43, the clothiers of these districts sent a petition to Charles I., who at that time held his court at York, strongly urging conciliation with his Parliament. On the departure of the king to Nottingham, where he raised the royal standard against the Parliament, he appointed the earl, afterwards marquis of Newcastle, his general-in-chief in

* Wardell's Municipal History of Leeds. Appendix, p. 14.

Yorkshire and the northern counties; with Sir William Savile of Thornhill Hall, as second in command. The Parliament nominated Ferdinando, Lord Fairfax, of Denton Hall, their general, with his much more distinguished son, Sir Thomas Fairfax, as second in command. At the commencement of the civil war, Leeds and Wakefield were garrisoned for the king. Bradford and Halifax were held by the parliamentary party; and the former town was attacked by the royalists on Sunday, December 18, 1642. After a severe contest they were repulsed at Bradford, and the parliamentary forces soon after marched to Leeds, and attacked and occupied the town.

At the beginning of the year 1642-43, Sir Thomas Fairfax, having repulsed the royalists at Bradford, and collected the parliamentary troops about Halifax and Bradford, marched upon Leeds, on Monday, the 23rd January. His forces consisted of six troops of horse and three companies of dragoons, under Sir Henry Fowlis, his lieutenant-general of the horse; and of nearly 1000 musketeers, with 2000 clubmen, under Sir William Fairfax, lieutenant-general of the foot. A company of parliamentary dragoons, under Captain Mildmay, with thirty musketeers and 1000 clubmen, marched on the south side of the river to Hunslet Moor, and threatened the royalists on that side; but the main body of the parliamentary army crossed the river Aire at Apperley Bridge, some miles above Leeds, and marched to Woodhouse Moor, a portion of Kirkstall Bridge having been broken down by the royalists, to interrupt the direct road from Bradford to Leeds. On arriving on Woodhouse Moor, Sir Thomas Fairfax sent a trumpeter to Sir William Savile, the king's commander, requiring him, in writing, to deliver up the town to the Parliament, or as the parliamentary commanders, and Parliament itself, then expressed it, "to the King and Parliament." Sir William Savile, having under his command 1500 foot, 500 horse, and two demi-culverins, or small cannon, refused both the first and a second summons to surrender, telling the Fairfaxes plainly that they would get nothing but by fighting. The attack then commenced, along a line of fortifications which the royalists had thrown up on the west side of the town, extending from the newly built church of St. John's to the river Aire. We have no account of the fortifications on the eastern side of the town; but as they were not attacked, they were probably stronger than those on the west and north. Every thing being prepared for the assault, five companies of the best-trained soldiers of the parliamentary forces, under Captains Forbes, Briggs, Lee, Frank, and Palmer, marched on St. John's church; and nearly at the same time a fierce skirmish commenced between the royal and the parliamentary musketeers, the latter of whom advanced under cover of a hill, through the fields before "the great long trench," on the west of the town. After considerable firing, without any important result, Sir Thomas Fairfax, with his two generals on one side, and Captain Forbes on the other, assaulted the outworks of the town, and in a hard fight of two hours' duration, drove the royalists from their works and took possession of them. About the same time another point of the intrenchments was carried, near the end of Buhr or Boar Lane; and soon after, the parliamentary forces advanced through Hunslet and attacked Leeds Bridge. The royalists, being thus assailed at three points, and being cut off from escape by the bridge, were broken and driven back to their works, near the parish church. Thence they attempted to escape across the Aire, and many of them succeeded in doing so; but Major Beaumont, and others, were drowned in the attempt. In this well contested engagement the parliamentary forces took 500 prisoners, four colours, two brass cannon, with arms and ammunition; and about forty men were killed, of whom twelve were on the Parliament side. Leeds was now garrisoned for the Parliament, and Sir Thomas Fairfax there dates his letter to the Speaker of the House of Commons, announcing his success. Soon after this defeat the royalist troops fell back on the city of York. This, however, was immediately followed by another advance of the royal army into the West Riding, by the battle of Adwalton Moor, in the parish of Birstal, not far from Leeds and Bradford, in which the parliamentary army, under Sir Thomas Fairfax, was defeated by the royalists, under the earl of Newcastle. This enabled the royalists to recover Leeds and Bradford, which they held until the Scottish army advanced to the assistance of the parliamentary party. On their advance the royalists retreated to York, and were immediately after defeated in the great battle of Marston Moor. No further military operations of much importance occurred in this neighbourhood. At the battle of Marston Moor one of the Leeds parliamentary regiments was commanded by Colonel Thoresby, the father of the Leeds antiquary, who seems to have behaved with very great courage in that fierce engagement.[*]

The register of the parish church of Leeds contains the following brief notice of the mortality caused by the conflicts between the parliamentary party and the royalists, in and about Leeds, in the years 1642-44:—23rd January, 1642-43, Leeds was taken by Sir Thomas Fairfax; eleven soldiers slain, buried 24th; five more slain two or three days after; six more died of their wounds. Buried 1st April, 1643, Captain Boswell, slain at Seacroft battle, and six soldiers. A gentleman and two common soldiers, slain in Robert Williamson's house, Hunslet, were buried 13th April, 1643. Five soldiers more slain. Nine more in May, 1643. Sixteen more in June, under Captain Lascelles, Major Gifford, Sir George Wentworth, Captain Thornton, and the earl of Newcastle. Twelve more in July, under General King, Sir Ingram Hopton, and Sir William Widrington. Twenty-six soldiers buried in July and August, 1644. A soldier buried in the Old School Garth. Several soldiers and Captain Cox, from Newcastle, slain at Bradford, February, 1643-44, also buried at Leeds.[†]

After the complete overthrow of the royalists, and the entire success of the parliamentary party, the episcopal form of religion was for a considerable time set aside in England, and the presbyterian established in its place. At the time of this change, Henry Robinson, who was the vicar of Leeds, was forced to retire from his home and living, and his place was taken by Peter Saxton. When the country had become somewhat more tranquil Mr. Robinson was allowed to settle at Swillington, in the neighbourhood of Leeds, where he discharged the duties of rector for fourteen years. He survived the restoration of church and king for three years; but though he was solicited to return to Leeds, and to resume his office, he declined to do so, apparently preferring the peace and tranquillity of the country. At his death, in 1663, he was interred in Swillington church, where there is a tablet to his memory, at the east end of the chancel. His son, Henry Robinson, was the principal founder of Trinity Church, Leeds; as his brother-in-law, John Harrison, had been the founder of St. John's.

Before the civil war was brought to a close, another and still more dreadful scourge fell upon the people of Leeds, and on many

* Thoresby's Diary.   † Whitaker's History of Leeds, vol. i. p. 73.

other towns in the north of England. The plague broke out in 1644, and continued to rage for more than a year, carrying off a fifth part of the population. Many of the inhabitants fled from the town, to cabins hastily built on Woodhouse Moor and other open grounds, to escape the ravages of the disease; and some cabins erected outside the town, on Quarry Hill, gave their name to another spot used for this purpose, thence called Cabin Closes. One of the plague troughs still exists in a wall on the Chapel Town Road. Into this trough, filled with water, the inhabitants threw their money, to pay for the provisions brought from the country; neither the buyers nor the sellers daring to touch or to come near to each other, from fear of infection.

The following are the particulars, in the parish register, of this fatal visitation:—

"March 11, 1644-45, was buried Alice, wife of John Musgrave of Vicar Lane. This woman was the first that was suspected to die of the plague. There were buried 131 persons in August, 1644, before the plague was perceived." Dr. Whitaker very naturally asks, what are we to think of the state of medicine, from these words?

"July 2, 1645, the Old Church doors were shut up, and prayers and sermon only at the New Church, and so no names of burials to be certified, but a few at St. John's, until Mr. Saxton came to be vicar, when prayers and sermon began again."

The extent of the calamity was awful indeed. The return of deaths made to Major-general Carter, governor of Leeds, from March 12, 1644-45 to December 25, 1645, amounted to 1325 persons. The disease raged most violently in Vicar Lane, and the Close Yards adjoining, from which several were buried, to avoid the danger of further removal, in the Vicar's Croft, and others in North Hall orchard; the plague was also very prevalent in Marsh Lane, the Calls, Call Lane, Lower Briggate, and Mill Hill. From March 12, 1644-45, to June 1 following, the number of persons who died was seventy-one, but in the month of June the disease attained its full malignity, and between the 1st and the 26th of that month the number of deaths was 127. From the beginning of June to the middle of September the pestilence raged with dreadful violence, the number of deaths varying from sixty to eighty-seven weekly; and in the week between the 24th and the 31st of June reaching 126. From the middle of

September the number of deaths weekly gradually decreased to forty-four, thirty-four, fourteen, eighteen, eleven; and in the month of December the number was fourteen. It is stated that at the time when the plague was most malignant, in the month of June, "the air was thick, very warm, and so infectious that dogs and cats, mice and rats, died; also several birds in their flight over the town dropped down dead." On this extraordinary statement Dr. Whitaker observes, "Appalled and confounded as the people must have been, no one appears to have been calm enough to observe with accuracy; and danger, we know, is one of the most powerful sources of credulity. From a much better attested account, however, of another plague, that of Athens, by Thucydides, it really appears that the infection extended to carnivorous birds at least; but there many bodies were left to be preyed upon, which in this instance is not likely."*

Leeds was represented in the Parliament of the Commonwealth by Captain Adam Baynes of Knowstrop Hall, Leeds, whose family, according to Thoresby, had been settled there for many generations.

The Second Royal Charter of Leeds.—After the restoration of King Charles II., in the year 1661, that king granted a second Royal Charter of Incorporation to the borough of Leeds. In this charter, which also included the whole parish within the borough, it was stated that the previous charter, granted by Charles I., had become without force and void in law, in consequence of which the body corporate and politic, in form aforesaid constituted, was declared to be dissolved. The charter granted by Charles II. proceeded to reconstitute it, and to provide that the town of Leeds should be under the government of "one of the more honest and discreet burgesses or inhabitants of the borough," who should be named mayor of the borough aforesaid; also of twelve of the more honest and discreet burgesses, who should be named aldermen; also of twenty-four other able and discreet men, who should be named assistants of the borough; which aldermen and assistants should hereafter for ever be, and be called, the common council of the said borough, and from time to time should be aiding, counselling, and assisting the mayor, for the time being, in the well ruling and governing the borough aforesaid. This charter also named the first mayor, aldermen, and assistants. Thomas Danby, Esq., was appointed "the first

* Dr. Whitaker's History of Leeds, vol. i. p. 76.

and present mayor," for the year 1662-1. The twelve aldermen named in the charter were—John Hopton, Esq., Benjamin Wade, William Marshall the elder, John Dawson, John Metcalfe, Henry Skelton, Francis Allanson, Daniel Foxcroft, Marmaduke Hicke, Edward Atkinson, Christopher Watkinson, and Godfrey Lawson. The names of the twenty-four common councilmen were— William Curtis, Richard Armitage, Gilbert Cooper, John Barker, John Killingbeck, John Simpson, Bryan Kitchinman, William Milner, Nicholas Lister, George Marshall, John Hodgson, William Fenton, William Busfield, Henry Walker, Samuel Child, Roger Pickering, James Netherwood, Henry Roades, Richard Midgeley, Lancelot Iveson, Adam Hargreave, William Foster, Charles Holdsworth, and Henry Mitchell. The mayor was to be elected by the town council every year; but both the aldermen and the assistants or common councilmen were appointed "during their natural lives, unless they were removed for their evil behaviour or evil carriage, or for some other reasonable cause." In case of the death of an alderman or an assistant, the mayor and the rest of the assistants were authorized to elect a successor, from the number of the aldermen or assistants, who was also to hold office for the term of his life. The charter also provided for the appointment of a recorder, and nominated Francis White, Esq., to that office; of a deputy recorder; and of a town clerk to be appointed by the king—George Banister being the first town clerk so appointed. It also provided for the appointment of a deputy town clerk.

The charter further established quarter sessions for the borough, and rendered the burgesses liable to serve on juries within the borough. It also appointed a coroner and clerk of the market; gave all fines to the corporation; freed the mayor, aldermen, and burgesses of the borough from liability to serve as jurors at assizes; authorized the mayor, aldermen, and burgesses to choose constables; further authorized them to construct a prison in the borough; to take assize of wine, bread, ale, and victuals (which was in effect to fix the retail prices of these articles, according to the average price of corn, cattle, malt, and wine in the cask); to hold a market on Tuesdays, as well as on Saturdays, and to impose needful taxes and assessments, for the necessary maintenance, support, dignity, defence, or preservation of the corporation and borough. At the commencement of this charter of Charles II. it is provided, that under the name of the borough of Leeds the whole parish of Leeds should be comprised, and that all and every the inhabitants of the town and parish of Leeds and their successors shall for ever continue one body corporate and politic. Such was the governing charter of the borough of Leeds, which continued in force, with some slight and temporary alterations until the Municipal Reform Act passed in the reign of her present Majesty, Queen Victoria.

Thoresby's Account of the Town of Leeds in the Reigns of Queen Anne and King George I., A.D. 1702-27—As Thoresby states, at the commencement of his "Ducatus Leodiensis," the greater part of the ancient and populous town of Leeds stands on the north side of the river Aire, rising with an easy ascent. He gives as a reason for commencing his description on the western side of the town, that of old there stood on that side "a famous castle," with a park adjoining. The site of the Park, though converted into lesser inclosures even in Thoresby's time (1714), retained the name of the Park, and, as he says, gave "denomination to Park Lane," on its northern side. Here were the shooting butts, at which the inhabitants practised archery before the introduction of gunpowder. The castle and park of Leeds remained in the crown for many ages; and there was a crown rent of £8 payable for the park and the mills, in the time of Queen Anne and King George I. They were then held by his Grace, Thomas Osborne, duke of Leeds, who had acquired most of the royal rights in the borough, and ultimately took his title from that flourishing town.*

The principal streets and public buildings existing at the time of the accession of the House of Hanover to the throne (1714), are described by Thoresby in the following order.

The Manor House.—The manor house which stood on or near the site of the old castle of Leeds, on ground rising from the river, known as the Mill Hill, was in the reign of George I. a capital messuage, and the ancient residence of the lords of the manor, and was held along with the park. In Thoresby's time it had formed part of the estate of Richard Sykes, Esq., who was the father-in-law of Ralph Thoresby; but when he published the "Ducatus" it belonged to Richard Wilson, Esq., barrister at law, of Gray's Inn, London, in right of his marriage with Eliza-

---

* Ducatus Leodiensis, or the Topography of the Town and Parish of Leeds, &c. By Ralph Thoresby, F.R.S., 1715. The second edition, with notes, by Thomas Dunham Whitaker, LL.D., vol. ii. p. 1.

beth, the eldest daughter of Richard Sykes. From him it passed through his sons and grandsons, one of whom was bishop of Bristol, to Richard Fountaine Wilson, Esq., for some time one of the members for the county of York, and a very liberal benefactor of the charities of Leeds.

The New Chapel and Almshouses.—A row of almshouses for sixteen poor people also stood near the manor house; and near to the style which then led into the park, at the western extremity of the town. This was at the foot of the present Park Row, and near the entrance to the Coloured Cloth Hall and railway station. There was a field attached to these almshouses, which was known by the name of the Almshouse Garth. Adjoining to this field, or garth, was the new chapel or meetinghouse, long known as Mill-hill Chapel. This chapel was erected by the Presbyterians resident in Leeds, almost immediately after the first indulgence of the nonconformists, in the reign of Charles II. and the year 1672. Thoresby says, that it was said to be the first in point of time, and that it was certainly one of the stateliest fabrics, built upon that occasion in the north of England. It was in point of fact a neat and commodious chapel; but on its site there has recently been erected one of the handsomest places of worship in Leeds.

The Bur, Burh, or Borough Lane.—Thoresby states that the street which leads from the castle to the town is called the Bur, Boar, or rather the Burrow Lane, from burg, *burgus,* or *castrum.* The original name seems to have been the Burh Lane, which is the Anglian and Saxon form of the present word borough. At the time when Thoresby wrote, about the year 1714, the Burh Lane was a suburban road leading from and to the park. He says, that from its not being so closely built as the rest of the town, several gentlemen had erected their houses there, amongst whom were Sir William Lowther, Bart. ; Sandford Arthington ; Cyril Arthington, Esq., who, says Thoresby, "has lately erected a noble hall, at Arthington" in Wharfedale ; Jasper Blythman, Esq. ; Mr. Robert Shaw ; Mr. John Skinner, merchant ; and John Atkinson, Esq., one of the magistrates of the West Riding.

Briggate.—In describing this wide and ancient street, Thoresby says, " In this ancient and spacious street, which from the bridge at the foot of it is called Bridge Gate or Briggate, stand many of the ancient burgage houses, granted by the early lords of the manor to their tenants in burgage. These paid a certain burgage rent to the lord of the manor of Leeds. Here also is situated the famous cloth market, the life, not of the town alone, but of these parts of England." This was held in Briggate, in the open air, twice every week, namely, on Tuesdays and Saturdays, early in the morning, having been removed from the bridge, to the street, in Thoresby's earlier years. Speaking of the cloth market as it was held about the year 1714, Thoresby says, that in every market several thousand pounds' worth of broad cloth was bought and, generally speaking, paid for; "and this with so profound a silence as is surprising to strangers, who, from the adjoining galleries can hear no more noise than the lowly murmur of the merchants upon the Exchange of London."

The Moot Hall.—At the top of Briggate was the Moot Hall, of which Thoresby says:—"The guild hall here is to this day called by the Saxon denomination of the Moot Hall, from mote or gemot, a convention or assembly, and healle, *Aula Palatium*, the Ruler's Hall. Folk-mote was originally a convention of all the inhabitants, which, if within a city or town, was called a Burghmote; if of all the free tenants within a county, was called the Shire-mote." Of the Moot Hall of Leeds, Thoresby says:—"Had Lady Danby's proposal been timely embraced, who, being relict of the first mayor of Leeds, offered a considerable sum towards the building of a new guild hall upon pillars and arches, as proposed by Mr. John Thoresby, we might have boasted of a stately *comitium*, whereas conveniency is now all that is pretended to. This bench, however, is honoured with the presence of persons of great quality at the county sessions, for which it is very convenient, being near the centre of the West Riding; and more frequently by our own magistrates." * *Pillory and Stocks.* —Directly before the moot hall were placed what, Thoresby informs us, our ancestors very significantly called the Hals Fang or Neck-holder, the Pillory, with the stocks adjoining, "that the justices from the bench may see the punishments inflicted upon malefactors." The shambles were on the other side of the Moot Hall, higher up the street. † *Paudmire Stone.*—This was an old boundary stone, chiefly remarkable as having given name to the house in which John Harrison, the most liberal of the benefactors of Leeds, was born, in the year 1579. *The Market*

---

* Thoresby's Ducatus, vol. ii. p. 18.   † Ibid.

Cross. — In the midst of the market-place, John Harrison, above mentioned, erected what Thoresby calls a stately cross, for the convenience and ornament of the market; not far from which place there stood in earlier times an old prison, which, being thought a blemish to the principal street, was pulled down, A.D. 1655, and a new one erected elsewhere, in Kirkgate. The old cross was taken down, and a much larger one erected in the year 1776.* *The Chantry.*—The corner house on the west side of Briggate, at the top of the street, which seems to have been the best in the town of that antiquity, was the chantry house of St. Mary Magdalene, founded by William Evers, vicar of Leeds, A.D. 1470.† In Thoresby's time the reserved rent of this charity, with other fee farm rents, were the property of the Right Honourable John Lord Somers of Evesham, the celebrated lord chancellor of England. Near here was the Talbot, a noted inn, which at one time boasted of a chamber curiously painted in fresco, with the arms of the nobility and gentry of the West Riding, as they were in Queen Elizabeth's time. Thoresby says that this venerable monument was defaced by the indiscretion of a tenant.‡

The Head Row.—The Head Row, says Thoresby, was so called by our predecessors from its elevated situation, or rather from its running across the head of the main street. It was of old one entire street, but was afterwards divided into the Upper and Nether, or Lower, Head Rows, by the New Street.

The Red Hall.—Near the West Bar, in the Upper Head Row, was the Red Hall, so called because it was the first house of any note that was built of brick, in the town of Leeds, A.D. 1628. Previous to that time, stone and timber were the only materials used. An apartment in this hall was called the king's chamber, in consequence of King Charles I. having been lodged therein, on his way from Newark to Newcastle, when a prisoner in the hands of the Scots. In the time of Thoresby the Red Hall was the residence of his friend Richard Thornton, Esq., recorder of Leeds; "whose noble collection of manuscripts," Thoresby observes, "had been of singular advantage to him in this undertaking."§

Rockley Hall.—In the Lowerhead Row was another capital messuage, called Rockley Hall, once the seat of an ancient family of that name, to which belonged the chapel of Rockley, in the

* Whitaker, vol. ii. p. 19.   † Ibid.   ‡ Thoresby's Ducatus.   § Ibid. p. 21.

parish church of Leeds. It was a timber building, and Thoresby says that it was of the most antique form of any that he had seen. Instead of deals or boards for the floors were oak planks, of so considerable a thickness that joists were made of them for part of the new brick building, which succeeded it in name as well as place.*

New Street.—The street, long known as New Street, but now forming a continuation of Briggate northwards, was built by John Harrison, about the reign of Charles I., and the rents were appropriated by him to pious uses. Near it was a very good and convenient house, which the founder built for the minister of St. John's church, also erected by him, with outhouses, croft, and garden; which last, says Thoresby, "is now (1714) replenished with great variety of very choice flowers, by the Rev. Mr. Bright Dixon, the present worthy incumbent."†

The Church of St. John's.—The church of St. John was founded by John Harrison, "a native and chief glory of this populous town, whose inhabitants were grown so numerous that the old church, though very great, could not contain them." ‡ Adjoining to the churchyard was a large quadrangular court; on the south side whereof was a chapel, designed for a person to read prayers to the poor of the almshouses, which were built on the west and north sides of the square, with convenience for forty poor people.

Lidgate and Tower Hill.—Thoresby says that the street adjoining to the North Bar was called Lidgate, even in his time. The name he derives from the Saxon words leod-gate, "the gate of the people." Thoresby also says that "this, being the highest part of the town in early times, was made choice of for building a tower." He adds that he had perused some manuscript surrenders, &c., belonging to the lords of the manor of Leeds, wherein it was called "the Tower Hill;" and adds, that in the year 1695, when the workmen were digging deep, to lay a secure foundation for the vast cistern which was to serve as a repository for the river water, that was then first conveyed in lead pipes from the bridge foot to this place, they found "prodigious large stones and the ruins of a great wall, which seemed to have been the groundwork of such a fabric;" that is, as the ancient tower.

North Bar.—" The North Bar was in early times the northern

* Thoresby's Ducatus, vol. ii. p. 29.   † Ibid. p. 28.   ‡ Ibid. p. 30.

gate, at the entrance of the town. In early times all English towns were surrounded with walls and gates, at which the burgesses were compelled to keep watch and ward from sunset to sunrise, taking it in turns, so as to secure safety without too much fatigue. This seems to have been the origin of the North Bar, the West Bar, and of four other bars at Leeds (making six in all), at the entrance of the main streets.* These were intended chiefly for purposes of police; but in time of war they were strengthened with trenches and additional works, generally extending from one bar to another, but sometimes formed considerably in advance of the original works. This seems to have been the case at York, Chester, and Leeds, in the great civil war, where new works of greater strength were constructed in front of the old fortifications.

The Free School and Library.—"In the place where now the Pinfold is," says Thoresby, "stood the free grammar-school, till the famous Mr. Harrison removed it from so inconvenient a situation to a pleasant field of his own, which he surrounded with a substantial wall, and then, in the midst of the quadrangle, built the present fabric of the school,† to which Godfrey Lawson, Esq. (mayor of Leeds, A.D. 1669), added a new apartment in the year 1692, in the lower room whereof is a conveniency for a fire for the scholars in winter; and in that above a growing library, wherein are some choice books of his gift and other charitably disposed persons."

More northward ("after we have passed by some pleasant seats of the merchants"), and at a little distance from the town, though within the main Riding, are Sheepscar and Buslingthorpe, "now [1714] mostly inhabited by clothiers."

The Sheepscar Beck.—"This," says Thoresby, "is the nameless water, that Mr. William Harrison, in his description of Britain, (published in the reign of Queen Elizabeth), mentions as running into Aire, on the north side of Leeds, from Wettlewood [as it is misprinted for Weetwood]. This beck proceeds from a small spring upon the moor, a little above Adle [Adel], and yet had some time ago [previous to 1714], eight mills upon it, in its four miles' course. The first is that of Adel (as it is written in some charts in my [Thoresby's] Collections), near unto which is the Roman camp, and the vestigia of the town lately discovered; and the last before its conjunction with the Aire is this at Sheepscar, which above eighty years ago [before 1714] was employed for

* Wardell's Municipal History of Leeds. † Thoresby's Ducatus Leodiensis.

the grinding of red wood, and making rape oil, then first known in these parts. It was converted into a corn mill in the late times, but upon the Restoration, when the king's mills recovered their ancient soke, it dwindled into a paper mill, not for imperial, but for that coarse paper called "emporetica," useful only for chapmen to wrap wares in. It was afterwards made a rape mill again, as it now stands."

After describing the western and northern parts of the town of Leeds, as they existed in the reign of King George I. (1714), Thoresby turns to the eastern or older part, which at that time was much more populous than the north or west. There he, or his ancestors before him, had lived for nearly 100 years, in their own house in Kirkgate, which at that time was a wide, open street, containing the vicarage and many other good houses, opening at the back into pleasant fields extending to Sheepscar beck and the open country. In the survey of the manor of Leeds, in the reign of James I., mention is made of two almshouses in the Vicar Lane, whose income, however, seems to have been trifling—only twopence a year. "These," adds Thoresby, "are near unto my garden wall, running back from Kirkgate; and the chamber over them is now converted into a dressing shop, and is in possession of Mr. Christopher Conder, who purchased it of Mr. Baynes, of Knowstrop, for 999 years."*

The old Parish Church of Leeds.—The old parish church of Leeds, dedicated to St. Peter, which was taken down in the year 1838 to make way for a much handsomer building, is described by Thoresby as being a very spacious and strong fabric, "an emblem of the church militant, black but comely. Being of great antiquity," says he, "it doth not pretend to the mode of reformed architecture, but is strong and useful. By whom it was first founded I can by no means learn, but hope my involuntary ignorance will be excused, seeing it is the common fate of most parochial churches, which perhaps were generally built, as they continue to be maintained, by the joint contributions of the inhabitants." Of the exterior of the old church, he says that it was plain, but venerable; the walls wholly of freestone, the roof entirely covered with lead, except that part of the quire only that belonged to the impropriator. It was built after the manner of a cathedral, with a large cross aisle, and the steeple or tower in

* Thoresby's Ducatus, vol. ii, p. 38

the middle of it. The dimensions of the old church were, in length 165 feet, breadth 97, height of the nave 51 feet, and that of the steeple 96 feet." *

Nether Mills and Stender.—Beyond the two fulling mills (the inheritance of Henry Smith, Esq., at the Survey) and stender, was the confluence of Sheepscar beck and the river Aire, at the foot of the ascent to Hill-house Bank, where in Thoresby's time was a large house, built by Mr. William Ingram. Upon this ascent, he says, "is Cavaliers' Hill, which has been so called ever since the marquis of Newcastle's army lay encamped there in the civil wars. From hence a road led by the nar [near] and far [farther] banks," which were then mostly inhabited by clothiers, or occupied by Grass Greens, to Knowstrop.

The Calls.—From the old church to Leeds Bridge there was in Thoresby's time a footpath way through the fields, by certain gardens, particularly Alderman Cookson's, "who had lately erected there a very pleasant seat, with terrace walks." The Calls, now Call Lane, Thoresby believed to be named from the Latin word *callis;* a word, he says, much used by Virgil and other Roman authors for a beaten path. *Calx,* "a flint," is probably the root of the name.

In the Call Lane, betwixt the back gates of the "quondam chantry and Mr. Harrison's garden," he says, "those of the Congregational persuasion built a stately chapel, or meeting house, with a turret upon the leaden roof, in the year 1691."

In the adjoining orchard, where was the grove and summer-house of which Mr. Harrison, at the time of his death, was proprietor, John Atkinson, justice of the peace for the West Riding and mayor of Leeds, in the year 1711, was building "a delicate house, that for the exquisite workmanship of the stonework, especially the dome, and for a painted staircase, excellently performed by Monsieur Parmentier, exceeded in beauty all in town." Dr. Whitaker, writing in the year 1816, says it was even then a handsome house, and having been durably built still remained entire. This house was the post-office of Leeds within the recollection of the author of this work, with a pleasant garden in front, and a row of elms at the side.

The Pitt Fall, Call Lane.—Thoresby says that here were formerly two fulling mills in his time, replaced by a rape mill and the water-

* Thoresby's Ducatus, vol. ii. p. 39.

engine. The engine was for conveying the river water, by lead pipes, to the different parts of the town. The water-works were erected in the year 1695, 8th William III., by Mr. George Surocold, whom Thoresby describes as "the great engineer, who has done the like at Macclesfield, Wirksworth, Yarmouth, Portsmouth, Norwich, King's Lynn, London Bridge, Deal, Bridgenorth, Islington New Water-works, and Bristol."

The Water-power of Leeds in the Seventeenth and Eighteenth Centuries.—Thoresby states that in the time of Anne of Denmark, the wife of King James I., who had the manor of Leeds as part of her dower, the corn mills of that town were held, *cum soca et secta*, by virtue of letters-patent under the seal of the duchy of Lancaster, by John Lindley of Leathley, Esq., at the yearly rent of £13 6s. 8d., but he adds, that they were "of the clear yearly value of £126 13s. 4d." In Thoresby's own time (in the reign of Queen Anne, the daughter of James II.) the mills were in the hands of William Neville, Esq., then of Holbeck, whose family held them down to the present century.

"Adjoining to the corn mills," says Thoresby, writing in the reign of Queen Anne or George I., "is lately rebuilt another mill, wherein, by the ingenious contrivance of Mr. John Atkinson of Beeston, one water-wheel carries [works] both the rape mill and a mill for grinding logwood, brasil, &c.; also a fulling stock for milling shalloons, serges, &c.; and a twisting mill with eighty bobbins; so also a stone for grinding scythes, sickles, whitesmiths' plates, &c.; it likewise throws water into a conveyance that fills the dyeing lead or pan; and also a throw for turning wood. This reminds me of an ingenious artist on the other side the bridge, namely, Jo. Armitage, who turns strong and large pieces of iron and steel in an engine for that purpose, useful in all strong machines and movements, as mills for plates, tobacco mills, malt mills, spindles for corn mills, &c. Jacks are also made after a new and curious method, the wheels and axles and all the moving parts (which formerly and now by most are filed), being all turned down to exactness, and the teeth cut in an engine; also fowling pieces, fine razors, scissors, and lancets, are made, grinded, and polished, &c." It is clear from these statements of Thoresby that the water-power, which is so abundant within the borough of Leeds, not merely in the river Aire, but in the large brooks, on one of which, namely, the Adel Brook, there were then eight mills, was now beginning to be used for a variety of new purposes, as well as the ancient one of grinding corn, to which it had been applied from before the Norman conquest, and the fulling of cloth, for which it had been used previous to the reign of King Edward III. Owing to these and other causes trade was increasing rapidly, and it became necessary about this time (1710-12) to build a Cloth Hall, for the sale of white or undyed cloth, at which the clothiers from the neighbouring villages, of whom more than 100 already attended the Leeds cloth markets every week, might sell their goods to the merchants, without being incommoded by the cold and wet, to which they had been so much exposed, when the Cloth Market was held on the old bridge, or even when it was in the open street of Briggate.

The First Cloth Hall Built at Leeds.—When Ralph Thoresby began business as a cloth merchant at Leeds, in the reign of Charles II. (1678-79), the only cloth market in that town was held in the open air, on Leeds Bridge, which was even then large enough for the purpose, though a marvellously inconvenient position, especially in wet and stormy weather. In the month of June, 1684, the cloth market was removed from the bridge to the open street of Briggate, where it was carried on, down to the year 1712, if not longer, on stands set up on the market day, by the side of the street, and in a position only a few degrees less inconvenient than that of the bridge. Speaking of the old cloth market held on Leeds Bridge, Thoresby says, under date of June 7, 1684, that he was that day "at the Bridge market, and afterwards at Denton Hall;" and on the 14th June, in the same year, he notes that he was "at the New Cloth Market, which by order of the mayor and aldermen is removed from off the bridge, to the broad street above (Briggate), to prevent the inconveniency from the cold air of the water in winter, and the trouble of carts and carriages in summer."

The first proposal to build a separate Cloth Hall at Leeds we find in Thoresby's "Diary," in the year 1710, when an alarm, lest the whole woollen trade should be carried off from Leeds by the public-spirited people of Wakefield, who had erected a cloth hall there for the accommodation of the clothiers of the surrounding country, roused the people of Leeds, and especially the cloth merchants, to a sense of the necessity of constructing a similar accommodation for trade in their own town. This was accordingly done, at the instigation of Thoresby and others, and with the warm support of

Lord Irwin of Temple Newsam, who appears to have taken an interest in everything relating to the prosperity of Leeds, with which his family was closely connected by a community of interest. With regard to this first Leeds Cloth Hall the following extracts from Thoresby's "Diary," in the year 1710, and succeeding years, show its origin and progress :—"August 14. Rode with the mayor, Cousin (Alderman) Milner, and others, to my Lord Irwin, about the erection of a hall, for the white cloths in Kirkgate, to prevent the damage to this town (the competition or superior advantage) of one lately erected at Wakefield, with design to engross that affair (the woollen trade), which is computed to bring about 100 tradesmen every market day, to this town." In the following year, 1711, April 22, Thoresby notes as follows :—"To see the new White Cloth Market in Kirkgate, *opened this day.*" In the next year, 1712, on the 23rd February, he mentions Cousin (Milner's) treat as alderman, as being the first made at the new White Cloth Hall; and in the year 1714, January 27, he has the following memorandum :—" Accompanied Cousin Milner and Lord Irwin to the Assembly "—which was no doubt held in the Assembly room attached to the White Cloth Hall.

The Rivers Aire and Calder made navigable from Leeds and Wakefield to the Ouse, the Humber, and the Sea.—The first very great improvement made at Leeds or in the West Riding of Yorkshire, in the means of conveying goods, merchandise, and minerals, was effected in the last few years of the seventeenth and the commencement of the eighteenth century, by rendering the river Aire navigable from Leeds to the Ouse, and so to the Humber, and the German Ocean ; and by, at the same time, making the river Calder navigable, from the town of Wakefield, to the point of the river Aire at which the Calder joins that stream. This was effected under the powers of the Act of the 10th and 11th William III., cap. 19, 1698–99, entitled an "Act for making and keeping navigable the rivers Aire and Calder, in the county of York."* This great improvement reduced the cost of transporting heavy goods, and especially minerals, to from a fourth, a fifth, and in some cases a tenth part, of the rates that prevailed previously, when goods were carried on the backs of pack-horses, or in heavy waggons, which travelled, with extreme slowness and difficulty, over the steep and

---

* "A List of Acts of Parliament relating to the borough of Leeds," in the Municipal History of Leeds, by James Wardell, Esq.

badly made roads of the West Riding. The effect of rendering the Aire and the Calder navigable was to substitute, what may still be regarded as the cheapest means of inland transport, for the dearest. It gave the manufacturers of Leeds comparatively cheap carriage for coal, iron, building-stone, and clay, as well as much lower rates than had previously prevailed for wool, logwood, oil, and other articles brought from great distances; and also gave them an easy outlet for their woollen goods to the port of Hull, and to Holland, which at that time possessed the greater part of the carrying trade of England and Europe. From that time the trade of Leeds with the continent, the eastern coasts of England, and Hull and London, which, along with Bristol, were the principal ports for the exportation and importation of the wools of England, Spain, and Saxony, before Australian wool was known or thought of, continued to increase rapidly. By this line of water carriage the manufacturing population of Leeds also obtained abundant supplies of corn, cattle, and provisions from Hull, Lincolnshire, and Nottinghamshire, whose produce came down the river Trent. This ultimately led to the establishing of large depots and markets of corn and cattle, partly at Leeds, but still more at Wakefield, which soon became one of the greatest markets for corn and cattle in the north of England. Large warehouses, with some of the conveniences of the modern warehousing system, were erected by the Navigation Company at both towns. About fifty years later the river Calder was still further improved, and was rendered navigable, by the construction or improvement of channels, natural or artificial, to the neighbourhood of Dewsbury, Huddersfield, and Halifax. Thus all the great towns of the manufacturing district of the West Riding, except Bradford, which was very inaccessible until the age of canals, were supplied with water carriage with each other, with the great corn-growing districts of the eastern and midland counties, and with the ports of Hull and London. No attempt was made to render the Aire navigable above Leeds to Bradford, perhaps owing to the difficulty of the gradients; but the Calder was made navigable almost to Halifax, and far above Dewsbury and the junction of the Colne near Huddersfield. But neither Leeds nor any other of the manufacturing towns of the West Riding had water carriage to Liverpool, the Irish Sea, and the Atlantic Ocean, until the later portion of the eighteenth century, when the genius of the great engineer, James

Brindley, devised, and taught others to apply, the means of carrying navigable canals over or through even lofty hills, by means of locks and tunnels.

As the rendering of the rivers Aire and Calder navigable to the tidewater of the river Ouse, and through the Humber to the great port of Hull, was the commencement of a long series of public works which have had an immense influence in developing the prosperity of Leeds, and of the West Riding, it may be well to give a few particulars as to the origin of that great improvement. Speaking of the events of the year 1697, Thoresby informs us, that proposals were now first made for rendering the rivers Ouse and Calder navigable to the Humber and the sea. This had been a subject of frequent discussion in the early part of the century, but it was not until very near its close, in the year 1697, that men were found capable of carrying out this great undertaking. On this occasion, says Ralph Thoresby, "I accompanied the mayor and Mr. Hadley, the hydrographer" (or, as we should say, the engineer), "to view the river." Justice Kirk of Cookridge Hall (like Thoresby, a member of the Royal Society), "measured it with his surveying wheel till they wearied, and left the rest to the servants and others. We lodged at Ferrybridge, ten miles by land, and twenty by water (from Leeds). Mr. Hadley affirmed it was the noblest river he had ever seen, that was not already navigable. The next day we went to Welland." Thoresby adds, " This journey brought me to a greater intimacy with the ingenious Mr. Kirk, who lent me his observations on the registers at Adel, and other curious papers to transcribe."*

About the same time, but more exactly in the year 1701, Thoresby mentions another great improvement relating to the whole of the West Riding, namely, the establishing of a public register of lands. On this subject he says, under date 17th September of that year :—" With Mr. Kirk at Cookridge, of whom glad to hear of the successful attempt for a public register of lands in the West Riding, which will be of use in future ages as well as the present."†

There do not appear to have been stage-coaches from Leeds to London, until after the beginning of the eighteenth century. Ralph Thoresby describes his early journeys between London and Leeds, up to the year 1709, as having been made on horseback, except one made luxuriously in the private carriage of Mr. Boulter

* Thoresby's Diary, vol. i. p. 220. † Ibid. p. 345.

of Harewood, a great friend of Thoresby's, and of his Museum. But about that time a coach was started between London and Leeds, which at once came so much into use, that Thoresby states, on one occasion, that all the places in the Leeds coach from London were taken up for a fortnight in advance. Sometimes in very bad weather the coach did not succeed in reaching Leeds, over the steep ridge of Rothwell Haigh; and on such occasions Thoresby and other travellers had to ride to Wakefield to join the coach, or to Leeds, after leaving it at Wakefield. The journeys generally took from four to five days, and after heavy rains were very dangerous, from the flooding of the rivers, which rendered the roads nearly impassable; as well as from numerous highwaymen, who rendered the approaches to London very perilous at all times. On one occasion Ralph Thoresby travelled to London with his cousin William Milner, afterwards the first Sir William Milner, Bart., of Nun Appleton, and M.P. for York, when they were eight days on the road. On that occasion they were also in double danger from floods and from highwaymen, and would scarcely have escaped the latter, if they had known that Alderman William Milner was carrying up to London several thousand pounds, to be by him invested in Government securities. It was this Alderman William Milner who at his own cost erected the statue of Queen Anne, which so long stood in front of the Moot Hall and Corn Exchange at Leeds, and which may still be seen in that new and handsome building, the Town Hall.

The Thoresby Museum.—Before taking leave of the excellent Ralph Thoresby, who died in the year 1725, after having not merely recorded, but aided in every improvement made in Leeds in his own times, we ought in justice to him and his gallant father, Colonel Thoresby, to add, that the museum formed by them in their house in Kirkgate, and thrown open to their fellow townsmen and the general public, without cost or charge, was one of the best museums ever formed by a private family. The breaking up of the museum, after Ralph Thoresby's death, was a great, and in some respects an irreparable misfortune, to Leeds and Yorkshire, of which it contained numerous ancient remains.

Improvement of Roads of Leeds and West Riding.—At the beginning of the eighteenth century, the only roads about Leeds and the other manufacturing towns of the West Riding, were packhorse roads, with a narrow strip of pavement, called a calsey, in the middle, or at one side only, along which strings of packhorses travelled, and occasionally heavy waggons, with very broad wheels, made their way slowly in the summer months, and when the ground was hardened by frost in winter. We have the following graphic account of the manner in which the inland traffic of Leeds, with other parts of the kingdom, was conducted, about the year 1727, at the commencement of the reign of George II., in Defoe's work, written at that time, entitled, "Travels of a Gentleman throughout Great Britain." Speaking of the trade of Leeds, Defoe says:—

"For the home consumption, their goods being, as I may say, every where made use of for clothing the ordinary people, who cannot go to the price of the fine medley cloths made in the western counties of England, there are for this purpose a set of travelling merchants in Leeds, who go all over England, with droves of packhorses, and to all the fairs and market towns over the whole island, I think I may say none excepted. Here they supply, not the common people by retail, which would denominate them pedlars indeed, but they supply the shops by wholesale and whole pieces; and not only so, but give large credit, to show that they are really travelling merchants, and as such they sell a very great quantity of goods. It is ordinary for one of these men to carry £1000 value of cloth with him at a time, and having sold it, at the fairs or towns where they go, they send their horses back for as much more; and this very often in a summer, for they choose to travel in the summer and perhaps towards the winter time, though as little in winter as they can, because of the badness of the roads." Thus the cloth brought to the markets of Leeds, and no doubt to those of Bradford, Halifax, Wakefield, and Huddersfield by the country clothiers, in single packages, on their own shoulders, or on ponies which most of them kept for that purpose, was conveyed on the backs of pack-horses, for sale in all parts of England.

It was about the time of Defoe's visit to Leeds, which corresponds with the twenty years of continued peace that the wise administration of Sir Robert Walpole secured to this country, in the reigns of George I. and George II., that the first great attempt began to be made to improve the high roads, in the neighbourhood of Leeds, and throughout England generally, under parliamentary powers given to joint stock companies, organized as turnpike trusts, to repair existing roads, and to make new ones; the promoters receiving tolls from horsemen, carts, and carriages, using the roads.

The first of numerous Acts for improving the public roads in the neighbourhood of Leeds, was passed in the fourteenth year of the reign of George II., 1740, and forms chapter 32, in the Acts of that year. The object of this Act was, first, to repair and enlarge the road from Leeds to the rising town of Selby, on the navigable part of the river Ouse; and second, to repair and enlarge the road from Leeds to Halifax, causing it to run in two separate branches, one through Bradford and Horton, and the other through Bowling and Wibsey, to the town of Halifax. In the same year (1740) another Act was passed for repairing the road leading from Leeds, up the valley of the Calder, to Elland, between Halifax and Huddersfield. The powers given by these Acts covered very extensive districts, reaching from the Humber and the Ouse to the entrance into the vale of Todmorden, and almost to the borders of Lancashire.[*] A few years later a third Act was passed, extending the powers of the previous Acts, and also giving powers to make an improved road from Leeds, to the neighbourhood of York. This was the 24th George II., 1750, cap. 32, which provided for making a road from Leeds, at a point on the Selby Road, by Halton Dials, through Seacroft, over Winmoor, through Kidhall Lane, and over Bramham Moor, to Tadcaster, on the borders of the Ainsty of York, and the banks of the river Wharfe. In the following year, 1751, an Act was passed for improving the roads running northward through "Harwood" to the south-west corner of the inclosures of Harrogate; and thence in two branches, one through Ripley, over Burage Green, and the other through Knaresborough and Boroughbridge, to Ripon; and from thence to the first rill of water, or water course, on Hutton Moor; and for repairing the sloughs or ruts on the said moor. Near the end of the same reign an Act was passed, in the 28th George II., 1754, cap. 60, for repairing and widening the roads from the town of Leeds to Otley, in Wharfedale; up the valley of the Wharfe, through Skipton, and over the hills of Craven to Colne, Burnley, Blackburn, and through Burscough Bridge to Walton-le-Dale, in the county of Lancaster; and from Skipton through Gisburn and Clitheroe to Preston, in that county. Four or five

[*] List of Acts of Parliament, relating to the Borough of Leeds, in Municipal History of Leeds, by James Wardell, Esq.

years later, in 1759-60, an Act was passed, for improving the road from Leeds through Wakefield to Sheffield, which afterwards became one of the great coach roads from Leeds to London, the other being through Doncaster. This was authorized by the Act of the 31 George II. cap. 63.*

The general result of the numerous Acts for improving turnpike roads passed in the reign of George II., was to give, at the accession of his successor, George III., nearly the whole of the towns of the West Riding, and the extensive lines of country between Leeds, Sheffield, Halifax, Preston, Ripon, Boroughbridge, and York, greatly improved means of communication with each other, and with London. At the same time, a similar process of improving the public roads was going on in almost every other part of the kingdom, and formed the great object of the local bills of that age. This was continued with increased energy during the long reign of George III, and of his sons, George IV. and William IV., along with Acts for forming navigable canals, and only ceased (if at all) when high roads and canals had reached perfection, and when the invention of railways introduced an entirely new means of communication throughout the country. At the time of the accession of George III. to the throne, in 1760, the coach journey from Leeds to London was made in two or three days; and in 1830-35, before the swiftest coaches were finally driven off the roads by the railways, to about twenty hours, instead of four or eight days as in 1709.

Neither the Jacobite insurrection of 1715 nor that of 1745 extended to Yorkshire, the insurgents having in both cases advanced and retreated through the county of Lancaster. But their intended line of advance and their movements being uncertain, large forces were collected in Yorkshire, the infantry principally at Leeds, and the cavalry at Doncaster, ready to advance in any direction to encounter the Jacobite army. The force of infantry assembled on the north side of Leeds, in 1745, was not less than 13,000 men, with twenty pieces of cannon.†

Wade Lane, Leeds, is generally supposed to have received its name from the circumstance of General Wade and his army having encamped there for some time, in 1745-46, prior to their march into Scotland, on the retreat of the Pretender. But this is a mistake, so

---

* List of Acts of Parliament relating to the Borough of Leeds, in Municipal History of Leeds, by James Wardell, Esq.

† Annals of Yorkshire, by John Mayhall, Esq., Clerk of the County Court, Leeds, vol. i. p. 125.

far as the name is concerned, for Wade Lane is mentioned in a lease of the reign of Charles II., quoted by Thoresby. Mention is also made in that lease of Wade Hall, situated in that lane, which stood until the end of the first twenty years of the present century, and was a handsome and picturesque house, probably built by some one of several members of the Wade family, who held the office of mayor of Leeds in the seventeenth or eighteenth century, and one of whom lived at New Grange, Headingley. There was a camp, near Camp Lane, in Thoresby's time, in the reign of Queen Anne, from which circumstance Camp Field was named. Thoresby mentions visiting the new camp of the soldiers.

Almost the only serious disturbance of the public peace that has occurred in the town of Leeds, in modern times, happened so long ago as the year 1753, and originated rather in the neighbouring country, than in the town itself. This disturbance was caused by the forming of turnpike roads, which, though one of the greatest improvements ever made in England, was very unpopular at the time, especially with the small farmers and carters, owing to the demand for tolls on roads which had previously been free, though detestably bad. The tolls were violently resisted, and led to several riots, one of the most formidable of which was locally known as "Leeds fight."

In the month of June, 1753, an attempt was made by a large body of rioters to pull down several of the new toll bars. The first attack was made on the bar near Harewood Bridge; but this was successfully resisted by Mr. Edwin Lascelles, afterwards the first Lord Harewood,* who armed his tenants and workmen, repulsed the rioters, and after some skirmishing took about thirty of them prisoners. A body of soldiers was sent from York to Leeds to support the toll collectors. Soon after their arrival a carter going through Beeston turnpike refused to pay toll, and was seized by the soldiers, who attempted to carry him before the magistrates and trustees, then sitting in judgment at the King's Arms Inn, in Briggate, nearly opposite to Boar Lane. This was the house built by the benevolent John Harrison, which afterwards became a hotel, and in the earlier part of the present century was the office of the *Leeds Mercury*.† But the carter was rescued by a mob of about 500 rioters, who assembled in Briggate, and began

---

* Burke's Peerage, Barons and Earls of Harewood.
† Annals of Yorkshire, by John Mayhall, Esq., Clerk of the County Court, Leeds, vol. i. p. 89.

to break the windows and shutters of the inn. The sentinel on guard having been knocked down, twenty of the soldiers were ordered to fire. This they did, at first with blank cartridge; but failing to produce any effect, they were ordered to fire with ball, and did so with fatal results, killing eight persons on the spot, and wounding fifty, of whom several afterwards died. Mr. Hebblethwaite, who lived to the age of upwards of ninety, and who was a boy playing on Woodhouse Moor at the time (1753), remembered the sound of the firing to the end of his life.

Smeaton the Engineer.—It was in this age that John Smeaton the great civil engineer, flourished. He was born at Austhorpe, near Leeds, in the year 1724, and from the time when he attained mature manhood, about the year 1750, to the end of his useful and active life, in the year 1792, he applied himself to the several branches of the science of civil engineering, which has done so much to promote the manufacturing and commercial greatness, and the social happiness, of the people of England. The early reputation of Smeaton was acquired in his native town of Leeds or in the neighbouring district; and he owed his admission to the Royal Society, which was at that time almost the only society that had the power of conferring honours on men of science, to papers written by him, on the application of the powers of wind and of water to the working of machinery. Smeaton might also claim the merit of having taken some part in the introduction of the still greater power of steam. The steam-engine of Savory and Newcomen, though far inferior to that of James Watt, was still an invention of great utility, and was applied with considerable success in Smeaton's time to the pumping of water from coal mines, and to other purposes of great value. An attempt to construct a steam-engine of this kind, and a turning-lathe, are said to have been amongst the first developments of those remarkable talents for engineering, which Smeaton afterwards displayed in their application to so many and such varied objects.

Building of the Coloured Cloth Hall.—About forty years after the building of the White Cloth Hall at Leeds, as described by Thoresby, and very near the close of the reign of George II., in the year 1758, the necessity of a cloth hall for the sale of coloured cloths began to be felt in Leeds, and Richard Wilson, Esq., the lord of the manor (the father of Dr. Wilson, bishop of Bristol, and ancestor of Richard Fountayne Wilson, Esq., who was member for Yorkshire in 1826), agreed to sell land on his estate, which had at one time formed a portion of the Park of Leeds, to the cloth merchants, for the purpose of building a new cloth hall, to which the name of the Coloured or Mixed Cloth Hall was given.

At the time when this land was purchased from the lord of the manor (it is said for the sum of £400),* it lay beyond the western limit of the streets and houses, and in a position to secure the most perfect lights for colours. Amongst the most westerly buildings in Leeds at that time was the Manor House, where the Wilsons, the lords of the manor, occasionally resided; where the ancient castle of Leeds had stood; and on or near to which the great railway station now stands. A little higher up what is now Park Row, but then consisted chiefly of open fields, was the Presbyterian or Mill Hill Chapel, built in the reign of Charles II., in the year 1672. About the time of the accession of George III., soon after the conquest of Canada, and the battle and capture of Quebec by General Wolfe, a set of good houses, long known as Quebec, were erected, at a short distance from the Old Manor House of the Wilsons, and from the new Coloured Cloth Hall. From that time the town began to extend westward, over the fields which had once formed the ancient Park of Leeds, in which, however, hedgerows, gardens, and grass fields contended with tenter-grounds, even in the first twenty years of the present century. The Coloured or Mixed Cloth Hall was a plain but large and solid building, composed of a main body and two wings, remarkably well lighted by large windows. It was divided into six long streets or aisles, and inclosed an open area. The building in its original form was $127\frac{1}{2}$ yards in length, and 66 in breadth. Each street contained two rows of stands, the freehold property of separate manufacturers. The stands were only twenty-two inches in front, and the number of stands in the building erected in 1758, was 1770. The number of clothiers who exposed their goods for sale in this market at the beginning of the present century, when factories were few, and home production was general, was estimated at about 2000. The Exchange, as it was sometimes called, adjoined the Mixed Cloth Hall, of which it was an appendage. It was a handsome building of an octagon form, built for the convenience of the cloth merchants, and

* Mayhall's Annals of Yorkshire, vol. i. p. 139.

was used for transacting the business of the cloth hall, by the trustees.*

The First Leeds Improvement Act.—Near the close of the reign of King George II. other improvements were effected in Leeds, besides building the Coloured Cloth Hall. In the year 1755 the first Leeds Improvement Act was passed (28th George II. cap. 41), which may be regarded as an epoch in the progress of the town, and shows what was its condition at that time. It was entitled an Act "for Enlightening the Streets and Lanes, and regulating the Pavement, in the town of Leeds, in the county of York." The preamble gave the following account of the condition of the town at that period:—" The town of Leeds," it stated, "is a place of great trade and large extent, consisting of many streets, narrow lanes, and alleys, inhabited by great numbers of tradesmen, manufacturers, artificers, and others; who, in the prosecution and carrying on of their respective trades and manufactures, are obliged to pass and repass through the same, as well in the night as in the day time;" hence several burglaries, robberies, and other outrages and disorders have lately been committed, and many more attempted, within the said town; and the enlightening the said streets and lanes, and regulating the pavements thereof, would be of great advantage, and tend not only to the security and preservation of the persons and properties of the inhabitants of the said town, but to the benefit and convenience of strangers and persons resorting to the several markets kept within the said town, and to others whose affairs may oblige them to pass and repass through the same, and also prevent the many mischiefs which might happen, as well from fires as burglaries, robberies, and other outrages and disorders." †

To prevent these evils the inhabitants resident within the bars, and rated at £3 a year, were authorized by the Act to meet yearly in the vestry of the parish church, and appoint fourteen of the principal inhabitants of the town to carry it into effect. These bars were six in number, namely, Burley Bar, in Guildford Street; Woodhouse Bar; North Bar, in North Street, opposite the Workhouse; East Bar, in Kirkgate, opposite Saint Peter's, or the parish church; South Bar, at the south end of the bridge; and West Bar, at the junction of (the present) Basinghall Street with Boar Lane. "The several sites," says Mr. Wardell, in his "Municipal History of Leeds," published in the year 1846, "are at present marked by boundary stones fixed in the walls, and inscribed with the name of each bar."

* Leeds Guide, 1806.   † List of Acts of Parliament relating to Leeds: Wardell's Municipal History of Leeds.

Under the powers of the Leeds Improvement Act of 1755, the fourteen commissioners so elected by the householders, together with the mayor, recorder, and justices of the borough, were authorized to appoint the requisite officers and to light the town, taking care that the public and most frequented streets should have their first attention. To defray the necessary expenses a rate was authorized to be levied upon all owners or occupiers of property, situate within the bars of the town, above the yearly rent or value of £3, such assessment not to exceed 8d. in the pound for the first year, or 4d. in the pound for any subsequent year. It was also provided by this Act, that the profits of the navigation of the rivers Aire and Calder, of the engine for supplying the town with water, or any tolls arising or payable within the said town and borough, or for or in respect of any lands or grounds not built upon, or any mills or tenters, or any houses, buildings, or tenements " in that part of the said town called the Tenters, which do not adjoin upon the bridge over the river Aire," should be exempt from assessment under this Act. The commissioners were also authorized to remove any nuisance or annoyance which might exist in the town; and also to order the streets lying and being within the bars, to be repaired and paved, by the respective owners thereof.*

Repairing of Leeds Bridge.—The last great improvement effected at Leeds in the reign of King George II., was accomplished under an Act for raising money for finishing and completing the repairing of Leeds Bridge. We have already stated that this bridge is mentioned as existing in the reign of King Edward III. in the year 1376, at which time it had a chapel or chantry, dedicated to St. Mary, attached to it, according to the custom of that period; and it is very probable that a bridge existed on the same spot long previous even to that, for some of the older parts of the work appear to be almost as old as the Norman conquest. Indeed, it is not unlikely, from the use of the word "brig," that the oldest bridge erected on the spot belonged either to the Anglian or the Danish times. Moreover, the remains of a still older structure, supposed to have been a causeway forming the approach to a Roman ford, have been discovered near the bridge, in the present century. That this is the point at which the river Aire was crossed, first by a ford, and afterwards by successive bridges, is highly probable, as there has been a town on the present site of Leeds at least from the date mentioned by the Venerable Bede, namely the year 616; and it is altogether incredible that a town could have existed on such a river for so many ages without being supplied with the usual means for crossing the stream.

The bridge at Leeds was widened in the year 1730, and again in

* The Municipal History of Leeds, by James Wardell, Esq.

the year 1760. The bridge is now, in the years 1872 and 1873, being entirely rebuilt. The object of the Act of 1758 was to raise money for finishing and completing the repair of the bridge, and for the purchasing and taking down the houses and buildings which straitened and obstructed the passage to and over it. In this Act, Leeds Bridge is said to be a county or riding bridge, and to stand on the public turnpike road leading from London to Edinburgh, by way of Derby, Sheffield, Wakefield, Leeds, Knaresborough, and Boroughbridge or Ripon. It is further stated that, from the increase of traffic, the bridge had fallen very much out of repair. We are told in the preamble of the Act, that "from the narrowness of the road, and the buildings and other encroachments made or set up at both the ends and abutments of the said bridge, the way or passage over the same was greatly confined and obstructed, and was become not only dangerous to passengers on foot and horseback, but also greatly prejudicial to the inhabitants, trade, and commerce of the town." In order to repair the bridge, the court of quarter-sessions of the West Riding had granted the sum of £1450; but this being considered insufficient, an Act was passed to enable the commissioners therein named to levy and collect a tax or assessment within the borough of Leeds, sufficient to raise a sum not exceeding £1500 in aid thereof. Amongst other improvements authorized, the commissioners were empowered to erect "a stone arch, over that part of the mill stream or goit passing under one arch of Leeds Bridge aforesaid, which runs between Mr. Green's house and the old school;" the latter being the chantry of St. Mary previously mentioned. The first meeting of the commissioners was held at the Moot Hall, on the 1st of July, 1760; and on the 4th of July of the same year, the corporation ordered that the sum of £350, part of their stock, should be lent to the treasurer for the purpose of carrying the Act into effect. The commissioners are named in the Act, and as they may be regarded as the leading men of the town during the first twenty or thirty years of the reign of King George III., it may be desirable to give their names in this work. They were Sir Henry Ibbetson, baronet (of Denton Park, who still retained the old family house in Kirkgate, Leeds), Charles Ingram (probably of the family of the Ingrams, Viscounts Irwin of Temple Newsam), John Atkinson, Edmund Barker, Charles Brandling (the owner of the collieries at Middleton, near Leeds), James Brooks, Anthony Cooke,

Jeremiah Dixon, Thomas Lee, Thomas Medhurst, Thomas Sawer, Henry Scott, Nicholas Torr, Richard Wilson, the lord of the manor of Leeds, and Richard Wilson, jun.—Esquires; Francis Blayds, John Blayds, Hans Busk, Thomas Cookson, Richard Cotton, Thomas Fenton, Joshua Hartley, Charles Gautier, Thomas Lodge, Richard Markham, John Medhurst, Darcy Molyneux, George Oates and Josiah Oates—Merchants; Samuel Harper, George Lumley, William Preston, Luke Sitchwell, Jervas Smith, James Smith, Richard Stephenson, John Suttell, William Tottie, Thomas Woolrich, Samuel Davenport, Benjamin Wynn, James Green, Samuel Howgate, Henry Smithson—Gentlemen; and Samuel Kershaw, Richard Bainbridge, John Murgatroyd, John Moore, and Christopher Topham—Clerks.

Leeds in the Reign of King George III.—The progress of the borough of Leeds was steady, and even rapid, during the first forty years of the reign of King George III., from 1760 to the close of the eighteenth century. It was during that period that many improvements in manufactures and machinery, and in the means of transport and communication, were introduced at Leeds, which produced great immediate fruits, and still more ample results in the early part of the present century. This was the age in which the steam-engine was invented, or brought to perfection, by James Watt; that machines for spinning cotton were constructed by Arkwright, Hargraves, and Crompton, which were afterwards adapted to the woollen and linen trades, and were brought into use in Leeds by the Marshalls, the Benyons, the Gotts, the Wormalds, the Fountaynes, and other enterprising manufacturers, who may be regarded as amongst the chief founders of the modern industry and prosperity of Leeds. It was in this age also, and during the first twelve years of the reign of George III., which after the first year or two was a period of peace both at home and abroad, down to the year 1774, that navigable canals and water carriage were introduced, by which, amongst other results, the town of Leeds was connected by means of canal navigation with the great port of Liverpool as well as with Hull, and through them with all the countries of the world. These were amongst the first and greatest steps towards the opening out of that world-wide trade and commerce since established, which now enables a quarter of a million of inhabitants to live within this borough, and to find food, employment, raw materials, and communication with markets at home and abroad, on a spot which, a hundred years ago, did not furnish such resources for more than the tenth part of the present population of Leeds.

The Leeds and Liverpool Canal.—Inland water carriage by navigable canals commenced in England about the year 1759-60, with Brindley's discoveries of methods of constructing and applying locks, tunnels, and other appliances, for carrying canals at varying levels through or over mountains and hills, at heights some hundreds of feet above the level of the sea. In about ten years after the constructing of the first Bridgewater canals, water carriage was adopted on a great scale at Leeds and Bradford, for the double purpose of connecting this part of Yorkshire with the Atlantic Ocean, and of completing the water communication across England, from the port of Hull to the port of Liverpool, by means of a canal carried through the hills which separate Yorkshire from Lancashire. The first of the Canal Acts of Leeds or the West Riding was that of the 10th George III. (1770) cap. 114, entitled "An Act for making and maintaining a navigable Cut or Canal, from Leeds Bridge, in the county of York, to the North Ladies Walk in Liverpool, in the County Palatine of Lancaster, and from thence to the River Mersey." It was long before this canal got either to Leeds Bridge or to the River Mersey; but it was commenced in the year 1772; some of the most important portions of it were opened about 1777; and it was carried out with energy from Leeds to Liverpool, through a course 128 miles in length, and through or over a range of hills rising, at the point crossed, 552 feet above the sea at Liverpool, and 446 feet above the level of the starting point of the canal at Leeds.* The Leeds and Liverpool Canal justly ranks as one of the greatest improvements and public works of the eighteenth century, and may be regarded as one of the principal sources of the rapid prosperity of the trade of Leeds, previous to the introduction of railways and steam, which were not applied to locomotion with full effect until sixty years later.

The General Infirmary at Leeds.—In the year 1767, a few years after the accession of George III. to the throne, and at a time of peace and prosperity, the merchants, manufacturers, and other inhabitants of Leeds, formed the happy idea of building a large infirmary, for the relief of unfortunate persons suffering from those sudden and dangerous accidents which occur so frequently amidst the varied occupations of a busy and crowded town. The original

* List of Acts of Parliament in Wardell's Municipal History of Leeds.

General Infirmary of Leeds, which has now been superseded by a still nobler institution of the same kind, ought not to be passed without notice. It was a spacious edifice; when built it was considered handsome; and it was situated in a large and pleasant open space, at the west end of the town. It was surrounded by a large court and garden, and was supplied with every requisite outbuilding. Howard the philanthropist, who visited Leeds in the year 1778, pronounced a marked eulogium upon it. He said that it was one of the best hospitals in the kingdom; that in the wards, which were fifteen feet eight inches high, there was great attention to cleanliness; that wide apertures, ventilators, and passages secured ample ventilation; and that many were cured of compound fractures in the Leeds' Infirmary, who would have lost their limbs in the unventilated and offensive wards of ordinary hospitals. The foundation stone of the original Infirmary was laid by Edwin Lascelles, Esq., afterwards Baron Harewood, in 1768, and it was opened for the reception of patients, March 5, 1771. The officers of this noble institution, in the end of the last and first part of the present century, were, as physicians, Dr. Walker, Dr. Hird, and Dr. Thorpe; as surgeons, Mr. Hey, F.R.S., Mr. Logan, and Mr. Chorley. Mr. Hare was apothecary; Mrs. Wilkinson, matron; William Cookson, Esq., treasurer; and Mr. Matthew Talbot, secretary—all of whom we mention in honour of their memory.*
We shall have to speak in a subsequent page of the still nobler institution which has now taken the place of the General Infirmary founded in the year 1767. Most of the other benevolent institutions of the town originated at the beginning of the present century, including the House of Recovery for the relief of fever patients. The same medical men superintended this institution, with the addition of Dr. Baynes, Mr. W. Hey, junior, then a comparatively young man; Mr. Teale, apothecary; Mr. Moxon, inspector; and Mr. R. Clark, secretary.

Founding of the Leeds Library.—Another noble institution, the Leeds Library, already rich with the accumulated stores of a hundred years, and every year becoming richer in the treasures of intellect, was founded in the year 1774. This was also one of the fruits of that bright period of the reign of George III., which preceded the first American war, and was distinguished in the annals of science, invention, literature, and benevolence.

* Leeds Guide, printed by Edward Baines for the Author, 1806.

Amongst the finest intellects which flourished in Leeds in that age were those of the first William Hey, an accomplished surgeon and member of the Royal Society, and of the Rev. Joseph Priestley, in his time the greatest of English chemists. Both of them were sincere lovers of everything that they believed to be true and useful to their fellowmen. They were amongst the leaders of society in this town, and amongst the founders of that useful institution, in which so many of its sons drew their earliest love of knowledge.

Corporation Festivities in 1765.—When George III. was a young man, and all the world was gay, the corporation regaled themselves in the quiet, amusing manner, described in the following extract from a memorandum book formerly belonging to Mr. Thomas Barstow the younger, who was appointed to the office of town-clerk in the borough of Leeds, in the year 1765:—"27th September.—To give notice of a court of mayor, aldermen, and assistants, to choose a new mayor (and assistants, if wanting), on the 29th, at three o'clock in the afternoon; afterwards the old mayor, the mayor-elect, and the rest of the court, go and drink a glass. The old mayor pays a guinea, the mayor 10s. 6d., the aldermen 2s. a piece, and the assistants 1s. each. What is spent above is paid by the treasurer, out of the corporation stock. Sunday after the last-mentioned day the new mayor goes to church with the old mayor, the former in a black and the latter in a scarlet day-gown, and dine together at the old mayor's. The first Sunday after the new mayor is sworn in is a gown day; the first whole week after Michaelmas, the quarter-sessions. Dine with the old mayor; go to court after dinner to swear the new mayor. Sup with the new mayor; waites (town musicians) playing before them from court. New mayor gives the Old Church ringers 10s., St. John's 5s., and Trinity 1s. The first adjournment in the forenoon, to dine with mayor. 5th November, a gown day; if not Sunday, waites to play before the mayor to church. Christmas Day, a gown day; Easter Day, a gown day; Whit-Sunday, a gown day; 29th May, a gown day, and if not Sunday, the waites to play before the mayor to church; 22nd June, a gown day, and if not Sunday, the waites to play before the the mayor to church. At court adjournment, the mace to be carried before the mayor; he to be in his black gown." *

The New White Cloth Hall.—In the year 1775, the 15th George III., the great increase of trade during upwards of twelve years of uninterrupted peace having rendered the old White Cloth Hall, built in the year 1711, insufficient for the trade in undyed cloths, it was determined to build a new and larger hall in the Calls. There was still a quantity of open ground between the Calls and the river, though the pleasant gardens, orchards, and summer-houses, which stood there in Thoresby's time, had

* The Municipal History of Leeds, by James Wardell, Esq.

mostly disappeared. The corporation contributed £100 out of their small funds for this object; and an Act was passed, 15th George III., cap. 90, 1775, for the sale and enfranchisement of certain copyhold tenements and premises, in the parish of Leeds, part of the estate belonging to the free grammar-school there, for the purpose of erecting a public Cloth Hall, and making avenues or passages thereto, and for applying the purchase money for the benefit of the said school.* The White Cloth Hall, then built, was a large square building, 297 feet in length and 210 in breadth. It was divided into five streets, each containing two rows of stands, the whole number being 1210. A few years later the number of master white cloth manufacturers using this hall was estimated at about 1300.†

Great Extension and Improvement of the Town. — The second period of peace in the reign of George III., which intervened between the close of the American War of Independence, in the year 1782, and the commencement of the wars of the French Revolution in 1793, was one of great prosperity. During that time many large schemes of improvement were commenced, and many noble institutions were formed, in Leeds. Amongst the improvements was the laying out of the fields, which had at one time formed the Park of Leeds, in streets, squares, and places, greatly exceeding in width, and in the size of the houses, any that had up to that period been seen in Leeds. Amongst these were Park Place, Park Square, Park Row, and South and East Parades. More within the town, but not in the Park, was Albion Street, built about the same time, chiefly inhabited by professional men; and then forming the line between the business and the residential parts of the town. It must be remembered that in those times there were no omnibuses or railway trains; and all families which were not rich enough to afford the expense of keeping a carriage, or which did not choose to incur that expense, found it pleasanter to live within easy walking distance of the business part of the town. The following account of what were the best streets and places of residence in Leeds, in the first ten years of the present century, shows pretty clearly what had been done, in the way of improvement, in the last twenty years of the previous century.

* A List of Acts of Parliament relating to the borough of Leeds, in Wardell's Municipal History of Leeds.
† The Leeds Guide, printed by Edward Baines for the Author, 1806.

Beginning the survey of Leeds at the west end of the town, the first object that then solicited attention was Park Place, which is described "as an elegant range of buildings, with a south aspect, and commanding a very pleasing view of the country, particularly of the river Aire." The houses in Park Place are spoken of as being built in superior style, and principally inhabited by affluent merchants, or gentlemen who had retired from business. Park Place was then the most pleasing promenade in Leeds, there being nothing in front of it but pleasure grounds, meadows, a narrow foot-path leading to detached gardens and to the new Bradford road, and in the distance a lofty row of weeping willows along the north bank of the river Aire, which was then a clear stream and a favourite bathing-place. Immediately behind Park Place was the new road to Bradford, opened for carriages in the year 1802, and formed chiefly to avoid the steep ascents of the road to Kirkstall, at Saint Peter's and Burley hills. On the north side of the new road to Bradford was Park Square, by some called St. Paul's Square, from the new church completed, in 1794, by and for the Rev. Miles Atkinson. Though the houses were not equal to those in Park Place, they are spoken of as being "well built, in the modern style," whilst the square was laid out with considerable taste. The Coloured Cloth Hall at that time formed one side of a very extensive square, or open ground. This having been built at various periods, had no general name; one side being called East Parade, another, South Parade, and a third, Park Row. The new, well-built street, Albion Street, we are told was at that time "perhaps the pleasantest in Leeds;" the houses are described as chiefly inhabited by professional gentlemen and persons in a wholesale line of business, no retail shops being then allowed in Albion Street. On the west side of the street was situated the Concert room; under which was a small cloth hall, for persons who were not members of the Coloured or White Cloth Halls.*

Public Buildings in Leeds at the close of the Eighteenth Century.—At the close of the last century, the public buildings in the town of Leeds were already tolerably numerous. Those for commercial and trading purposes consisted of the Mixed Cloth Hall (1758), the Octagon adjoining, sometimes named the Exchange† (1758), the White Cloth Hall, the New Cloth Hall in Albion Street, the Post Office, the large warehouses of the

* The Leeds Guide: printed for the Author by Edward Baines, 1806. † Ibid.

Aire and Calder, and the Leeds and Liverpool Canal Companies. The buildings for purposes of justice were the Moot Hall; the Rotation Office, where the borough magistrates sat in rotation to hear cases; and the prison, in Kirkgate, described as "a wretched building," in which Howard the philanthropist, on being informed that no one was confined in it for more than a day or two, answered, that no one ought to be confined for a single hour in such a place. The public buildings connected with charity and humanity were the General Infirmary, already described, the House of Recovery for fever patients, the Charity School, Sunday schools, "attended by 2000 children," the School of Industry, the old alms-houses, the new alms-houses, and the work-house. The public institutions connected with education, instruction, and amusement, were the circulating library, already containing a large and excellent collection of books; the Free Grammar School; the theatre, which was long in the hands of Tate Wilkinson and his son; the concert room, the assembly room, and the Riding School for the instruction of young horsemen.

The Manufactures of Leeds and the District connected with it at the End of the Eighteenth Century.—There were few woollen factories in the town of Leeds before the end of the eighteenth century. The clothing business, strictly so called, was divided into the two branches of the manufacture of cloth, from dyed wool, and from wool in its native state. Both of these were carried on extensively in the manufacturing villages about Leeds, the clothiers of which places brought their goods to the Leeds market. The former of these descriptions of cloth was manufactured principally by the clothiers who lived within the parish of Leeds, and at the villages of Morley, Gildersome, Adwalton, Driglington, Pudsey, Farsley, Calverley, Eccleshall, Idle, Baildon, Yeadon, Guiseley, Rawdon, and Horsforth, in or bordering upon the vale of Aire, chiefly west of Leeds; and at Batley, Dewsbury, Osset, Horbury, and Kirkburton, west of Wakefield, and in or near the vale of Calder. We are told that at this time (1806) not a single manufacturer was to be found more than one mile east or two miles north of Leeds; also that there were not many in the town of Leeds, and those only in the outskirts. The white cloths manufactured in 1806, were principally produced at Alverthorpe, Osset, Kirkheaton, Dewsbury, Batley, Birstall, Hopton, Mirfield, Hartshead, Cleckheaton, Little Town, Bowling, and Shipley—a tract of country described as forming an oblique belt across the hills that separate the vale of Calder from the vale of Aire, beginning about a mile west of Wakefield, leaving Huddersfield and Bradford a little to the left, terminating at Shipley on the Aire, and not coming within less than about six miles of Leeds on the right. The districts of the white and coloured manufactures were generally distinct, but were a little intermixed at the south-east and north-west extremities. The cloths were then sold in their respective halls, rough as they came from the fulling mills. They were finished by the merchants, who employed dressers, dyers, &c., for that purpose. The clothiers were generally men of some small capital, and often annexed a small farm to their other business; many had a field or two in the villages to support a horse and a cow, and they were for the most part blessed with the comforts, without the superfluities of life. Down to the year 1806 the number of clothiers and merchants who sold or bought cloth in the Coloured Cloth Hall was estimated to be about 2000; whilst the number of those who sold their cloth in the White Cloth Hall, was estimated at about 1300. There was also another small Cloth Hall in Albion Street, for the accommodation of those who had not served a regular apprenticeship to the trade, and therefore were not permitted to sell their cloth in the other Halls.*

Arthur Young, while collecting information for his "Annals of Agriculture," appears to have visited Yorkshire, and gives a brief account of the manufactures of Leeds, and of the condition of the inhabitants of the town, in the year 1796. He states that there were then at Leeds six or seven steam-engines used in woollen mills, and one in a drying house; and that the machines which had done so much for the cotton trade were being rapidly introduced into the woollen manufacture of Leeds. He adds that the wages of spinners in Leeds at that time were from 10$d.$ to 1$s.$ a day; and that hand-loom weavers were earning from 9$s.$ to 12$s.$ a week. The wages of the highest class of workmen employed in finishing woollen cloth, such as croppers, shearmen, and knappers were from a guinea to 30$s.$ a week.† Some idea may be formed of the progress which machinery had made in the town of Leeds, from the evidence given by Mr. Benjamin Gott, then a young man, before a committee of the House of Commons, in the year 1800. He then stated that fifteen years

* Leeds Guide, p. 58.   † Mayhall's Annals of Yorkshire, vol. i. p. 200.

before it would have required 1634 persons to do that which was then done by thirty-five persons in a week, in the process of scribbling and spinning by machinery. He also said that the average wages in the woollen manufacture at that time were, for men, 16s. to 18s. per week; old men, from 9s. to 12s.; women, from 9s. to 12s.; children and young people of from fourteen to eighteen years of age, 5s. to 6s.; and young children, 3s. per week. Children were thus already profitable to their parents, as well as able to earn a good living for themselves.

Rapid Progress of Leeds in the Nineteenth Century.—Leeds at the commencement of the nineteenth century, according to the census of 1801, was a flourishing municipal, though not yet a parliamentary borough, of 53,162 inhabitants, of which number the township of Leeds contained 30,669, and the out-townships 22,493 persons. In the seventy years that elapsed between the census of 1801 and that of 1871, the population of the whole borough increased from 53,162 to 259,200 persons, of whom, in 1871, 139,349 were resident in the township of Leeds, and 119,851 in the out-townships. In the last decennial period, from 1861 to 1871, the increase of the population of the borough was no less than 52,051, giving an average yearly rate of increase of more than 5000, which rate is supposed to be still rather augmenting than decreasing. Comparing the population of 1801 with that of 1871, the increase in seventy years was 206,038, the numbers having thus increased nearly four-fold in that time.

It required a period of nearly 1200 years, from the time when Leeds is first mentioned by the Venerable Bede, in the year 616, to that of the first census of the nineteenth century, made in the year 1801, to raise Leeds to the position of a borough of 53,162 inhabitants, whilst seventy years from the latter date increased that number to upwards of a quarter of a million. This wonderfully rapid increase of numbers within the "threescore years and ten," forming the ordinary term of life—and being far less than the time granted to some few men of unusual strength, like the late Sir Thomas Beckett, Bart., a member of one of the most distinguished families of Leeds, who has just died (1872) at the age of ninety-three years—can only be accounted for by an immense increase of profitable employment in the town and neighbourhood, drawing multitudes together to this spot from other districts, sustaining the people in comfort, and promoting marriages. First, amongst these causes of increased employment, as already mentioned, was the invention of the steam-engine by James Watt, in the early part of the reign of George III., which first enabled this country to grapple with the trade of the world, followed as it was by the early and extensive application of steam-power on that rich portion of the Yorkshire coal field, of which Leeds is the capital. Second, was the invention by Arkwright and others, about the same time, of machines for spinning and weaving all kinds of raw materials, with their boundless power of production, and their early introduction into Leeds by the Gotts, the Marshalls, the Wormalds, the Fountaynes, and others. Third, was the peopling of Australia, a country capable of furnishing unlimited supplies of wool, suited for the manufactures of Leeds and the West Riding. Fourth, was the opening of the trade with North and South America, South Africa, British India, and many other countries, also capable of supplying wool, cotton, silk, and other materials for textile industry, and of consuming immense quantities of English goods. Fifth, was the great increase in the quantity of British wool produced (though this more affects the manufactures of Bradford than those of Leeds) under the system of drill husbandry, turnip cultivation, the breeding of improved varieties of sheep, and a greatly increased demand for clothing at home. Sixth, the invention of railways, and means of steam locomotion on land by George Stephenson and his pupils, and of steam navigation at sea, which now renders it easier and cheaper to travel 100 miles to or from the great seats of industry, either by land or sea, than it was to travel twenty miles in former times. Seventh, the application of the abundant supplies of iron found in this part of the West Riding to numerous purposes of construction, for which timber only was used in former times, which application was commenced in Leeds previous to the year 1806, in our largest flax mills. Eighth, the increased power of working coal mines, which has raised the total supply of coal in Yorkshire alone to 12,800,000 tons yearly, and that of the Leeds district to about 2,500,000 tons.

The promptitude and energy with which the manufacturers of Leeds and the labouring population of the town availed themselves of these new and previously unequalled advantages, must be regarded as amongst the most powerful local causes of the immense increase of trade and employment that has taken place in Leeds during the present century. To these may be added many great social and political causes, not indeed confined to this town, but which had a large share in giving a sudden and lasting impulse to its industry and its numbers. Amongst these were internal order and freedom; security from foreign invasion; seas always open to furnish supplies of raw materials from abroad, and to distribute the products of industry over the whole world; more than fifty years of almost uninterrupted peace (a blessing unknown during the two preceding centuries, when peace seldom lasted for more than ten or a dozen years at a time, and wars continued for many years, two of them lasting, with a brief interval of rest, for twenty years—from 1689 to 1714, and from 1793 to 1814); the recognizing of the principles of free trade and commerce with all nations, and the removal of exclusive privileges both in this country and wherever British influence is felt. It is very honourable to the corporation of Leeds that it should have placed on record in its books, so early as the year 1793, the following emphatic declaration against monopolies:—"Resolved, on the 28th January, 1793, by the corporation of Leeds, at a court held on that day, that monopolies are inconsistent with the true principles of commerce, because they restrain at once the spirit of enterprise and the freedom of competition; and injurious to the country where they exist, because the monopolist, by fixing the rate of both purchase and sale, can oppress the public at discretion." The declaration was ordered to be inserted in the Leeds, Manchester, and Liverpool newspapers.* This resolution against monopoly was passed immediately before the breaking out of the war. William Pitt, who had adopted many of the soundest principles of Adam Smith's political economy, was still wishful to apply them to the commercial intercourse between England and France.

Manufactures in Leeds in 1806.—Already, in the first ten years of the present century, there were in Leeds able and spirited manufacturers, seeking to adapt the new inventions of the age to all the branches of industry; and we find from contemporary records that in the year 1806, the Gotts and Wormalds were applying these inventions to the woollen trade of Leeds; the Marshalls and Benyons to the linen manufacture; the Hartleys to the manufacture of pottery; the Cawoods to the improvement of brass-founding; the great firm of Fenton, Murray, and Wood, to the construction of steam-engines and machinery, and the Brandlings to the cheapening of the

* Municipal History of Leeds, by James Wardell. Esq., p. 86: Extracts from Corporation Records.

carriage of coal on iron railways; whilst an active local Press was preserving and extending the knowledge of all improvements made, and discussing all national and local questions with freedom and intelligence. It was about this time that the two Leeds newspapers passed into the management of able and spirited young men, one of whom, Griffith Wright, rose to the position of mayor of Leeds, the other, Edward Baines, to represent the town in several parliaments.

The following account of the principal manufactures existing at Leeds, written and printed in the year 1806, will show what were the branches of industry then in progress, and who were amongst the chief leaders in the race of industry.*

There was already a very large establishment for the manufacturing of woollen cloths on the banks of the river Aire, at Bean Ing, on the west side of the town of Leeds. This had been erected in 1793 by Messrs. Wormald, Fountayne, and Gott. It was burnt down in 1799, and re-erected by the firm of Messrs. Wormald, Gott, and Wormalds. Here the whole process of the manufacture of cloth, from the first breaking of the wool to the finishing of the piece, ready for the consumer, was conducted on a very extensive scale. We are told that the mill was pleasantly situated on the banks of the Aire, and that many other establishments of a similar kind, but less in extent, had lately been erected in the town of Leeds.†

The Marshalls were the founders of the linen trade of Leeds. Previous to the year 1796, the linen manufacture had attained a high position there, and was chiefly conducted in extensive factories. The first of these was erected by Messrs. Marshall and Benyon, in Water Lane, near Holbeck; and we are told that there the manufacture of canvas, linen, linen yarn, and thread yarn, was already carried on extensively. In the year 1796 this manufactory was burnt down, by which accident six or seven persons lost their lives, from the sudden falling of one of the walls. Soon after this fire a very large factory was erected by Messrs. Benyon and Bage, in Meadow Lane, for the manufacture of linen, which was completely fire-proof, no timber whatever being used in the building, its place being supplied by cast iron. The floors were on arches raised upon cast iron beams supported by iron pillars, the

---

* The Leeds Guide, printed by Edward Baines for the Author, 1806, p. 100.
† Leeds Guide, p 103.

whole firmly united. It must have been amongst the earliest applications of iron to that purpose. There was also a manufactory for canvas and linen yarn at the Bank, carried on by Messrs. Moore, Shaw, & Co.; a linen yarn and thread manufactory at the bottom of George Street, belonging to Messrs. Millburn, Clayton, and Gersed; also one for making sacking and canvas, belonging to Messrs. James and Joshua Kaye, situated in Water Lane. The whole number of persons employed in the linen manufacture of Leeds in the year 1806 was computed to be 2000, including children. There were also at that time in the neighbourhood of Leeds a considerable number of persons employed in the spinning of cotton; but the yarn was not generally wrought up into finished goods, at Leeds. Iron works were beginning to be established in Leeds, on an extensive scale, at the beginning of the present century. We are informed that several foundries had recently been established in that neighbourhood, one of which belonged to Messrs. Fenton, Murray, & Wood, and was upon an extensive scale, there being a considerable manufacture of steam engines and machinery carried on there. It is stated in the Leeds Guide of 1806, that Mr. Murray had risen from the situation of a common smith, to his then high position, by his extraordinary mechanical genius. A foundry of cast iron and brass was also carried on by Mr. Prior; another by Mr. Warwick; and Messrs. Cawood & Son had an extensive brass and iron foundry, in Marsh Lane. The making of pottery was also carried on at Leeds at this time. A very large manufactory of earthenware had for some years been conducted by Messrs. Hartley, Green, & Co., which had been turned into a prosperous joint stock company. Fortunately for the stability of the trade of Leeds, the financial and banking interest of the town was mainly developed and directed by the first Sir John Beckett, Bart. (then John Beckett, Esq.), by his partner Mr. Blayds, and by one or two other financiers of the soundest judgment, whose influence, and that of their successors, has had a beneficial effect on the banking affairs of the town of Leeds for nearly a hundred years.

The Introduction of Tramways and the Earliest Railways at Leeds.—We hear of railways as being employed in Leeds and the neighbourhood in the year 1806. But they were not worked with locomotive steam-engines until 1811, when Mr. Blenkinsop's steam locomotive was introduced, between Leeds and the Middleton collieries of Mr. Brandling. We are told, in 1806, that "The Pottery," as it was called by way of eminence (though there were several in the neighbourhood), was very advantageously situated "near the iron railway leading to Middleton Colliery, from which it was distant nearly two miles, and about one mile from Leeds." In 1806 coals were conveyed in waggons on an iron railway, from the collieries at Middleton to a staith in Hunslet Lane, from which point they were sent to every part of the town, at a rate precisely fixed, and from which no deviation was allowed. Each person who wished to have coals sent to him from the staith had his name and place of abode, and the quantity of coals entered in a book, which orders were executed in rotation—a regulation that prevented all complaints of partiality. "Coals," we are told, "were then delivered at· the staith, at the rate of $7\frac{1}{2}d.$ a corfe, the weight of which was 210 lbs."*

But before the steam-engine was improved by James Watt, many years before steam locomotion on common roads was introduced by Trevithick, and long before the swift passenger-carrying railway locomotive was perfected by George Stephenson, Acts of Parliament had been passed, at the instigation of ingenious and adventurous persons connected with the town of Leeds, for the purpose of improving the tracks or roadways, on which coals were conveyed from the collieries of Middleton into the town of Leeds. As early as the year 1758, an Act of Parliament (32nd George II. cap. 22) was passed, entitled "An Act for establishing agreements made between Charles Brandling, Esq., and other persons proprietors of lands, for laying down a waggon way, in order for the better supplying the town and neighbourhood of Leeds, in the county of York, with coals." About twenty years later, in the 19th George III. (1778), cap. 11, another Act was passed, for rendering more beneficial the above Act, and to enable Charles Brandling to supply annually a larger quantity of coals to and for the use of the said town and neighbourhood, and for regulating the prices of carrying coals from the repository at Casson Close. A third Act, similar to the above, was passed in the 33rd George III. chapter 86 (1792-3); and in the year 1803, 43rd George III. chapter 12 (1803), another Act was passed for the better supplying of the town and neighbourhood of Leeds with coal. The above Acts were all intended to create means of estab-

* Leeds Guide, p. 117.

lishing a road, with some of the advantages of a tramroad, in the neighbourhood of Leeds; and in 1806, as we have said, there was an iron railway carrying coals from the collieries at Middleton to Leeds.

Anticipations of the Modern Railway System.—That part of the principle of modern railways which depends on the using of a firm and unyielding tramway of iron, instead of a roughly paved or deeply rutted highway, seems thus to have been adopted in bringing coals into Leeds from the Middleton Colliery, from the beginning of the reign of George III.; and so early as the year 1802, if not some years earlier, there were public writers who anticipated the introduction of railway travelling on a much greater and more perfect plan. The following paragraph from the *Leeds Mercury* of 1802 will show the hopes that already began to excite the minds of men, of improvements which were far more than realized in the next thirty years:—

"*Iron Railways.*—Richard Lovell Edgeworth, Esq., so well known as an author, has published an essay on railroads, of which he claims the invention. He states that in 1768 he presented models to the Society of Arts, for which he received their gold medal. He recommends an experiment to be made which shall demonstrate their advantages beyond the possibility of doubt or cavil. He proposes four iron railways to be laid on one of the great roads out of London, two of them for carts and waggons, and two for light carriages. To accommodate coaches and chaises he would have cradles, or platforms with wheels, adapted to the railway, on to one of which each carriage would drive up an inclined plane erected at the end of the road for that purpose. The carriage would then be drawn, not upon its own wheels, but upon the wheels of the platform or cradle. He calculates that a stage coach, with six inside and six outside passengers, would travel at the rate of six miles an hour with one horse. Gentlemen's carriages with two horses would go at the rate of twelve or fifteen miles an hour; and if a railway were laid from London to Edinburgh the mail-coach would go in thirty hours. Even at this great speed the most timid female might trust her delicate frame with most perfect security, for the carriage could not possibly be overturned. Any obstruction from hills would be easily overcome. Mr. Edgeworth proposes to plant a steam-engine at the top of every hill, which would move forward the carriages by a chain, to which they would be connected or detached from at pleasure"

Progress of the Woollen Manufactures.—The first forty or fifty years of the reign of George III., from 1760 to 1805, and, indeed, the whole of that reign, was a period of great progress in the woollen manufacture of Leeds, and the other towns of the West Riding. Between 1788 and 1805 the yearly production of broad cloth increased from 4,244,322 yards to 9,987,252 yards; that of narrow cloth having also increased in the same period from 4,208,303 to 5,460,179 yards. On the whole, the increase between the year 1788 and the year 1805 had been such as to more than double the quantity of woollen cloth produced in the West Riding; and if we go back to the year 1769, the increase had been still greater, for in that year the quantity of broad cloth stamped in the West Riding was not more than 1,771,667 yards, the increase in the production of broad cloth, from 1769 to 1805, having thus been more than five-fold.

The bulk of the woollen manufacture of the Leeds district still consisted of the coarser kinds of cloth. Although the manufacture of superfine cloths had greatly increased, still they were not equal to the cloths made in the West of England. About that time also a number of fancy articles were made in the same neighbourhood, such as swan'sdown, toilonets, kerseymeres, and a very rough kind of cloth, called duffles. But none of those articles were exposed for sale in the Leeds cloth halls, which were exclusively for the sale of mixed and white cloth.*

Years of Scarcity, and Inclosing of Commons in the Parish of Leeds.—Although there was seldom, if ever, a time during the present century when the trade of Leeds did not increase, yet the change from domestic to factory labour from 1801 to 1820, the long continuance of war and war expenditure, the frequent interruptions of trade, and more than twenty years of scarcity and dear bread, produced great misery among the poorer classes, especially towards the end of the war. Wheat had been repeatedly sold at from £4 10s. to £6 a quarter between 1795 and 1810. In 1812, the time of the Luddites, the blockade of all the ports of Europe and America caused wheat again to rise to the famine price of £6 2s. per quarter, besides closing the best market for British goods; and in 1813, when we were still at war with the United States, and when more than a million of men were in arms in Europe, there was little amendment; wheat selling at £5 13s. a quarter.

* Leeds Guide, p. 109.

The Inclosure of Commons at the end of the last Century, and the beginning of this.—At the beginning of the present century the town of Leeds, strictly so called, only extended about a mile and a half in length, and half a mile in breadth, so that it was easy at that time for people of all classes to get into the country for an evening walk, and at least to breathe the fresh air on Sunday, on the wide commons and in the pleasant lanes which were to be met with in all directions. The town at that time did not cover the fifth part of the ground which it occupies at present, when vast and apparently interminable lines of streets extend in all directions from the centre of population, and render it difficult to find either fresh air or a pleasant walk, within any reasonable distance of the more thickly-peopled parts of the town. This evil was very much aggravated in the beginning of the present century and the close of the preceding one, by the rage that everywhere prevailed for inclosing commons and waste lands. This originated in a great degree in the excessive dearness of corn, and of all the products of the soil, caused by the rapid increase of the population, the cost of military and naval operations abroad, and the impossibility of obtaining any adequate supplies of food from abroad, either from the continent of Europe, which was wasted by continual wars, or from America, which at that time only contained a few millions of inhabitants, unable to supply the urgent wants of the thickly-peopled countries of Europe. In these years of scarcity many hundreds, and indeed some thousands of inclosure Acts were passed, and on the whole proved highly beneficial to the country. But in the eagerness to secure every piece of waste land that could be found, many beautiful commons situated in the immediate neighbourhood of large towns were inclosed, which could very well have been spared, and which it has been found necessary to replace with parks and other places of recreation in more recent times. Happily the great increase of wealth, of public spirit, and of regard for the health of the labouring classes, has rendered this possible, though expensive.

In the neighbourhood of Leeds the inclosing of waste lands and commons commenced about the beginning of the present century, or a few years earlier. One of the first inclosure Acts, relating to the borough and parish of Leeds, which are conterminous and of great extent, stretching, according to the Ordnance Survey of 1847-53, over an area of 21,572 acres,* was passed in the year

* Report of Boundary Commissioners for England and Wales, 1868.

1789-90, the 29th George III., which by cap. 53 authorized the inclosing the commons and waste grounds within the manor or township of Bramley, in the parish of Leeds. A few years later, 1792-93, an Act of that year, cap. 61, authorized the dividing and inclosing the common and waste grounds within the manor or township of Armley. In the 43rd George III., 1802-3, cap. 102, an Act was passed for inclosing the commonable lands within the manor and township of Potter Newton-cum-Gipton, also in the parish of Leeds. Somewhat later the most beautiful common in the neighbourhood of Leeds, namely, that of Chapel Allerton, which is said to have formed 300 acres of the finest grass land in the West Riding, and which everywhere commanded beautiful prospects, was inclosed by an Act, cap. 6 of that year, for inclosing lands in Chapel Allerton. By a somewhat remarkable coincidence, an Act of Parliament was passed in the same year, for making and maintaining a road from Leeds to Roundhay, the seat of the large and beautiful park recently purchased by the corporation of Leeds, and thrown open to the inhabitants of the town and the public in the year 1872. But by a subsequent Act the wild heath-covered lands in the manor and township of Headingley-cum-Burley, in the parish of Leeds, were inclosed so recently as the 10th George IV., 1829-30. Even later than this, in the 3rd and 4th William IV., 1834-35, an Act was passed for inclosing lands in the township of Wortley. Happily for the health and recreation of the people of Leeds, they and their public authorities have never allowed any encroachment on Woodhouse-moor, which is still what it has been from the remotest times, a delightful breathing place for the people of Leeds, scarcely at all changed during the last fifty years, except in the withering of the whins and gorse, the recent planting of ornamental plantations, and in the erecting of handsome buildings beyond the limits, though commanding views of the moor, which it is to be hoped will be as faithfully and diligently preserved in future as it has been in past times.

Local Coinage during the French War.—This was the time (1797 to 1819) when even the Bank of England was compelled to suspend cash payments; when a gold guinea was looked on as a rarity; when the silver money of the country was rubbed so smooth that not a single mark could be seen upon it; and when even the copper money was scarce and bad. The small and necessary change for carrying on retail trade was confined to the old currency, struck principally during the great recoinage of silver in the reign of William III., which, in the course of 100 years, had been worn smooth with constant use. This debased currency was further increased by a quantity of light hammered silver, agreeing in nothing but size with what it pretended to be. From the accession of George III. in 1760 to the year 1787, only £50,000 was coined in silver; and from that time to 1816 the coinage of silver was entirely stopped. The copper coin was equally bad; not half the amount in circulation had been issued from the mint, though there was a spurious imitation. In 1787 permission was given by the government to trades-people to issue copper tokens; of these, as well as of the whole of the coins or tokens struck in Leeds during the last two centuries, there are engravings in Mr. Wardell's excellent "Municipal History of Leeds." Richard Paley, soap-boiler near the Old Church, issued one in 1791, having on one side a standing figure of Bishop Blaize, holding a crozier and wool comb, and on the reverse the arms of Leeds. Henry Brownbill, silversmith, in Briggate, issued a halfpenny in 1793, having a bust of Bishop Blaize, with a wool comb in front on one side, and on the reverse a view of the Mixed Cloth Hall. Samuel Birchall had one struck in 1795, with the Birchall Arms on the obverse, and a fleece on the reverse; but this was not intended for circulation, a few impressions only being made for the amusement of collectors. By license of the privy council in 1797, the governor and company of the Bank of England were empowered to issue Spanish dollars, stamped with a small head of George III. (the same as was used for stamping silver plate), which were then circulated at 4s. 9d. This was the first time that this prerogative of royalty had been thus suspended. The price of silver again rising, the stamped dollars were taken back by the bank in 1804 at 5s., and were entirely re-struck, with the king's head on the obverse, and the figure of Britannia on the reverse. In 1811 the dollar rose to 5s. 6d., when the bank issued large quantities of three shilling and eighteenpenny tokens, being the half and quarter dollar. This issue not being sufficient for small change, a further relaxation was made, by allowing private persons to issue silver tokens. At Leeds, Messrs. John Smallpage and S. Lumb issued a shilling, in 1811, having the Arms of Leeds on one side, and a figure of Justice standing on the other. In 1812 they issued a shilling and sixpence, and in the same year the overseers of the poor issued a shilling, having on one side the arms and supporters of the borough of Leeds. The private tokens were cried down at the end of 1813 and those of the Bank of England in 1816, after the extensive issue of silver coinage in that year. A beautiful new silver coinage was one welcome sign of the return of peace.

During the wars of the French revolution the demand for soldiers was unceasing, and every market day the streets of Leeds and other manufacturing towns resounded with the drums and fifes of the recruiting parties, who marched through them with colours displayed, and raised recruits for the army by beat of drum. The militia also raised even greater numbers of men by enrolment, and every large town had its regiment or regiments of volunteers. From the year 1794, when the war with France which broke out in the preceding year was thoroughly kindled, to the year 1815, when it finally closed amidst the triumphs of Waterloo, the demand for soldiers never ceased, except during the very short breathing time, given by the peace of Amiens in 1802–3. In the year 1794 Colonel Forbes intimated to the corporation of Leeds that some regiments were about to be raised under the countenance and support of the corporate towns of the kingdom, and requested the sanction and support of the corporation towards raising a regiment for his Majesty's service. This was very willingly given; and in the same year the corporation passed a vote of thanks to the volunteer corps of this borough, for their readiness in enrolling themselves for its defence; and also ordered an elegant sword to be purchased and presented by the mayor, in the name of the corporation, to Thomas Lloyd, Esq., colonel-commandant of the volunteers. The cost of the sword, as appears by the treasurer's account, was £84. This regiment remained in commission until the close of the war with the French Republic, and was dissolved at the peace of Amiens in 1802. But short was the period of peace, for before the end of the year 1803 the regiment was raised again, on the breaking out of the war with what soon became Imperial France, under the first Napoleon. When that event occurred the corporation ordered two pairs of colours to be purchased and presented to the Leeds corps; which was accordingly done, the colours being presented to the regiment on the moor at Chapel Allerton, in the presence of the mayor, recorder, and corporation, and a great number of other influential persons. Colonel Lloyd held the command of the regiment to the month of February, 1807, when he was compelled to retire from failing health, after which the command of the corps was conferred on Lieutenant-colonel Smithson. A deputation, comprising the mayor and three other members of the corporation, was appointed to present a vote of thanks to Colonel Lloyd, for the public spirit which he had shown during a crisis of unparalleled difficulty and danger. No one who was not alive at that time can form any conception of the excitement that then prevailed, and which induced nearly a million of men to take arms to fight in defence of their country, on sea and land. Even those who were mere children at the time will remember the constant drill and frequent parades of the infantry, the sound of the cavalry trumpets at the corners of the streets, and the grand reviews of horsemen on Woodhouse and Chapeltown moors. The defeat of Napoleon in Russia, the battle of Leipsic, Wellington's victories in Spain, and the crowning deliverance of Waterloo, were celebrated with illuminations in every street and house.

Leeds Improvement Acts during the reigns of George III. and George IV.—We have already mentioned the first Leeds Improvement Act, passed in the reign of King George II., for the purpose of lighting the streets and lanes and regulating the pavements in Leeds. Several Acts of a similar kind were passed in the reigns of George III. and George IV. In the 30th George III. (1789-90, cap. 68), an Act was passed for the better supplying of the town and neighbourhood of Leeds with water, for more effectually lighting and cleansing the streets and other places within the town and neighbourhood, and for removing and preventing nuisances, annoyances, encroachments, and obstructions therein. Another Improvement Act was passed in the 49th George III. 1808-9 (cap. 122), entitled an Act to amend and enlarge the powers of an Act passed in the thirtieth year of his present Majesty (George III.), for better supplying the town and neighbourhood of Leeds with water; for more effectually lighting and cleansing the streets and other places within the said town and neighbourhood, and for removing and preventing nuisances and annoyances therein; for erecting a court-house and prison for the borough of Leeds; and for widening and improving the streets and passages in the said town. A fourth Improvement Act was passed, 55th George III., 1814-15 (cap. 48), entitled an Act to amend and enlarge the powers and provisions of an Act of his present Majesty (George III.), for erecting a court-house and prison for the borough of Leeds and other purposes; to provide for the expense of the prosecution of felons in certain cases; and to establish a police and nightly watch in the town, borough, and neighbourhood of Leeds. The first Act for introducing the brilliant light of gas into the town of Leeds, in the place of the darkness visible produced by the old oil lamps, was passed in the 58th George III., 1817-18 (cap. 22), and this Act was extended in the 5th George IV., 1824-25 (cap. 110). In the same year, by cap. 124, another Act was passed for lighting, cleansing, and improving the town and neighbourhood of Leeds.*

Enlargement of the Town of Leeds after the French War.—Almost immediately after the close of the war with France under the first Napoleon, extensive improvements, arising out of the rapid growth of the population and the increased hopefulness of the public mind, began to be made in Leeds. In the years 1816 and 1817, the 57th George III., by cap. 51, an Act was passed for making and maintaining a road from Quebec in the parish of Leeds, to Homefield Lane End in the same parish, with a bridge or bridges across the river Aire, on the line of such road. Two or three other Acts were afterwards passed for extending this plan, namely, the Acts 4th and 5th William IV., passed in the year 1834-35, that of the 5th and 6th William IV., and that of the 1st and 2nd Victoria (1837-38). It was under the powers of this Act that the road known as the Wellington Road, with the adjoining streets, was formed from the neighbourhood of what is now the Midland railway station to the new Bradford Road, and to Bramley. By this great alteration a number of pleasant fields, lying between Park Place and the river, were turned into roads, and ultimately into streets, and the Aire itself from being a clear country stream was changed into a great manufacturing river. In order to preserve some portion of the pleasantness of this neighbourhood Richard Fountayne Wilson, Esq., the chief landowner, whose family had been owners of the manor house and of most of the land forming the ancient park, and who possessed some portion of the old manorial rights (though much subdivided), made a grant of a large and pleasantly-situated portion of the fields along the line of Wellington Road to the public, and more especially to the Leeds Infirmary, in order to insure quietness and fresh air to that institution, and to afford a pleasant place of exercise and recreation to the inhabitants of the many good streets and houses in the neighbourhood.

* Wardell's Municipal History of Leeds: Appendix, p. 199.

A somewhat similar gift of land had been made by his father, Dr. Wilson, bishop of Bristol, who gave the ground on which St. Paul's Church was built, and who must have had a share in drawing out the plans on which Park Square and Park Place were formed, and their fine open spaces were laid out. Previous to the making of the Wellington Road the ground through which it was run contained great numbers of very pleasant gardens, belonging to gentlemen and merchants residing in the town, who with their families used to go out in summer evenings to enjoy the pleasures of fresh air and of gardening. This was a favourite practice at Leeds so early as the time of Ralph Thoresby, in the reign of Queen Anne. He had two gardens (one at the back of his house in Kirkgate, then an open and pleasant situation, and another by the side of the river), which he planted with choice flowers, reared by a well-known florist in the village of Tong. The Spring Gardens on the banks of the river already existed in Thoresby's time, as well as the original North Hall Gardens, which were, however, at the north end of the town, although in the first twenty years of the present century there was another set of gardens, known as the North Hall Gardens, between the new Bradford and the Burely roads. It was not until about the year 1830 that the population of Leeds began to extend on all sides into the neighbouring villages—a great improvement, originating partly in the increase of population, and partly in the introduction of railways and omnibuses.

The Leeds Literary and Philosophical Society.—The preliminary meeting at which this most valuable and successful institution took its origin, was held on the 11th December, in the year 1818, and it was then resolved to form a philosophical and literary society, somewhat on the plan of the societies of a similar kind which already existed in the towns of Manchester and Liverpool, but on more comprehensive principles, calculated to bring within the institution members possessed of every kind of literary and scientific knowledge. It was in a great measure owing to the largeness of the principles on which the institution was founded that it had so strong a vitality, and that, at the end of fifty years, it could boast of still possessing the support of the principal lovers of literature and science in the town of Leeds. On the 3rd of May, 1870, this society celebrated the fiftieth anniversary of its formation, when some two or three of the original members were present, supported by most of the leading inhabitants, devoted to the noble objects for which this society was formed.

At this meeting the past history of the society was traced by the chairman and the few remaining founders of the society; and we are ourselves able to add a few particulars to their statements, from the recollection of the first thirty years of the present century.

Amongst the founders of the Leeds Philosophical and Literary Society was one of the best and greatest men whom Leeds ever produced—William Hey, F.R.S., then in his eighty-third year, and within three months of his death. He united the present with the past, having been one of the principal founders, and for more than forty years one of the medical advisers of that excellent institution, the Leeds Infirmary; having been a member, along with Dr. Priestley, of a small and comparatively private scientific society, which existed in this town many years before the Leeds Philosophical and Literary Society was formed, and having been amongst the founders of that valuable institution, the Leeds Library. Associated with him in the founding of the Leeds Philosophical and Literary Society in the year 1818, were Mr. Marshall, Mr. Gott, Mr. Tottie, Mr. George Banks, Dr. Thorp, Mr. John Bischoff, Mr. Thomas Blayds, Mr. W. Hey, jun., Mr. Michael Thomas Sadler, Mr. John Atkinson, surgeon, Mr. Jonathan Wilks, Mr. W. Osburn, Dr. Payne, Dr. Hunter, Mr. C. T. Thackrah, Mr. J. Gott, Mr. West, Mr. Edward S. George, Mr. Samuel Clapham, Mr. J. S. Tennant, the late Edward Baines, M.P., and his son, the present Edward Baines, M.P., the latter of whom had the honour and happiness of presiding in 1870, as chairman at the fiftieth anniversary of the society, which he assisted in founding in the year 1818.

The beautifully classical hall, designed by Mr. Chantrell, architect of Leeds, for the meetings and the museum of the Leeds Library and Philosophical Society, was not opened until the 6th April, 1821, although several meetings were held, papers read, and discussions took place, in the interval between the forming of the society and the opening of the hall. The first president was Mr. Marshall, the inaugural address was read by Mr. Charles T. Thackrah, and Mr. West and Mr. Edward S. George gave jointly the first course of scientific lectures that was delivered in the institution. Subsequently courses of lectures were delivered by many of the leading men of science of the age, including in the early days of the Society, John Dalton, the Rev. Professor Sedgwick,

Professor John Phillips, and at a more recent time Professor Owen, Sir John Herschel, Professor Huxley, and many others. Single lectures, or series of lectures, were also given by James Montgomery, the poet; Dr. Whewell, master of Trinity; Sir H. Rawlinson; Sir John Bowring; and Sir Gilbert Scott. The first curator was Mr. John Atkinson, surgeon, of Park Square, who lost his life in making investigations in comparative anatomy; and he was ably assisted by Mr. Henry Denny, who held the office of assistant curator for nearly fifty years. To Mr. Denny's indefatigable attention the society was indebted for a large portion of the fine collection of objects which now adorn and enrich its museum.

Amongst the earlier contributors to that museum was Charles Waterton, of Walton Hall, near Wakefield, who presented it with some specimens of the most beautiful tropical birds, captured by himself in the forests of South America, and preserved by him with a skill that has never been matched. He was the discoverer of the art of preserving the most beautiful shades and colours of tropical birds, and other objects of natural history; and we remember his informing the society, in his usual humorous way, that the whole secret of preserving natural objects, in their original brightness and beauty, consisted in washing them in a strong solution of ingredients which no insect could touch without being poisoned. He observed that if that was done, and the poison was made strong enough, no insect would touch a specimen washed in it, however hungry it might be, any more than a London alderman would eat even the most tempting slice of a haunch of venison served up with arsenic sauce. Charles Waterton was not only a liberal contributor to the Leeds Museum, but he also drew up an interesting account of his adventures in the forests of Demerara, and upon the River Orinoco, for the society. This was read by one of his friends, Mr. Waterton accompanying it with a most characteristic representation of the manner in which he had fished out the cayman or alligator from the river Orinoco, and of the manner in which he had caught an enormous serpent, whilst it was taking an afternoon nap in the same forest. Both the cayman and the serpent were present, or at least their skins, to contradict him if he had at all exaggerated the dangers that he had run in capturing them; but his adventures were as truthful as they were surprising.

Amongst the earliest resident members of the Leeds Philosophical and Literary Society, who were present when it was formed in the year 1818, when it was opened in 1821, and who were still living when the fiftieth anniversary was celebrated in the year 1870, was Mr. William Osburn, who, in the early days of the society, was one of the first persons to bring before the English public the great discoveries in the art of reading and interpreting the hieroglyphics forming the sacred language of Egypt. Only a few years previously the meaning of these signs had been deciphered by Champollion and by Thomas Young, both much assisted by the discovery of the Rosetta Stone, which had been captured by the French savans in Napoleon's expedition to Egypt, but had been recaptured by the British army of Sir Ralph Abercromby, and had found its way to the British Museum, instead of the Louvre at Paris. The subject was still very obscure in 1818-20, and amongst the men of science and learning, who were then endeavouring to elucidate the language in which these oldest written and engraved memorials of the human race were recorded, and on which the great works of Lepsius and Bunsen have been founded, as well as other questions of oriental literature, was Mr. William Osburn. If we were to give even a list of the members of this society, whose essays on almost every branch of science and literature we had ourselves the pleasure of listening to in the early years of the society, we should have to mention the names of almost every man of literary and scientific celebrity connected with the town of Leeds and the neighbouring district. Mr. Michael Thomas Sadler, M.P., a man of remarkable eloquence, was one of the number, and another was W. M. Smith, the discoverer of the laws of geological stratification, who wrote an early account of the geology of Yorkshire. The public meetings, which were attended both by ladies and gentlemen, will be remembered by all who were then alive, and who had the great advantage of attending them, with lasting pleasure. This was the commencement of what may be regarded as a new era in the intellectual history of the town of Leeds.*

Only three of the actual founders of the society were present at

---

* Proceedings at the Fiftieth Anniversary of the Leeds Philosophical and Literary Society, including the speeches of the chairman, Edward Baines, M.P., Mr. Hey, and those of Dr. Heaton, the president, Canon Woodford, the Rev. Charles Wicksteed, Mr. Denny, Mr. Alderman George, and others long connected with the Society.

the fiftieth anniversary held in the year 1870, namely, Mr. Samuel Clapham, then eighty-three years of age, Mr. Hey, and Mr. Baines M.P.; but a communication was read from Mr. William Osburn, which showed his continued interest in the society, to which his great attainments had done so much honour.

The Leeds Mechanics' Institute.—About six years after the Philosophical and Literary Society had been founded, the Leeds Mechanics' Institute was formed, chiefly by the instrumentality of the enlightened men who had taken part in forming the above Society. This we shall speak of more fully in a subsequent part of this work.

Leeds from 1821 *to* 1831.—Leeds is described, in the year 1823, as the principal seat of the woollen manufacture in England. "Its situation," we are told by a very competent judge, "was peculiarly favourable for trade and commerce," and its natural advantages had been improved by great public works: the river Aire, which passed through the town, towards its southern boundary, being navigable from the Humber; and the Leeds and Liverpool Canal being open through the whole of its course, from the port of Liverpool, and having a direct communication with the navigation of the Aire, within a quarter of a mile of Leeds Bridge. Placed, therefore, in the middle of that line of fine inland navigation which here extended across the island, Leeds was equally open to the eastern and the western seas. At that time these great commercial facilities were still increasing by the continued improvement of roads, canals, and river navigation. The undertakers of the Aire and Calder Navigation were, in 1823, forming a new canal from Knottingley Lock to the river Ouse at Goole, capable of admitting vessels drawing six feet and a half of water, and with an eighteen feet beam. In connection with this an alteration was taking place in the locks of the Aire and Calder Navigation, from Leeds to Castleford, which were to be made eighteen feet wide, and "by which it was hoped that Leeds would become a port for vessels fit to navigate the German Ocean." *

Already the communication from Leeds to all parts of England, both by land and water, was very active; and the following account of the means of personal travelling and conveying merchandise from and to Leeds, in the year 1823, will show the point that had been reached in the years almost immediately preceding the introduction

* History, Directory, and Gazetteer of the County of York, by Edward Baines, 1823.

of the modern system of railways. Previous to the establishment of railways the Aire and Calder Company's fly-boats were despatched every evening (Sundays excepted) from the company's warehouse in Simpson's Fold, Leeds, to Selby, where they arrived in twelve hours. There they delivered their cargoes on board a steam packet (for steam navigation was already introduced on the Humber), which sailed every morning, and landed packages at Hull the same afternoon. Thence the goods were conveyed by contract vessels, employed by the Aire and Calder Company, by sea to London, Lynn, Wisbeach, Boston, Yarmouth, Newcastle, and other places along the east coast; and also up the rivers Ouse, Derwent, and Trent, to York, Malton, Gainsborough, Lincoln, and Nottingham. In connection with the Aire and Calder Navigation there were also canal boats, running by the Dearne and Dove Canal from Wakefield and Barnsley to Sheffield.

From the town of Leeds to the Atlantic and the Irish Sea, at Liverpool, there were at that time three lines of water communication. The first of these was that of the Leeds and Liverpool Canal, 128 miles in length, which gave constant employment to about forty vessels in transporting goods. This spirited company despatched fly-boats that sailed every day, and conveyed goods to Liverpool in four days. At the same time the Union Company's vessels sailed daily from Leeds to Manchester, following the line of the Aire and Calder Navigation, by way of Wakefield to Sowerby Bridge, near Halifax, and then crossing the hills by the Rochdale Canal, proceeding to Manchester by branch lines connected with that canal. But the swiftest method of sending goods from Leeds to Manchester and Liverpool at that time, was to despatch them from Leeds to Dewsbury, by light vans, which started at nine o'clock every evening from Leeds, shipped the goods carried by them on the Calder at Dewsbury, and sent them forward by fly-boats through the Huddersfield Canal to Manchester, where they arrived in sixty hours after leaving Leeds. Manchester was a great canal centre to all parts of the kingdom, and thence goods were immediately forwarded to the port of Liverpool, and by canal to London, Birmingham, and all parts of England.

The modes of conveying goods from Leeds to London by land carriage were various, and continued to improve to the last. Daily post waggons from Leeds to London made the journey in four days; Pickford and Deacon's caravans, as they were called, provided with springs and guarded like coaches, conveyed parcels to London in thirty-six hours. These vans started from Leeds daily, at half-past one o'clock at noon, through Sheffield, Nottingham, Loughborough, Leicester, and Northampton, reaching London in thirty-six hours; and started on the return journey to Leeds at ten o'clock on the following morning. This was about the swiftest mode of conveying goods from Leeds to London that existed previous to the introduction of the railway system, and it was of great value, especially in long frosts. The goods thus received at Leeds from numerous points, or prepared on the spot, were transported to all parts of Yorkshire by about a hundred country carriers, who started from well-known houses in Leeds, and made their way as quickly as they could to every part of the county. The Leeds and Masham waggon, which for want of a coach was sometimes used from Ripon to Masham by passengers, made the journey of thirty-six miles in two days.

Coach travelling previous to the introduction of railways was the principal means of personal communication with other parts of Yorkshire, and of the kingdom generally. There were eight coaches every day from Leeds to London, and eight from London to Leeds, capable of carrying four inside and eleven to thirteen outside passengers; and the swiftest of these coaches, before they were finally driven off the roads by the railways, made the journey of 186 miles in about twenty hours. The journey from Leeds to Newcastle-on-Tyne was made in one day, between the hours of half-past five in the morning and eight in the evening. From Leeds to Hull the journey was made between seven in the morning in summer, and eight in winter, and half-past five in the evening; and to Liverpool, through Halifax, Rochdale, and Bolton, between six in the morning and eight in the evening. All these coaches were a little accelerated before the railway system was introduced, but the hours stated were the general hours of travelling until the prospect of the coming railways induced them to put on their utmost speed. Within ten years after the opening of the Liverpool and Manchester Railway in 1829, this mode of travelling had almost ceased to exist; yet it was wonderfully well organized, and as perfect as well-built coaches, well-bred horses, smart coachmen, and active guards could render it.

The Streets of Leeds Previous to the Improvement Act of 1825.—The principal business street of Leeds was still Briggate, "a very broad and spacious street, extending from the foot of the bridge to the Moot Hall, a distance of about 450 yards." "At this point," says a writer, describing Leeds in 1823, "it is divided by a row of houses, for the distance of 120 yards, into two miserable streets, or rather alleys: that to the east is the Shambles; the other is called Back of the Shambles, and was formerly the wool market." The same writer adds, "When the buildings attached to the Moot Hall are removed (a consummation devoutly to be wished), this street will probably be equalled by few out of London, as the distance from the bridge to the top of Cross parish is near half a mile. The buildings to the east of Briggate may properly enough be termed the Old Town, those to the west the New Town; the latter generally forming the residence of the wealthier part of the inhabitants, the former that of the labouring classes."

Modern System of Railways.—The years 1830 and 1831 witnessed the preparations for and the commencement of the modern system of railway transport and travelling, in the neighbourhood of Leeds. During the previous five years the construction of the Liverpool and Manchester Railway, under the direction of George Stephenson, had been watched with intense interest in this part of England; and no sooner was it ascertained, near the close of the year 1829, that the hopes of that great engineer were more than realized, by the swiftness, the smoothness, and the astonishing power of the new mode of steam locomotion, than the most active steps were taken to introduce railway carriage and transport in the crowded district of the West Riding. In a few years all the lines of country which we have already described as having been supplied in the previous century, and in the earlier part of the present, first with excellent lines of highways, and afterwards with extensive lines of inland navigation, were furnished with railways. Everywhere the steam railway train took the place of the mail coach, the stage coach, the post chaise, and the heavy waggon; and the shrill whistle of the railway train was heard where the cheerful horn of the mail guard had so long resounded.

The necessity and great advantage of connecting the large manufacturing town of Leeds with the navigable part of the river Ouse, and through it with the estuary of the Humber, and of thus forming a line of steam communication from Leeds to the port of Hull, partly by railway and partly by steam navigation, led to the passing of the Act for forming the Leeds and Selby Railway in the year 1830, the 11th George IV. and 1st William IV., sec. 59. In the year 1835, the 6th and 7th William IV., cap. 107, an Act was passed for making a railway from Leeds to Derby, to be called the North Midland Railway. This was the commencement of a group or system of railways which now extends, under various names, over many hundreds of miles.*

Progress of Leeds in the first Thirty Years of the Nineteenth Century.—In the first thirty years of the present century the population of Leeds had increased from 53,162 to 119,345. This was the time at which many great local, as well as national changes, were fully ripe for accomplishment.

Leeds made a Parliamentary Borough.—In 1832 all the larger and more populous boroughs of England, as yet unrepresented, including the great towns of the West Riding, obtained the right of returning members to Parliament, by the Act of 2nd William IV., cap. 45, entitled "An Act to amend the Representation of the People in England and Wales," under which the borough of Leeds was empowered to return two members to Parliament. That was the largest number given to any English borough under Earl Grey's Reform Act of 1832. But when the Reform Act of the Earl of Derby and Mr. Disraeli was passed, in the year 1867, a few of the largest towns of England were authorized to return three members each; and Leeds being in the first class, both as to population and wealth, received an additional member, and since then returns three members to Parliament. We give a list of the members who have been returned for the borough of Leeds, from the passing of the Act of 1832 to the present time, joining to it that of Captain Adam Baynes, of Knowstrop Hall in the borough of Leeds, who was returned in the time of the Commonwealth:—

A LIST OF MEMBERS RETURNED TO SERVE IN PARLIAMENT FOR THE BOROUGH OF LEEDS.

——	—— Commonwealth,	Adam Baynes.
11th December,	1832, 3 William IV.,	{ John Marshall, the younger. { Thomas Babington Macaulay.
14th February,	1834, 4 William IV.,	Edward Baines, *vice* Macaulay.
6th January,	1835, 5 William IV.,	{ The Right Hon. Sir John Beckett, Baronet. { Edward Baines.
27th July,	1837, 1 Victoria,	{ Edward Baines. { Sir William Molesworth, Bart.
1st July,	1841, 4 Victoria,	{ William Beckett. { William Aldam, the younger.

* Wardell's Municipal History of Leeds; List of Acts relating to the Borough of Leeds, pp. 202, 203.

July,	1847, 10 Victoria,	{ William Beckett. James Garth Marshall.
July,	1852, 15 Victoria,	{ Sir George Goodman. Right Hon. Matthew Talbot Baines.
March,	1857, 20 Victoria,	{ Right Hon. Matthew Talbot Baines. Robert Hall.
June,	1857, 20 Victoria,	George Skirrow Beecroft, *vice* Hall.
April,	1859, 22 Victoria,	{ Edward Baines (the Younger). G. S. Beecroft.
July,	1865, 28 Victoria,	{ G. S. Beecroft. Edward Baines.
November,	1868, 31 Victoria,	{ Edward Baines. Robert Meek Carter. W. St. James Wheelhouse.

The increase made in the constituency of Leeds by the Reform Act of 1867 was very great. Previous to the passing of that Act no candidate had polled more than 3223 votes, whilst at the election of 1868, Mr. Edward Baines polled 15,941, Mr. Alderman Carter 15,105, and Mr. St. James Wheelhouse polled 9437 votes.

Local Government of Leeds before and under the Municipal Reform Act.—When Leeds became a borough under the charter of Maurice Paganel, in the reign of King John and the year 1208-9, it was governed by an officer appointed by the lord of the manor, who is described by the Latin title of prætor in that charter, but whose functions bore more resemblance to those of an Anglian boroughreeve, such as existed at Manchester, or a Norman high bailiff, like the one at Birmingham, than to a Roman prætor. He was appointed yearly by the lord of the manor, but in the charter he had a good set of local laws to regulate his conduct. Such a bailiff, boroughreeve, or prætor, was probably the acting governor of the town for many ages, for mention is made of the bailiffs of Leeds, Snaith, Kellam, and Beverley, amongst the persons who took part in the disastrous Pilgrimage of Grace, in the reign of King Henry VIII., 1536, which cost so many people their lives.* The bailiff of Leeds is also mentioned in some legal proceedings relating to the duchy of Lancaster, to which Leeds at that time belonged; and Leeds is spoken of as the Bailiwick or Manor of Leeds, in a deed by which John Harrison gave up his right in five-ninths of it, in trust for the use of the corporation. But in the second year of the reign of Charles I. Leeds became a borough, having then received a charter from the king in 1626, under which the government of the borough was placed in the hands of a town council, nominated by the king himself, and renewable for ever by self-election. This charter perished amidst the confusion

* Wardell's Municipal History of Leeds, pp. 16, 18, 19.

of the great civil war; but soon after the Restoration of Charles II., in the year 1662, another charter was granted by that king to the borough, which, like the previous one, gave the mayor, the aldermen, and the town councillors, then named by the king, the power of renewing their numbers by self-election, without any reference to the choice of the inhabitants.

But in the 36th year of the reign of Charles II., 1684–85, and when his brother, afterwards James II., had attained a complete ascendancy, the corporation of Leeds, in common with most of the corporations of the kingdom, was summoned by his notorious tools, Jeffreys and Sunderland, to surrender their charter to the king, and to accept, in place of it, a new one, giving the crown the power of dismissing the mayor, or any member of the town council, without trial or appeal. Most of the members seem to have submitted to this unconstitutional change; but the corporation records state, that William Lowther, Esq. (the ancestor of the Lowthers of Swillington), who had a house in Leeds, appeared before the corporation on the 29th of September, 1687, accompanied by, and on the behalf of Robert Baynes, the younger, Esquire, of Knowstrop, to endeavour to prevail on the court to excuse Mr. Baynes from serving as town councillor, to which office he had been elected, but which he refused to accept under King James' charter. Mr. Lowther seems to have given great offence to the municipal body by the freedom of his speech, as it is recorded in the court book, that he "cast several reflections upon the court and the members thereof; and, in particular, said that he cared not for the records of the court, for they were false and not to be trusted; and again, that no person in the court knew when reason was offered." This plain speaking, as might have been foreseen, produced an effect the opposite of that intended, and Mr. Baynes was fined for his contumacy and contempt of the court, in not accepting the office to which he had been elected.* But neither Mr. Lowther nor he had to wait long for their revenge, for in the following year James II. was dethroned by the rising of the nation in the Revolution of 1688, and William and Mary were proclaimed king and queen of England, amongst other places, in front of the Moot Hall at Leeds, where all the opponents of James and his charter may have listened to the downfall of the incurable house of Stewart.

* Wardell's Municipal History of Leeds, p. 55.

After the overthrow of James II., the charter of the 13th Charles II. was restored to the corporation. The declaration published by William and Mary on occupying the throne, contained a long list of evils that had been practised during the late reign, amongst which the seizure or compulsory surrender of corporation charters was enumerated; and it was declared that the late charters by which the election of burgesses was limited, contrary to the ancient custom, should be considered null and of no force, and that all boroughs should again return to their ancient prescriptions and charters. Accordingly, in the 1st William and Mary, 1689, the charter of incorporation of the borough of Leeds, of the 36th Charles II., 1684, was superseded, and the previous one of the 13th Charles II., 1662, was restored. Under this charter Leeds was governed until the year 1835, and that charter is still in force except where it is inconsistent with or contrary to the provisions of the Municipal Corporation Act of 1835, or to subsequent Acts. In that year the whole system of municipal government was reconstructed throughout the cities and boroughs of England, and a uniform system was adopted, under which the burgesses of each borough, of course including Leeds, elected their own town councillors, who elected the aldermen; both town councillors and aldermen joining in the election of the mayor. Previous to the Municipal Reform Bill, the corporation of Leeds consisted of a mayor, twelve aldermen, and twenty-four common councillors; under the Municipal Reform Bill, it consists of a mayor (who is one of the aldermen), sixteen aldermen, and forty-eight town councillors. The town council is, and always has been, assisted by a recorder, who is a barrister of standing, by a town clerk, and a deputy recorder.

The township of Leeds was anciently arranged in six districts or divisions, namely, Leeds Town, Leeds Briggate, Leeds Kirkgate, North part of Leeds Main Riding, South part of Leeds Main Riding, and East part of Leeds Main Riding. Subsequently the districts or divisions of the town were thirteen in number; namely, Kirkgate division, South-east division, East division, South division, South-west division, Lower North-west division, Upper North-west division, North-east division, Upper North-east division, Lower North-east division, High Town division, North division, and Millhill division. The out-townships in both cases were the same as at present, with the exception of their not being classed in wards.

In the year 1834 the royal commission issued for the purpose

of obtaining information as to the constitution of the municipal corporations of England visited Leeds; and after making a full inquiry reported "that the close constitution of the corporation was obvious, all vacancies in each branch of the corporation being filled by the select body, which gave to that body absolute and uncontrolled self-election," adding, however, that "the great respectability of the then existing members of the corporation, and their impartial conduct as justices, were universally acknowledged." *
The Municipal Corporations Act, giving the right of voting to the burgesses, having passed both Houses of Parliament, received the royal assent on the 9th of September, 1835; and in pursuance of the 39th section of that Act, Thomas Clarkson and Charles William Heigham, Esquires, barristers-at-law, having been duly appointed to revise the lists of burgesses, divided the borough into wards, and also assigned the number of councillors to be elected therein respectively. The following is a list of the wards, both in Leeds township and in the out-townships, as given under the respective hands of the revising barristers, on the 6th November, 1835, and approved by an order of his Majesty, William IV., in council, on the 4th December following:—

LEEDS TOWNSHIP.
1 Mill-hill Ward.
2 West Ward.
3 North-west Ward.
4 North Ward.
5 North-east Ward.
6 East Ward.
   Hamlet of Osmondthorpe.
   Hamlet of Skelton.
   Hamlet of Thornes.
7 Kirkgate Ward.
8 South Ward.

OUT TOWNSHIPS OF LEEDS.
9 Hunslet Ward.
   Township of Hunslet.
10 Holbeck Ward.
   Township of Holbeck.
   Township of Wortley.
11 Bramley Ward.
   Township of Bramley.
   Township of Armley.
   Township of Farnley.
   Township of Beeston.
12 Headingley Ward.
   Township of Headingley-cum-Burley.
   Township of Chapel Allerton.
   Township of Potternewton.

Mr. Wardell in giving this list observes, "It will be perceived that in thus dividing the borough, the Hamlet of Cold Cotes has not been apportioned by the revising barristers to any ward."

The last mayor of Leeds elected under the charter of King Charles II. was Griffith Wright, Esq., who was elected in 1834, and continued in office in pursuance of the Act of Parliament then recently passed, until the 1st January, 1836. George Goodman, Esq., after-

* See Extract of Report in Mr. Wardell's Municipal History of Leeds.

wards Sir George Goodman, M.P., was the first mayor of the borough of Leeds under the Municipal Corporations Act. The following is a list of the gentlemen who have held the office during the present century, from 1801 to 1873 :—

LIST OF MAYORS OF LEEDS FROM THE YEAR 1801 TO THE YEAR 1873.

UNDER THE CHARTER OF CHARLES II.

1801 William Cookson.
1802 William Hey.
1803 Thomas Ikin.
1804 Wade Browne.
1805 John Wilson.
1806 Richard Ramsden Bramley.
1807 Edward Markland.
1808 Thomas Tennant.
1809 Richard Pullan.
1810 Alexander Turner.
1811 Charles Brown.
1812 Henry Hall.
1813 William Greenwood.
1814 John Brooke.
1815 Whittell York.
1816 William Prest.
1817 John Hill.
1818 George Banks.
1819 Christopher Beckett.
1820 William Hey, F.R.S.
1821 Lepton Dobson.
1822 Benjamin Sadler.
1823 Thomas Tennant.
1824 Charles Brown.
1825 Henry Hall.
1826 Thomas Beckett (afterwards Sir Thomas Beckett, Bart).
1827 Thomas Blayds.
1828 Ralph Markland.
1829 Christopher Beckett.
1830 Robert William Disney Thorp.
1831 William Hey.
1832 Thomas Tennant.
1833 Benjamin Sadler.
1834 Griffith Wright.

UNDER MUNICIPAL CORPORATIONS ACT, 5 AND 6 WILLIAM IV. CAP. 76, 1835.

1836 George Goodman, January 1st to 9th November.
1836 James Williamson, M.D.
1837 Thomas William Tottie.
1838 James Holdforth.
1839 William Smith.
1840 " "
1841 William Pawson.
1842 Henry Cowper Marshall.
1843 Hamer Stansfeld.
1844 Darnton Lupton.
1845 John Darnton Luccock.
1846 G. C. Maclea, *resigned;* George Goodman, elected in his place.
1847 Francis Carbutt.
1848 John Hope Shaw.
1849 Joseph Bateson.
1850 Sir George Goodman.
1851 " "
1852 John Hope Shaw.
1853 John Wilson.
1854 Joseph Richardson.
1855 Thomas Willington George.
1856 John Botterill.
1857 Peter Fairbairn.
1858 Sir Peter Fairbairn.
1859 William Kelsall.
1860 James Kitson.
1861 " "
1862 James Ogdin March.
1863 Obadiah Nussey.
1864 John Darnton Luccock.
1865 Henry Oxley.
1866 A. Fairbairn.
1867 { Sir A. Fairbairn.[*] / Thomas Willington George.
1868 T. Willington George.
1869 William Glover Joy.
1870 John Barran.
1871 " "
1872-73 Henry Oxley.

[*] Sir A. Fairbairn retired from the mayoralty in order to contest the borough, and Mr. George was elected in his stead for the remainder of the year, and afterwards re-elected for the following year.

RECORDERS OF THE BOROUGH OF LEEDS FROM THE YEAR 1626 TO THE YEAR 1873.

13th July,	1626, John Clayton.	23rd August,	1776, Samuel Buck.
2nd November,	1661, Francis White.	15th September,	1806, John Hardy.
18th November,	1692, Jasper Blythman.	9th April,	1833, Charles Milner.
31st December,	1707, Richard Thornton.	18th February,	1837, R. Baynes Armstrong.
28th February,	1711, John Walker.	1st May,	1839, T. Flower Ellis, jun.
18th December,	1729, Richard Wilson.	April,	1861, John Blossett Maule.
25th June,	1761, Richard Wilson.		

TOWN CLERKS OF THE BOROUGH OF LEEDS FROM THE YEAR 1626 TO THE YEAR 1873.

13th July,	1626, Francis Bellhouse.	13th November,	1755, Thomas Barstow, the younger.
2nd November,	1661, George Banister.		
4th January,	1662, Samuel Brogden.	18th April,	1792, Lucas Nicholson.
18th October,	1684, Castilian Morris.	31st January,	1812, James Nicholson.
"	" John Jackson.	8th July,	1836, Edwin Eddison.
28th December,	1702, Henry Adam.	19th July,	1843, John Arthur Ikin.
18th November,	1725, John Lazenby.	24th October,	1860, John Edward Smith.
2nd May,	1753, Thomas Atkinson.	6th March,	1867, Capel Aug. Curwood.

Leeds Improvement Acts and Public Improvements since the passing of the Municipal Act of 1835.—We have given an account of the Improvement Acts passed under the corporation constituted by the charter of 1662. Many additional Acts of Parliament for objects of great public importance have been passed and carried out, since the passing of the Municipal Reform Act of 1835. Amongst these was an Act passed in the year 1835-36, for better lighting the town and neighbourhood of Leeds; an Act of 1837-38, cap. 39, for building a bridge over the river Aire at Leeds, and for making convenient roads, avenues, and approaches thereto; an Act of the 7th King William IV. and 1st Victoria, 1837-38, for the better supplying of water to the town and neighbourhood of Leeds; an Act of the 2nd and 3rd Victoria, 1839-40, cap. 17, for discharging the inhabitants of the manor of Leeds, in the township and parish of Leeds, from the custom of grinding corn, grain, and malt, at certain water corn mills in the manor of Leeds, and for making compensation to the proprietor of the said mills; an Act of the 3rd and 4th Victoria, 1840-41, cap. 26, for making and maintaining a new bridge over the River Aire at a place called Crown Point, with suitable approaches thereto; an Act of the 5th and 6th Victoria, 1842-43, for providing additional burial grounds in the parish of Leeds; an Act of the same year, cap. 104, for better lighting, cleansing, sewering, and improving the borough of Leeds; an Act of the 7th Victoria,

1843-44, cap. 30, to enlarge the powers and provisions for lighting with gas the town and neighbourhood of Leeds. In the 7th and 8th Victoria, 1844-45, cap. 108, an important Act was passed, entitled an Act to authorize the division of the parish and vicarage of Leeds in the county of York into several parishes and vicarages.

IMPROVEMENT ACTS.

Leeds Improvement Amendment Act (11th and 12th Vic. cap. 102)	1848
Leeds Improvement Amendment Act,	1856
*Leeds Improvement Amendment Act,	1866
Leeds Improvement of Becks Act,	1866
Leeds Improvement Act,	1869
Leeds Corporation Gas Act (for the acquisition of the gas-works),	1870
Leeds Corporation Gas and Improvements, &c., Act (authorizes corporation to start opposition gas-works, if those of the company be not acquired under previous Act, also for Sanitary Improvements),	1870
*Leeds Improvement Act (Street Improvements, &c.),	1872

Extension of the Water-works of Leeds.—When the original water-works of Leeds were formed in the year 1695 by Sorocold, who was the great engineer of the reign of Queen Anne, and whose numerous works for supplying large towns are mentioned in Thoresby's Diary, the water, which was drawn from the river Aire at Leeds, and pumped up near the bridge by an engine that conveyed it into a reservoir in the highest part of the town, was excellent in quality, as well as most abundant in quantity. The waters of the river Aire, after leaving the limestone beds of Craven, never possessed the brilliant clearness that is or was seen in the waters of the Wharfe, the Nidd, and the Ure, which flow over beds of rock, where there is little earth or clay to affect their transparency; still it was very clear and pleasant until about the year 1825. Yet even at that time precautions had been taken for catching the water in a tunnel above the King's Mills, in order to save it from the impurities to which it might have become subject, lower down the stream, from dye-works and other manufacturing establishments, which began to increase rapidly about that time. Soon afterwards the water of the river Aire became unfit for domestic use, owing to the increase of manufactures in and above the town; and in the year 1837 an Act was passed for obtaining water from a purer source, namely, from the Adel Beck, near the point where it issues from the moors and pleasant fields in which it rises. The quality of this water is very

* Under these two Acts money was borrowed for the purchase of Roundhay Park.

good, but the quantity was small for the wants of a rapidly-increasing town, containing nearly two hundred thousand inhabitants. In the first attempt to impound the water of the Adel springs, in a reservoir at Black Hill, the banks of the reservoir broke, and the water rushed down the course of the Adel Beck into the river Aire, causing a similar scene, though on a less disastrous scale, to those which were afterwards witnessed at Holmfirth and at Sheffield. Though the reservoir covered an area of from twenty to twenty-five acres, and the embankment was about fifteen feet high, the reservoir emptied itself in two hours into the river Aire. The flood even surpassed the well-known flood of 1807, which, from its occurring at the close of the great county election, was remembered at Leeds, for many years, as the Milton Flood. *

From this source the supply was taken for some years, but in 1851 the town suffered, in common with many other towns in Yorkshire, from excessive drought, and it was found necessary to procure an increased supply. In 1852 the corporation purchased the water-works, and shortly afterwards there was a protracted discussion in the council, as to whether the increased supply should be taken from the Wharfe, by pumping at Arthington, or by gravitation from the Skirfare, one of the streams flowing into the Wharfe. The pumping scheme was adopted, and power was obtained to take 6,000,000 gallons per day from the Wharfe, at Arthington. By this plan a supply of water of fair quality was secured, but in a few years it proved to be inadequate; and the pollution of the Wharfe by the drainage from the rising towns of Otley and Ilkley, and the intervening villages, forced the corporation to look to other sources for the future water supply of the borough. An extensive survey of the surrounding district was made, and in 1867 it was decided to apply to Parliament for powers to expend £500,000 on works in the Washburne Valley, whereby a supply of 20,000,000 gallons per day would be obtained. The scheme was recommended by Mr. Filliter, C.E., at that time the borough surveyor. The Washburne is one of the tributaries of the Wharfe, entering it from the north, a few miles below Otley. The bill was passed through Parliament, and in August, 1869, the first sod of the new works was cut, the drawings having been prepared by Mr. Thomas Hawksley, C.E.

* Mayhall's Annals of Yorkshire, vol. i. p. 347.

These works consist of four immense reservoirs, formed by draining the Washburne valley at Lindley Wood, Swinsty, Fewston, and Thurscross. The first will have a capacity of 750,000,000 gallons, the second of 961,000,000, the third of 870,000,000, and the fourth of 540,000,000 gallons. The works are still in course of construction in 1873, and will not be completed for some time. Meanwhile, the supply from the Wharfe has been augmented from the lower part of the Washburne. The water of that stream is of good quality.

Street and Town Railway Improvements.—Amongst other improvements which have been made since the establishment of the present system of municipal government in Leeds, we may mention the following:—Powers were obtained in the Improvement Acts of 1866 and 1869, for widening and straightening the chief business streets. Under these powers the corporation had expended up to 1873 nearly half a million of money, including £78,530 paid for the abolition of tolls on the roads and bridges within the borough. More than a quarter of a million has been spent in widening and extending old streets, and in opening out new ones. Amongst the more important of the improvements have been the widening of Boar Lane, at a cost of more than £70,000; the extension of Briggate northward, at a cost of £30,638; the extension of Albion Street, at a cost of more than £27,000; and the opening of new streets between Duncan Street and Vicar Lane, and Wellington Street and King Street. Large sums have also been expended in enlarging the Kirkgate Market, and in improving the Central Market, as well as in widening and straightening the brooks or becks, the beds of which have been laid with masonry, to secure a more rapid flow of water into the river Aire. In connection with these varied improvements may also be mentioned the construction of the short line of the North-eastern Railway, connecting the Leeds Northern and the Hull and Selby section, so as to secure through communication on the North-eastern system. The line passes through the heart of the town from the new station in Wellington Street, to the old Hull and Selby station in Marsh Lane, and crosses Briggate, Call Lane, Kirkgate, York Street, and Marsh Lane. It was completed in 1869, and the line was opened for traffic on the 1st of April in the same year; the new station being jointly built and occupied by the North-eastern and the London and North-western companies.

Rebuilding and Widening of Bridges.—The bridge now (1873) in course of construction across the Aire, at the bottom of Briggate, and connecting that great thoroughfare with Hunslet Lane, the chief southern entrance to and exit from the town, was designed by Mr. T. D. Steele, C.E., of Newport, and when completed will be a handsome and substantial structure. It is to be almost entirely of iron, the buttresses alone being of stone. It is slightly askew, and consists of one arch, having a span of 102 feet 6 inches, the centre being thirteen feet above the ordinary water level. The road-way is to be thirty-six feet wide, and the causeways twelve each. The cost is estimated at from £15,000 to £20,000, towards which the West Riding has contributed £2000. The foundation stone was laid on the 20th of September, 1871, by the then mayor (Mr. John Barran). The reconstruction of this bridge has rendered necessary other improvements, such as widening the approaches, and alteration of the levels, and these involve a total estimated cost of £59,270. The following is a list of the bridges across the Aire, within the borough of Leeds, all of which have been freed from toll by the corporation:—Leeds Bridge (iron), now in course of construction; Wellington Bridge, about to be rebuilt (stone); Victoria Bridge (stone); Crownpoint Bridge (stone); Kirkstall Bridge (stone); Monk Bridge (iron suspension); Suspension Bridge (iron suspension). The Corporation, in January, 1873, accepted the tender of Messrs. Fearnley and Wilson, contractors, for erecting a new bridge, in place of the existing Wellington Bridge, at a cost of £3150. The new structure, when completed, will be a great advantage to the neighbourhood, as the present bridge, owing to its narrowness, causes much inconvenience. The approaches are already widened, and the completion of the improvement will consist in widening the bridge, to correspond with the road. There will be a clear width of road and path of about forty-five feet from parapet to parapet. The span of the bridge, which, as already stated, will be rebuilt with stone, is 100 feet.

The Town Hall of Leeds.—The Town Hall of Leeds is a very handsome and commanding structure in the Italian style of architecture, built at a cost of £140,000, from designs by Mr. Cuthbert Brodrick. The foundation stone was laid on the 17th of August, 1853, by Mr. John Hope Shaw, who was then mayor, and the building was opened on the 7th of September, 1858, during the mayoralty of Sir Peter Fairbairn, by the queen, who was accompanied by Prince Albert and other members of the royal family, the late Lord Derby being in attendance as the minister of state. It is situated at some distance to the north-west of Briggate; the southern or principal façade, fronting to Park Lane, having a large open space between the line of street and the main entrance. The building covers an area of 5600 square yards, the external form being that of a parallelogram, 250 feet in length by 200 feet in breadth. Standing on a lofty platform, it is surrounded by Corinthian columns and pilasters, supporting an entablature with balustrades, altogether about sixty-seven feet in length. The principal façade is approached by a fine flight of steps with projecting buttresses on each side, leading to a deeply recessed portico of twelve columns; ten being in front and two recessed. Rising above the centre of this façade is a dome and tower 225 feet in height, containing a large bell, by Warner, and a clock by Dent. In the tympanum of the archway is an emblematic group of figures representing Leeds, in its commercial and industrial character, fostering and encouraging the arts and sciences, by Thomas of London. The two sides and the north end of the building are somewhat similar to the front, excepting that the columns and pilasters are near to the walls. The interior of the building is admirably arranged. On the ground floor there is a splendid hall, 161 feet long by seventy-two feet wide, and seventy-five feet in height, called the Victoria Hall, the entrance from the front being through a fine domed vestibule, the floor of which is laid with encaustic tiles; also a council chamber, a borough court, and two assize courts, occupying respectively the four corners of the parallelogram; with various offices for the town-clerk and other officials. On the floor above, which is reached by a broad and effective staircase at each corner, are a handsome suite of rooms called the mayor's rooms, the West-Riding magistrates' court, and other offices. Both on the ground floor and on the first floor spacious corridors run round the building. The basement is occupied by the police, including cells and the various offices necessary for the administration of the force. The Victoria Hall, which is very elaborately decorated by Crace of London, interspersed with mottoes and legends suggested by Mr. Edward Baines, M.P., is divided into five bays by composite Corinthian columns and pilasters resting on a sur-base, and supporting an enriched entablature running round the hall, from which springs a semicircular ceiling, also divided into five bays corresponding with the columns, panelled and highly ornamented with conventional foliage. It is lighted by ten semicircular windows near the ceiling, and at night by ten handsome glass chandeliers. The north end of this hall is semicircular in plan, coved at the top; and in the recess thus formed there is a splendid organ, built by Messrs. Gray & Davidson of London, at a cost of £6000, from designs by Messrs. Smart & Spark. The hall will accommodate 2500 people seated, and is in every respect one of the handsomest in the kingdom. In the second bay from the main entrance is a marble statue of the late Mr. Edward Baines, M.P., by Behnes, and on the opposite side is a similar statue of the late Mr. Robert Hall, M.P., by a local artist; both originating in public subscriptions. In the vestibule are marble statues of the Queen (presented by Sir Peter Fairbairn) and Prince Albert, erected by subscription; and busts of the prince and princess of Wales, presented by Mr. James Kitson—all the pieces by Noble. In the council chamber, the mayor's rooms, the borough magistrates' room, and the corridors, are several presentation portraits by Grant, R.A., and Waller, and other paintings; including a fine allegorical piece by Armitage, representing the suppression of the Indian mutiny, Milton dictating "Paradise Lost" to his daughters, by Sir A. Calcott, and Mary Queen of Scots by Haydon. In the open space in front of the hall is a subscription statue of the duke of Wellington by Marochetti; the buttresses surmounted with lions couchant by Keyworth of London. It may be mentioned here that there are bronze statues of Sir Robert Peel, by Behnes, in Park Row, near the Post Office, and of Sir Peter Fairbairn, by Noble, in Clarendon Road. One of the first results of the opening of the town hall and the visit of the queen, was a movement to transfer the West Riding assize business to Leeds. After many failures the movement was successful, and by an order in council, dated 10th June, 1864, the county of York was divided for assize purposes, and Leeds made the assize town for the West Riding. The first assizes were held on the 7th August, 1864, the judges being Mr. Justice Blackburn and Mr. Justice Keating.

The Borough Goal at Armley.—This prison was built by the corporation, from designs by Messrs. Perkin & Backhouse, at a cost of £43,000, and covered an area of more than ten acres. It was commenced in 1843, and completed in July, 1847. It is a castellated structure, occupying a prominent position on the right bank of the Aire, about two miles from Leeds, with a frontage to the north. The cells are placed in three wings radiating from the centre, one for males, one for females, and one for juveniles, communicating with a central hall by corridors running from a circular staircase. The exercise yards are placed between the wings. In the front there is a chapel, together with residences for the governor and chaplain. Accommodation was originally provided for about 300 prisoners. It has since been enlarged, and will now accommodate 501 prisoners, namely, 359 males and 142 females. When the West Riding assizes were removed to Leeds, it was constituted a common gaol for the delivery of prisoners and for assize purposes. In other respects it is simply a borough gaol. Productive labour was early introduced in the management of the prison, and the manufacture of cocoa-nut matting has been carried on extensively for many years. The sum total of the profits received from the earnings of prisoners amounted in 1872 to £1411; more by £203 than that of the previous year. The governor of the gaol, in his last report, states that the enlargement of the prison for females has been satisfactorily completed, and that the building is now of dimensions which may reasonably be expected to meet the requirements of the borough for many years.

Organization of the Police.—The very great and rapid increase of the population of Leeds has rendered it necessary to add materially to the numbers of the police force. Some years previous to the Municipal Reform Act, there were a chief constable and constables of divisions, namely, the Upper, the Middle, the Mill Hill, the South, the Kirkgate, the East, the Upper North-east, the Lower North-east, the Upper North-west, and the Lower Northwest divisions, as well as a town beadle and a deputy constable. The nightly watch consisted of thirty-eight men, and the patrol of sixteen, under the command of the captain of the watch and patrol. There was also a constable in each of the ten out-townships. The police force of the borough at the present time, 1873, consists of a total of 315 officers and men. It is commanded by 1 chief constable, having under him 4 superintendents of divisions, 1 detective superintendent, 11 inspectors, 4 sub-inspectors, 32 sergeants, 1 detective sergeant, 6 officers of constables, and 255 constables, making a total strength of 315. The numbers have been increased with the amount of the population, having advanced from 279, in the year 1869, to 315 in 1872. The net cost of the police in the last-named year was £15,058 10s. $11\tfrac{1}{2}d$: the cost of each constable being

£47 15s. 5½d.; and the number of offences affecting property in that year was 1417. The per centage of property recovered on the amount of first loss was rather more than 30; the total number of persons apprehended 4234; the number of persons summarily disposed of by the magistrates was 5796; and the number committed for trial was 242.*

The Leeds Soke Act.—The Corporation created by the Municipal Reform Act of 1835, felt itself strong enough to free the town from the old feudal obligation to grind the whole of the corn of the borough and manor at what were long known as the King's Mills. This obligation had probably existed from the time of the Norman conquest, if not from a more remote period. In that age the mill dam, known as the Bondman Dam, had been erected in the river Aire by the labour of the villani or bondmen of the manor of Leeds; and from that time all the other residents of the manor had been compelled by law to grind their corn at that mill only, and to pay fees for so doing, which greatly exceeded the amount of service rendered by the owner of the soke or manorial rights. Previous attempts, all of them unsuccessful, had been made to free the inhabitants of Leeds from this obligation; but these only served to show that the obligation had a legal origin, and could only be got rid of in the manner in which other abuses of a legal kind are removed in this country, namely, by the buying up of the existing rights. The Leeds Soke Act for this object received the royal assent on Tuesday, the 14th May, 1839. It provided for the payment of a sum of £13,000, as compensation to Mr. Edward Hudson, of Roundhay, the proprietor of the King's Mills, in four yearly instalments. The money was raised by an assessment on the inhabitants of the town. The Act further provided for the appointment of nineteen trustees and two auditors to carry out its provisions, and these trustees and auditors were appointed on Monday, the 24th of June of the same year.

Manufactures in Leeds.—The history of the woollen manufacture in Leeds and the district has already been published in the first volume of this work, from the pen of Mr. E. Baines, M.P. It may here be added that the industry of Leeds has during the last quarter of a century been materially developed, and at the same time has undergone great and important changes. Whilst retaining the position it has held for many generations as the capital of the

* Leeds Constabulary Report and Criminal Statistics for the year ending September 29, 1872.

woollen manufacture of Yorkshire, Leeds has become the seat of
other industries only second to it in importance, whether viewed
in reference to the capital invested or the number of workmen
employed. The effect on the general stability and wellbeing of
the town has been most valuable; for it rarely occurs that all the
branches of industry carried on within its boundaries suffer simul-
taneously, and the result is an average of trade, which prevents
that general depression and consequent distress so frequent in towns
and districts dependent exclusively upon one trade. The woollen
manufacture, however, is still its chief and pre-eminent industry,
though it is of a more limited character than formerly. According
to a parliamentary return, dated the 9th August, 1871, obtained
by Mr. Baines, there were, when the return was prepared, 954
woollen factories, 60 shoddy factories, 516 worsted factories, and
70 flax factories in Yorkshire. Of this number there were in Leeds
130 woollen factories, 13 shoddy factories, and 4 worsted factories,
employing about 10,000 hands, and 29 flax factories, employing
about 8000 hands. In the Batley district there were 30 woollen
and 2 shoddy factories, employing 5000 hands; and in the Dewsbury district 48 woollen and 5 shoddy factories, employing 7000
hands. Altogether there are in Leeds and the Leeds clothing
district about 250 woollen and shoddy factories, employing about
30,000 hands. The trade, which was formerly transacted so largely
in the cloth halls, is now chiefly carried on in the merchants' warehouses. The Coloured Cloth Hall still stands where it has so long
stood, but its associations—and they are part of the political as well
as the commercial history of the West Riding—belong to the past
rather than the present. It is an unsightly building, certain sooner
or later to be removed or rebuilt. The White Cloth Hall had to be
removed a few years ago, in consequence of the North-eastern
Railway passing through it; and a new building has been erected
in the old Infirmary gardens, having a frontage into King Street.
It is a large and commodious structure, but has no architectural
pretensions. It was opened in July, 1868. The principal warehouses are in Wellington Street, King Street, and York Place, in
close proximity to the two halls. The market-days are Tuesday
and Saturday, but in the early part of 1873 it was decided to
open the Coloured Cloth Hall daily. Next in importance to the
woollen trade is the flax and linen manufacture, which employs
several thousand hands. Ranking not far short of these great

branches of textile industry, are the ironworks of the town and district. The manufacture of iron is an ancient industry here. On the occasion of the visit of the British Association to Leeds in 1858, Mr. James Kitson, jun., one of the proprietors of the important ironworks at Monk Bridge, Leeds, read a paper in the section Statistics and Economics, on "The Iron Trade of Leeds." *
It contained some highly interesting and valuable information, both as to the manufacture of iron in this locality in the past, and as to the enormous development of this branch of industry within the past quarter of a century. Mr. Kitson observes, that the evidences of iron having been worked in this district in ancient times are abundant. Scoriæ from iron furnaces, the fires of which must have been extinguished many centuries ago, have been found at Middleton, Whitkirk, and Horsforth, all places within the borough of Leeds. There is near the last-named village, marked on the Ordnance maps, a patch of ancient timber bearing the name of Iveson and Clayton Wood. Not quite twenty years ago, in disafforesting this piece of land, extensive agglomerated masses of scoriæ were discovered; and in not a few instances these were found to be penetrated by the roots of trees of great size and age. Many persons are inclined to think that these relics of ancient iron smelting date from the period of Roman occupation of this island.† This opinion, of course, has no better foundation than probability, based upon a few collateral facts. There can, however, be no doubt of this, that the iron furnaces, of the existence of which those heaps of scoriæ inform us, were in operation many centuries ago, but how many can only be conjectured. It may be mentioned here that in excavating for the foundations of the Leeds Corn Exchange, some years ago, shafts that had evidently been employed in working iron ore and coal, which here lie in contiguous seams, were found. Of these vestiges of mining industry, discovered at a spot on which the most ancient part of the town stands, no record exists to inform us when working operations were first prosecuted here, or when they ceased. There is reason to believe that the monks of Kirkstall had works for smelting iron ore, obtained from the seams which now supply the well-known works at Farnley and Low Moor with their best qualities of iron. As successors of the monks, the extensive ironworks at Kirkstall Forge have a high reputation for steam-hammers, malleable shafts, and other products in iron. A

* Proceedings of British Association for 1858, p. 183. † See Murray's Handbook of Yorkshire, p. 314.

few years ago, in making extensions at the forge, excavations revealed, at an unsuspected depth beneath the present surface, the remains of ancient charcoal refineries. Within a short distance there are the works of the Farnley Iron Company (Limited), which are associated with the names of the Armitages as the founders of the undertaking. This company has blast furnaces, at which the ore obtained from the coal measures in the locality is made into pig, and afterwards is advanced on the premises adjoining, stage by stage, until it assumes its ultimate manufactured shape and passes into the hands of the customer. The Airedale Foundry in Hunslet is an important establishment, which, like many others of a similar description in Leeds, dates its prosperity from the era which witnessed the commencement of such a marvellous development of our railway system. The machinery produced at these works consists principally of locomotives, orders for which have been carried out for the most distant countries. The Railway Foundry, established in 1836, and subsequently absorbed by the Airedale Foundry, was the first manufactory in Leeds at which the construction of locomotives on a scale of importance was commenced. Mr. Kitson, sen., the chief proprietor of Airedale Foundry, which stands at the head of the locomotive engine works of this district, is now the senior builder of locomotives in the world; the Stephensons (father and son) and the brothers Hawthorn having passed away. The Monk Bridge Ironworks are mentioned above. These extensive works are the property of Mr. Frederick and Mr. James Kitson, sons of Mr. Kitson of the Airedale Foundry, who, following the example of their father at the older establishment, have introduced many improvements in the manufacture of iron at Monk Bridge. Amongst these mention may be made of the manufacture of steel on a large scale by the gas process, invented by Mr. Siemen. The chief products of the Monk Bridge works are steel tires, boiler plates, and axles for locomotives and waggons. Another important firm is that of Messrs. Manning, Wardle, & Co. (which has recently undergone a change of partners), Boyne Engine Works, Hunslet. Perhaps more novel mechanical inventions have been constructed here than in any other engineering works in Leeds. Amongst these mention may be made of a Fell centre-rail locomotive for overcoming the steep gradients of a Brazilian railway, and the elegant little engine employed on the single-rail line at Aldershot Camp. The machine works of Messrs

Fairbairn, Kennedy, and Naylor, are known wherever the manufacture of flax is prosecuted. Messrs. S. Lawson & Sons, Mabgate, produce large quantities of machinery and machine tools; Messrs. Taylor Brothers & Co., Clarence Ironworks, Hunslet, carry on an extensive trade; Messrs. Greenwood & Batley have turned their attention successfully to the manufacture of arms of precision; and there are many other firms of almost equal importance to those enumerated, engaged in the various branches into which the manufacture of iron is divided. The manufacture of steam ploughs was introduced into Leeds in 1860 by Messrs. Fowler & Co., the ploughs being, in the first instance, made at the Airedale Foundry. In 1863 the Messrs. Fowler removed to their present works, and their machinery has since obtained a high reputation, and their ploughs are now extensively used in all parts of the world. The establishment was the first of its kind, and in this special branch of manufacture it continues to be the largest and most important in the county. Of late years the firm has added the construction of locomotives, and the manufacture of mining machinery. The works are situated at Hunslet, and now cover about nine acres of ground, and employ 1200 workmen. According to the return obtained by Mr. Baines and referred to above, there are 15,000 persons employed in metal works in Leeds, of whom between 8000 and 9000 are engaged in iron mills, foundries, and machine shops. There are also between 600 and 700 persons employed in the manufacture of nails and in brass-finishing, and 6629 in "miscellaneous" articles of metal. Nominally, the iron trade holds a position second to that of the woollen trade; but it is rapidly increasing, and if we take into consideration the capital invested, and the amount paid in wages, its actual importance is scarcely inferior to that of the textile industry of the town.

The other important branches of industry, which are of comparatively recent origin, are the boot and shoe trade, employing about 3000 hands, and the leather trade, employing about 2500 hands. The cloth cap trade is also extending rapidly and becoming a great branch of industry. There are in addition to these large manufactories of tobacco, extensive chemical and glass works, important works for the making of sanitary tubes, fire-bricks, &c., and of late years the lucifer match trade has also been introduced into Leeds.

Mineral Wealth of the Leeds District.—Amongst the greatest sources of the wealth of Leeds are its abundant supplies of coal and iron, and these natural advantages have been rapidly developed, especially during the last fifty years, by the intelligence and skill with which those great instruments of labour have been applied to the purposes of producing and working machinery. The mineral wealth of the United Kingdom for the year 1871, according to the last official account, published in the month of November, 1872, was of the enormous value of £47,494,400 (previous to the recent rise of prices), of which no less than £35,205,608 was derived from coal, and £7,670,572 from iron. This represents the value of these articles at the pits' mouth, before it had been increased by the cost of carriage, or by any of the innumerable industrial purposes by which that value is increased at least fourfold. The value of the lead ore produced in England, and much of it in Yorkshire and Derbyshire, in the same year (1871), was £1,155,770. The county of York takes a very conspicuous position in furnishing the mineral wealth of the empire. In the great article of coal, which may be regarded as the mainspring of the modern industry of Great Britain, Yorkshire furnished in the year 1871, 12,801,260 tons, of the total amount of 117,352,028 tons of coal produced in the United Kingdom. In the same year Yorkshire supplied no less than 4,989,898 tons, of the whole quantity of iron ore produced in the United Kingdom, amounting that year to 16,334,888 tons, 14 cwts. Thus this county furnished above one-tenth part of the coal raised in the United Kingdom, and one-fourth part of the iron ore. The number of the Yorkshire collieries worked in the Leeds district in the year 1871, amounted to not less than 99. The number in the other districts of Yorkshire, from the highest to the lowest numbers, in the same year were—in the Bradford district, 49; in that of Wakefield, 48; Barnsley, 44; Sheffield, 36; Dewsbury, 31; Halifax, 29; Huddersfield, 26; Rotherham, 25; Holmfirth, 12; Pontefract, 7; Normanton, 6; Peniston, 6; Bingley, 4; and in the district of Saddleworth, 1. This made the total number of collieries in Yorkshire, in the year 1871, 423; with a total produce of coal amounting to 12,801,260 tons. The names and positions of the ninety-nine collieries existing in the Leeds district, in 1871, were given as follows, by Mr. Frank N. Wardell, the inspector of collieries for the county of York, in his official return rendered in 1872.

NAMES AND POSITIONS OF COLLIERIES IN THE LEEDS DISTRICT, WORKED IN THE YEAR 1871.

Adwalton Lane, Adwalton Moor, Allerton Main, Astley, Baildon Moor, Balaklava (Morley), Beeston (3), Beeston Road, Beverley (Armley), Birkhill (Birkenshaw), Blue Hills Lane (Wortley), Britannia Main (Adwalton), Brook House (Gomersal), Brown Moor, Bushey (Drighlington), Calverley, Churwell (2), College (Birstal), Cross Green, Crow Trees (Gomersal), Dartmouth, Dean Hall (Morley), Doles Wood (Drighlington), Dye House (Gomersal), Ellerby Lane, Farnley, Farnley Wood, Foxholes (Methley), Garforth, Gelderd Road, Gildersome, Gildersome Street, Green Man (Hunslet), Greville (Rawden), Harchills, Holbeck, Howden Clough, Howley Park (Morley), Hunslet, Killingbeck (York Road), Kippax, Lanes Wood (Gomersal), Little Gomersal, Lumb Wood, Manston, Manston Lodge, Micklefield, Middleton, Morley, Morley Main, Mount Pleasant (Adwalton), Muffitt Lane, Nethertown, Neville Hill, New Hall (Middleton), Newmarket (Adwalton), Oakwell, Osmondthorpe, Owlet Hall (Adwalton), Potternewton, Primrose Hill (Liversedge), Quaker Lane (Liversedge), Robert Town (2), Robin Hood, Rock (York Road), Rothwell Haigh, Scotland (Gomersal), Seacroft, Smithies (Birstal), Smithy Hill (Liversedge), Spring Gardens, Stanley Main (Liversedge), Strawberry Bank (Liversedge), Sykes (Drighlington), Tanhouse Mill (Liversedge), Toft Shaw Moor, Tong Moor, Victoria (Morley), Victoria (Adwalton) (2), Waterloo, Waterloo Main, Water Loose (Adwalton), Wellington, West Yorkshire (Birstal), West Yorkshire (Manston), White Horse (York Road), White Lee, Wortley (2), York Road.

Iron Mills and Forges.—The following is the return, published in 1872, of the number of iron mills and forges at work in the Leeds, Bradford, Sheffield, Cleveland, and other districts of Great Britain:—

MILLS AND FORGES IN LEEDS, BRADFORD, SHEFFIELD, CLEVELAND, ETC., IN 1871.

County.	No. of Works.	No. of Puddling Furnaces.	No. of Rolling Mills returned.
ENGLAND :—			
Northumberland,	2	54	5
Cumberland,	6	95	15
Durham,	21	951	65
Yorkshire (Cleveland District),	11	542	34
" (Leeds and Bradford District),	13	247	59
" (Sheffield and Rotherham District),	10	353	54
Derbyshire,	5	94	19
Somersetshire,	1	19	2
South Staffordshire,	122	2,037	320
North do.	8	429	40
Shropshire,	9	218	28
Lancashire,	10	154	35
NORTH WALES,	3	54	6
SOUTH WALES :—			
Glamorganshire,	17	613	92
Brecknockshire,	2	86	7
Monmouthshire,	12	553	42
SCOTLAND,	14	339	44
Total,	266	6,838	864

The Leeds Chamber of Commerce.—The Leeds Chamber of Commerce was formed in the year 1851, and has rendered essential service in watching over national and local legislation connected with the interests of trade and commerce. Previous to the formation of this society, the old proverb which says that "what is every man's business is no man's business" was realized in Leeds and other places, where many questions arose, not directly or at all in some cases connected with municipal government, but which had a great influence on local prosperity. This extensive class of subjects is now looked after by the Chamber of Commerce, together with questions immediately and obviously connected with the interests of trade. Suggestions are also made by this and other similar institutions as to the principles as well as to the details of commercial legislation, which are often of great value in that branch of legislation. The following is a list of the presidents of the Chamber since its formation, with the dates of their appointment:—

1851 Sir George Goodman.	1858 Mr. Darnton Lupton.
1854 Mr. Henry Cowper Marshall.	1873 Mr. John Barran.
1857 Mr. William Beckett.	

The Churches, Chapels, Schools, Libraries, and other Educational Institutions of Leeds.—During the last fifty years there has been a greatly increased desire for education, especially in the large and wealthy towns of England. Under the term education we include every form of instruction—religious, moral, scientific, literary, and artistic. The proof of this is found in the rapid increase that has taken place in that period in the number of the churches, chapels, schools, libraries, and educational institutions of every kind. We have now reached the time when it is no longer unreasonable to hope, that the whole mass of the English people will become, at least, as well educated as the people of any other country of Europe or America. The law now provides for the universal education of the people. But this was not the case until very recently; and up to that time the instruction of the poorer classes, such as it was, depended partly on a few old endowments, but chiefly on the spontaneous zeal of the more educated classes, in furnishing the means of instruction, and on men of intelligence, who devoted themselves to the honourable and useful art of instruction. The following is a brief and rapid sketch of the various establishments and institutions for religious, moral, and intellectual instruction of the people, which have gradually sprung up in this great and busy seat of industry. We shall take the churches and chapels first, and then give some brief account of the institutions for promoting and extending general education.

Churches and Chapels in Leeds.—In the first ten years of the present century, the number of churches and chapels in the town of Leeds is said to have been not more than eighteen or twenty.* In a list of these churches and chapels published in the year 1806, we are told that there were at that time five churches belonging to the English establishment, one Scottish kirk, three Independent chapels, one meeting-house of the Society of Friends, two Presbyterian chapels, one Baptist chapel, three Methodist chapels, one Roman Catholic chapel, and a chapel belonging to the less known body of the Inghamites. According to a statement published very recently, the number of churches and chapels of all sizes and denominations existing in Leeds at the present time is 203, and is thus composed :—Established churches, 51 ; Presbyterian, 2 ; Congregationalists, 24 ; Baptists, 15 ; Society of Friends, 5 ; Unitarians, 6 ; Wesleyan Methodists, 30 ; United Methodist Free Churches, 20 ; New Connection, 13 ; Primitive Methodists, 21 ; and Plymouth Brethren, 1. The increase since 1801 is thus four or five fold, or equal to the increase of the population during the same period.†

The Parish and other Churches.—St. Peter's, the parish church in Kirkgate, stands on the site of the old church, which, after an existence of many ages, was pulled down in the year 1838, and entirely rebuilt, in three years' time, at a cost of £38,000. The great expense of this costly structure was defrayed by voluntary subscription, stimulated by respect for Dr. Hook, then vicar of Leeds, now dean of Chichester. A greater work than the building of a church is due to Dean Hook. By surrendering the half of his living, he was enabled to create several ecclesiastical districts formed out of his parish, for each of which a church has since been built. St. Peter's is Gothic in style, with an interior made rich in effect by dark oak carvings and stained glass windows. The painting over the altar represents the "Agony in the Garden." At the end of the north aisle is a monument by Flaxman of "Mourning Victory," erected in honour of Captain Walker and Captain Beckett of Leeds, who fell at Talavera. Thoresby, the antiquary, and first historian of Leeds, who lived in Kirkgate, then a pleasant open street, was buried in the choir.

* The Leeds' Guide, 1806. List of Churches and Chapels, p. ix. † See Appendix.

The fact was unrecorded in any monument in the old church—an omission supplied in the new edifice, where, under the arch of a piscina of the fourteenth century, preserved from the old building, a memorial to Thoresby is appropriately placed. In the walls of the old church broken crosses of great antiquity were found; whence it is highly probable that a minster or church stood here in very ancient times, and Symeon of Durham is quoted as recording that Eanbald, a Saxon archbishop of York, died at Leeds in 769. One of the crosses discovered possesses an extraordinary interest, belonging to the age (937), and apparently erected in honour of King Olaff or Onlaf, known also as Onlaf Helga or the Holy, or St. Olave, who was the first Christian king of Norway, Denmark, Iceland, and of that part of England known by the name of the Danelagh, which included Yorkshire and all the country north of the river Humber. On this subject Mr. Mayhall says, "On taking down the old parish church of Leeds in 1838, a most interesting discovery was made of several sculptured stone crosses of the Anglo-Saxon (or Danish) period. The largest cross was thirteen feet in height; the others were less, and broken into fragments. One of the crosses contained in Runic characters the name of a king. The inscription was Cuni(g) Onlaf; that is, King Onlaf. Onlaf the Dane entered the Humber in 937, and subsequently became king of Northumbria, and a Christian."* One of the principal objects of his policy was to introduce or promote Christianity amongst the people in his extensive dominions, and we are told by Snorro Sturleson, in the "Lives of the Kings of Norway," that "in the spring of the year, Olave, named Helga or the Holy, had his fleet prepared, in which he was accustomed in the summer months to make his voyages through the southern regions" (including portions of the British islands), "holding solemn assemblies, in which he decided questions in dispute, and prescribed laws to the people. He also collected tribute where it was due. He further pursued his voyages in the autumn towards the most distant regions, where he initiated the inhabitants in the mysteries of Christianity, in his extensive territories, and promulgated statutes and laws. Having sent out embassies, he made many friends in Iceland, Greenland, and the Faroe Islands. He also sent the timber needful for building a temple in Iceland, where a temple was afterwards built, at a place called Thingwall (Tingwalla), where solemn courts of justice were

* Annals of Yorkshire. By John Mayhall. Vol. i. p. 16.

held yearly."* There are very ancient churches at York, London, and other places in England, dedicated to St. Olave; and it would give an additional interest to the history of the parish church at Leeds to find that it was in any way connected with him. We have already given Ralph Thoresby's account and description of the old church of Leeds in the reign of Queen Anne, and some slight notices which have been preserved from earlier times, in a previous part of this work. After the downfall of the Danes and the Saxons in England there was still a church and a presbyter in Leeds, mentioned in the Domesday Survey, and since that time the church has been rebuilt more than once. The following is a list of the vicars of Leeds from 1220 to 1873:—

LIST OF THE VICARS OF LEEDS.

Hugo,	1220	Johannes Thornton,	—
Alanus de Shirburn,	1242	Chr. Bradley,	1556
Johannes de Feversham,	1250	Alexander Fascet, or Fawcett,	1559
Galfridus de Sponden,	1281	Robert Cooke, B.D.,	1590
Gilbertus Gaudibus,	1316	Alex. Cooke, B.D.,	1614 / 1615
Alanus de Berewick,	1320		
William Brunby,	—	Henry Robinson, B.D.,	1632
Wm. Mirfield,	1392	Peter Saxton, M.A.,	1646
Johannes Snagtall,	1394	William Styles, M.A.,	1652
Robert Presselew,	1408	Johannes Lake, D.D.,	1661
Robert Newton,	—	Marmaduke Cooke, D.D.,	1663
William Saxton,	1418	Johannes Milner, B.D.,	1677
Johannes Herbert,	1424	Johan. Killingbeck, B.D.,	1690
Jacobus Baguley,	—	Josephus Cookson, M.A.,	1715
Thomas Clarel,	1430	Samuel Kirshaw, D.D.,	1746
William Evre, B.D.,	1470	Peter Haddon, M.A.,	1786
Johannes Frazer, Bp. of Ross,	1482	Richard Fawcett, M.A.,	1815
Martinus Collins,	1499	W. F. Hook, D.D.,	1837
Robert Wranwash, B.A.,	1500	James Atlay, D.D.,	1859
William Evre,	1508	Canon J. R. Woodford, D.D.,	1868
Johannes Thompson,			

St. John's Church.—The second of the Leeds churches, namely, that of St. John's, was built in the reign of King Charles I., and in the year 1638, entirely at the expense of John Harrison, the benefactor of all the best institutions of Leeds. Ralph Thoresby pronounced rather a warm eulogium on the architectural beauties of St. John's church, which gave rise to a somewhat severe and disparaging criticism by Dr. Whitaker, in his "Loidis and Elmete." Without interfering in this controversy, it may be well to give the following remarks on the subject by Sir Gilbert Scott, whose judg-

* Heimskringla, or Lives of the kings of Norway, Part 7.

ment strongly confirms the eulogium of Ralph Thoresby. He states "that the church stands alone among all the churches in this country, as an instance of the old feeling for church architecture extending to the days of King Charles, carried out with a richness, costliness, and beauty, which would do honour to the best periods of ecclesiastical architecture." He recommended that the church should be carefully repaired, retaining jealously every old feature, and disturbing nothing unnecessarily. "You will thus," he said to the trustees, "be handing down to many generations a rare and beautiful specimen of the church architecture of the Reformed English Church, erected at a period of which the specimens are more scarce than any other."* The church has been thoroughly repaired, the richly-scrolled panels of the roof being in good preservation. The living is a vicarage worth £500 per annum, in the patronage of the vicar, mayor, and three aldermen. Trinity Church was built chiefly by the contributions and solicitations of the Rev. Henry Robinson, the nephew of John Harrison. Like his father and his uncle, the founder of Trinity Church was a man of distinguished benevolence, expending nearly the whole of his income on public objects. This church was erected in the year 1721. The next church erected in Leeds, namely, that of St. Paul's, was built by the Rev. Miles Atkinson, on ground in Park Square which was the gift of Dr. Wilson, bishop of Bristol. It was opened in the year 1794. St. James's Church, a large octagonal building, was opened for divine worship in 1794. The worship here was for some time conducted on the Countess of Huntingdon's plan, by the original proprietors, who named it Zion Chapel. It was afterwards, however, purchased by the Rev. Mr. King, and consecrated by the archbishop of York in September, 1801.

Churches Erected in the Present Century.—During the first thirty years of the present century few churches were built in Leeds. One of them, St. Mark's, Woodhouse, was erected between the years 1823 and 1826, at a cost of about £10,000. At the close of 1872 it underwent extensive internal renovation. It contains a rich stained-glass window, illustrative of the leading events in the life of our Saviour, and a fine carved font of Caen stone, presented by Alderman Maclea, in 1853. St. Mary's, Quarry Hill, was erected in 1823–27, at a cost of about £12,500. In 1826 Christ Church, Meadow Lane, was built at a cost of about £10,457. These three were all built under parlia-

* Annals of Yorkshire, by John Mayhall; vol. ii. p. 684.

mentary grant, and have a general similarity of architectural style. St. Matthew's, Holbeck Moor, was erected by government in 1829-32 at a cost of nearly £4000, upon a site given by the marchioness of Hertford. The old church was an ancient structure. It is said to have been mentioned in a bull granted by Pope Alexander to Ralph Pagnell, who lived in the time of William the Conqueror. It appears to have been rebuilt, for Whitaker, in his " History of Leeds," says, " It was a mean building of uncertain antiquity, no remnant of the *original* structure now appearing." The register books commence in 1717. After the reconstitution of the diocese of Ripon in 1836, church building became much more active under the stimulus of systematic local effort. Towards the end of 1838 St. George's Church was consecrated. It was built by subscription at a cost of about £11,000, and is the principal evangelical church in the town. It contains a fine altar-piece by C. W. Cope, R.A. The church of Stanningley, in the parish of Leeds, is built in the Norman style, and was consecrated in 1841. The noble and ancient parish church of Leeds (St. Peter's) was in the same year re-opened (as already mentioned), after having been rebuilt and enlarged at a cost of £38,000. The tower contains a peal of thirteen bells, weighing upwards of eight tons. St. Luke's church, North Street, was also consecrated in 1841. It was intended chiefly for the use of the soldiers at the barracks. An interval of four years elapsed before any additional churches were opened in Leeds. That of St. Andrew, Cavendish Street (erected from designs by Sir Gilbert Scott, of London, as a monument to the memory of Mrs. Sinclair, wife of the Rev. W. Sinclair, the first incumbent of St. George's Church), was consecrated in 1845; as was also St. Saviour's Church, Ellerby Road. The latter was built by an anonymous benefactor, known to sympathize with Dr. Pusey and the Oxford Tracts' party, and was the first High church erected in the borough, the original cost being about £10,000. It was for many years the representative church of this section of the High Church party, and some years after it was opened a great sensation was caused by the secession of several of the curates to the Roman Catholic Church. The windows are filled in with stained glass of the finest quality, and the subjects are richly and most artistically treated. In 1847 St. Philip's Church was consecrated. It was built by subscription, at a cost of about £5000, upon a site given by Messrs. Gott. Meanwood Church, opened in October, 1849, was erected and endowed under the late Sir Robert Peel's Act, by the late Misses Beckett. All Saints' Church, Pontefract Lane, was opened in 1850. St. John's, Holbeck, dates from the same year, and was built from designs by Sir G. G. Scott, after the plan of the Temple Church, London. It was erected at the expense of the Messrs. Marshall, who endowed it with £150 per annum and £500 Three per cents. as a perpetual repair fund. The internal carving is very fine. St. Matthew's Church, Camp Road, was opened in 1851; St. Thomas', Melbourne Street, in 1852 (at the expense of Mr. M. J. Rhodes); St. Jude's, Hunslet Road, in 1853; New Wortley and Moor Allerton, both in 1853; St. Michael's, Buslingthorpe, in 1854; also in the same year, Burmantofts and Burley churches. In 1855 St. Barnabas', Holbeck, was opened, and was the last of the Leeds churches consecrated by the late Archbishop Longley, before his translation to the diocese of Durham. During the episcopate of Dr. Bickersteth the work of church building has continued active in Leeds, and indeed throughout the whole diocese. Amongst the churches which the bishop has consecrated in the parish of Leeds, are St. Mary's, Hunslet (rebuilt in 1864); St. John Baptist, New Town, in November, 1867; St. Chad's, Headingley, in January, 1868 (a beautiful church, erected in memory of the late Mr. William Beckett); St. Peter's, Hunslet Moor, in July of the same year; St. Clement's, Sheepscar, in September, 1868; St. Silas, Hunslet, in November, 1869; St. Wilfrid's Chapel (Grammar School), in January, 1870; St. Augustine's, Wrangthorn, in November, 1871; and, in 1872, Christ Church, Upper Armley; St. Luke's, Beeston Hill; and Holy Trinity, Armley Hall. Towards the cost of these churches the Church Extension Society has contributed at least £50,000, in some cases providing the site and endowment. Great as the work thus done has been, it forms only part of the work undertaken by the church in Leeds; for in connection with every new church there has grown up a school, and there has been developed a variety of spiritual agencies for extending religion and improving the moral character of the people.

Nonconformist and other Denominations.—The religious activity referred to above was not confined to the Church of England. The zeal and enthusiasm which resulted from the preaching of the two Wesleys and of Whitfield, affected the Nonconformist churches of Yorkshire even more directly and actively than the Church of

England. Life was given to the inert feeling existing amongst the masses of the people, and it has never again wholly slumbered. There have been periods of inactivity, times of apathy, when the religious denominations outside the pale of the church suffered from the same lethargy which prevailed within it; but these were simply the varying pulsations of life, and not its cessation. Nowhere has this new life manifested itself more vigorously than in the West Riding, and especially in Leeds. The history of Nonconformity in this part of Yorkshire would be the history of civil and religious liberty, and the result is seen in the influence which the Wesleyans, the Congregationalists, the Roman Catholics, the Unitarians, and the other religious denominations, exercise upon its public life. The older denominations in the town have a special history of their own. The mention of Mill Hill Chapel, built by the Presbyterians in 1672, and of Call Lane Chapel, built by the Independents in 1691, carry the mind back to a time when religious liberty, and even religious toleration in Leeds, were something very different from what they are now. After many changes the latter place of worship has been destroyed, to make way for a much needed improvement; and the former was rebuilt, in 1848, on its old site, by the Unitarians, and is now one of the handsomest churches belonging to that body in the north of England, whilst its congregation is one of the most wealthy and intelligent. Salem Chapel, a large, substantial, stone building, was finished in the year 1791. Albion chapel, which was for several years occupied by that brilliant and accomplished orator and excellent man, the Rev. Richard Winter Hamilton, D.D., was built in the year 1796. In 1836 Dr. Hamilton removed to the new chapel built for him in Belgrave Street, and he continued his pastorate there until his death in 1848; Albion Chapel in the meanwhile, and to the present (1873), being used by the Swedenborgians. East Parade Chapel, a fine building, Grecian Doric in style, was built in 1841, at a cost of £18,000, and for many years its pulpit was filled by the Rev. John Ely, one of the most eminent nonconformist ministers of the first half of the century. Queen Street Chapel was built in 1825 for the Rev. Thomas Scales, another of the old nonconformist worthies of Yorkshire. After a long interval a handsome chapel was erected at Headingley, chiefly by members of the Queen Street and East Parade congregations. It was opened in 1865. There are also chapels belonging to this body in Marshall Street, Holbeck, at Beeston Hill, and at Potternewton; and there are preaching rooms at Kirkstall and in other parts of the borough. The Baptists remained stationary for many years; but greater activity has lately been manifested, and two or three new chapels have recently been built. Their principal places of worship are in South Parade, Woodhouse Lane, and North Street. Of the more modern religious denominations the Wesleyan body occupy by far the most important position in the borough, both as regards the number of its members and the liberality of its congregations. John Wesley visited Leeds in 1745, and laid the foundation of the society as it now exists; and in 1771 the first chapel, afterwards known as the "Old Chapel," was erected in Boggart Fields, near St. Peter's Street—Albion Street Chapel, now occupied as a warehouse, being erected in 1802. The society has continued to progress, and there is a sense in which Leeds may now be considered the head quarters of Wesleyanism; for the munificence of its missionary collections have given it a pre-eminence of which it is justly proud. The pulpits of its several chapels have been held from time to time by the most distinguished members of Conference; and amongst the lay members of the body the name of the late Mr. William Smith, of Gledhow, the founder of what is known amongst Wesleyans as the "Gledhow Missionary Breakfast," is held in affectionate remembrance, as one of its most liberal and zealous supporters. The borough is divided into four circuits, including thirty places of worship, containing 22,025 sittings. The principal chapels are Brunswick, containing a fine organ erected at a cost of between £2000 and £3000, opened in 1826; Oxford Place, opened in 1836; St. Peter's, built on the site of the Boggart Fields' Chapel, and opened in 1835; Meadow Lane, opened in 1816; Hanover Place (1847), Richmond Hill (1849), and Roscoe Place (1862). There are also chapels connected with the body in all the out-townships, and it has (1873) been decided to erect three additional chapels, at Chapeltown, Roundhay, and Woodhouse Carr. In 1867 a handsome building was erected at Headingley, at a cost of nearly £20,000, as a training college for students for the ministry. It was opened in 1868; the Rev. John Farrar, formerly principal of Woodhouse Grove School, being appointed governor. The different sections of Wesleyans which have at different times seceded from the main body, have also chapels in the borough. The Primitive Methodists, the Methodist New Connection, and the Methodist Free Church are the most important of these; and the Belle-vue Chapel, the Woodhouse Lane, and Lady Lane chapels are amongst the most commodious places of worship in the town. The Society of Friends, who for more than a hundred years had a meeting house in Water Lane, removed in 1867 to a new and more commodious place of worship, erected in Woodhouse Lane. The Presbyterians, the Plymouth Brethren, the Bible Christians, and other minor religious denominations, have also several chapels, or preaching rooms. All these bodies have special organizations, as schools and missionary agencies, for promulgating their religious views. It may also be mentioned that the Jews have a synagogue in Belgrave Street. Distinct from these religious denominations, the Roman Catholics hold a position of growing importance. Leeds having recently been selected as the residence of the Bishop of Beverley, it has become the centre of ecclesiastical influence for that diocese. The first bishop was Dr. Briggs, and the present holder of the see is Dr. Cornthwaite. Apart from this, the church is increasing in numbers, mainly from the augmentation of the Irish population, but partly also from the unwearied zeal of its priests and religious orders. The first of the existing churches belonging to the Roman Catholics in Leeds was built in York Road, having a burial-ground attached to it. It was dedicated by the name of St. Patrick, and opened in 1832. The church in Park Row, dedicated by the name of St. Ann, a good example of the perpendicular style, was opened in 1838, and was then and is still the principal church in this part of the diocese. In 1853 a very handsome church was commenced on Richmond Hill, at the east end of the town, but it was not opened for several years, the chapels first opened being consecrated by Cardinal Wiseman. It was originally intended as a cathedral church; but the first design has not been entirely adhered to, and it is still (1873) incomplete. The cost so far has been about £20,000. It has been dedicated as the church of the Immaculate Conception. As in the case of St. Ann, many of the windows are filled in with rich stained glass, and it contains several very fine shrines; there is a conventual establishment and schools connected with it. A church was also built at Hunslet some years later, and still more recently one was erected in the Leylands. The Little Sisters of the Poor have a large establishment, still in course of construction, in Belle-vue Road, at the west end of Leeds.

It is estimated that during the ten years, from 1862 to 1872,

£133,680 was expended in improving the religious accommodation of Leeds, of which the members of the various denominational bodies contributed £71,380. This general outline, for it is nothing more, will give the reader some idea of the religious activity which has prevailed in this important town for two or three generations past.

The Leeds Library in 1873.—In Commercial Street is the old library, called the Leeds Library (founded in 1768), already mentioned. It is a proprietary library in the hands of 500 members, who are shareholders; and is governed by a president and committee. The number of works at the present time is upwards of 50,000, and it is one of the best-selected libraries in England. Some of the books bought nearly a century ago have now become very rare, especially the topographical works that were issued from the press of Bowyer and Nichols, about the time of the French revolution. The Hopkinson MSS. of Yorkshire and Lancashire pedigrees are most valuable. These are copies from Hopkinson's originals at Eshton Hall, made by Thomas Wilson, who added some particulars of his own. Wilson was a contemporary of Thoresby, and his copy of the Ducatus Leodiensis, with his notes, is also in the Leeds library. A collection of civil war tracts, and one of German and Latin tracts bearing upon the Reformation, deserve mention.

Leeds Public Library.—In addition to the Leeds library above described, a public library was formed at Leeds in the year 1868, under the powers of the Act which authorizes municipal corporations to establish libraries of that description for the general benefit of the public. In January, 1873, the number of volumes in the library exceeded 33,000, and the following table will show how extensively the advantages of the Leeds public libraries have been appreciated by the inhabitants:—

LEEDS PUBLIC LIBRARIES.
BOOKS LENT FOR HOME READING.*

Central Lending Library, from opening, April to December, 1872,	145,712
Hunslet Branch Library, from opening, October, 1870, to December, 1872,	65,840
Holbeck Branch Library, from opening, October, 1870, to December, 1872,	59,736
BOOKS CONSULTED.	271,288
† Reference Library, from opening, October, 1871, to December, 1872,	34,250
	305,538

* In nine months the stock, which was about 8000 at the commencement and is now about 10,000, has been issued more than fifteen times. The system of location, which is original, works admirably, the remaining stock left always being within reach of the attendant. The fiction shelves appear to the public almost empty.

† Newspapers and novels have been restricted from this room, therefore the issues are not quite so large as might be expected, as is also the case in the Birmingham Library, which is imitated in this respect.

VISITORS TO THE CENTRAL AND DISTRICT READING AND NEWS ROOMS (PERIODICALS).
Central Library, from opening, October, 1871, to December, 1872, ... 45,943
* Hunslet Library, from April, 1870, to December, 1872, ... 117,611
* Holbeck Library, from April, 1870, to December, 1872, ... 106,571
                                                                      270,125

The Philosophical Hall and Museum.—The Philosophical Hall, in Park Row, the home of the Leeds Philosophical and Literary Society, already fully described, was opened in 1821, as before mentioned, but greatly enlarged in 1862. It contains a handsome theatre for lectures, in which men of eminence are invited to lecture on the chief subjects of science and literature. Many gifts have been made to the museum, which is admirably arranged and well furnished, both with antiquities and objects of natural history. The collection of coins bequeathed to it by Mr. George Baron, of Drewton, is very valuable. The series of mammalia in the zoological room is said, by no less an authority than Professor Owen, to be "the most complete serial exposition of the class existing in England." The plants from the coal strata, exhibited in the geological room, have a special interest in this place, so rich in minerals. The library is well stocked with scientific books. There is a small industrial museum of specimens of the materials used in the local manufactures, which needs further development.

The Leeds Mechanics' Institute.—This valuable institution, as we have already stated, was established soon after the Literary and Philosophical Society had been instituted, and to a great extent by the same public-spirited men by whom the previous institution had been formed. Up to that period comparatively little had been done, either at Leeds or anywhere else, to raise the intellectual character of the labouring classes, or to establish amongst them those habits of thought and intelligence which have since that time so greatly advanced the social and political position of the mechanics and working classes of this and other large towns of the kingdom. In the list of the first officers of the Leeds Mechanics' Institution, established on the 1st December, 1824, we find the following names:—Benjamin Gott, Esq., president; John Marshall, Esq., and John Luccock, Esq., vice-presidents; John Darnton, Esq., treasurer; Mr. Todd, secretary; and the following directors:—The Rev. George Walker, head master

* The above reading rooms were opened in April, 1870.

of the Free Grammar School, (a man of the highest literary attainments); Mr. John Cawood, Mr. George Rawson, Dr. Williamson, and Dr. Hunter (at that time two of the leading physicians of Leeds), Mr. E. S. George, and Mr. William West (two eminent chemists), Mr. Edward Baines, jun., Mr. John Heaps, Mr. S. Petty, jun., Mr. Thompson, Mr. J. O. March, Mr. Joshua Dixon, Mr. Wood, and Mr. W. Davis. Originally the members of this valuable institution met in a confined and remote locality at the back of Park Row; but when it combined with the Literary Society, it removed to a commodious building in South Parade. "The ground floor," as Mr. Mayhall informs us, "was occupied for schools connected with the institute, and the upper consisted of a large room used as a lecture and news room, and also as a library. At the end was an elevated platform, from which the lectures were delivered. The walls were adorned with busts of literary and scientific men, and with an excellent full-length portrait of the late Edward Baines, M.P. (who was one of the best friends of the institution), painted by Richard Waller, of Leeds. The portrait was presented by subscribers, chiefly confined to the members of the institution. In a few years the number of books forming the library increased to 11,000 volumes, many of them of a scientific character, and circulating widely amongst the members. The officers of the society at this time consisted of a president, two vice-presidents, a treasurer, two honorary secretaries, and eighteen directors." *

The present Mechanics' Institute is a handsome building in the Italian style, designed by Mr. Cuthbert Brodrick, the architect of the town halls of Leeds and Hull, and situated in Cookridge Street. It is one of the most important institutions of its class in the north of England. Connected with it is a prosperous School of Art. The present building was raised in 1865, the old one having been found insufficient for its increasing number of members. The spacious theatre will accommodate 1500 persons, while the well-furnished library and reading-room are generally filled with readers. The Leeds Mechanics' Institution and Literary Society commenced its operations in the year 1842, by the union of the above two societies, and carried on its work for twenty-six years in the premises in South Parade. In June, 1868, the new building in Cookridge Street was opened, and the work of the institution transferred to it. Its

* The Annals of Yorkshire, compiled by John Mayhall, Esq., Clerk of County Court at Leeds, vol. i. p. 308.

course consists of the following literary and educational departments :—The library, reading room, lectures, and evening classes. From the foundation of the institution, the members and subscribers have had the power to elect the managing committee from year to year, and to make such alterations in the work of the society as they in general meeting assembled might decide upon. The members and subscribers to this department number 2273, many of whom are students in the evening classes. The great work, however, is of an educational character, and the various departments and classes have been added from time to time as necessity required. 1st, The elementary work in evening classes for reading, writing, and arithmetic, the pupils being adults and above thirteen years of age. There are (1873) 200 male and 100 female pupils attending these classes, taught by competent certificated teachers. The boys' department is now under the inspection of the Whitehall Department of Education. 2nd, The School of Art, under the supervision of the South Kensington Department, numbers 599 pupils. 3rd, The School of Science, in which the following subjects are taught :— Practical plane and solid geometry, building construction, machine construction, mathematics, chemistry, acoustics, light and heat, animal physiology and metallurgy : there are 129 pupils. 4th, French and German classes, numbering 64 students. 5th, Day schools. The committee have established day schools for the middle classes, both for boys and girls. A great want was felt in this respect so far as Leeds was concerned, and the results have fully justified the committee in the step thus taken. There are 290 boys and 190 girls attending these schools. The schools are a source of profit to the committee, and assist greatly in aiding it to carry on artistic, scientific, and elementary evening class work, which is at all times of a non-remunerative character. In 1872 the library contained 16,000 volumes.

The Yorkshire Union of Mechanics' Institutes was established in the year 1837 by Mr. Edward Baines and a few other friends of education, and of the best interests of the working classes. Its first annual meetings were held in Leeds. In 1838 the organization embraced sixteen institutes and about 4000 members. Its subsequent anniversaries have been held in nearly every considerable town in the county. Mr. Baines has remained its president from the first. It now numbers 113 mechanics' institutes, working men's clubs, and young men's institutes in its union, with an aggregate body of nearly 30,000 members, of whom about 1900 are females. The libraries of seventy institutes contain 135,259 volumes, the annual issue in 1872 having been 303,430. By the reports from these seventy institutes we find that 771 periodicals and 968 newspapers were taken in. Thirty-five institutes have had 196 lectures. Seventeen institutes have penny banks connected with them, in which £36,241 18s. 9d. was deposited in 1872, and the accumulated savings amounted to £51,063 18s. 1d. Thirty-four of the institutes are connected with the science and art department at South Kensington. Seventeen have grants from Whitehall for elementary teaching. Many of the institutes have very handsome buildings. The Leeds institute, as mentioned above, cost £27,000; that of Bradford, including several shops), £32,500; Saltaire, £25,000; and Keighley, £16,300. There are free libraries in connection with those at Sheffield, Middlesborough, and Hunslet. Keighley has a trade school in connection with it. There is also a prosperous institution at Huddersfield, having a fine building of its own, and upwards of 1000 members attending its evening classes—nearly all operatives. In connection with the union a circulating village library has been established, now containing about 2500 volumes. In 1854 Prince Albert gave £50 worth of books to the library, and her Majesty has since given a similar sum. Twenty-three villages avail themselves of this agency. The committee of the Union, consisting of delegates from the principal centres of population, meet monthly in Leeds or some other large town. The time of the agent, Mr. Frank Curzon, is wholly devoted to the Union, and in 1872 he paid above 200 visits to the institutes, his work being chiefly that of organization and superintendence. In 1872 a similar union of church institutes in Yorkshire was organized in Leeds.

The Leeds Church Institute, which has a beautiful building in Albion Place, and the Young Men's Christian Institute, in South Parade, possess valuable libraries, and are conducted on similar principles, as to classes and lectures, with those of the Mechanics' Institute, while they have in addition a decidedly religious character. The former is confined to members of the Church of England, but the latter is open to members of all religious denominations, and indeed to the public generally. The operations of the Young Men's Christian Institute include out-door work, undertaken with the view of promoting the moral and religious welfare of the neglected portions of the population, particularly of the young. About three years ago the secretary, Mr. Hind Smith, aided by Mrs. Smith, originated a movement for providing houses of resort for the working classes free of charge, where no intoxicating liquors should be sold, but where refreshments can be obtained at the option of the customers. These houses, under the general title of "The British Workman," or "public houses without drink," are now to be found in many large towns of the kingdom.

The Leeds Grammar School.—Immediately after the Reformation, in the year 1552, the 5th and 6th King Edward VI., the Grammar School of Leeds was founded by Sir William Sheafield, a clergyman or priest. The first school was built on an open spot in the suburbs, but the site of the school afterwards was occupied by the Pinfold in Edward Street. In 1624 the school was removed to the site on which it so long stood, at the North Town End, where it was erected or rebuilt in the year 1624, by John Harrison, the great benefactor of Leeds, in a pleasant field adjoining his own residence. There it remained until the present generation, being more than once enlarged and rebuilt. In the year 1856 a new and much finer site was found for this excellent institution on the borders of the great open space of Woodhouse Moor (a place dedicated to the health and enjoyment of the people of Leeds), where, in 1859, a handsome building, decorated English in style, was erected at a cost of £11,000, from designs by Mr. E. Barry, adding to its beauty. At a later period, a chapel in the same style was erected at the east end of the school. During the period of more than three hundred years, which has elapsed since it was first erected, this school has been a nursery of sound knowledge, in which a considerable portion of the most distinguished citizens of Leeds have been educated.

HEAD-MASTERS OF THE LEEDS FREE GRAMMAR SCHOOL SINCE THE SECOND ENDOWMENT BY HARRISON, IN 1624.

1624	{ Samuel Pullen, D.D., afterwards archbishop of Tuam.	1755	John Moore, M.A.
		1764	Samuel Brooke, M.A.
1630	Joshua Pullen, D.D. (his brother).	1778	Thomas Goodinge, LL.D.
1651	John Garnet, M.A.	1790	Joseph Whiteley, M.A.
1662	Michael Gilberts, M.A.	1815	George Page Richards, M.A.
1690	Edward Clerke, M.A.	1818	George Walker, M.A.
1694	Miles Farrer, M.A.	1830	Joseph Holmes, D.D.
1698	Thomas Dwyer, B.D.	1854	Alfred Barry, B.D., Cambridge.
1706	Thomas Dixon, M.A.	1862	{ William George Henderson, D.C.L., Oxon.
1712	Thomas Barnard, M.A.		
1750	Richard Sedgwicke, M.A.		

Mr. Mayhall gives the following account of the origin of this school:—" The first endowment of the Free Grammar School at Leeds is contained in the will of Sir William Sheafield, priest, dated 6th of March 1552, by which he vested in Sir John Neville, knight, and sixteen others as co-feoffees (co-possessors), certain copyhold lands situate near Sheepscar Bridge, 'for finding sustentation and living of one honest, substantial, and learned man to be a schoole maister, to teach and instruct freely for ever all such younge scholars, youths, and children as shall come and resort to him from time to time, to be taught, instructed, and informed in such a school house as shall be founded, and erected, and builded by the paryshioners of the said town and parish of Leeds; upon condition that if the parishioners should not find a school house, and also purchase unto the school master for the time being a sufficient living of other lands together with his gift, to the clear yearly value of £10 for ever, within four years after his decease, that the feoffees should stand seized to the use of the poor inhabitants of Leeds.' The testator directed that his feoffees and their heirs for ever should have the nomination, election, and appointment of the said schoolmaster, and gave them power to put him out for reasonable cause at their discretion; the best man's voice to take no more place than the honest poorest man of them.' In 1554 certain copyhold premises were surrendered by Richard Bank and his wife for the use and support of the school. In 1555 a feoffment was made by Sir William Armistead, with this curious declaration annexed to it, that 'the feoffees should employ the profits towards the finding of one priest, sufficiently learned to teach a free grammar school within the town of Leeds for ever, for all such as should repair thereto, without taking any money, more or less, for teaching of the said children or scholars, saving of one penny of every scholar to mention his name in the master's book, if the scholar have a penny, and if not enter and continue freely without any paying.' In 1595 certain copyhold premises were surrendered by John Moore and others, for the use and support of the same institution; and Christopher Hopton and others also surrendered a close, denominated the Calls, containing three acres, for the same purpose. Subsequent endowments in houses and lands were made by other parties. When the grammar school was first founded by Sir William Sheafield the building which was used for the purpose was in a very incommodious situation, where the Pinfold some years since stood, by the workhouse. Six years after, viz., in 1558, the 'New Chapel,' which, in spite of its name, was a very old building, was purchased of Queen Elizabeth and used as the grammar school, and there the operations of the institution were carried on for the period of sixty-six years."[*]

Endowed and Public Schools in Leeds.—Under the authority of the Schools Inquiry Commission of 1864, Mr. J. G. Fitch was appointed to inquire into the state and condition of the schools of Yorkshire. His general report was published in volume ix., and his special reports in volume xviii. They give a very full and carefully prepared account of the schools inspected by him. His inquiries in Leeds included the grammar schools, the two schools connected with the Mechanics' Institution, and an endowed school for primary education. Since his report was published, the Church of England has established middle class schools for boys and girls on the same principle as the schools connected with the Mechanics' Institution, and steps have been taken for erecting a suitable building for their accommodation. These include the whole of what may be called the public schools in the borough, distinct from mere elementary schools. The foundation of the grammar school dates from 1552, and its gross revenue from endowments in 1866 was £2454. Mr. Fitch says—"This rich and important school has long enjoyed a high reputation." The scheme which now (1873) governs it came into force in 1855, but it is understood that it will undergo further revision by the Endowed Schools Commissioners. The scheme provides four exhibitions of £50 each, tenable for four years each, at Oxford, Cambridge, or Durham. The curriculum of the school includes a classical and a commercial department; the foundationers pay ten guineas a year in the upper school and five in the lower; the non-foundationers fourteen guineas, if under fourteen years of age, and sixteen if above that age. The other endowed school was founded in 1705, and has a gross income of £470, of which £285 is applied for education, including donations of £10 each to eighteen national schools. The balance is applied for "other benefit of scholars." The education is at present confined to girls. The scheme of this foundation will also come under the revision of the Endowed Schools Commissioners. The schools connected with the Mechanics' Institution and the Church of England middle-class schools give, in the boys' departments, a

[*] Annals of Yorkshire, by John Mayhall, Esq., vol. i. p. 49.

commercial and mathematical education, with instruction also in Latin and modern languages; and in the girls' department, an education suitable to the position in life of the scholars, with instruction in French, drawing, and music. The West Riding Educational Board, of which Mr. H. H. Sales, of Leeds, is the secretary, has been established to promote and extend the elementary examination of scholars, in co-operation with the Society of Arts, the Department of Science and Art, and the universities of Oxford, Cambridge, and Durham. It has since its formation taken an active part in promoting secondary education in Yorkshire; and in 1872, as one of the results of its labours, a scheme was issued for the establishment at Leeds of "The Yorkshire College of Science," for the purpose of supplying instruction in those sciences which are applicable to the industrial arts, particularly in their relation to manufactures, engineering, mining, and agriculture. It is proposed to raise £60,000 for this object, and in the beginning of 1873 several munificent donations were promised, the total amount exceeding £22,000.

Elementary Education in Leeds.—The Elementary Education Act was introduced into Leeds in 1870, the first school board being elected on the 28th November of that year. The election was attended with a good deal of excitement, political and denominational feeling running very high. The result was a denominational rather than a political board, seven of the members being Churchmen, three Wesleyans, and two Roman Catholics; the other members belonging respectively to the Independent, Methodist, and Unitarian denominations. The following is a list of the first board:—

Sir Andrew Fairbairn (chairman).	George Patrick Kelly.
John Jowitt (vice-chairman).	Rev John Hutton Fisher Kendall.
William James Armitage.	William Long.
William Barker.	William Middleton.
William Beckworth.	James Wilson, jun.
John Ellershaw.	Jabez Woolley.
Edwin Gaunt.	
John Deakin Heaton, M.D.	T. T. Dibb (solicitor).
William Glover Joy.	W. Lee (clerk).

As soon as the board could get into working order, it was decided to make a thorough investigation into the school provision and requirements of the borough. The result of this inquiry is shown in the following table:—

Sub-district.	Total Population, Census 1871.	Children to be provided for.	Available Accommodation.		Deficiency
			Existing.	Projected	
South-East and Whitkirk,.	29,505	5,426	4,428	976	22
North,	49,624	9,498	3,455	2,141	3,907
West,	60,615	10,159	7,000	1,188	1,971
Kirkstall,	13,941	2,307	1,456	298	553
Chapeltown,	7,314	1,196	642	527	27
Hunslet,	37,284	7,244	2,279	1,630	3,335
Holbeck,	19,927	3,680	2,561	531	588
Wortley,	31,110	5,942	3,827	1,206	909
Bramley,	9,880	1,888	1,082	425	381
	259,200	47,340	26,730	8,922	11,693

It was decided to make provision for this deficiency, and there are now (1873) forty-five school departments under the control of the board, having fifty-two certificated teachers, thirty-four assistants, and 180 pupil teachers. Nearly the whole of the present schools are provisionally occupied. Sites for eighteen new schools have been secured at an average cost of about 5s. per yard. Three schools are in course of erection, and plans are prepared for four others. The effect of the labours of the board on the education of the district, is shown in the following analysis of the increase in attendance from November, 1870 :—

DENOMINATIONAL SCHOOLS.				BOARD SCHOOLS.			
	Nov.1870.	Jan. 1873	Increase.		Nov 1870	Jan. 1873.	Increase.
I. Existing in 1870. Number on Roll,	21,193	22,327	1,134	I. Schools existing in 1870 transferred to the School Board. Number on Roll,	1,181	2,458	1,277
II. New Denominational schools since Nov. 1870. Number on Roll,		4,497	4,497	II. New Board Schools. Number on Roll,		7,801	7,801
Total Denominational Schools,		26,824	5,631	Total Board Schools, . .		10,259	9,078

Grand Total on Roll, 37,083. Increase in two years, 14,709, being 66 per cent.
Grand Average Attendance, 21,990. Increase in two years, 8475, being 63 per cent.

The board has worked with complete harmony, and it has been enabled in consequence to carry out the Act without serious difficulty.

Men connected with Literature, Science, Invention, and the Arts in the Borough of Leeds.—The great object with which men assemble in vast numbers in large manufacturing and commercial towns, such as those that exist in Yorkshire and Lancashire, and which have so wonderfully increased in population, wealth, and intelligence during the last hundred years, is the carrying on of the useful arts affecting the daily wants of all classes of society. But great cities and towns have always been nurseries of intelligence, from the time of Tyre, Athens, and Florence, which were seats of knowledge and the fine arts, as well as of trade and commerce. The cities and towns of England have produced many men of eminent learning and great literary and scientific attainments, as well as numerous inventors and promoters of the useful arts. Leeds has had its fair share of men of this description; and now that intelligence and education are so widely diffused amongst the populations of our large manufacturing cities and towns, there is every reason to hope that the number will increase. Our limits will not allow us to do more than enumerate the natives of this town who have taken a considerable part in increasing the general amount of knowledge, intelligence, science, and art.

Sir William Sheafield, the first founder of the Grammar School at Leeds, in the year 1552, well deserves to be mentioned at the head of the men of letters. At that time Latin was everywhere the great instrument of communicating thought and knowledge; and though the English, French, German, and Italian languages have all of them since taken a very high position, they have not superseded the value either of Latin or of Greek, in their influence in refining the taste and in extending the knowledge of mankind. Sir William Sheafield lived at the time when the English intellect was beginning to expand into freedom of thought, and he, and the other distinguished men who gave to the minds of their contemporaries the direction which they have since taken, deserve to be regarded as amongst the benefactors of their race. The same praise is due to John Harrison, and other liberal benefactors of the Leeds Grammar School, who, though not themselves scholars, expended the fruits of their industry in encouraging learning, religion, and every object that exalts humanity.

Amongst the early scholars connected with this town was the Right Reverend Ralph Baynes, said by Thoresby to have been born at Knowstrop, near Leeds. In 1554 he was raised to the bishopric of Lichfield and Coventry. The most remarkable circumstance in his history was his early knowledge and cultivation of the Hebrew language, which, after having been almost forgotten in Europe for several centuries, was revived in Germany by the distinguished Hebrew scholar Reuchlin, who in the year 1506 published his great work entitled "De Rudimentis Hebraicis," at Pforzheim, in that country. It was only very slowly that this language, which contains the ancient records of the human race, made its way in France and in England; and Ralph Baynes, though a zealous Roman Catholic, appears to have been one of the first persons in England who studied the language with sufficient care to write an account of its grammatical structure. The first and second vicars of Leeds after the Reformation seem also to have been distinguished scholars, as well as zealous supporters of the reformed religion. The Rev. Robert Cooke, B.D., born at Beeston, near Leeds, in the year 1550, and who was appointed vicar of Leeds in 1590, was educated in Sir William Sheafield's foundation, the original Grammar School at Leeds, and was, according to Anthony à Wood (the author of "Athenæ Oxonienses"), "the most noted disputant of his time." His principal work was on patristic literature, and was entitled "Censura Patrum." Ralph Thoresby describes him as the glory of the place (Leeds). He died in the year 1614, and was interred in his own church. The Rev. Alexander Cooke, B.D., who was a brother of the preceding eminent man, and succeeded him as vicar of Leeds, is described by Anthony à Wood as "being admirably read in the controversies between the Protestants and Papists, versed in the fathers and schoolmen, witty and ingenious, but a great Calvinist." Ralph Thoresby says that he was a "person of great learning, reading, and judgment, of prodigious industry in consulting so great a number of authors, and of great sagacity in making so accurate observations on them." He died June, 1632, and was interred in the chancel of his parish church, near the remains of his brother, but without any memorial.[*]

Amongst the laity of Leeds, the first who displayed any great superiority in literature and the arts were Christopher Saxton (the chief geographer of the reign of Queen Elizabeth, whom Camden describes as a most excellent chorographer), and the Thoresbys, father and son. John Thoresby, the father of Ralph, was a merchant at Leeds, afterwards an alderman of the borough, and in the great civil war commanded a regiment of trained

[*] Leeds Worthies, by the Rev. R. V. Taylor, p. 60.

bands in support of the Parliament. According to an eye-witness[*] he was one of the few officers of the trained bands who stood resolutely by Sir Thomas Fairfax, in the battle of Marston Moor; and this was either the commencement or the renewal of the warm friendship between the Fairfaxes and the Thoresbys, which continued undiminished until the death of Ralph Thoresby, fifty years later. Alderman, or Colonel, John Thoresby was the founder of the Thoresby Museum at Leeds, which was, in the opinion of the learned Spanheim, one of the finest collections of coins ever made by a private collector, and also contained a very large collection of objects of natural history. Although the science of geology could scarcely be said to exist at that time, the geology of the age consisting chiefly of extravagant theories as to the formation of the earth, unsupported by any sufficient evidence, yet a few men were beginning to lay a solid foundation for this great science, by collecting specimens of extinct plants and races of animals, and by comparing and contrasting them with still existing species and varieties. Dr. Martin Lister, a physician of great eminence, residing at York at this time, is regarded by Humboldt as one of the founders of this branch of geology; and his observations must have been greatly facilitated by the fine collections of geological specimens made by the Thoresbys and other collectors, who preserved everything at all curious that was brought to them, under the general name of natural curiosities, and even sent their surplus specimens to the Ashmolean Museum at Oxford.

The age of Ralph Thoresby, which terminates with the reign of George I., seems to have been a period marked by great intelligence in this part of England as well as in London, where it was regarded as the Augustan age of English literature, of which William Congreve, the dramatist, said to have been born at Bardsey-Grange, near Leeds, was one of the brightest ornaments. Thoresby mentions with some pride that there were then six members of the Royal Society connected with the county of York, and that the same county had produced several archbishops and bishops within a single generation. Amongst the members of the Royal Society thus referred to were Ralph Thoresby himself, whose forte was antiquities, and who was not only a good Latin scholar, but also very well acquainted with the Anglo-Saxon language and literature. Another member of the Royal Society was Cyril Arthington, the

[*] Robert Gledhill, of Cromwell's Life Guards or Ironsides, Thoresby's Diary, vol. i. p. 331.

builder of Arthington Hall, in Wharfedale, but who had also a town house in Boar or Burh Lane, Leeds. A third member was Mr. Kirk, a Leeds merchant, and one of the projectors of the Aire and Calder Navigation, who resided at Cookridge Hall, about five miles from Leeds, where he formed grounds, commanding some of the finest views in Yorkshire, and laid them out on the plan of landscape gardening that prevailed in the time of Louis XIV. He also collected much information as to the Roman and other ancient remains found at Adel; and examined the registers of Adel church, with a view to describing the laws of population. The fourth and most distinguished of the Yorkshire members of the Royal Society at that time was Dr. Bentley, the greatest Greek scholar and critic of his age, who was a native of Oulton, near Leeds, and a friend and frequent visitor of Ralph Thoresby. Another member was Sir Joseph Copley, Bart., then of Sprotborough Hall, near Doncaster; and the sixth was the Hon. Mr. Molesworth, the author of an interesting account of Denmark, in which country he had served with the embassy. Amongst the archbishops and bishops whom Thoresby speaks of as natives of Yorkshire were Dr. Sharp, archbishop of York, a native of Bradford; Dr. Tillotson, archbishop of Canterbury, a native of Sowerby bridge, near Halifax; Dr. Margetson, archbishop of Armagh, a native of Drighlington, between Leeds and Bradford; Dr. Bramhall, archbishop of Armagh, a native of Pontefract; and Dr. Lake, bishop of Chichester, a native of Halifax, and for a time vicar of Leeds. Amongst other men of learning, at Leeds and in the neighbourhood, mentioned by Ralph Thoresby, were Mr. Bathurst, a good translator of Italian poetry; the Rev. Mr. Milner, vicar of Leeds, the first person who kindled the love of antiquities in the mind of Ralph Thoresby, by remarking in one of his sermons in the parish church, that Leeds was mentioned nearly a thousand years ago by the Venerable Bede. Thoresby assisted in drawing plans of Leeds, and gives a picture or sketch of the town in his "Ducatus;" he also assisted in making the surveys for the Aire and Calder Navigation. In every way he appears to have contributed to the mental development and the social improvement of his fellow-townsmen. He kept up a friendly intercourse with a learned tradesman of Leeds, whom he describes as the "Saxon saddler," and he has preserved numerous particulars of all the Yorkshire antiquaries of that age; including Hopkinson, the great collector of Yorkshire records, who resided at Lofthouse, near Wakefield; Dr. Sharp, archbishop of York, and all the Sharps of Horton, near Bradford, his relatives, who were a family of extraordinary talent; Abraham de la Pryme, a native of Thorne, who wrote the first history of the town and port of Hull; Dean Gale of York, an antiquary of almost unrivalled learning; and every man of any literary note who resided within the county of York in his time.

Almost immediately after the time of Thoresby, John Smeaton, who may be justly regarded as one of the principal founders of the science of civil engineering, was born at Austhorpe, near Leeds, and spent great part of his life in enriching the county of York, as well as the kingdom in general, with magnificent public works, including the Eddystone Lighthouse, the works for upholding London Bridge, and the higher and more difficult parts of the Calder Navigation from Wakefield to Halifax. In a different but not less useful and necessary branch of science was William Hey, F.R.S., a native of Pudsey, near Leeds, but who was educated and spent the whole of his honourable and useful career in that town, and for more than half a century held the highest rank amongst the professors of medicine and surgery in this part of England. About the same period Dr. Joseph Priestley (born at Birstall, near Leeds, and long resident in the town as minister of Mill Hill Chapel), one of the greatest of English chemists, tried at Leeds many of those experiments, which earned for him so high a rank amongst the founders of the modern science of chemistry. In the year 1720 Leeds produced that accomplished painter, Benjamin Wilson, F.R.S., the father of the gallant General Sir Robert Wilson. At an earlier period William Lodge had also acquired a high reputation as an artist; and Birkenhout, the son of a Dutch merchant, but himself born in Leeds, displayed great learning in natural history, and in several branches of literature.

In the present century Leeds has produced, or enrolled amongst its sons, many men whose talents have exercised a lasting and beneficial influence on society. Amongst these we place great inventors, or introducers of new inventions, whose skill, judgment and perseverance have enabled them to establish new forms of industry, which have had a lasting influence on the communities amongst which they have dwelt. In the first rank in this class we place John Marshall, who was afterwards one of the members for the county of York, and Benjamin Gott, who held for half a century the highest position amongst their fellow-townsmen. They were amongst the great organizers of the most important branches of modern industry, and were also great promoters of knowledge and education amongst the labouring classes. Mr. Marshall was the author of an interesting work, entitled "The Economy of Social Life," which was intended to explain, to the working classes more especially, some of the most important doctrines of political economy. Amongst the inventors of the useful arts who have taken part in the business of Leeds during the present century, we may mention Mr. Matthew Murray, an eminent engineer, who began life as an engine-smith or machine-smith in the neighbourhood of Newcastle-on-Tyne, but who came to Leeds when a young man, and was so fortunate as to obtain the friendship of Mr. Marshall, and to assist in carrying out, and also in suggesting, improvements in the manufacture of flax. This was the commencement of a most successful career, in the course of which he attained the highest rank in his profession. He it was who made the first locomotive that worked regularly upon any railway, namely, the engine erected by him for Mr. Blenkinsop to work the Middleton Colliery Railway, near Leeds. He was the inventor of a heckling-machine, in the year 1805, for which he received a gold medal from the Royal Society, presented by the duke of Sussex. He also was one of the earliest English builders of a steam-boat, which was tried on the river Aire. The invention of the locomotive by Mr. John Blenkinsop, from a patent taken out by him in the year 1811, and placed by him in the hands of Messrs. Fenton, Murray, and Wood, was also one of the greatest steps towards the establishment of the modern railway. Mr. Blenkinsop's engine began running on the railway from the Middleton Colliery to the town of Leeds, a distance of about three miles and a half, on the 12th of August, 1812. And it was the first commercially successful engine ever laid upon any railway. We have already mentioned the long-continued and persevering efforts of the Brandling family, the owners of the Middleton collieries, to establish a railway from those collieries to the town of Leeds. We well remember the interest that was excited by the opening of Mr. Blenkinsop's railway; and a few years later, in 1820, Mr. Thomas Gray, a native of Leeds, published a work on the adoption and extension of the railway system, the general views of which greatly resemble those put forth by Mr. Richard

Lovell Edgeworth, and quoted in an earlier part of this work. Mr. Gray's work was entitled "Observations on a general Iron Railway or Land Steam Conveyance, to supersede the necessity of Horses in all Public Vehicles, showing its vast superiority in every respect over all the present pitiful methods of Conveyance by Turnpike Roads, Canals, and Coasting Traders." Although the plans thus indicated have since been carried out with immense advantage to the nation and the world, they did nothing to promote the interests of Mr. Gray; but since his death Queen Victoria, with her usual kindness and benevolence, granted a small pension to his widow, which may be accounted as a national and royal acknowledgment of real services to the country. In somewhat more recent times the reputation of Leeds, as a scene of manufacturing invention, has been upheld by several very eminent men. Amongst them we may mention the late Sir Peter Fairbairn, the brother of Sir William Fairbairn, Bart., and the father of Sir Andrew Fairbairn, of Leeds, a member of a family which will ever hold a high rank in the records of British industry and invention. Together with him we may name the late Charles Gascoigne Maclea, Esq., for many years a member of the firm of Maclea & March. We may also mention amongst the engineers whose genius has done honour to the town of Leeds, the late John Fowler, the inventor of the steam-plough, an instrument which will probably change the character of agriculture in all parts of the world. Along with mechanical inventions we may include the discoveries in the science of chemistry, especially such as have tended to advance the industry of this and other districts. Amongst the most promising of the young men who took part in that great advance in science, art, and literature, which attended the forming of the Leeds Philosophical Society, was Mr. Edward S. George, F.L.S., the honorary curator of the Leeds Philosophical Society, and a leading member of the well-known firm of Messrs. Thomas George & Sons. He died at the early age of twenty-nine, having only had time to show the superiority of his talents. His friend and associate in science, William West, F.R.S., had a longer time to develop his eminent talents, and in the year 1846 the fellowship of the Royal Society was conferred upon him for distinguished attainments in chemical science.

In general literature we may mention the following writers, whose names deserve to be remembered :—John Luccock, one of the first English travellers who visited South America after the removal of the seat of government from Lisbon to Brazil, and who wrote interesting "Notes on Rio Janeiro and the Southern Parts of Brazil in 1808-18," having, before he left England, published an "Account of the Nature and Properties of Wool, with description of the English Fleece," published at Leeds in the year 1805. Matthew Talbot, the author of an "Analysis of the Holy Bible," a work of extraordinary labour, and which occupied the mind and the time of its author for many years, and is still the source from which other works on the same subject have been drawn. A few years later Dr. Thomas Dunham Whitaker, who had resided in Leeds in his early years, and was descended by the female line from the Thoresbys, produced through the press of Leeds some of his many learned and tasteful works. He was a copious as well as an elegant writer, and his works entitled "Thoresby's History of Leeds, with additions," published at Leeds in 1816, and his "Loidis and Elmete, or a History of the Lower Portions of Airedale, Wharfedale, and the Vale of Calder," published in 1816, are alike distinguished by taste and learning. He was an accomplished scholar and a man of fine taste; but he had a prejudice against manufactures which somewhat interfered with the value of those portions of his works which relate to the manufacturing districts. At a somewhat later period Michael Thomas Sadler, M.P., F.R.S., who was born in Derbyshire in the year 1780, but who came to reside in Leeds while still a young man, published a number of works, chiefly upon questions affecting the interests of the labouring classes, which attracted great attention at the time, and were amongst the causes of his being elected a member of Parliament at three successive elections, in the years 1829-30-31. His works were entitled "Ireland, its evils and their remedies," and two volumes on the Law of Population, in opposition to the opinions of Malthus. Mr. Sadler was a very eloquent and brilliant speaker, although he went into Parliament comparatively late in life, having been elected in 1829, and having died in the year 1835, in the fifty-sixth year of his age. We have already spoken of the learning of Mr. Sadler's friend and associate, Mr. William Osburn. His works entitled "History of Egypt," published in the year 1854, and his "Account of the Religions of the World," are of permanent interest.

In addition to Dr. T. D. Whitaker's topographical works, many works on similar subjects have appeared in Leeds in the present century. The first Edward Baines devoted a considerable period of his time to the history of his native county of Lancaster, which still holds a high position amongst the topographical works of the age. He had the same pleasure in writing the history of his native county of Lancaster, that his third son has had in producing the present history of his native county of York. He was also ably assisted by his second son, the present member for the borough of Leeds, in writing his "History of the Reign of George III.," a period of sixty years of unrivalled interest in the history of this country; and since that time the younger Edward Baines has written the "History of the Cotton Trade," has supplied the history of the woollen trade contained in this work, and has taken an active part in advancing the intellectual improvement of his fellow-townsmen, who showed their appreciation both of his and of his father's services, by conferring upon both of them the greatest honour which they had the power to give, namely, that of representing them in Parliament for a long course of years. Dr. Hook, the dean of Chichester, was for twenty-two years the vicar of Leeds, and during his residence published a "Church History," "Ecclesiastical Biography," "Devotional Library," and other works. Since his removal to Chichester he has been engaged on the "Lives of the Archbishops of Canterbury." James Wardell, the author of the "Municipal History of Leeds," has written several minor works on archæological subjects, all displaying considerable research and patient study.

The Local Press of Leeds.—Leeds was one of the first provincial towns that availed itself of the establishment of the freedom of the press, on the accession of the house of Hanover, to support and encourage the establishment of a local press for the instruction of its inhabitants, and to promote that free discussion which is one of the principal instruments for forming and directing public opinion in this country. The *Leeds Mercury* was first established by Mr. James Lister in the year 1718; and after having been discontinued for some time, it was re-established in 1767 by Mr. Bowling, who conducted it for twenty-seven years. He was succeeded by Messrs. Binns and Brown, who disposed of it to the first Edward Baines, in the year 1800. In his hands it became an instrument for free yet temperate discussion, in addition to its previous service as a means of diffusing local and general knowledge. The first Edward Baines continued his connection with the *Leeds Mercury* to the close of his life, assisted by his sons Mr. Edward and Mr. Frederick Baines. The *Leeds Mercury* has thus been in his family for upwards of seventy years, and is now published as a daily morning paper. The *Leeds Intelligencer* was also in the hands of the first Mr. Griffith Wright and his descendants for not less than seventy years, having belonged successively to the first Griffith Wright, to Thomas Wright his son, and to the second Griffith Wright, the son of the above, from the year 1754 to the year 1818. It was then transferred to other proprietors, and is now conducted as a daily morning paper under the title of the *Yorkshire Post and Leeds Intelligencer*. The *Leeds Times* was established by Mr. Edward Bingley in the year 1838, and afterwards passed into the hands of the present proprietors. Amongst the men of ability connected with the local press of Leeds we may mention, in addition to those already named, Alaric Alexander Watts, a poet of considerable taste, who conducted the *Leeds Intelligencer* for some time, whilst it belonged to Messrs. Robinson and Hernaman. We may also mention amongst the conductors of the *Leeds Times*, Mr. Robert Nicoll, a young but able man, with a fine poetical taste, as well as a good prose writer, who published in 1835 a volume of poems which was well received, and which has passed through several editions, and who edited the paper until he was cut off by a premature death; and Dr. Samuel Smiles, the popular author of "Self-help," and the "Lives of George Stevenson" and of many of our greatest engineers. The *Times* is still issued as a weekly journal. There are also two evening papers, the *Leeds Express*, established in 1867, and the *Leeds Daily News*, established in 1872.

Progress of Leeds from 1861 to 1873.—The Preliminary Report of the Census of the United Kingdom, taken in the year 1871, and published at the end of the year 1872, shows that the population of Leeds, Sheffield, Bradford, Halifax, Huddersfield, Dewsbury, and Wakefield; of the seaports of Hull, Scarborough, Whitby, and Middlesborough; and that of the county of York generally— increased with almost unexampled rapidity during the ten years which intervened between the census of 1861 and that of 1871. The following returns from the tables given in the Preliminary Report of the last census, show what has been the progress of population during the last ten years, and what is now the population of each of the Yorkshire parliamentary and municipal boroughs :—

YORKSHIRE:

HOUSES AND POPULATION, IN THE CITIES AND BOROUGHS OF YORKSHIRE, HAVING DEFINED MUNICIPAL OR PARLIAMENTARY LIMITS, IN 1861 AND 1871.

Note.—Towns not being either corporate under the Municipal Reform Act, nor sending Members to Parliament, do not appear in this table.

City or Borough.		Inhabited Houses.		Population.		Increase or Decrease of Population between 1861 and 1871.
		1861.	1871.	1861.	1871.	
Bradford (Yorks.),	M & P*	22,518	29,413	106,218	145,827	39,609
Dewsbury,	M	3,639	4,999	18,148	24,773	6,625
	P (n)	—	11,196	—	54,943	
Doncaster,	M	3,594	4,872	16,406	18,758	2,352
Halifax,	M (a)	} 7,807	{ 13,795	} 37,014	{ 65,124	28,110
	P (e)		13,795		65,124	28,110
Hedon,	M (i)	—	231	—	992	—
Huddersfield,	M (l)	—	14,752	—	70,253	
	P (e)	6,955	15,612	34,877	74,358	39,481
Hull,	M	} 19,516	{ 25,134	} 97,661	{ 121,598	23,937
	P (e)		25,455		123,111	25,450
Knaresborough,	P	1,318	1,271	5,402	5,205	— 197
Leeds,	M & P	44,651	55,943	207,165	259,201	52,036
Malton,	P	1,694	1,699	8,072	8,168	96
Middlesborough,	M (a)	3,117	6,827	18,992	39,585	20,593
	P (n)	—	8,026	—	40,643	—
Northallerton,	P	1,058	1,084	4,755	4,961	206
Pontefract,	M	1,122	1,149	5,346	5,372	26
	P	2,596	2,616	11,736	11,242	— 494
Richmond (Yorks.),	M	863	904	4,290	4,443	153
	P (e)	1,046	1,104	5,134	5,364	230
Ripon,	M & P	1,382	1,406	6,172	6,805	633
Sheffield,	M & P	38,052	48,521	185,172	239,947	54,775
Thirsk,	P	1,205	1,300	5,350	5,735	385
Wakefield,	M	4,781	} 5,632	23,350	} 28,079	4,729
	P (e)	4,773		23,150		
Scarborough,	M & P	3,940	5,161	18,377	24,244	5,867
Whitby,	P	2,464	2,842	12,051	13,082	1,031
York City,	M	8,242	9,441	40,433	43,796	3,363
	P *	9,162	10,268	45,385	50,761	5,376

The following note is attached to the official census return by the Author of these Preliminary Remarks :—The minus sign (—) prefixed to any of the numbers in this column, indicates that the population decreased between 1861 and 1871 to the extent stated. It must be borne in mind, in reading this column, that as regards all cities and boroughs whose designations (M or P)* are followed by an italic letter within brackets, the increase of their population is partly due to the extension of their areas.

The author of the Preliminary Census Report, from which the above official return of the population of Leeds and the other parliamentary and municipal cities and boroughs of Yorkshire is taken, makes the following general observations on the progress of Yorkshire, from 1861 to 1871 :—

"Relatively," he says, "the increase in Yorkshire is much greater than it was in the previous ten years, 1851-61; and greater than

* Municipal and Parliamentary.

the increase of Lancashire in the last ten years. The reason is easily explained: the American war, which was Lancashire's difficulty, was Yorkshire's opportunity, of which her sagacious heads not slowly availed themselves. The rise in the cost of cotton raised the demand for woollen stuffs, and wool was attracted in large quantities, as the Board of Trade returns show. Independently of this circumstance, the supply and demand for wool, short and long, invaluable as the staple of clothing in these climates, and produced in immense quantities by our colonists, increased. The Board of Trade returns show, comparing the three years 1858–60 with the three years 1868–70, that the average annual import of wool (sheep, lamb, and alpaca) rose from 136,000,000 to 258,000,000 lbs. Adding wool of home growth and deducting wool exported, no less than 288,512,000 lbs. were left, according to the estimate of Mr. A. Hamilton ("Journal of Statistical Society," December 1, 1870), for home consumption in 1869. The increase of production has been greater than the increase of workers, for the obvious reasons that coal power is so largely converted into work by the steam engine and improved machinery."

Sources of Supply of Wool in 1872.—The imports of wool, the greatest material of the manufactures of Leeds, in 1872 amounted to more than one million bales; and were derived from the following countries, none of which, except Spain and Germany, supplied England with any considerable quantity of wool at the beginning of the present century:—Australia and Van Diemen's Land, 418,125 bales; New Zealand, 104,584 bales; Cape of Good Hope, 138,892 bales; Germany, 24,276 bales; Spain, 2983 bales; Portugal, 12,815 bales; East Indies, 67,440 bales; Peru and Chili, 42,009 bales; River Plate, 17,343 bales; Iceland and Denmark, 6639 bales; United States, 1638 bales; coasts of the Mediterranean, 64,035; and other countries, 15,376 bales. Adding to this amount of wool 32,558 bales of alpaca and 30,502 of mohair, we have a total of 1,018,169 bales. Large as this quantity is, it is less than the import of 1871 by 82,000 bales.

"Since the census of 1861 the population of Huddersfield and that of Halifax nearly doubled (in some degree owing to the extension of their limits); Bradford has increased largely; and Leeds, also the centre of the principal manufactures. Sheffield, the great city of steel and cutlery, has an ample increase; so has Hull, the great eastern port. Scarborough, the delightful watering-place of the north, is increasing every year in attraction and population. Guisborough district, in the North Riding, south of the Tees, is increasing rapidly in population; so also are parts of the Whitby and Pickering districts. Yorkshire is in some respects a northern compendium of England; it has the marshes, the alluvial soil, and the chalk cliffs of the south, the oolitic formation of the midland counties; the new red sandstone formation; the limestone and the rich coal measures; it has mountains, crags, moors, wolds, and fair vales, adorned by many an abbey; there are Craven, Cleveland, Wharfedale, Wensleydale, and Teesdale; its waterfalls are among the finest known; the rivers, with the Ouse as their chief, fed by many sister streams, water the whole land, supply the canals, and are discharged into the estuary of the tidal Humber, on which Hull and Grimsby are harbours. Yorkshire occupies the whole region of the Humber and of its affluent streams, except the Trent. Railways connect all its great centres of population."

PROGRESS OF POPULATION OF THE BOROUGH OF LEEDS IN THE DECENNIAL PERIOD FROM THE CENSUS OF 1861 TO THE CENSUS OF 1871.

Wards, &c.	Houses.			Persons.			Population in 1861.	Increase.
	Inhabited.	Uninhabited.	Building.	Male.	Female.	Total.		
East Ward,	4,589	171	15	10,096	10,548	20,644	18,954	1,690
Kirkgate Ward,	476	31	3	1,070	1,201	2,271	3,088	—
South Ward,	1,418	79	2	3,289	3,305	6,594	7,154	—
North Ward,	3,026	111	5	7,396	7,332	14,728	14,554	174
North-east Ward,	7,330	403	84	17,561	17,339	34,900	26,579	8,321
West Ward,	6,946	377	37	15,269	17,212	32,481	25,361	7,126
North-west Ward,	5,231	204	91	11,523	12,704	24,227	16,561	7,666
Mill-hill Ward,	745	25	1	1,783	2,119	3,902	5,312	—
Hunslet,	8,142	363	91	18,486	18,803	37,289	25,763	11,526
Templenewsam (pt. of)	74	3	—	215	170	385	271	114
Holbeck,	3,843	124	41	8,335	8,830	17,165	15,824	1,341
Beeston,	587	15	—	1,394	1,368	2,762	2,547	215
Bramley,	2,157	76	34	4,799	5,083	9,882	8,690	1,192
Armley,	2,047	83	19	4,545	4,679	9,224	6,734	2,490
Farnley,	623	39	4	1,491	1,473	2,964	3,064	—
Wortley,	4,179	155	28	9,472	9,451	18,923	12,058	6,865
Headingley, Burley, Kirkstall,	3,004	146	72	6,378	7,564	13,942	9,674	4,268
Chapel-Allerton,	819	13	24	1,870	1,977	3,847	3,083	764
Potternewton,	663	61	6	1,453	2,004	3,457	1,878	1,579
Seacroft (part of),	2	—	—	6	4	10	—	10
Total,	55,901	2,479	557	126,431	133,166	259,597	207,149	55,335
Deduct decrease in Kirkgate, South, Mill-hill, and Farnley Wards,								2,887
Total increase in Borough,								52,448

PAST AND PRESENT.

The following series of tables relate to the different Unions :—

LEEDS UNION.

Districts.	Houses.			Persons.			Population in 1861.	Increase.
	Inhabited.	Uninhabited.	Building.	Male.	Female.	Total.		
Leeds,	29,687	1,398	238	67,772	71,590	139,362	117,566	21,796
Kirkstall (including Headingley and Burley),	3,004	146	72	6,378	7,564	13,942	9,674	4,268
Chapel-Allerton,	819	13	24	1,870	1,977	3,847	3,083	764
Potternewton,	663	61	6	1,453	2,004	3,457	1,878	1,579
Roundhay,	117	4	—	260	323	583	570	13
Seacroft,	283	9	—	630	600	1,230	1,235	—
Total in Leeds Union,	34,573	1,631	340	78,363	84,058	162,421	134,006	28,420

HUNSLET UNION.

Districts, &c.	Houses.			Persons.			Population in 1861.	Increase.
	Inhabited.	Uninhabited.	Building.	Male.	Female.	Total.		
Hunslet,	8,142	363	91	18,486	18,803	37,289	25,763	11,526
Middleton,	216	13	—	559	499	1,058	902	156
Rothwell,	775	42	10	1,878	1855	3,733	3,220	513
Oulton - cum - Woodlesford,	454	9	7	1,019	1023	2,042	1,851	191
Templenewsam,	454	34	2	1,080	1033	2,113	1,806	307
Thorpe Stapleton,	7	—	—	15	24	39	44	—
Totals,	10,048	461	110	23,037	23,237	46,274	33,586	12,693
Deduct decrease for Thorpe Stapleton,								5
Net increase of Union,								12,688

BRAMLEY UNION.

Districts.	Houses.			Persons.			Population in 1861.	Increase.
	Inhabited.	Uninhabited.	Building.	Male.	Female.	Total.		
Armley,	2,047	83	19	4,545	4,679	9,224	6,734	2,490
Bramley,	2,157	76	34	4,799	5,083	9,882	8,690	1,192
Farnley,	623	39	4	1,491	1,473	2,964	3,064	—
Gildersome,	729	40	4	1,741	1,707	3,448	2,701	747
Wortley,	4,179	155	28	9,472	9,451	18,923	12,058	6,865
Total,	9,735	393	89	22,048	22,393	44,441	33,247	11,294
Deduct decrease in Farnley township,								100
Net increase in Union,								11,194

HOLBECK UNION.

Districts.	Houses.			Persons.			Population in 1861.	Increase.
	Inhabited.	Uninhabited.	Building.	Male.	Female.	Total.		
Holbeck,	3,843	124	41	8,335	8,830	17,165	15,824	1,341
Beeston,	587	15	0	1,394	1,368	2,762	2,547	215
Churwell,	355	14	14	846	844	1,690	1,564	126
Totals,	4,785	153	55	10,575	11,042	21,617	19,935	1,682

Gildersome is outside the borough; and the population in 1871 for the four townships within the borough is 40,993, as against 30,546 in 1861. The net increase in that portion of the Union within the borough is, therefore, 10,447.

The following table, giving a summary of the population and houses within the borough to every decennial period since the commencement of the century, will be found interesting, as showing the continued prosperity of Leeds:—

	Houses. Occupied, Empty, and Building.			Population.		
	In Leeds Township.	In Out-Townships.	Total in the Borough.	In Leeds Township.	In Out-Townships.	Total in the Borough.
1801	6,882	—	—	30,669	22,493	53,162
1811	8,220	5,634	13,854	35,951	26,583	62,534
1821	11,223	8,039	19,262	48,603	35,143	83,746
1831	15,308	11,346	26,654	67,554	51,791	119,345
1841	20,213	14,005	34,218	88,741	63,313	152,313
1851	22,247	15,770	38,017	101,331	70,927	172,258
1861	25,808	20,366	46,174	117,566	89,599	207,165
1871	31,323	27,537	58,860	139,362	119,850	259,212

It will be seen that the increase in houses in the Leeds township during the last ten years is 5515, against an increase of 3561 in 1861. The proportional increase for the out-townships is still greater, being 7171, against 4596; and the proportional increase on the totals for the two periods is 12,686, against 8157. As regards population, there is an increase this year in the Leeds township of 21,796, against an increase of 16,235 in 1861; an increase of 30,251, against 18,672 in the out-townships; while the totals show a difference in the one increase over the other of 17,140 —the increase in 1861 being 34,907, and in 1871, 52,047.

The years 1872 and 1873 will be memorable in the history of Leeds as the years in which the new Royal Exchange of Leeds was built, and in which the great and noble People's Park was formed, and thrown open for the use of the people.

The Royal Exchange of Leeds.—This building is intended to supply the place of the Leeds Commercial Buildings, which for many years was one of the finest public buildings in Leeds, and was erected in the years 1826-29, at a cost of nearly £35,000. It was built at the north-west corner of Boar Lane, at the junction of that street with Park Row, and was a prominent object on entering the town from the railway stations. It was Ionic in style, in the form of a parallelogram, and had a handsome circular tetrastyle portico, surmounted by an attic concave. It included a series of spacious rooms, one of which was used for several years as a commercial news-room. When the corporation decided to improve Boar Lane this building was pulled down, the portions of the site not required for the improvement being ultimately sold to the Royal Exchange Company, Limited, for the purposes of a public exchange and news-room. The foundation-stone of this new building, still (1873) in course of construction, was laid by Prince Arthur, on the 20th of September, 1872, in the presence of the corporation, the Burmese Embassy, and a large assembly of the inhabitants. Within a cavity in the lower stone a bottle was placed, containing a list of the directors and shareholders of the new exchange engrossed on vellum, a copy of the articles of association of the company, a list of the Leeds corporation, copies of the Leeds newspapers, and the coins of the realm. The brass-plate covering the cavity bore the following inscription:—

THE FIRST STONE
OF
THE LEEDS EXCHANGE
WAS LAID BY
HIS ROYAL HIGHNESS PRINCE ARTHUR,
K.G., K.T., K.P., &c.,
ON THE 20TH DAY OF SEPTEMBER, A.D. 1872.

Chairman—OBADIAH NUSSEY, ESQ., J.P.
Vice-Chairman—JOSEPH HIRST, ESQ., J.P.

Directors:

JOHN BARRAN, ESQ., Mayor.	EDW. IRWIN, ESQ., J.P.
WILLIAM BAXTER, ESQ.	RICHARD NICKOLS, ESQ.
RILEY BRIGGS, ESQ., J.P.	JAMES STABLES, ESQ.

WILLIAM WATSON, ESQ.
Architects—T. H. and F. HEALEY, Bradford.
Solicitor—HENRY SNOWDON, ESQ.
Secretary—WILLIAM HIRST.

The following is a description of this building:—The style selected for the new Exchange is perpendicular Gothic, picturesque in outline, and assimilating somewhat in this respect to buildings that may be seen in many parts of Flanders. The structure, four stories in height, will be in harmony with the architecture of Mill Hill Chapel, which it adjoins. The principal entrance, at the junction of Boar Lane with Park Row, is composed of three arches resting on polished granite shafts, forming a kind of outer porch. Access is gained by eleven steps in two flights, reaching the level of the News Room and the Exchange floor. To the left is the News Room, forty-five feet by twenty-four feet, with a height of seventeen feet six inches, lighted by large windows looking into Park Row and the chapel yard, an arrangement having been made by which light is obtained in the latter direction. The Exchange in the centre of the block—and cut off by the shops from the noise of traffic in the streets—is circular in form, about sixty feet in diameter, with a supplemental area in the north-east angle, next to Basinghall Street. Externally the building will have a handsome appearance. The façade is tastefully treated, and the general effect is pleasing and harmonious to the eye. Over the central arches of the entrance will be an oriel window, and over this again a two-light window with broad mullions. In the spaces between the arches shields may be placed bearing the Leeds arms. Provision is made in the upper stage of the tower for an illuminated clock, facing towards the Midland Railway Station. Above the clock is a deep-moulded cornice, enriched with shield, and a pierced tracery parapet with crocketed pinnacles. The total height of the tower from the ground to the top of the finial is 118 feet, and below the latter is a richly designed lantern, with lucerne lights in the sides of the spire. In the centre of the Park Row front an oriel window is shown, a chimney gable breaking the outline of the roof. The angle next to the chapel yard is treated as a turret, surmounted by a conical spire, covered with slate, and rising to a height of eighty-four feet. The entrance to the suite of club rooms is in Boar Lane, immediately adjoining the Exchange entrance. The outer walls of the staircase slightly project into the street. The staircase is lighted by windows "ramped" or stepped up in stages, and it is to be covered with a high-pitched roof. The front of the three shops is composed of stone pillars, bearing ornamental iron girders, over which are carried arches of masonry. There are two-light windows in each of the stories, each window being finished with an enriched parapet and crocketed gables. The roof will be covered with green Coniston slate. The cost of the entire structure is estimated at £18,000, including fittings. There will be eight shops in all, in addition to the Exchange and News Room and the other portions of the pile.

The New People's Park at Roundhay, near Leeds. — One of the greatest improvements that has been made, either in Leeds or any other of the large towns or cities of England in the present generation, has been effected by the purchasing and consecrating to the public use and enjoyment of the beautiful park of Roundhay, with its charming lakes, woods, and grassy turf, which, having been formed by one of the most tasteful of the merchant princes of this district, has now become the property of the people of Leeds. The ceremonies on the opening of this beautiful park, which were attended by one of the princes of the royal family, Prince Arthur, third son of her Majesty, will long be remembered in Leeds, and will form an epoch in the history of that great and flourishing town. The entire Roundhay Park estate comprised 1364 acres. The park proper—comprising 601 acres, one rood, twelve perches—was purchased by Mr. Alderman Barran, then mayor of Leeds, and the principal and most active promoter of the park, for the sum of £107,000 on behalf of the borough of Leeds. Another portion of the land of the Roundhay estate—containing 173 acres, two roods, and twenty-five perches—was also bought, to secure an approach worthy of the park, for the sum of £32,000. Thus, at a cost of £139,000, this splendid demesne was secured by the borough—that is to say, by the people of Leeds. No finer, larger, or more beautiful public park has been formed in any of the great manufacturing and commercial towns of England during the present century, than that thus secured to the people of Leeds by the public spirit and enterprise of Mr. Alderman Barran and the town council of that large, wealthy, and public-spirited community. The site is beautiful, the park being visible even from Meanwood, Cookridge, and the most distant parts of the borough, and the woods and lakes, constructed and trained by the labour and growth of many years, presenting almost every beauty which art can develop amidst the charms of nature.

APPENDIX.

LEEDS VICARAGE—LIST OF PATRONS WITH THEIR ADDRESSES.

William Hey, Esq., Gledhow, near Leeds.
James Garth Marshall, Esq., Headingley House, near Leeds.
Thomas Benyon, Esq., Myton, Warwickshire.
William Dinsley Skelton, Esq., St. George's Terrace, Leeds.
Jas. Brown, Esq., Rossington, near Doncaster.
Robert John Ellershaw, Esq., 8 The Crescent, Scarbro'.
Thos. Tennant, Esq., Blenheim Ter., Leeds.
The Rev. Canon Barry, D.D., King's College, London.
Henry Cowper Marshall, Esq., Weetwood Hall, near Leeds.
George Young, Esq., 3 Pulteney Buildings, Weymouth.
Chas. Chadwick, Esq., M.D., Park Sq., Leeds.
Richard Bickerton Turner, Esq., Bank of England, Leeds.

Walker Joy, Esq., Queen's Square, Leeds.
Edmund Maude, Esq., Middleton Lodge, Leeds.
George B. Nelson, Esq., Hanover Sq., Leeds.
Sir Andrew Fairbairn, Knight, Goldsbro' Hall, Knaresbro'.
Thomas John Kinnear, Esq., Horsforth Hall, Leeds.
Joseph Teale, Esq., The Ridding, Bentham, Lancaster.
Thomas Pridgin Teale, Esq., Headingley, near Leeds.
John Ellershaw, Esq., Kirkstall, near Leeds.
John Rhodes, Esq., Potternewton, near Leeds.
Thomas Greenwood Teale, Esq., Meanwood, near Leeds.
Thomas Wolryche Stansfield, Esq., Weetwood Grove, near Leeds.
Henry Chorley, Esq., 8 Park Square, Leeds.

Chapels and Churches in Leeds.—The following statistics with regard to the number of churches and chapels in Leeds recently appeared in the *Nonconformist* newspaper:—

Religious Denominations.	1851. Population, 172,270.		1871. Population, 259,201.		Increase between 1851 and 1872.	
	No. of Places of Worship.	No. of Sittings.	No of Pl. of Worship, 1872.	No of Sittings, 1872.	Places of Worship.	No. of Sittings.
Church of England,	36	25,436	51	36,700	15 a	11,264
Presbyterian,	—	—	2	600	2	600
Congregationalists,	11	8,305	24	9,960	13 b	1,655
Baptists,	13*	5,781	15	5,560	2 c	dec. 221
Society of Friends,	1	1,100	5	1,650	4 d	550
Unitarians,	3	1,240	6	1,770	3 e	530
Wesleyan Methodists,	26	20,475	30	22,025	4 f	1,550
Un. Meth. Free Churches,	14	4,554	20	8,400	6	3,846
New Connection,	7	2,717	13	3,700	6 g	983
Primitive Methodists,	13	3,900	21	6,070	8 h	2,830
Brethren,	2	250	1	300	dec. 1	50
Roman Catholics,	2	1,220	7	5,400	5	4,180
Jews,	2	140	1	350	dec. 1	210
All others,	7	1,370	7	1,750	7 i	380
Total,	137	76,488	203	104,235	75	28,849

* These included several varieties of Baptists.
a Including two mission stations (320).
b Including four mission stations (710). Others with more than 1000 sittings not included.
c Including school (500) with regular worship. Since 1863 three new chapels built (1250).
d Including two mission rooms (350).
e Including two mission rooms (420).
f Including two mission rooms (350).
g Including one mission room (100).
h Including one mission room (100).
i Including Christians (200), Inghamites (150), Swedenborgians (500), Apostolic Church (350), Free Gospel (150), and two Mormons (400).

DATES OF THE PRINCIPAL EVENTS CONNECTED WITH THE HISTORY OF LEEDS.

Roman and British Period, A.D. 97 to 616.—Leeds supposed by Thoresby and Whitaker to be the Loid, or Caer Loid Coit, the "city of Loid in the Forest," mentioned by Nennius.—Yorkshire: Past and Present, vol. ii. p. 91.

616.—Loidis, Loidis, or Leeds, mentioned by the Venerable Bede as the chief place in the British kingdom of Leodis and Elmete, afterwards conquered by the Angles.—Vol. ii. p. 91.

655.—Great victory of the Christian army of the Angles of Northumbria over the pagans at Winweyd, in the district of Leodis or Leeds.—Vol. ii. p. 94.

500 to 800.—Present names of places in parish of Leeds, chiefly derived from the Anglian, a branch of the Germanic language.—Vol. ii. p. 96.

867.—Conquest of this part of England by the Danes and Norwegians.— Many names of Danish or Scandinavian origin in and about Leeds.—Vol. ii. p. 97.

930 (about).—Cross with name of King Olaff or St. Olave, king of Norway, Iceland, and Northumbria, found recently amongst the foundations of the old parish church of Leeds.—Vol. ii. p. 200.

1084–86.—Leeds at the time of the Domesday Survey, about twenty years after the Norman Conquest.—Population supposed to have been less than 1000.—Value of Leeds at that time, about £115 of modern money.—The Bondman's Dam on the river Aire.—Grant of Leeds to Ilbert de Laci, by William the Conqueror.—Vol. ii. p. 99.

1089 (about).—Grant of Leeds to Ralph Paganel by Ilbert de Laci.— Advowson of church of Leeds given to priory of the Holy Trinity at York, by Ralph Paganel.—Castle built at Leeds by the Paganels, with park attached to it.—Vol. ii. p. 102.

1207–8, the 9th King John.—Maurice Paganel grants charter of liberties to his burgage tenants at Leeds.—Copy of charter of Maurice Paganel.—Trade and condition of Leeds at that time.—Vol. ii. p. 104.

1217.—Leeds passes to the earl of Chester, Ranulph de Blondeville.—Vol. ii. p. 109.

1251, 35th Henry III.—Edmund de Laci, earl of Lincoln, obtains charter of free warren in Leeds and neighbouring manors.—Vol. ii. p. 109.

1272, 57th Henry III.—Woollen manufactures of Leeds mentioned in Pipe Rolls or High Sheriff's Account of this year.—Vol. ii. p. 111.

1311, 4th Edward II.—The manor of Leeds passes to Thomas Plantagenet, earl of Lancaster, by his marriage with Alicia de Laci, heiress of the earls of Lincoln; and afterwards to the earls and dukes of Lancaster.—Vol. ii. p. 110.

1373, 47th Edward III.—Fulling mills of Leeds leased to Thomas Burgers. —Vol. ii. p. 111.

1376, 50th Edward III.—Leeds Bridge, with the adjoining chantry, mentioned in the reign of King Edward III.—Vol. ii. p. 110.

1399, 1st Henry IV.—Leeds becomes the property of the Crown, by the accession of Henry of Bolingbroke, duke of Lancaster, to the throne of England, as King Henry IV.—Vol. ii. p. 111.

1536, 27-8th Henry VIII.—Leeds described by Leland as "a pretty market-town, standing by clothing."—Vol. ii. p. 112.

1536, 28th Henry VIII.—Valuation of tithes of the parish of Leeds.—Vol. ii. p. 116.

1538, 30th Henry VIII.—Advowson of parish church of St. Peter's, in Leeds, sold to Thomas Culpepper by King Henry VIII.; afterwards, in the reign of Queen Elizabeth, to Preston and Darnley, the latter of whom sold it to the parishioners of Leeds for £113.—Vol. ii. p. 114.

1574, 16th Elizabeth.—Camden's account of Leeds.—Parish register of Leeds commences.—Population of the parish supposed by Dr. Whitaker not to have exceeded 4000 persons in the reign of Queen Elizabeth.—Vol. ii. p. 112.

1609, 7th James I.—Sale of King's Mills, one fulling mill and two corn mills, at Leeds, to Edward Ferrers and Francis Philips, of London.—Vol. ii. p. 116.

1611.—Manor of Leeds part of dowry of Anne of Denmark, queen of James I., afterwards sold to Mr. Alderman Sykes and other leading inhabitants.—Vol. ii. p. 124.

1617, 15th James I.—Lord Bacon confirmed Sir John Saville, of Howley Hall, near Leeds, and twenty-four of the principal inhabitants of Leeds, as holders and patrons of the advowson of the parish.—Vol. ii. p. 115.

1626, 2nd Charles I.—The first charter from the Crown to the borough of Leeds, granted by King Charles I. this year.—List of names of first alderman who acted as mayor, and of principal burgesses of the borough of Leeds.—Vol. ii. p. 115.

1642–44, 18th and 20th Charles I.—Part taken by Leeds in the great civil war.—Numbers slain in various engagements in and around Leeds.—Vol. ii. p. 117.

1644, 20th Charles I.—Leeds regiment commanded by Colonel John Thoresby, at the battle of Marston Moor.—Vol. ii. p. 119.

1644–45, 21st Charles I.—Many hundred persons destroyed by the plague at Leeds.—Vol. ii. p. 121.

1652.—Leeds represented in Parliament by Captain Adam Baynes, of Knowstrop Hall, Leeds, in one of the Parliaments of the Commonwealth.—Vol. ii. p. 122.

1654.—John Harrison and others, conveyed five-ninths of the bailiwick or manor of Leeds to the Corporation.—Vol. ii. 178.

1661–62, 13th and 14th Charles II.—The second royal charter of Leeds, granted by King Charles II. after the Restoration.—Mayor, aldermen, and common councillors of Leeds, named in this charter.—Vol. ii. p. 122.

1663, 16th Charles II.—Number of tenements in Leeds parish paying hearth money 1431; at five persons to each house, giving a population of 7155.

1672, 23rd Charles II.—Mill Hill Chapel built 1672; rebuilt, enlarged, and beautified in the year 1848.—Vol. ii. pp. 125, 205.

1684–85, 37th Charles II. and 1st James II.—Leeds deprived of its charter by James II. and Judge Jeffreys.—Opposition of William Lowther of Swillington, and Richard Baynes the younger of Knowstrop Hall, to James' charter.—Vol. ii. p. 179.

1689.—The Revolution.—William and Mary proclaimed king and queen of England, in front of the Moot Hall, Leeds.—Vol. ii. p. 179

1695.—Water-works constructed at Leeds.—Vol. ii. p. 132.

1697.—The rivers Aire and Calder rendered navigable.—Vol. ii. p. 134.

1701.—The water-power of the river Aire and of the brooks within the borough of Leeds.—The manufactures of Leeds in the reign of Queen Anne, as described by Thoresby.—Vol. ii. p. 132.

1702-27.—Thoresby's account of Leeds, written in the reigns of Queen Anne and King George I. Places described:—The Manor House (occupied by the Wilsons, afterwards the Fountaine-Wilsons, as heirs and representatives of Richard Sykes, senior lord of the manor); the New Presbyterian Chapel (Mill Hill); the alms-houses; the Burgh, Borh, or Borough Lane, Briggate; the Moot Hall, the Market Cross, the Head Row, the Red Hall, Rockley Hall, the New Street, the Church of St. John's, Lidgate and Tower Hill, the Free School and Library, the Sheepscar Beck and the mills upon it, Kirkgate, the Old Parish Church of Leeds, the Nether Mills, the Calls, the Independent Chapel built there, the New Water-works, &c., &c.—Vol. ii. p. 124.

1709.—Coaches established between Leeds and London.—Vol. ii. p. 137.

1710.—The first White Cloth Hall built.—Vol. ii. p. 133.

1727.—Daniel Defoe's description of the town of Leeds and of its manufactures.—The trade of the Leeds merchants, by pack-horses, with all parts of England.—Vol. ii. p. 138.

1718, 4th George I.—*Leeds Mercury* established by Mr. James Lister.—Vol. ii. p. 226.

1727, 1st George II.—Trinity Church built in Boar (or Burh) Lane.—Vol. ii. p. 202.

1740, 14th George II.—Commencement of improvement of high roads, from Leeds to all parts of Yorkshire.—Vol. ii. p. 139.

1745, 18th George II.—Army assembled at Leeds to resist the Pretender and the Highlanders.—Vol. ii. p. 140.

1753, 27th George II.—The riots against toll bars, known as "Leeds fight."—Vol. ii. p. 141.

1754, 28th George II., July 2.—The *Leeds Intelligencer* established by the first Griffith Wright.—Vol. ii. p. 227.

1755, 29th George II.—The first Leeds Improvement Act passed.—Vol. ii. p. 144.

1756, 30th George II.—Richard Wilson, Esq., of the Manor House, sells land to clothiers for site of Mixed or Coloured Cloth Hall.—Vol. ii. p. 143.

1758, 31st George II.—Coloured or Mixed Cloth Hall built.—Attended by 2000 clothiers, at the beginning of the present century.—Vol. ii. p. 143.

1759, 32nd George II.—First Act for making waggon way to convey coals from Middleton collieries to Leeds.—Vol. ii. p. 160.

1760, 1st George III.—Leeds at the commencement of the reign of King George III.—Vol. ii. p. 147.

1765, 5th George III.—Corporation festivities at Leeds.—Vol. ii. p. 150.

1767, 7th George III.—The General Infirmary at Leeds founded.—Vol. ii. p. 148.

1770, 11th George III.—Act for making the Leeds and Liverpool Canal.—Vol. ii. p. 148.

1774, 15th George III.—The Leeds Library founded.—Vol. ii. p. 149.

1775, 16th George III.—New White Cloth Hall opened.—Vol. ii p. 151.

1778, 18th George III.—Second Act for conveying coals by waggon from Middleton to Leeds.—Vol. ii. p. 160.

1782, 23rd George III.—Great extension and improvement of town of Leeds.—Vol. ii. p. 151.

1788, 28th George III.—Commencement of inclosing of commons around Leeds.—Vol. ii. p. 162.

1792-93, 32nd to 33rd George III.—Third Act for conveying coals from Middleton to Leeds.—Vol. ii. p. 160.

1793, 33rd George III.—French revolutionary war commenced.—Vol. ii. p. 166.

1794.—Leeds regiment of volunteers raised.—Vol. ii. p. 166.

1795.—Great reviews of West Riding volunteers on Woodhouse and Chapeltown Moors.—Vol. ii. p. 166.

1796, 36th George III.—Arthur Young's account of Leeds.—Vol. ii. p. 154.

1799, 40th George III.—Villages in which the woollen trade was carried on for the Leeds market at the beginning of the present century.—Vol. ii. p. 153.

1800, 41st George III.—Public buildings in Leeds at the close of the eighteenth century.—Mr. Gott's evidence as to the progress of machinery.—Vol. ii. p. 154.

1801, 41st to 42nd George III.—Rapid progress of Leeds in the nineteenth century.—Chief causes of progress.—Vol. ii. p. 155.

1803, 44th George III.—Fourth Act for better supplying Leeds with coal, by waggon road.—Vol. ii. p. 160.

1806, 46th George III.—Principal manufactures and banks in Leeds at this time.—Messrs. Gott's woollen mill, at Bean Ing.—Messrs. Marshall's flax mill.—Iron-works of Messrs. Fenton, Murray, and Wood.—The Leeds Pottery.—The first railways at Leeds.—Messrs. Beckett's bank.—Vol. ii. pp. 157-159.

1807, 47th George III.—Retirement of Colonel Lloyd, commander of Leeds volunteers.—Thanks for long-continued services.—Vol. ii. p. 166.

1809, 50th George III.—Another Leeds Improvement Act passed, enlarging powers of Act of 1760, and authorizing the building of a new court-house and gaol, for the borough of Leeds.—Vol. ii. p. 167.

1815, 56th George III.—Another Improvement Act passed.—Vol. ii. p. 167.

1816, 57th George III.—Issue of new coinage, and withdrawal of local coins.—Vol. ii. p. 164.

1817.—Enlargement of Leeds and extensive improvements under the 57th George III., and subsequent Acts.—Vol. ii. p. 168.

1818, 59th George III.—Leeds Philosophical and Literary Society founded—Vol. ii. p. 169.

1824, 4th George IV.—Act for lighting and cleansing the town; Act for removing and pulling down the Middle Row and the Moot Hall in Briggate. ; Act for abolishing vicarial tithes in the borough of Leeds, and substituting a payment in money.—Vol. ii. pp. 168, 176.

1831, 1st and 2nd William IV.—Progress of Leeds in the first thirty years of the nineteenth century.—Vol. ii. p. 177.

1832.—Leeds made a parliamentary borough, returning two members to Parliament.—List of members returned to serve in Parliament for the borough of Leeds.—Vol. ii. p. 177.

1835.—Local government before, and under, the Municipal Reform Act. —Vol. ii. p. 178. List of mayors of Leeds from 1801 to 1873.—Vol. ii. p. 182. Leeds Improvement Acts, and public improvements since the passing of the Municipal Act.—Vol. ii. p. 183.—The Leeds Soke Act. Manufactures of Leeds.—Vol. ii. p. 191.

1837.—The Yorkshire Union of Mechanics' Institutes.—Vol. ii. p. 211. The Leeds grammar school.—Vol. ii. p. 213.

1851.—Extension of waterworks.—Vol. ii. p. 184. The Leeds Chamber of Commerce.—The churches, chapels, schools, libraries, and other educational institutions of Leeds.—Vol. ii. p. 198.

1858.—The Town Hall of Leeds.—Vol. ii. p. 187.

1861.—Street and town railway improvements.—Vol. ii. p. 186.

1862.—The Philosophical Hall and Museum.—Vol. ii. p. 209.

1864.—Endowed and public schools in Leeds.—Vol. ii. p. 215.

1867.—Leeds authorized to return three members to Parliament.—Vol. ii. p. 177.

1868.—List of the vicars of Leeds. Vol. ii. p. 201.

1870.—Elementary education in Leeds.—Men connected with literature, science, invention, and the arts, in the borough of Leeds.—Vol. ii. p. 217.

1872.—Mineral wealth of the Leeds district.—Vol. ii. p. 195. The Royal Exchange of Leeds, foundation stone laid by his Royal Highness, Prince Arthur. —Vol. ii. p. 233. The new Peoples' Park at Roundhay, near Leeds, opened by his Royal Highness, Prince Arthur.—Vol. ii. p. 235.

1873.—Leeds public libraries.—Vol. ii. p. 208. The local press of Leeds. —Vol. ii. p. 226. Progress of Leeds from 1861 to 1873.—Houses and population in the cities and boroughs of Yorkshire, having defined municipal or parliamentary limits, in 1861 and 1871.—Vol. ii. p. 228. Progress of population of the borough of Leeds in the decennial period, from the census of 1861 to the census of 1871. Vol. ii. p. 230.

APPENDIX.

Patrons of vicarage of Leeds.—Churches and chapels in Leeds.—Vol. ii. p. 236.

Dates of principal events in the history of Leeds.—Vol. ii. pp. 237 to 241.

CHAPTER III.

THE HISTORY OF THE BOROUGH OF BRADFORD.

BRADFORD, the first in population and importance of the municipal and parliamentary boroughs engaged in the worsted trade, the second occupied in the several textile industries of Yorkshire, and containing, at the census of 1871, 145,827 inhabitants, is one of the most flourishing of the manufacturing towns of England; the increase of its population having been no less than 39,609 persons, between the census of 1861 and that of 1871.[*] Its growth, during the whole of the present century, has been very rapid. All the sources of its prosperity continue in undiminished activity, whether derived from large supplies of coal, iron, steam-power, and machinery; from the energy and industry with which raw materials, both new and old, have been brought together from, and new markets have been sought in, the most distant regions of the world; or from the skill with which both domestic and foreign materials have been applied to the purposes of industry. Hence it has the promise of a continued and at least as rapid a rate of progress, as that which has been witnessed during the first seventy years of the present century. "The town of Bradford lies in a valley which may justly be considered a branch of Airedale, though from a remote period it has borne the distinctive appellation of Bradford Dale. This valley, stretching from the moorlands above Thornton to the Aire at Shipley, forms at Bradford a considerable bend; and being at this point joined by two small dells, the town appears to be seated at the junction of four valleys."[†] Three abundant brooks or becks, as they are locally termed, unite their waters at Bradford, flowing thence down Bradford Dale in a collected stream to the Aire, about four miles distant. These overflowed the valley after heavy rains, and produced a wide marsh,

[*] Return of Houses and Population in the Cities and Boroughs of Yorkshire, having defined Municipal or Parliamentary Limits, in 1861 and 1871, from the Preliminary Census Report for 1871, given in vol. ii. p. 228 of this Work. In another Return the increase is made 39,597.

[†] The History and Topography of Bradford in the county of York, with Topographical Notices of its Parish, by John James: London, Longmans; Bradford, Charles Stanfield, 1841.

only passable by a broad ford, from which Bradford is supposed by James and other local authors to have taken its name.

Bradford is an Anglian or English town in name, and probably in origin, although the roads and works of the Romans have been clearly traced within the parish, in the neighbourhood of the iron mines of Bierley,* where the Romans had workings, the remains of which were examined and described by Dr. Richardson, of Bierley Hall, early in the last century. Amongst the remains of these mines were found coins of the reigns of Diocletian, Constantius, Constantine, and others of the later emperors, from A.D. 284 to A.D. 337. Other coins of as early a date as the reign of Trajan, A.D. 98–117, have also been discovered amongst the hills in the neighbourhood of Bradford, as well as a third set, filling up the interval between these two periods. Dr. Richardson, in a letter to Hearne the Oxford antiquary, says, "That iron was made in this neighbourhood" (Bierley, near Bradford) "in the time of the Romans, a late discovery has sufficiently convinced me. Upon removing a heap of cinders to repair the highways, a quantity of copper Roman coins were discovered, some of which I have now in my possession. They were of Constantine, Constantius, Diocletian, and the usurper Carausius. This country abounds with such heaps of cinders, though we have not so much as a tradition that iron was made [here] then."

The modern name of Bradford is evidently derived from the Anglian words brad or broad, and ford, a passage across a stream or marsh; and the names of the townships and villages in the parish are nearly all of Anglian origin, or have Anglo-Saxon terminations. Thus wic or wyke, which is the name for an Anglian or Saxon camp,† is found in the parish of Bradford, as well as in many other places in Yorkshire. The Anglian termination of ton, meaning originally an inclosure, but afterwards a town or village, occurs in Allerton, Clayton, Heaton, the two Hortons, and Thornton. Names ending in the Anglian word ley, a field or inclosure, are found in North Bierley and Shipley: and names derived from other well-known Anglian words, such as ford, hill, worth, burg, or bury, and ham or hame, occur in the names of Bradford, Eccleshill, Haworth, Stanbury, and Manningham. The termination of the word Bowling is also Anglian, and is probably derived from the name of a meadow,

---

* Ordnance Map, No. 88, Yorkshire, published 1843.
† See Account of Anglian Wics or Military Stations, vol. i. p. 391 of this Work.

which was ing; whilst the word or syllable ing, in the name of Manningham, appears to be that form of the Anglian word, which is equivalent to a tribe or sept; Manningham probably meaning the home of the Mannings.* Almost the only British termination amongst the names of the townships of Bradford is Wilsden, the wild den, and that is both Teutonic and Celtic. The den in this word is the British name for a valley, or deep recess, and was perhaps given to this township when it was still inhabited by some ancient British tribe, by the Angles, who themselves afterwards adopted the same word den for the name of a glen or valley. The names of Leventhorpe, Oxenhope, and Denholme are probably Norse in their origin; and though the great preponderance of names of places in the district of Bradford is Anglian or Teutonic, the name of the lord of the manor of Bradford, immediately before the Norman conquest, was Gamel or Gamall, which is a Danish or Scandinavian name, signifying The Old.†

Little or nothing is known of Bradford from records or books previous to the Domesday Survey. Bradford, or as it is there written Bradeford, is described in the Domesday Record, made between the years 1084 and 1086, as containing the manor of Bradford, and also six berewicks or subordinate manors. The names are not given, but they are supposed on good evidence to have been Great and Little Horton, Manningham, Stanbury, Haworth, and Oxenhope.‡ Even before the wasting of this district in the wars of the Norman conquest, Bradford was valued only at the insignificant sum of £4 a year, equal to about fifteen times as much, or £60 a year, in the money of the present time; not equal to £400 of present money, as stated by James in his History of Bradford, for Sir Thomas Duffus Hardy, and other writers of authority, fix the proportion between the pound of Domesday, which was a weight of 12 oz. of silver, and the present pound (£) of 20s. at 15 to 1, allowing for difference in weight, and in the exchangeable value of silver. Much of the district was still waste and deserted when the Domesday Survey was made, nearly twenty years after the Conquest. In addition to the arable land there was a wood or forest, half a mile in length, and seven and a half furlongs in breadth. The following is the description of Bradford, and of the neighbouring manors and vills, given in the Domesday Record. The word carucate,

---

* See Account of Anglian Hams or Hames, vol. i. p. 394 of this Work.
† Gamall or Gamel, *refus*. Haldorsens' Norse Dictionary.   ‡ James' History of Bradford, p. 39.

so often used in this description, is sometimes estimated as high as 180 acres, and sometimes as low as 120. In these early times it was an estimate or guess, at the quantity of land that a yoke of oxen could work in a year, and must have varied with the strength of the land and the oxen. It afterwards was fixed in Fleta and some other works at 180 acres.

BRADFORD AT THE DOMESDAY SURVEY.

Bradford.—"A Manor. In Bradeford, with six berewicks [or subordinate manors], Gamel had fifteen carucates of land to be taxed, where there may be eight ploughs. Ilbert [De Laci] has it, and it is waste. Value in King Edward [the Confessor's] time, four pounds [£60 of present money]. Wood pasture half a mile long and half a mile broad. *Bowling.*—Manor. In Bolline, Sindi had four carucates of land, which pays to the geld [Danegeld], where there may be two ploughs. Ilbert has it, and it is waste. Value in King Edward's time, five shillings [£3 15s. present money]. *Bierley.*—Manor. In Birle, Stainulf had four carucates of land to be taxed, where there may be two ploughs. Ilbert has it, and it is waste. Value in King Edward's time, ten shillings [£7 10s. present money]. Wood pasture half a mile long and half a mile broad. *Bolton.*—Manor. In Bodeltone, Archil had four carucates of land to be taxed, where there may be two ploughs. Ilbert has it, and it is waste. Value in King Edward's time, ten shillings [£7 10s. present money]. This [the following land] belongs to this manor, Celeslau [Chellow], Alretone, Torentone, Claitone, Wibetesa [Wibsey]. To be taxed together ten carucates of land, where there may be six ploughs. It is waste. Value in King Edward's time, forty shillings [£30 present money]; now [1084-86] nothing. *Shipley.*—Manor. In Scipleia, Ravenchil had three carucates of land to be taxed, where there may be two ploughs. Ilbert has it, and it is waste. Value in King Edward's time, ten shillings [£7 10s. present money]. Wood pasture one mile long and one half broad." *

Bradford in the Hands of the De Lacis, Earls of Lincoln.—After the Conquest, Bradford, with Leeds, Huddersfield, and about 150 other manors in the West Riding, were granted by the Conqueror to one of his warlike followers, Ilbert de Laci, whose descendants became earls of Lincoln, and whose family held them for 230 years;

---
* Bawdwen's Translation of Domesday, as relates to Yorkshire.

that is, from about the year 1080 to 1311. There is evidence that the De Lacis erected a manor-house at Bradford, and Dr. Whitaker speaks of a fort, or castle, as having been built by them at that place. He says that after the Norman conquest the De Lacis became possessed of the honour of Clitheroe, and erected the castle there; that within a few years the Conqueror put them in possession of the fee and castle of Pontefract; that from Pontefract to Clitheroe was a space of somewhat more than fifty miles, the greater part of which extends (or then extended) over a bleak and desolate country; that a line drawn from one of these points to the other would pass nearly over Bradford; that at Leeds the De Lacis had a castle, and at Colne a manor-house; but that those places being fifty miles from each other, an intermediate resting-place was wanted and was formed at Bradford. The name of "Burgenses" or Burgesses, Dr. Whitaker remarks, occurring in an early inquisition as to Bradford, proves that there had been a burg or castle there, though there was then only a manor-house. "Some of the earlier Lacis," he concludes, "must have erected a small fortress at Bradford, and the protection afforded by a fortress always attracted inhabitants." Whether this reasoning, as to the existence of a burg or castle at Bradford in the time of the De Lacis, is sound or otherwise, there is no doubt that they erected there a manor-house and established courts of justice; that they let part of their land on burgage and other free tenancies; and that they granted, or obtained for the inhabitants of Bradford, some valuable privileges from the crown, which would materially assist in developing the prosperity of the town. When the De Lacis obtained possession of Bradford, in the time of William the Conqueror (1084–86), they found nothing there but ruins, which they had themselves probably assisted in making, in a war of conquest; but when Henry the last earl of Lincoln, of that family, died, in the reign of King Edward II. and the year 1311, Bradford had become a place of considerable trade and activity, and the interest of the Lacis in this and the immediately adjoining manors was valued at a sum equal to £600 a year of modern money. Something was probably due to the liberality of the lords of that great and noble family, who soon forgot Normandy, and became thorough Englishmen. John de Laci, one of those lords, was amongst the twenty-five barons who were appointed by the whole body of the English Peers to enforce the great charter of English freedom, Magna Charta, extorted by the barons and the citizens of London from King John, at Runnymede.

Early Progress of Bradford.—The following facts enable us to trace the progress of Bradford, during the time when the lordship and manor were in the hands of the De Laci family. In the year 1246, the 30th Henry III., Bradford paid a tallage or tax to the crown of four marks, equal to about £40 of present money, and more, by one and a half marks, than was paid by Leeds at the same taxation. *Grant of Market to Bradford.*—In the year 1256, 40th Henry III., the king granted to Edmund de Laci, and to his tenants and burgesses of Bradford, the valuable privilege of holding a market every week in that town, which could not then be done without consent of the crown or lord. This charter must have given a fresh impulse to the progress of Bradford, by making it the centre of the trade of that portion of Airedale, and of the adjoining hills and dales, which extends from Bingley, if not from Skipton, to Leeds in one direction, and to Halifax in another. The following is a copy of the charter:—" The King to the Archbishops, &c., greeting—Know ye that we have granted, and by this our present charter confirmed, to our beloved servant, Edmund de Laci, that he and his heirs for ever shall have a market every week, on Thursday, in his manor of Brafford (Bradford) in the county of York, unless that market should be to the injury of the neighbouring markets. Witnesses, Ralph son of Nicholas, Bertram de Criol, Master William de Kilkenny, archdeacon of Coventry, Artaldo de Sco Romano, Robert le Norreis, Stephen Banthan, Anketin Mallore, and others. Dated at Merton, 20th day of April,"* 1256, 40th Henry III.

When King Edward I. succeeded to the throne in the year 1273, he made a strict inquiry into his own rights and those of all the great tenants of the crown, including the Lacis, in Bradford, and their many other manors. The following was the report of the commissioners, who evidently put the De Lacis on their proofs, and claimed everything for the crown to which they could not clearly establish their right:—

"They [the jurors] say that the townships of Clayton, Thorneton, Allerton, and Heton, were taxable to the lord the king (not to the earls), and were appropriated to the liberty of the Lord Edmund de Lascy, by John de Hoderode, late steward of the said Edmund.

* James' History of Bradford, p. 48.

Hitherto, the said customs are kept by Henry de Lascy, earl of Lincoln [Edmund's successor]. And they say that Peter de Saunton, steward of the said Henry de Lascy, appropriated [to the earl] the towns of Wyk [Wyke] and of Bolling, in the last days of the lord the King Henry [III.], father of the now king, and that service he hath withdrawn from the king, and appropriated to the earl. Concerning those who have liberties [or seignorial rights], they say that Henry de Lascy hath many liberties in the town of Bradeford; to wit, a gallows [the right of inflicting capital punishment on criminals], assize of bread and beer, a market, and a free court from ancient times; a sheriff's turn [or court] made by his steward; and the debts of the lord the king levied by his own bailiffs. Also, they say that as well the steward of Alesia de Lascy as of the said Henry, use liberties otherwise than they ought to do, and have taken toll of things bought and sold without the market-place of Bradeford, at the gates, of the sellers and buyers, and that toll is called Dortol and Huctol; and if the sellers and buyers have in anything opposed them, they amerce them; and other things they do contrary to ancient usage. Concerning new approvements, &c., they say that Hugh de Swillington approved [improved] for himself a certain inclosure in the Rodes, in a place called Jordansal, in the time of King Henry, father of the now king [Edward I.], but by what warrant they are ignorant. Concerning sheriffs and bailiffs they say, that Gilbert de Clifton, steward of Henry de Lascy, in the time of King Henry, father of the now king, amerced William de Whiteley of Wilsenden for not coming to the turn [court] when there were sufficient persons to make inquisition. Of those who have felons (in custody), they say that Nicholas de Burton, steward of Henry de Lascy, had Evan, weaver (*text'icem*) of Gumersal in the prison at Bradeford, and took from him two cows, and permitted him to go without judgment."*

Bradford in Testa de Nevill.—Bradford is mentioned in the ancient account of the royal rights existing in various lordships, known as Testa de Nevill, drawn up by Johand de Nevill, a judge or justice itinerant in the reign of Henry III., at some time or times between 1216 and 1272. Every manor then formed a knight's fee, or part of one, and was liable on the summons of the king to the lord of the manor, or to the superior lord of the fee, to furnish a certain number

* Hopkinson's MSS. quoted in James' History of Bradford, p. 50.

of soldiers to the king's armies, in time of war. The De Lacis held seventy knight's fees in about 150 manors in the West Riding, and they or their tenants had to supply seventy times as many soldiers as an ordinary knight. Their lands in Bradford rendered them liable to furnish half the soldiers required from a knight's fee; the knight's fee in Yorkshire being about 2000 acres of land, though considerably less in the south of England, where the land was then more valuable:—

"The copy of Testa de Nevill, in the King's Remembrancer's Office, shows that the earl of Lincoln (De Laci), his sub-tenants, and others, had in Bradford and the immediate neighbourhood the following fees:—In Bolling, one third part of a knight's fee. William de Swillington (in Bierley) held one fourth of a fee. The abbot of Kirkstall held, in Allerton, one half of a fee. Robert de Horton held one third part of a knight's fee. Gilbert the younger, of Horton, held the tenth part of a knight's fee. In Bradfordale (vallis de Bradeford) was one half of a fee held by the earl of Lincoln. In Clayton there was due for the tax called scutage, 11s. 8½d. The whole of the scutage for the honour of the earl of Lincoln was 79s. 2d, or about £55 of modern money." *

Charter for holding a Market and Fair at Bradford, 1294.—In this year King Edward I. confirmed to Henry de Laci, earl of Lincoln, and his heirs, the right to hold a weekly market at Bradford every Thursday; and also conferred upon him and his heirs the right to hold a fair in Bradford every year, to continue for five days, namely, on the eve and on the day of St. Peter ad Vincula, and for three days following. The witnesses to this charter were Edmund (earl of Lancaster), the king's brother, the bishops of Durham, Bath and Wells, and others. The charter was dated at Westminster, 6th June, 1294 (22nd Edward I.). The privilege of holding a fair was then of great value, as in those ages nearly all the trade of the country, except in articles of daily food, was carried on in fairs, which were specially guarded, and were attended by buyers and sellers of wool, cloth, lead, iron, and other articles, from all parts of the kingdom.

The Parish of Bradford at the time of Pope Nicholas' Valuation, 1291.—We also obtain a very interesting account of the value of the rectory, vicarage, and tithes of Bradford, in the year 1291, the 19th Edward I., in what is called Pope Nicholas' Valuation. In the year 1288, Pope Nicholas IV. condescended to grant the tenths

* Testa de Nevill, in James' History of Bradford.

of all ecclesiastical benefices in England to King Edward I. for six years, towards defraying the expense of an expedition to the Holy Land ; and that they might be collected to their full value, a taxation by the king's precept was begun in that year, which was completed in the province of Canterbury in the year 1291, and in that of York in the following year. This taxation was for many ages a most important record, as most if not all the taxes of the clergy, both to our kings and to the popes, were regulated by it, until the 26th year of the reign of King Henry VIII., 1534-35, when the new valuation, well known as the *Valor Ecclesiasticus*, was established. The taxation of Pope Nicholas also possesses great historical interest, as showing what was the supposed value of the tenths of all ecclesiastical benefices in England, in the year 1291, and thus enabling us to form an approximate estimate of the value of the produce of the parishes, of which the tithes were the tenth part. Thus in the case of the parish of Bradford, it appears that the value of the rectory at that time was £53 6s. 8d., and that of the vicarage £13 6s. 8d. These sums amount together to £66 13s. 4d., and by adding to them the other nine-tenths we obtain an amount of £666 and a few shillings, as the approximate yearly value of the landed produce of Bradford at that time. But as we have already stated, the value of money, of the same denomination, was fifteen times as great in 1291 as it is at present, so that the annual value of the tithable property of the parish of Bradford in the year 1291, in modern money, was fifteen times £666, or about £10,000.

Bradford when it passed into the hands of the House of Lancaster, in 1311.—Much the best account of Bradford in these early ages, is contained in the Inquisition or Inquiry into the value of the De Laci property, in the manor of Bradford and its berewicks, made on the death of Henry de Laci, the last earl of Lincoln of that family, which event occurred in the year 1311, the 5th of the reign of King Edward II. Inquisitions of this kind were held on the death of every great tenant of the crown, in order to ascertain what was the value of his estates, and what rights, if any, accrued to the crown from the decease of its tenant. These inquiries were made with more than ordinary care when, as in this case, the estates passed to a minor or a female ; the crown having in those cases the control of the estate until the heir reached his majority, or until the heiress was married to a husband selected by the king. In this case Alicia or Alice, the sole heiress of Henry the last earl of Lincoln, married Thomas Plantagenet, the son of Edmund the first earl of Lancaster, and a grandson of King Henry III. This was a wretched and disgraceful marriage, attended with all kinds of scandals, and ended in a separation before the death of the earl of Lancaster, who was himself beheaded at Pontefract for high treason ; and in the marriage of Alicia, after a variety of discreditable adventures, to Ebulo L'Estrange (said to have been an old lover), with a most liberal allowance of 5000 merks per annum, or not much less than £50,000 a year of modern money. But the estates of the De Lacis, including Bradford, were subsequently given by Edward III. to his cousin Henry, the second earl of Lancaster, and ultimately descended to the duchy of Lancaster, and through it to the Crown. The account of that portion of the estates which was in Bradford and the neighbourhood is as follows :—

INQUISITIO POST MORTEM, ON THE DEATH OF HENRY DE LACI, THE LAST EARL OF LINCOLN, 1311, 5TH EDWARD II.

After the death of Henry De Laci, the usual Inquisition as to the value of his lands and other territorial possessions was taken at Pontefract, on the 3rd day of March, 1311. The following is a translation of this document, so far as relates to the possessions of the deceased earl in the manor and neighbourhood of Bradford. We are informed that :—

"The earl had at Bradford a hall (*aulam*) or manor-house with chambers, and it is nothing worth beyond necessary repairs [manor-houses and castles were not taxed in these Inquiries], and there are there forty acres in demesne (land), demised to divers tenants at will, the value whereof yearly is 8*d.* an acre, . . £ s. p. 1 6 8*

And there are there 156 acres of land approved [reclaimed from the waste], demised to divers tenants at will, and valued by the year at 4*d.* an acre,† . . 2 11 0

And there are there four acres of wood which is separate, and the value of the herbage yearly is 0 2 0

And there is there one water mill, valued by the year at 10 0 0

And a fulling mill, which is worth yearly 1 0 0

And there is there a certain market, every seventh day, upon the Lord's day, the toll of which is worth yearly ‡ 3 0 0

And there is there a certain fair which is held yearly upon the Feast of St. Andrew the Apostle, the toll of which is worth yearly 3 0 0

And there are certain villeins (bondage tenants) who hold twenty-three oxgangs of land in bondage, and render yearly at the Feast of St. Martin (4*s.* for every oxgang), (8 to 24 acres),§ 4 16 0

* All these amounts ought to be multiplied by fifteen, to show their value in present money.
† About five shillings an acre of modern money.
‡ This is rather remarkable, for the day mentioned in both the charters is Thursday.
§ Nicholas, Notitia Historica p. 134.

		£	s.	d.
And the same villeins do work in autumn, which is worth yearly, for every oxgang, 3d.,				—
And the same villeins hold certain parcels of land approved [reclaimed from the waste], and render therefor at the term aforesaid,		0	18	3
And there are there certain tenants at will, who hold three oxgangs of land, and render therefor yearly, at the term aforesaid (that is, for every oxgang, 5s.),		0	15	0
And there are there certain burgesses (*burgenses*) who hold twenty-eight burgages, and two parts of one burgage, and an eighth part of one burgage, and render therefor yearly at the term aforesaid,*		1	17	6
And there are there certain free renters or farmers (*liberi firmarii*), who hold certain messuages and certain parcels of land approved [reclaimed from the waste], rented at their true value, and render therefor yearly at the term aforesaid,		1	11	4
And there are there certain free tenants (*liberi tenentes*) who hold their tenements of the said earl, and render yearly their rents and services at the Feast of St. Martin, according to the particulars thereof under written :—				
Ade de Eton, for a messuage and three oxgangs,		0	7	4
Robert de Northcrofte, for a toft and croft,		0	4	8
Roger Carpenter, for two messuages,		0	0	6
Hugh, son of Luke, for two messuages,		0	0	7
William de Poleover, for six acres of land,		0	0	2
Adam, son of Robert the Clerk, for two oxgangs of land,		0	2	9
William Brome, for three oxgangs of land,		0	3	10
William Grey, for one oxgang of land,		0	1	4
Walter Heris, for two oxgangs of land,		0	3	10
William Baume, for ten acres of land,		0	4	4
William Childyonge, for ten acres of land,		0	3	4
Ade de Eton, for ten acres of land,		0	3	4
Hugh de Benecliffe, for ten acres of land,		0	3	4
Ralph de Rachdale, for two oxgangs of land in Horton,		0	2	3
Luke de Horton, for two oxgangs of land,		0	2	3
William de Clayton, for ten oxgangs of land in Clayton, and four oxgangs of land in Oxenhope,		0	14	10
Jordan de Bierley, for eight oxgangs of land in Clayton, and one librate with all the appurtenances,		0	1	0
William de Horton, for four oxgangs of land in Oxenhope,		0	4	0
The heirs of John de Haworth, for four oxgangs of land in Haworth, and for five oxgangs of land in Manningham,		0	7	0
Thomas de Thornton, for land in Allerton, yielding 5s. yearly, and work in autumn,		0	17	10
William de Scholes, for an oxgang of land,		0	3	1
John King, of Horton, for one oxgang and a half,		0	6	6
And the same renders work in autumn,		0	0	2½
John Lemon, for one oxgang of land,		0	2	2
And renders work in autumn yearly,		0	0	1½
Ralph de Hill, for one oxgang of land in Horton,		0	1	0
And the same renders work in autumn for the same,		0	0	1½
William Crementor, for two oxgangs of land in Horton,		0	0	3
Theobaldus de Thornhill, for one essart [piece of reclaimed land] in Horton,		0	0	2
The abbot of Kirkstall, for four oxgangs of land in Horton, a pair of white spurs.				
Robert de Northrop, for one oxgang of land in Manningham,		0	0	9

* The rent of burgage land was generally one shilling an acre, equal to fifteen shillings of modern money, and often more, the tenure being so much more permanent and valuable than that of land held at will or for short terms.

	£	s.	d.
Robert de Manningham, for two oxgangs of land in Horton,	0	0	3
Village of Wike, for work in autumn from ancient times, yearly,	0	2	0
Land held by the church of Bradford, eight oxgangs of land in Bradford for work in autumn,	0	0	8
Adam de Windhill, for essart [piece of reclaimed land] in Allerton,	0	2	0
And the same earl hath a certain free court (held from three weeks to three weeks), and other pleas or perquisites of court, yearly,	0	14	4
The whole sum,	£39	9	6

The sum of £39 9s. 6d. given in this interesting return ought to be multiplied by fifteen, to show its value in our present money, when it will be seen that the value of the De Laci estates in Bradford and the immediate neighbourhood, in the year 1311, was about £600 a year. The classes of persons mentioned as holding land are, twenty-eight burgesses, thirty-five free tenants, thirty free farmers, and twenty-three villeins or bondage tenants. This gives a total of about 100 tenants of the classes named; and taking their families at an average of five, the whole number of persons is from 470 to 500. Mr. James estimates the population of Bradford at this time, 1311, at 650. There may have been other residents not included in this return, but the chief distinction at that time was that of bond or free. The extent of the essarts, or newly inclosed land, shows that cultivation was spreading around Bradford.

Bradford in the hands of the Plantagenets, Earls and Dukes of Lancaster.—Bradford passed to the Plantagenets, earls of Lancaster, by marriage with Alicia de Laci and subsequent grant from King Edward III., to Henry the third earl of Lancaster; afterwards into those of other earls or dukes of Lancaster; still later into those of John of Gaunt, duke of Lancaster, the fourth son of King Edward III., on his marriage with Lady Blanche Plantagenet, the only surviving child of Henry, duke of Lancaster; and ultimately into those of Henry of Bolingbroke, son and heir of John of Gaunt, who made himself king of England, with the title of Henry IV. Whatever tendency there may have been, in the population of Bradford, to increase under its old or new lords, was effectually kept down for nearly fifty years, in the reigns of the three Edwards, by an incessant drain of able-bodied men of the town and neighbourhood, raised for the purpose of carrying on destructive wars in Scotland. In Edward I.'s Scottish campaign of 1299, a commission was issued to raise 400 chosen men in the wapentake of "Barkeston" Ash, the liberties of Bradford, and the soke of Snaith, all to be at

Carlisle, on the day of the Assumption of the Blessed Lady (August 15). Nor was Bradford alone in these merciless and murderous conscriptions, for the same number of men were also demanded, and perhaps drained away, for the same purpose, from each of the wapentakes of Agbrigg, Morley, Skyrack, and Claro. In the campaign of 1299, near 6000 soldiers were raised, or at least demanded, in Yorkshire alone. In times like those, war, famine, and pestilence conspired to keep down the numbers of the people; hence the increase was almost incredibly slow, and was sometimes stopped altogether. Between the time of the survey of Bradford given above, as made in the year 1311, the 5th Edward II., and the survey made in the time of Henry Plantagenet, earl of Derby, afterwards duke of Lancaster, in the year 1342, the population of this part of Yorkshire must have been much more than decimated by the slaughter of the battles of Dunbar, Stirling, Bannockburn, and Halidon Hill; and after Bannockburn the country had to undergo the misery of a general invasion, by a justly enraged enemy. It is said that the invading army of Bruce, commanded by Randolph, had their head-quarters in the hundred of Morley, near Leeds and Bradford, and laid waste the country at its pleasure. At an inquisition of the manor, taken in the year 1342, the value of the estates in Bradford had sunk to about one-half their previous amount. In a third survey made in 1361, on the death of Henry the first duke of Lancaster, there was some recovery, the fortune of war having again turned in favour of England, and invasion being no longer added to the waste of foreign war; but the effect of these sanguinary wars was long felt in this and every other part of the north of England.

As already mentioned, four earls or dukes of the royal house of Plantagenet held the lordship of Bradford, with the other estates which had belonged to the De Lacis in Yorkshire, before they became the property of the crown in the person of Henry of Bolingbroke, duke of Lancaster, afterwards King Henry IV. Inquiries supplying some information as to the nature and value of their estates in Bradford and elsewhere took place in the time of each earl or duke. The following are summaries of the information obtained at these inquisitions:—

In the year 1342 Bradford belonged to Henry, earl of Derby, afterwards duke of Lancaster. According to a valuation made that year, the manor included a messuage or manor-house, in ruins, worth 2s.; a certain meadow called the Halling, containing one acre, valued at 3s.; forty acres of land in demesne, 40s.; a wood of sixteen acres, 2s., and underwood, 1s. 8d.; pannage for the swine of the *nativi* (serfs); one fulling mill open (*discoopta*) to every house, valued beyond repairs at 8s., and held by William the Walker (or Fuller) and James the Walker for 10s.; also a corn mill sufficient for all the houses, which, exclusive of the cost of repairs, was valued at £6 6s. 8d. a year; the toll of the fair on the day of Saint Andrew the Apostle, £5 13s. 4d.; the perquisites of the court held every three weeks, 13s. 4d.; two sheriff's terms yearly, £1 13s. 4d.; fees on the marriage of female serfs, 13s. 4d.; also a parcel of land called Bolleshagh, containing thirty acres by estimation, besides ten at an inferior rent—10s.; sum total, £18 6s. 8d. Another inquisition as to the value of the lordship, was made in the year 1361. In that year Henry, duke of Lancaster, died at Leicester, leaving two daughters, Maude and Blanche, the younger of whom married John of Gaunt, the fourth son of King Edward III., first created Earl of Richmond, and afterwards Duke of Lancaster. An inquisition was taken on the estates of Duke Henry, at York, on Saturday, the Feast of St. George, 1361. In this inquest the jurors stated that there was at Bradford the site of one capital messuage, one acre and one rood of meadow, forty acres of demesne held by tenants-at-will, who paid 33s., at the feast of St. Martin, for the whole year; one water mill and one fulling mill, with the toll of market and fair, paying £12, at two equal terms; that the free tenants and the *nativi* or bondmen paid £11 4s. 6d.; that at Bradford, Stanbury, and Manningham the *nativi* paid £4 4s.; that the pannage or mast for feeding the hogs of the *nativi* yielded 24s.; that the herbage of Bradford Bank and Rohagh was worth 2s.; and that the perquisites of the courts, with the profits of the two sheriffs' turns or courts, were 40s. Mr. James says that Bradford Bank was the hill or bank to the north of the church, and that Rohagh was the same as the uninclosed wood mentioned in the extent, and a remnant of the wood recorded in Domesday Survey.

The last twenty years of Edward III. were comparatively prosperous, for he had vanquished all his enemies, had introduced Flemish manufactures into England, and had opened a great trade in wool with Flanders.

Amongst other acts of ownership performed at Bradford by

John of Gaunt, duke of Lancaster, was the making or confirming of a grant of lands to John Northrop of Manningham, on condition of attending upon the duke and his successors when he or they passed through Bradford, and of remaining there for thirty days, armed with a spear and attended by a greyhound, receiving yeoman's board, namely, a penny (15*d.*) for himself, and a halfpenny for his dog. The land was afterwards granted to the Rushworths of Horton.

The following is a copy of this curious grant:—"Know all present and future that I, John of Gaunt, duke of Lancaster, have given and granted, and by this my present charter have confirmed, unto John Northrop of Manyngham, three messuages and six oxgangs of land, and sufficient common of pasture to the same belonging, in Manyngham aforesaid, lying and abutting there upon one brook, running between Manyingham and Horton on the south; upon one small brook called Bull-royd Syke on the west; on the north, between Manyngham and Heaton, to the height where the rain-water divides (*aqua pluvialis dividit*); and on the east upon one small brook called Shaw Syke, to the water which runneth by Bradford; with all and singular the liberties and easements in Manyingham aforesaid: to have and to hold the aforesaid three messuages and six oxgangs of land, with sufficient common to the same belonging and appertaining, with all the conveniences, to the aforesaid John Northrop, his heirs and assigns, of the chief lord of the fee thereof, by his services due and of right accustomed: rendering therefor yearly to me and my heirs, coming to Bradford, one blast with his horn (*unum flatum cornu*) upon St. Martin's day in winter, and attending upon me and my heirs, coming to Bradford from Blackburnshire, with one lance and hunting dog (*cane venatico*) for the space of forty days, having yeoman's board, one penny for himself, and a halfpenny for the dog, per day, and rendering as well one of his best cattle (*averia*), on the day of death for relief, and going with my receiver, or bailiff, to conduct him with his friends safe to Pontefract, whenever the same shall be faithfully required. And I truly, the aforesaid John of Gaunt, and my heirs, the aforesaid three messuages and six oxgangs of land, with sufficient common and all other the premises before mentioned, to the aforesaid John Northrop and his heirs, against all men will warrant and for ever defend. In witness whereof I have to this present writing put opposite my seal.—Dated at Lancaster, 4th of August, Edward III."

Mr. James says, "The original horn," which was mentioned by

Gough, the editor of Camden, "is now (1841) in the possession of Mr. Jonathan Wright." It is now (1873) owned by Sir Titus Salt, Bart., of Saltaire, near Bradford. It had, previous to coming into the hands of these gentlemen, been handed down from generation to generation, by the possessors of the Hunt Yard (part of the land in question). Since the time of Gough (who wrote about the middle of the last century), it had been reornamented with silver, and Mr. James says of it, "It is one of the most beautiful specimens of ox horn that I have ever seen. Its colour is a dappled grey. The length on the outer side, from the tip to the end, is twenty-eight inches; the girth of the extremity at the wider end nine inches, tapering beautifully to the tip. This horn has connected with it many associations which are interesting to the inhabitants of Bradford. It is probably coeval with the origin of Bradford Arms, which without a shadow of doubt took their rise from the above-mentioned singular tenure. These arms are now, according to the current representation, Gules, a chevron or, between three bugle horns strung sable; crest, a boar's head erased—and evidently point at the slaying of the woody boar, and the blowing of the horn on Saint Martin's Day."*

With regard to the custom of holding lands by the possession and the blowing of a horn, it is of extreme antiquity, and goes back to the time when the Angles and Saxons conquered this country. A considerable portion of the lands of York Minster were held by the possession of the horn of Ulphus, an ancient Anglian king of Deira or Northumbria. The date of this grant is about A.D. 700, but the horn of Ulphus is still amongst the treasures of the Minster. The horn of the Puseys is as old as the time of King Canute, and numerous cases of the tenure of lands by the blowing of a horn, on the arrival of the chief lord or his representative within a lordship, are given in Testa de Nevill, which, as already mentioned, was drawn up in the reign of John of Gaunt's ancestor, King Henry III. The object of this grant was to secure to the lord the personal attendance of a guard of his own military followers, in his journeys from his castles in Lancashire to his great castle at Pontefract. To insure this, it was required that they should come armed to the place of meeting, that they should remain thirty days on duty, and that they should be accompanied by a hunting-dog, for the purposes of sport. The latter was also a very frequent condition in ancient

* James' History of Bradford, p. 97.

grants of land, and according to Domesday Book the whole of the lands between the river Ribble and the river Mersey were held by the tenants of the crown, on condition that they should attend the great hunting parties of the lord, who a few years before the Domesday Survey was King Edward the Confessor, as great a hunter as Nimrod himself, though not a hunter of men. John of Gaunt, and all the earls and dukes of Lancaster, entertained claims to the throne, which were finally carried out by Henry of Bolingbroke, and which required that they should always be sure of the assistance of their most warlike supporters. John of Gaunt himself had many knights and gentlemen in his pay, to some of whom he gave lands on mere nominal terms, and others of whom he paid by liberal grants of money. Thus Rankin of Ypres, in Flanders, received £10 a year, equal probably to more than £100 a year of present money, on condition of supporting John of Gaunt in all his military undertakings; and that was no doubt the real object in the case of the grant of lands to John Northrop of Manningham and Bradford. These lands had previously been held by the payment of a money rent.

King Edward III., in the thirty-eighth year of his reign, granted to John of Gaunt, Blanche his wife, to their heirs, and to their tenants in Bradford, as part of their duchy of Lancaster (which included the whole of the estates that had belonged to the De Lacis), freedom from local tolls and charges on roads, bridges, and markets (known in that age as passage, pontage, and stallage), throughout England. This exemption continued in force for two or three centuries; for in the year 1690 the inhabitants of Bradford obtained letters patent, in which, after reciting the grants of Edward III. to John, duke of Lancaster, it was commanded "that our men and tenants, inhabitants of and resident of and within our manor of Bradford, in the county of York, parcel of our said duchy (of Lancaster), shall have, use, and exercise all the liberties in the above grant contained, according to the effect of the above-mentioned grants and statutes; and that they be not molested, provided that all and singular the aforesaid men and tenants do pay toll, pontage, lastage, &c., in all fairs, markets, and places within the said duchy, wherein the same hath heretofore been paid, as is just."* These exemptions were no doubt valuable when they were granted, but they lost their value in modern times. In the same age

* James' History of Bradford, p. 99.

John of Gaunt granted the manor of Bradford to his son by Catherine Swinford, John de Beaufort, marquis of Dorset, one of his sons of doubtful legitimacy, from whom, however, Henry VII. was descended. In the twenty-first year of Richard II. this John de Beaufort obtained a grant, or rather a confirmation of the ancient right, to hold a fair at Bradford, on the eve and day of Saint Peter ad Vincula, and on the day next following, and to hold a market every Thursday.

Bradford in the hands of the Plantagenet Kings, 1399–1400 to 1482.—Bradford passed to Henry of Bolingbroke, son of John of Gaunt, and afterwards King Henry IV. of England, in the year 1399–1400, and no doubt shared in the miseries of the wars of York and Lancaster, which originated in the rival claims to the throne of two of the descendants of Edward III., the heads of the houses of York and Lancaster. These wars raged with little interruption for more than fifty years. At that time the house of York held nearly one-half of the West Riding of Yorkshire, including the towns of Wakefield and Halifax; and the house of Lancaster held the greater part of the other half, including Bradford and Leeds. In this county the Yorkists held all the estates that had belonged to the earls of Warren, of which Sandal castle, near Wakefield, and Coningsboro' castle, between Wakefield and Sheffield, were the chief feudal fortresses; and the house of Lancaster held those that had belonged to the De Lacis, earls of Lincoln, of which Pontefract and Tickhill castles were the chief places of strength. It is not certain that there was at that time any castle either at Leeds or at Bradford, a circumstance which may have kept the war in Yorkshire away from both, and caused it to spend its fury on Wakefield, York, and the intervening country. In the reign of King Edward IV., the great champion of the house of York, a charter was granted, or rather confirmed, to the people of Bradford, entitling them to hold a market every Thursday, and two fairs yearly.

Bradford in the Time of the Tudors.—At the close of the wars of York and Lancaster, Bradford, like most of the towns in the West Riding of Yorkshire, began to advance in prosperity, partly to the restoration of tranquillity at home, and partly to the opening of a great trade with Flanders, and the influx of large quantities of gold and silver from America, which country was discovered in the year 1492, seven years after Henry VII. gained the English throne by the battle of Bosworth Field, fought in the year 1485. In the reign of Henry VII. the fairs of Bradford had become very extensive. We are told in a bill filed in the Duchy Court of Lancaster by Sir Richard Tempest, John Rawson, John Bowett, Christopher Rawson, and others, in this reign, that there were at that time three fairs held at Bradford, of great resort by merchants, pedlars, chapmen, and the inhabitants of the surrounding country, but that such fairs were much less attended, and the town thereby greatly hurt, by reason of the excessive and unlawful toll demanded by the king's bailiff there. In another bill of a still earlier date, filed by the inhabitants of Manningham against John Clerk the king's auditor, the complainants stated that they or their ancestors had occupied certain oxgang land at 4s. 5d. (about £2 10s.), an oxgang (ten to twenty acres), for the space of 300 years, and had done several services, such as repairing the mill dam, and had carried great quantities of stone and other materials to repair the said dam; that they paid fines on heirships; "that they have hard fare and living;" and that John Clerk, the king's auditor, had put them out of their lands and increased their rents, as well freeholders as copyholders; that they had formerly had common of pasture, on the moors and commons adjoining to the town of Bradford, but that "the said auditor hath lately inclosed great part of them, and left little to the said tenants of Manningham."

We also obtain some further information as to the condition of Bradford, in the 9th Henry VII., 1493-94, from a bill filed in the Duchy Court of Lancaster by inhabitants of Bradford against William Bradford, otherwise Rawson, complaining of him, that he had built a fair place upon a piece of ground holden of the king by copy of court roll, after the custom of the manor of Bradford; that his son, John Bradford, was holding inquiries as to copyhold tenements held by the king, and that "there is now one Bryan Bradford, otherwise Rawson, who is clerk of the Court of Bradford and keeper of the court rolls, which Bryan is brother of the said John, and now has all the court rolls, and no tenant can get to them but by his license, and he may make all to his brother's advantage." By the formation of this family compact, which furnished the brothers with an opportunity of playing into each other's hands for their mutual interest, they certainly laid themselves open to suspicion, and the complaint of the inhabitants seems to have been well-founded. It is thus satisfactory to know that jobbing came within the range of the wisdom of our ancestors, just as instances of it occasionally turn up among their descendants, who in so many other things have profited by their lessons, and shown themselves true to the instincts of the race.

Leland's Account of Bradford.—Leland in his "Itinerary," published about 1536, in the reign of King Henry VIII., speaks of Bradford as an active, rising, town. He says:—"Bradford [is] a pretty, quick, market town, *dimidio autem amplius minus Wackefelda* [one half or more less than Wakefield]. It hath one parish church, and a chapel of St. Sitha. It standeth much by clothing, and is distant six miles from Halifax and four miles from Christial Abbey (Kirkstall Abbey)." He further describes it as a quicker or more active town than Leeds. Leland speaks of the brooks which flow through Bradford, down Bradford Dale into the Aire, as follows:—

"There is a confluence in this toune (Bradford) of three brokes. One riseth above Bouline Haul (Bowling Hall), so that the head is a mile and a half from the town, and this at the town hath a bridge of one arche; another riseth a two mile off, having a mille and a bridge. The third riseth four miles off." James, in his "History of Bradford," says that the whole of these brooks are inconsiderable streams; but there can be no doubt that they supplied the water-power which was absolutely necessary for the working of the woollen mill erected there by the De Lacis, earls of Lincoln, in the time of the Plantagenet kings, and to which, as we are expressly informed, the whole of the burgesses and free tenants had access. Mr. James states that the first of these brooks is formed by rills rising in the Roughs and Park Side between Bowling and Bierley, and feeding the pond below Bowling Hall. The second brook, he states, has its source upon Bradford Moor. The third or main stream, known as Bradford Beck, rises at Bell Dean or Old Allen, in the township of Allerton. In the progress of the brook down Allerton valley, it receives several tributary streams and divides the townships of Allerton and Thornton, being called Allerton Beck. In its progress down to Bradford it is joined by Horton Beck, and running past Bradford it falls into the river Aire, at Shipley. "None of the three streams, which unite at Bradford, have from ancient time had any definite appellation. At least, in the charters and old deeds this is not the case. Even the largest of them, in the early charters, is merely described as "the water which runneth from or through Bradford." Yet these streams were of great value both in ancient and in modern times, not merely in furnishing water-power for the infant manufactures of the town, but in supplying more recently the water, or a portion of it, for the Bradford Canal, which connected the town with the Leeds and Liverpool Canal, and conferred upon it the immense advantage of water-carriage, from near the end of the last century.*

Bradford in the Great Civil War, 1640–1645.—Bradford, with Leeds, Halifax, and the clothing district of the West Riding, took a very active and determined part in the civil war between Charles I. and the Long Parliament, Bradford being the chief stronghold of that party, in the West Riding. None of those towns were then directly represented in Parliament, except as forming portions of the county constituency of Yorkshire; but they were already the chief places in the West Riding, and as such took a leading part in all public affairs. The Fairfaxes, the Lamberts, and other great parliamentary families of Yorkshire, several of which resided within a few miles of Bradford, were looked upon as the natural leaders of the people in that great contest, and led them to ultimate victory. At the beginning of the civil war, Sir Thomas Fairfax, the representative of a race of soldiers, and a man of dauntless courage and great military talent, assumed the command of the parliamentary party in the neighbourhood of Bradford; whilst his father, Fernando Lord Fairfax, was appointed governor of the fortress of Hull, and was recognized as the commander-in-chief for the Parliament, in all those parts of Yorkshire which upheld the authority of that assembly and resisted the demands of the king. Thus Hull was the head-quarters of Lord Fairfax, and Bradford the head-quarters of his much abler son, at the commencement of the civil war. But those places are more than sixty miles distant from each other, and it was with great difficulty that they kept up communications across the county, for they were constantly threatened by the royal army, under the marquis of Newcastle, whose head-quarters were at York; and for some time by the royalist garrisons at Leeds and Wakefield, as well as those in Sandal and Pontefract castles. Their chief line of communication, when they had one, was through Leeds and Selby; but on more than one occasion it was closed by the royalists,

* James, p 7.

and it was never permanently secured until the spring of 1644, when the Scottish army advanced from the border, and joined the armies of the Fairfaxes, and those of Manchester and Cromwell, under the walls of York. From the beginning of the year 1643, to the middle of 1644, the parliamentary party in the West Riding was very severely pressed by the royalists. Both Bradford and Leeds were more than once taken, and the parliamentary forces were on one occasion driven back beyond Halifax to the borders of Lancashire. There they were joined and assisted by the parliamentary forces of Lancashire and Cheshire. In return for this service the parliamentary army of Yorkshire, under the command of Sir Thomas Fairfax, occasionally joined the parliamentary forces of Lancashire and Cheshire, and aided them in gaining some very considerable victories. Amongst those was the victory of Nantwich in Cheshire, in which the royal army, organized in Ireland by the earl of Strafford, brought over to Chester by Lord Byron, and aided by the royal forces of Cheshire, was completely defeated by the Yorkshire, Lancashire, and Cheshire parliamentary forces, under the chief command of Sir Thomas Fairfax. There it was that Fairfax and Monk first met; the former as commander of the victorious parliamentary army, the latter as a prisoner in the Irish army organized by Lord Strafford. Many years later they again met at York; and there arranged the restoration of Charles II.

At the beginning of the great civil war on the 9th of January, 1643, Sir Thomas Fairfax, being in command of the parliamentary forces near Bradford, wrote to his father, Lord Fairfax, then in command at Hull, a letter which shows the resolute spirit of the people of Bradford, and the surrounding district. "I am sure," he says, "I shall have 600 muskets if I summon the country to come in; besides 3000 and more (men) with other weapons, that would rise with us." The result showed that he was not mistaken; for the royalists, who had then possession of Leeds, having attacked the parliamentary forces at Bradford, the latter not only held their ground, but succeeded in repulsing the assailants, and opened a communication with Lord Fairfax and the Hothams at Hull. Sir Thomas Fairfax's narrative of the commencement of the civil war in this district is very interesting. He says: "The first action we had was at Bradford. We were about 300 men, the enemy 700 or 800, and two pieces of ordnance. They assaulted us; we drew out close to the town, to receive them. They had the advantage of the ground, the town being encompassed with hills, which exposed us more to their cannon, from which we received some hurt; but our men defended those passages by which they were to descend so well that they got no ground of us; and now the day being spent, they drew off and retired to Leeds. A few days after, Captain Hotham, with three troops of horse and some dragoons (from Hull and Selby), came to us. Then we marched to Leeds; but the enemy having notice of it, quitted the town, and in haste fled to York." Leeds, however, was not taken by Sir Thomas Fairfax without a resolute defence, in which the royalists were at length driven from the town with loss. We have already given an account of the storming of Leeds, by Fairfax, in the history of that town.

But the early triumphs of the Bradford parliamentarians did not last long. The superior numbers, discipline, and equipments of the king's army, 7000 to 8000 strong, under the command of the earl, afterwards marquis, of Newcastle (William Cavendish), proved too much for them; and the Yorkshire parliamentary army under Fairfax was totally defeated on Adwalton Moor, in Birstal parish, near both to Bradford and Leeds. After narrating his adventures at other points, Fairfax, in his "Short Memorial," proceeds to give the following account of his adventures at Bradford, after his defeat by Newcastle at Adwalton:—"The earl of Newcastle," he says, "spent three or four days in laying his quarters about the town of Bradford, and brought down his cannons, but needed not to raise batteries; for the hills, within half musket shot, commanded all the town. Being planted in two places, they shot furiously upon us, and made their approaches, which made us spend very much of our little store, being not above twenty-five or twenty-six barrels of powder, at the beginning of the siege. Yet the earl of Newcastle sent a trumpet to offer us conditions, which I accepted, so they were honourable for us to take and safe for the inhabitants. We sent two captains to treat with him, and agreed to a cessation of hostilities during that time, but he continued working still; whereupon I sent forth the commissioners again, suspecting a design of attempting something upon us. They returned not till eleven o'clock at night, and then with a slight answer." The royalists had profited by this parley, to get their cannon into position near the heart of the town.

"Whilst they (the commissioners) were delivering the answer to us, we heard great shooting of cannon and muskets; all ran presently to the works, which the enemy was storming. Here for three quarters of an hour was very hot service, but at length they retreated. They made a second attempt; but were also beaten off. After this we had not above one barrel of powder left, and no match. I called the officers together, when it was advised and resolved to withdraw presently, before it was day, and to retreat to Leeds, by forcing a way, which we must do, for they had surrounded the town. Orders were despatched and speedily executed. The foot, commanded by Colonel Rogers, was sent out through some narrow lanes, and they were to beat up the dragoons' quarters, and so go on to Leeds. I myself, with some other officers, went with the horse, which were not above fifty, in a more open way. I must not here forget my wife, who ran the same hazard with us in this retreat, and with as little expression of fear; not from any zeal or delight in the war, but through a willing and patient suffering of this undesirable condition. I sent two or three horsemen before, to discover what they could of the enemy, who presently returned and told us there was a guard of horse close by us. Before I had gone forty paces, the day beginning to break, I saw them upon the hill above us, being about 300 horse. I, with some twelve more, charged them. Sir Henry Fowlis, Major-general Gifford, myself, and three more, brake through. Captain Mudd was slain, and the rest of our horse being close by, the enemy fell upon them and soon routed them, taking most of them prisoners, amongst whom was my wife; the officer, William Hill, behind whom she rid, being taken. I saw this disaster, but could give no relief; for after I was got through, I was in the enemy's rear alone." This high-spirited woman, who afterwards appeared in Westminster Hall to protest against the condemnation and execution of Charles I., was of the noble and warlike family of the De Veres. The marquis of Newcastle, a fine specimen of an English royalist, sent back Lady Fairfax to her husband in his own coach, accompanied by a lady of honour. "Those," continued Fairfax, "who had charged through with me went on to Leeds, thinking I had done so too; but I was unwilling to leave my company, and stayed there till I saw there was no more in my power to do, but to be taken prisoner with them. I then retired to Leeds. The like disaster fell among the foot, that went the other way by a mistake; for after they had marched a little way, the van fell into the dragoons' quarters, clearing their way; but through a cowardly fear, he that commanded these men being in the rear, made them face about and march again into the town, where the next day they were all taken prisoners; only eighty or thereabouts of the foot that got through came to Leeds, mounted on horses which they had taken from the enemy, where I found them when I came thither; which was some joy to them all, they concluding that I was either slain or 'taken prisoner. At Leeds I found all in great distraction; the [parliamentary] council of war newly risen, where [at which] it was resolved to quit the town and retreat to Hull, which was sixty miles off, many of the enemy's garrisons being in the way. This, in two hours after, was accordingly done [commenced], lest the enemy should presently send horse to prevent us; for they had fifty or sixty troops within three miles. But we got well to Selby, where there was a ferry, and hard by a garrison at Cawood, and so to Hull."

After Fairfax's retreat the people of Bradford were thrown into great terror, by a rumour that Newcastle had ordered his men to give only "Bradford quarter," that is, no mercy at all, to the inhabitants. The origin of the phrase, and supposed motive for the order, was the reported slaughter of a young royalist, said to be a son of Lord Newport, who on claiming quarter was stated to have been struck down by his assailant, a townsman, who exclaimed derisively, "I'll give you Bradford quarter." The murderer of Lord Newport's son, if such a person existed, deserved to be shot; but the earl of Newcastle was much too noble-spirited a man to destroy the population of a whole town, to punish a single crime. Lord Newcastle's purpose, says a popular legend, was changed by a spiritual visitation at his lodgings at Bowling Hall. A figure appeared, and saying, "Pity poor Bradford! pity poor Bradford!" kept pulling the clothes off his bed, until he had reversed his orders. This story must have been invented by some credulous person, incapable of appreciating mercy and generosity in an enemy. The earl of Newcastle, Sir Thomas Fairfax, Sir Ralph Hopton (another distinguished Yorkshire royalist), and General Lambert, were all noble specimens of the race of English gentlemen, some of the royalist, others of the parliamentary party. We may say of them in the words of Shakspeare, that in the great civil war—

"Naught did they in hate, but all in honour."

Besides the disheartening loss of his wife, Sir Thomas Fairfax had to encounter the greatest difficulties in getting his little daughter, afterwards (unfortunately for herself) duchess of Buckingham, to a place of safety. He was wounded by a musket ball in the wrist, was without food and in the saddle for some forty-eight hours, and saw his child swoon several times from fatigue and privation, before he was able, mangled and exhausted as he was, to place her in security in Hull. His wife was restored to him in a few days, the duke of Newcastle having, as already stated, sent her back in his own coach, attended by a maid of honour. Besides Fairfax's " Short Memorial," there are three rare and curious tracts that illustrate this period of the history of Bradford. They are entitled respectively: — "The Rider on the White Horse [Sir Thomas Fairfax] and his Army, their late good success in Yorkshire; or a true and faithful relation of that famous and wonderful victory at Bradford, obtained by the clubmen there, with all the circumstances thereof; and of the taking of Leeds and Wakefield by the same men," &c.; "The Autobiography of Joseph Lister of Bradford, in Yorkshire;" "A true Relation of the Passages at Leeds, on Monday the 23rd January, 1642-43." A volume containing copies of these tracts was published, in London, in 1842; but Fairfax's truthful and modest history of the events is the most reliable of all the accounts of these spirit-stirring times. An excellent account of these and all the other great events in his history will be found in Clement Markham's "Life of the Great Lord Fairfax," published in the year 1871, in which justice is done to that noble patriot and most gallant and able soldier.

After the great victory of the parliamentary armies on Marston Moor, in July, 1644, the triumph of the parliamentary cause was complete in Yorkshire, except behind the almost impregnable walls of Pontefract Castle, the ancient abode of the De Lacis, and in Scarborough and some other strong castles, where small bodies of the Yorkshire royalists made most gallant but unsuccessful struggles against the victorious armies of Fairfax and Cromwell. Fairfax was alike opposed to the execution of Charles I. and to the military tyranny of Oliver Cromwell. Had it been possible either to trust the king or control the Protector, the great civil war might have ended as happily as the Revolution of 1688; and in that case a second revolution would not have been necessary to secure such institutions as those under which this country has long been so happy, free, and prosperous. After the death of Cromwell the people of Yorkshire consented to receive Charles II. as their king; but when he and his brother, James II., had shown their determination to govern in defiance of laws and of Parliament, they joined Lords Danby, Fairfax, and the leading gentlemen of Yorkshire, in again deposing the house of Stewart. But they did not receive what they had every right to ask (the right of returning members to Parliament), until long afterwards, in the year 1832, when it was given to them, together with all the other great towns of the kingdom.

Progress of Bradford from the Great Civil War, 1644, to the Accession of King George III., 1760.—The progress of population and industry in the town of Bradford was steady, but not rapid, during this long period. The persevering industry of the inhabitants, and the abundant supplies of water-power, of coal, and of building stone found in the neighbourhod, maintained Bradford in its position as one of the great manufacturing towns of the West Riding, but did not enable it to advance at much more than the tenth part of the rate, judging from the increase of the population, that has been witnessed during the present century. Bradford must have been a town of at least 5000 to 6000 inhabitants at the time of the great civil war, say in the year 1644; but did not more than double its population in the next hundred years. It can scarcely have had more than 10,000 inhabitants at the accession of George III. in the year 1760, as it had only 13,264 at the census of 1801.

During the whole of that period Bradford suffered from two great evils. In the first place it had no water communication, by navigable river or canal, with the other towns standing on the Yorkshire coal-field, or with the more distant parts of the kingdom, including the two great seaports of Hull and Liverpool, through which it now draws a considerable portion of its most valuable materials of industry, and by which it diffuses its numerous and beautiful manufactures over the surface of the globe. In this respect Bradford was in that age much less favourably situated than Leeds, which obtained the advantages of water carriage, by the navigable river Aire, about the year 1700. This was nearly seventy years before Bradford had water carriage of any kind.

Another very great disadvantage under which Bradford suffered during the period above mentioned was that it had no representation of its inhabitants, either in the Parliament of the United Kingdom or in any town council or other public body, speaking their opinions and capable of carrying out their wishes and directing the public expenditure. When the sagacious Daniel Defoe travelled through Yorkshire, about the year 1725, he remarked that the town of Wakefield, though containing a population which was then estimated to be nearly as great as the population of the city of York, had no local government, except that of a constable appointed by the lord of the manor as in any country village. The same observation would at that time have applied to Bradford, Halifax, Huddersfield, and Dewsbury, and indeed to Manchester and Birmingham. All these towns grew up into manufacturing and commercial greatness without any local government worth mentioning; and that is the principal reason why many things connected with the public health and comfort, and even with the industrial prosperity of those places, which now form the legitimate and most important duty of their municipal governments, were then neglected. The general laws of the country, which were free and good, produced an independent and high-spirited people; but in local administration almost every one did what seemed good in his own eyes, without regard to the general interests of the community amongst which he dwelt. Leeds and Sheffield were the only large manufacturing towns of the West Riding that possessed even moderately good local governments, previous to the passing of the Municipal Boroughs Act in the reign of William IV.

Daniel Defoe's Account of Bradford.—The best account that we have of Bradford in this age is contained in Daniel Defoe's "Tour through the Whole Island of Great Britain, by a Gentleman," published in the year 1727. That most sagacious observer and admirable describer of life and manners, made three long tours on horseback through Yorkshire, in the course of which he carefully examined every thing of interest in the large manufacturing towns of the West Riding, as well as in the city of York, the port of Hull, and the agricultural and pastoral districts of the county. He says, "In my first journey I came only west from York to Wakefield, and then turning south by Barnsley and Doncaster, went away still south to Rotherham, Sheffield, Chesterfield, Chatsworth, and the Peak. In the second journey I came out of the western part of England, namely from Cheshire through Lancashire, and passing east over those Andes of England called Blackstone Edge, and the mountains which, as I stated before, part Yorkshire and Lancashire, and reach from the High Peak (of Derbyshire) to Scotland, I came to Halifax, Bradford, Huddersfield, Leeds, Wetherby, Pontefract, and Borough Bridge, and so went away into the East Riding. The third journey I went from the Peak in Derbyshire again, and traversing the same country as I returned by in the first journey, as far as Wakefield, went on again north to Leeds, and thence over Harwood [Harewood] Bridge to Knaresborough Spaw [Harrogate], thence to Ripon, and through that old Roman streetway called Leeming Lane, to Pierce Bridge, thence to Durham, and so into Scotland." "If," says Defoe, "by all these circuits, and traversing the country so many ways, which I name for reasons above, I am not furnished to give a particular account of the most remarkable things, I must have spent my time very ill, and ought not to let you know how often I went through it." Describing the manufacturing district of the West Riding generally, Defoe observes :—"As the Calder river runs by Halifax, Huddersfield, and through Wakefield, so the Aire runs by Skipton, Bradford, and through Leeds, and then joins the Calder at Castleford Bridge, near Pontefract, so in a united stream forming that useful navigation, from this trading part of Yorkshire to Hull, to the infinite advantage of the whole county, and which as I took a singular satisfaction in visiting and inquiring into, so I believe you will be no less delighted in reading the account of it, which will be many ways both useful and very instructive."[*] At the period described by Defoe, he says "that the kersey and shalloon trade was confined to Halifax, and the towns, already named, of Huddersfield and Bradford." In making his journey from Halifax to Leeds he remarked that everywhere, to the right hand and the left, the country appeared busy, diligent, and even in a hurry of work, though they [the people] were not scattered and dispersed as in the parish of Halifax, where the houses stand one by one, but in villages; those villages large, full of houses, and those houses thronged with people; for [as he adds] the whole county is infinitely populous. All this part of the county is so considerable for its trade, that the post-master-general has thought fit to establish a cross-post through

[*] Tour through the Whole Island of Great Britain, divided into Circuits or journeys, by a Gentleman (Daniel Defoe), vol. iii. p. 88 (1727).

all the western part of England into it, to maintain the correspondence of merchants and men of business, of which all this side of the island is so full. This cross post leaves Plymouth in the south-west part of England, and ends at Hull, passing through Bristol, Gloucester, Shrewsbury, and Chester, to Liverpool, and then through Manchester, Bury, Rochdale, Halifax (Bradford), Leeds, and York."

Making of the Lancashire and Yorkshire, or Leeds and Liverpool, Canal.—But it was not until the year 1768, the 9th George III., that the grand project of forming a navigable canal through Yorkshire and Lancashire, from Leeds to Liverpool, running within three miles of Bradford, and joining the Aire and Calder Navigation, so as to give that town access to most of the great towns of Yorkshire and Lancashire and the ports of Hull and Liverpool, was originated. Scarcely ten years had then elapsed since the new plans of construction, of the great Brindley had been tried on the duke of Bridgewater's and the Staffordshire canals, and had shown that it was possible to carry navigable canals, by means of locks and tunnels, over or through hills of considerable height. The project of forming this canal was eagerly taken up by the inhabitants of Bradford, to whom it supplied the greatest of all requisites for their further prosperity; namely, a connection with the interior, and with the western and eastern coasts of England, by the cheapest of all modes of transport, water carriage. On the 30th December, 1768, the following announcement was published in the Liverpool and Yorkshire newspapers:—"Whereas at two numerous meetings, in pursuance of announcements of the public papers, of the gentlemen, merchants, landowners, and others of the county of York, held at Bradford, the 5th of this instant December, and of the county of Lancaster, held at Liverpool, the 9th, called to receive and consider Mr. Brindley's report of his survey of the proposed navigable canal from Leeds to Liverpool, it was unanimously agreed that the said canal is very practicable, and will be of great public utility, and application should be made to Parliament, in the present session, for leave and power to effect the same. A meeting is therefore desired of the nobility, gentlemen, merchants, landowners, manufacturers, and others, who are disposed to promote this most beneficial undertaking—for the county of York, at the Sun Inn, Bradford, on Monday the 9th day of January next; and for the county of Lancaster, at the Exchange in Liverpool, on the same day—when and where a subscription will be opened upon the following scheme [terms], being nearly the same as those of the Staffordshire, Coventry, and other canals, for which Acts have been lately obtained: namely, that the power be vested in a company under the name of the proprietors of the Yorkshire and Lancashire Canal; that the capital sum be divided into shares of £100, and each subscriber have a vote for every share he is possessed of, but no person to be allowed more than 100 shares; that such shares be made personal estate and transferable as such; that the money subscribed be made payable by different calls or instalments; that no call shall exceed ten per cent. at one time, and between every call there shall be at least an interval of three months; that an interest of £5 per cent. be regularly paid at a stated day in every year, to attend the sum advanced upon every call; and that when the whole navigation is completed, every proprietor shall become entitled to a proportion of the full profits of the shares he is possessed of." *

The progress of that part of the Leeds and Liverpool Canal which extends from the neighbourhood of Bradford up the valley of the Aire to Bingley, and down that valley to Leeds, was very rapid, and that also was the case with the part of the line extending from the Lancashire coal-field, at Wigan, to the town and port of Liverpool; but it took many years to complete the middle part of the line, across the hills of Yorkshire and Lancashire. The portion of the work between Bradford and Bingley was opened on the 21st March, 1774, and was considered to be the greatest work of the kind that had ever been effected in that part of England. "From Bingley, and about three miles down the valley of the Aire," says a writer of that age, "the noblest works of the kind that perhaps are to be found in the universe are exhibited—namely, a five-fold, a three-fold, a two-fold, and a single lock, making together a fall of 120 feet; a large aqueduct bridge of seven arches over the river Aire; and an aqueduct on a large banking (embankment) over Shipley valley. On the day on which this part of the canal was opened five loaded boats passed the grand lock, the first of which descended through a fall of sixty-six feet in less than twenty-nine minutes. This much wished for event was welcomed with ringing of bells, a band of music, the firing of guns by the neighbouring militia, the shouts of spectators, and other marks of public rejoicing." In the same year, 1774, on the 19th of October,

* History of Liverpool, by Thomas Baines, p. 437.

the Lancashire end of the canal from Wigan to Liverpool was opened with equal rejoicing at Liverpool, Wigan, and all along the line. But the progress of some portion of the works was very slow, owing partly to the great difficulties of the country, and partly to the imperfect engineering skill of that age. It was not until the year 1796 that the Leeds and Liverpool Canal was finally completed, on Tuesday the 9th of May. On that day the grand tunnel on the Leeds and Liverpool Canal at Foulridge, between Colne and Burnley, was opened. Its length was 1630 yards, and it took five years to complete it. The rejoicings on that occasion were very general and lively. From that time water carriage through this part of England was fully established—a circumstance which had a great effect in advancing the progress of all the towns along the line, and of the whole district extending from Bradford to Hull on one side of the island, and from Bradford to Liverpool on the other. The reduction in the cost of transport, which followed on the substitution of water carriage for land carriage, was equal to about four-fifths of the whole amount: that is to say, for a hundred miles the reduction in the cost of conveying a ton of goods was from about £5 to £1. This was the case even in the more level districts of England, but in the more hilly and mountainous districts it was very much greater; and thus many branches of trade which could not previously be carried on with much profit, and some which could not be carried on at all, began to extend at a rate never before witnessed. At that time the chief supplies of foreign wool were imported into Hull, and the chief supplies of cotton into Liverpool, both of which ports were brought into cheap and easy communication with Bradford and Leeds, by the opening of the Leeds and Liverpool Canal. Alpaca and some other of the finer textile materials, since brought into use at Bradford, were then unknown in England.

The Bradford Canal, connecting that town with the Leeds and Liverpool Canal, was opened in the year 1774. It commenced at Bradford, and extending along the east side of Bradford Dale, joined the Leeds and Liverpool Canal at Shipley. Its length was three miles, with a rise from the Leeds and Liverpool Canal of eighty-six and a quarter feet, effected by means of ten locks. The locks were of the same dimensions as those of the Leeds and Liverpool Canal, namely, sixty-six feet in length, and fifteen feet two inches in width. The depth of water was five feet. At the time when the Act of Parliament for forming the Bradford Canal was obtained, the subscribers consisted of twenty-eight persons, who were incorporated by the name of "The Company of Proprietors of the Bradford Navigation." They were empowered to raise among themselves £6000, in sixty shares of £100 each. The works were not to commence till the whole sum was raised; and if more capital should be required, they were empowered to raise an additional sum of £3000, by the admission of new subscribers. In order to obtain a better supply of water, the proprietors were obliged to buy up mills and land contiguous to the banks, and so to increase by calls the price of their shares to £250 each. After sixty to eighty years of the greatest public usefulness, during which time the population and buildings of Bradford increased more than ten fold, an injunction in chancery was obtained against the proprietors of the Bradford Canal, compelling them either to let the water off, or to fill the canal with pure water. As they could not see their way to get a sufficient supply of pure water, the canal was allowed to run dry in 1867, and it remained unused for five years. But eventually a new company was formed; the canal from Northbrook Street, Bradford, to Shipley, was purchased and supplied with pure water, was thoroughly repaired, and partially re-opened on the 1st of May, 1872. New wharves were constructed at the Bradford end, and on April 15, 1873, the canal was once more in full working order. The supply of water is derived from streams flowing from the adjacent hills, and by pumping water from other sources where a pure service can be obtained. The scheme is expected to prove highly remunerative in the conveyance of heavy materials. The old bed of the canal at Bradford has been filled up, and several streets formed through it. The new company expended £25,000 in the purchase and repair of the navigation, and in the construction of wharves. On Easter Tuesday, 1873, the *Enterprise*, a screw steamer, sailed up the canal from Shipley to Bradford, in the presence of a large concourse of people, this being the first steamer that had ever reached Bradford. The new works were constructed under the superintendence of Mr. W. B. Woodhead, of Bradford.

Progress of Bradford to the End of the Eighteenth Century.—The forming of this great line of water communication in the neighbourhood of Bradford, giving it cheap and easy transport at home and with distant countries; the constructing of numerous turnpike roads; James Watt's great improvement of the steam-engine; and Arkwright's and Hargreaves' inventions of spinning machinery, applicable to worsted and wool as well as to cotton—gave a great impulse to the progress of the trade of Bradford in the last thirty years of the eighteenth century. The Piece Hall of Bradford was erected in the year 1773, just before the commencement of the American war of Independence. Previous to that time the small manufacturers, from the out districts, attending the Bradford markets, resorted with their goods to a popular public house, the White Lion Inn, where their customers, the merchants, met and dealt with them. As trade increased a want was felt, which only the erection of a Piece Hall could satisfy, and a large and, for the times, commodious hall was raised by subscription. This hall was about fifty yards in length by eleven broad, the lower room being divided into two by a brick wall running from one end of the building to the other. Against this wall were fixed about 100 show-boards for the display of goods, with closets to store them, which were at first reserved for the original subscribers to the edifice, and were used by them as a safe place of deposit for their goods from market to market. The upper room was also closeted for the convenience of non-subscribers, who had to pay rent for the use of the closets. "Hither," says Mr. James, writing so late as the year 1841, "are brought great numbers of pieces of different kinds, besides worsted tops and gross yarns, which are exposed to sale every market day. This is on Thursday, precisely at ten in the morning, when a bell, hung in the cupola for the purpose, announces the opening of the market. It lasts till half past eleven, when the same bell announces the close of business. At two in the afternoon of the same day the market is again opened, for the sale of worsted tops and gross yarn, being finally closed at half past three, by ringing of bell." There is no Piece Hall now. The premises are used for other purposes, and manufacturers have either warehouses or piece rooms in different parts of the town. These piece rooms are now very numerous; and the warehouses of the merchants are palatial in size and appearance.

Introduction of Steam-power into Bradford.—About twenty years after the perfecting of Watt's steam-engine, in the year 1793, Mr. Buckley, a spirited manufacturer at Bradford, proposed to introduce steam-power into his mill, but he was deterred from doing so by a threat of an action at law on the part of some very respectable, but not very far-seeing inhabitants of the town, on the ground that the smoke from the engine furnace would be a nuisance. Five years later, in 1798, Messrs. Ramsbotham, Swaine, and Murgatroyd, proved more resolute, and saw their new building raised, and a steam-engine set up within it, in spite of all opposition. This was the commencement of a new era in the history of Bradford.

The Ironworks near Bradford.—One of the most important results of establishing cheap water carriage between Bradford, London, Liverpool, Hull, and other parts of the kingdom, was to bring into use the rich mineral ores existing in this neighbourhood. The extensive ironworks of Bowling were commenced before the canal was altogether completed. In the year 1789 a partnership was formed between John Sturges the elder, of Wakefield, John Sturges the younger, of Bowling (or Bolling) Hall, Richard Paley, of Leeds, Richard Sturges, of Datchett (Bucks), and John Elwell, of Fall-Ing, in Sandal Magna, near Wakefield, for carrying on the business of iron-founders, at Bowling and Fall-Ing, for forty years. The foundry at Bowling was erected on land purchased of Madam Rawson, of Bradford, and her son Benjamin. In 1792 this partnership was dissolved, so far as John Elwell was concerned; and in the year 1800 another and more numerous partnership was formed for carrying on the Bowling Ironworks.* The works eventually passed into the hands of a limited liability company, and in 1873 were conducted with great vigour. The manufacture of steel was prosecuted in conjunction with that of iron, the works being largely extended. Nothing but the best quality of iron is made at Bowling, and the early fame obtained by the Bowling iron has been maintained by the new proprietors. About the same time, namely, in the year 1788, the manor and mansion of Royds Hall were purchased by Messrs. Hird, Dawson, Jarratt, and Hardy, for the sum of £34,000. The land was then worth between £800 and £900 a year, and the colliery was valued at £950 a year. The proprietors of the Low Moor Ironworks are the present lords of the manor of Royds.† The Bierley Ironworks were commenced shortly after 1800, when the coal and ironstone under the estates of Miss Currer, of Bierley Hall, were leased to Henry Leah, Esq. and others, for a term of forty-six

* James' History of Bradford, p. 319.   † Ibid. p. 328.

years. After the death of Mr. Leah the Bierley Ironworks were purchased by the Low Moor Company, and in 1873 were still in their possession. Mr. James, in mentioning the commencement, observes that it is well known that the eminent success of this undertaking was in a great measure due to the able management of Mr. Leah. Writing on the same subjects in the year 1841, Mr. James observes, that "for half a century Royds Hall had been the residence of the Dawsons. Joseph Dawson, Esq., one of the first proprietors of the Low Moor Ironworks, the father of the present possessor, was the intimate friend of Dr. Priestley; and what is worthy of observation, part of the apparatus is yet at Royds Hall, with which that great philosopher made his discoveries respecting the qualities of air and the phenomena of electricity."* Mr. G. N. Smythe, who was connected with the works, resided at Royds Hall in 1873. The Dawson family had removed to Wharfedale. In that year the works had been largely extended, the concern had not changed hands, and the business was prospering. It may be mentioned, in connection with this proprietary, that at one time three members of the firm occupied seats in Parliament. The late Mr. H. W. Wickham sat for Bradford, Mr. John Hardy for Dartmouth, and the Right Hon. Gathorne Hardy for Oxford University.

Bradford at the Commencement of the Nineteenth Century.—The growth of Bradford, from the position of a town of 13,000 inhabitants to that of a great city, commenced with the discoveries and undertakings above named, and may be dated from the beginning of the present century. In 1803, although it did not then contain more than from 14,000 to 15,000 inhabitants, the advancing progress of the town was both shown and promoted by the passing of an Act of Parliament, to provide for the purposes of cleansing, lighting, and watching. There being then no town council, a body of commissioners was appointed to superintend the carrying out of the Act. But the town was lighted with oil lamps until the year 1822, when the Bradford Gaslight Company was formed. Beginning with 600 shares, value £25 each, the company in little more than twenty years had increased its capital three-fold. The price charged at one time for the gas was as much as 11s. 6d. for 1000 feet, a quantity for which not more than 3s. was paid in 1872. The company have three stations; in Mill Street, Thornton Road, and at Valley Road, respectively. But in the

* James' History of Bradford, p. 324.

year 1871 the Gaslight Company was dissolved, the Corporation purchasing the shares, plant, and other rights of the company, for the sum of £210,000. The Corporation bought an estate at Bowling in 1872, with the view of erecting new works. Power was obtained, in the Bradford Improvement Act, 1873, to borrow £50,000 for the extension of the gasworks.

Bradford Fifty Years ago.—When Bradford was described rather more than fifty years ago by the first Edward Baines, he stated that the town was pleasantly situated at the junction of three beautiful and extensive valleys; that it was built almost entirely of stone; that the soil was dry, the air sharp and salubrious, and the annual mortality not much exceeding one in fifty. Worsted stuffs, he stated, formed the staple manufacture of the town and neighbourhood; but broad and narrow cloths, wool-cards, and combs, were also made here to a considerable extent, and the cotton trade from Lancashire had found its way into the district. No manufacturing town in England had then suffered so little from the depression of trade as Bradford. In war and in peace it had been alike prosperous, and within the preceding ten years the population of the town had increased by 5297 persons. At that time most of the business was done in the Piece Hall, which was attended not merely by the manufacturers of the town itself, but by numerous others from the neighbouring towns and villages of Allerton, Apperley Bridge, Baildon, Bierley (East and North), Bingley, Birkenshaw, Bolton, Bowling, Bradley Mills, Bramhope, Burley, Burley Wood Head, Calverley, Clayton, Coley, Cottingley, Cullingworth, Denholme, Eccleshill, Eldwick, Esholt, Frizinghall, Fulneck, Guiseley, Halifax, Harden, Haworth, Heaton, Hipperholme, Horton (Great and Little), Idle, Keighley, Lightcliffe, Manningham, Morton, Northowram, Oakenshaw, Otley, Ovenden, Pot Ovens, Rawden, Shelf, Shipley, Stanningley, Sutton, Thornton, Tong, Wibsey, Wike, Wilsden, Windhill, Wrenthorp, and Yeadon. [*]

Manufactures of Bradford.—An account of the rise and progress of the worsted trade of Bradford from the earliest times to the year 1868 will be found in the first volume of this work, pages 673 to 696. It will be seen from that acccount that the trade has become centred in Bradford, which is justly styled the "metropolis of the worsted trade." In addition to worsted fabrics the Bradford merchants, especially those engaged in the foreign trade, transact a

[*] History and Gazetteer of the County of York, by Edward Baines: vol. i. p. 60, 1823.

large and increasing business in woollen goods. Linen yarns are also merchanted in Bradford. One of the largest silk mills in the country is in course of erection at Manningham, by Messrs. Lister & Co., on a scale of size and splendour rarely seen in manufacturing establishments, and not even surpassed by the remarkable works at Saltaire, already described. Mr. S. C. Lister, the improver of the woolcombing machine, which has done so much to meet the wants of the trade of Bradford, not satisfied with his efforts in this direction, turned his attention to the manufacture of silk and velvet. After spending some of the best years of his life in experiments, he was at length successful in perfecting machines for the manufacture of these goods, which enabled him speedily to realize all that he had attempted. He then commenced the building of a new mill at Manningham, designed by Messrs. Andrews and Pepper, covering nearly eleven acres, the cost of which, when completed, will not be less than half a million sterling. A new town has risen round the works; and as the buildings stand on high ground, and are crowned by a chimney of great size, height, and even beauty, Manningham Mills form one of the most conspicuous objects in Bradford. Reckoning the several stories of the mill and warehouse, they give a total extent of flooring of about sixteen acres. A portion of these works, where the velvet manufacture is carried on by the aid of a new power-loom, has been in operation for some years. The manufacture of silk and velvet promises to become an important part of the future trade of Bradford. The Chamber of Commerce, established in 1851, has been the means of great service to the trade of Bradford and the worsted district generally. Its operations are described in another part of this work. That district now extends for several miles round the town in every direction, and as far as Colne and Nelson, in Lancashire. All the manufacturing firms in the worsted district have market rooms in Bradford.

The Steam-Power of Bradford.—We have seen that the steam-engine was first introduced into Bradford in the year 1798. The steam-engine thus planted, though only of fifteen horse-power, was the first of a numerous host, and the creator of many new forms of industry in the town. In 1819 the steam-engines employed in mill-work in Bradford and its immediate neighbourhood, had increased to 492 horse-power; in 1830 to 1047; in 1841 to upwards of 2058; and it appears by the latest return, that the three factories which stood in the town in 1800 have multiplied until the number reached in 1872 was 186, and the strength of steam 5176 horse-power. But this return is supposed to be very incomplete, and much below the amount of the steam-power in use at present. Statistical information respecting the position of the worsted trade, except in the export department, and that is a mere declaration of values,. is very difficult to obtain. The Bradford Chamber of Commerce has urged the importance of correct data being yearly registered of the state and position of the various departments; but up to 1873 nothing of this kind, which it is very desirable should be done regularly, had been attempted in the worsted trade. The number of persons employed has increased proportionately with the machinery, and the annual produce of all their labour, if judged by its sale alone, has advanced in the present century from about 150,000 pieces to upwards of 3,000,000 a year. Saltaire alone finds work for 4000 people. The staple stuffs of Bradford are manufactured from long wool, as cloth is made from short wool. These worsted goods go into the markets of the world, under various shapes, colours, and names. There are merinos, Saxony cloths, shalloons, moreens, Orleans cloth, figured crapes, and alpacas. Bradford also supplies most of the worsted yarn required by other manufacturers in the several trades peculiar to Nottingham, Huddersfield, Kidderminster, Rochdale, Paisley, and Glasgow. The town is not without its cotton mills, dye-houses, cloth factories, and machine-making establishments; but worsted is its main production. Its success in industry has drawn into its bosom wealthy merchants from Leeds, Liverpool, and Manchester, and there are also many German merchants, owning some of the largest and richest concerns in the borough, who contribute to the progress of the town, and are ever ready to participate in any public enterprise that promises advantage or improvement to their fellow townsmen.

Value of the Trade of Bradford.—It is due to these gentlemen to state, that they were among the pioneers in the erection of the magnificent stuff warehouses which are so great an ornament to Bradford. Mr. Leo Schuster, an enterprising merchant of Manchester, was the founder of the first foreign stuff concern in the town. This firm existed in 1873 as Messrs. Leo Schuster, Brothers, & Co., and occupied one of the largest and handsomest warehouses in the city, at the corner of Leeds Road and George Street. About 1836 Mr. Schuster gave what was then thought an extravagant price for about 1000 yards of land, fronting to Charles Street and Brook Street, paying 30s. a yard for the land fronting to the former street, and 20s. for the latter, and expending between £7000 and £8000 in the erection of the first foreign stuff warehouse. This erection was the forerunner of the grand piles of buildings now occupied by the Bradford merchants. Mr. Schuster's old warehouse in Charles Street was to be sold in May, 1873, and was valued at £20 a yard. The principal firm of home stuff merchants in Bradford in 1824—said by some persons to be the only one in the town at that period—was Messrs. T. & J. Mann, who had their place of business in Mann Yard, Kirkgate, occupied in 1873 by Messrs. T. Arton & Co. The late Mr. Robert Milligan, founder of the firm of Milligan, Forbes, & Co., the owners of the largest warehouse in the town in 1873, had in 1824 a retail draper's shop in Kirkgate, and he also sold goods wholesale, having a small warehouse in the Talbot Hotel Yard. Mr. Milligan began life in Bradford as a travelling draper, and died one of the wealthiest men in the town. In 1834 there were twelve stuff merchants in Bradford, but in 1873 the number had increased to 252, and in addition to these there were a large number of commission agents connected with the worsted trade. We have it on the authority of gentlemen of eminent position in Bradford, who have been in business there from their youth upwards, and have entered into careful calculations on the subject, that an approximate estimate of the total value of the business transacted in the year 1872, in the warehouses of the home and foreign merchants, amounted to between £40,000,000 and £50,000,000 sterling. To this amount will have to be added some millions in value of goods sent from the Bradford district by manufacturers to other places, and which are not merchanted in Bradford. Mr. Jacob Behrens, an excellent authority, informs us that when he came to reside near Bradford, early in the present century, the value of the trade done in the warehouses of the town in one year did not exceed £300,000. Stuff goods were in those days manufactured in Bradford, and were purchased by merchants in Leeds and other places. The total estimated value of the wool grown in the United Kingdom, consumed in the worsted district in 1872, was £11,112,500. The import of colonial wool into Bradford in 1872 was estimated to amount to from 80,000 to 100,000 bales, and the value of the wool consumed in the district in the same year would be from £2,250,000 to £2,500,000. In the same period the value of mohair imported into Bradford was estimated at £1,000,000, and that of alpaca at from £450,000 to £500,000, all consumed in the district. In 1872 the aggregate value of cotton warps consumed in the Bradford trade was calculated to amount to £5,000,000, and there was also a comparatively small but growing demand for China grass for manufacturing purposes. It must be distinctly understood that these estimates are approximate. They have all been prepared by leading merchants in the several departments, who have kindly obliged the author with the results of their calculations, and the estimates are believed to be rather under than over the mark.

The Water-Works of Bradford. — Although surrounded with rills and streams, Bradford long continued to be ill supplied with water, chiefly from the want of a proper local government to provide for the increasing wants of a large town. An Act of Parliament was passed in 1842, which authorized the forming of a joint stock company to supply the town with water. The company drew their supply from an excellent spring at Manywells, in the Hewenden valley. The water was conveyed to two storage reservoirs at Chellow Dean, and was supplied to Bradford from the service reservoir at Whetley Hill. This supply was found insufficient for the wants of the town. The Corporation applied to Parliament and obtained an Act in 1854 authorizing them to purchase the works of the company, and to take over a new scheme for which the company had secured an Act, to obtain a supply of water from the watersheds of the rivers Aire and Wharfe. The sum of £215,000 was paid by the Corporation for the entire undertaking. "The result of these exertions," says Mr. James, "was the formation of the New Bradford Water-works, which constitute one of the mightiest triumphs of this engineering age, and surpass the greatest of the famous aqueducts which supplied imperial Rome with water. From the chief feeder at Hebden, near Grassington, to Bradford, the works extend twenty-four miles, intersecting deep glens, crossing high mountains, and piercing the hills by many miles of tunnel. Difficulties of no ordinary magnitude had to be surmounted in completing the work [and it is not even now, 1873, completed], on account of the rugged nature of the country, and the porous quality of the strata on which the reservoirs rest." The supply of water is, however, abundant, and of the best quality both for manufacturing and domestic purposes. There are on this line of service the compensation reservoir at Grimwith, and the reservoirs of Barden (storage, unfinished), Chelker (storage), Silsden (compensation), and Heaton (service for the town). Subsequently the Corporation extended their works into the watersheds of the Hewenden valley. They constructed Stubden storage reservoir on Thornton Moor, at an elevation of about 1030 feet above sea-level, to supply the population residing on the high levels round Bradford, 600 and 800 feet above the sea. They also formed Doe Park compensation reservoir on Stubden beck, and afterwards the Brayshaw service reservoir at Horton Bank Top, to increase the high-level supply. Another large storage reservoir at Horton Bank was in course of construction in 1873, and it was intended to make one on Thornton Moor, above Stubden. In addition to these immense works, a stone conduit, strong and massive as the work of the Romans, was being carried underneath Thornton Moor into the Oxenhope or Worth valley, where, at Leeming and Leeshaw, two compensation reservoirs were being made. The Corporation possess powers to make five more service reservoirs—at Stairs and Shady Bank, at the head of the Worth Valley; at Thornton Moor, and at Bowling and Bunker's Hill, near Bradford. Various Acts have been obtained to increase the borrowing powers of the Corporation on account of the waterworks; the total amount authorized to be borrowed, up to 1873, being £1,300,000. Of this large sum, £1,043,923 had been spent on land and works up to December, 1872. The revenue from water, which, in 1856, was £10,225, in 1872 had risen to £52,000. Of late years the works have been constructed from the designs and under the superintendence of Mr. C. Gott, C.E., borough surveyor and waterworks manager, and are certainly among the finest series of waterworks in the kingdom. The following table gives some interesting particulars respecting them in a condensed form. It will be seen from it that the Corporation possessed powers in 1873 to increase the number of reservoirs to twenty. Of these fourteen were for the town service, on the high, intermediate, and low levels; and six were for compensating mill-owners and others whose water supply had been taken by the Corporation. Those marked with an asterisk were in progress in 1873, and those to which a dagger is appended had not been commenced. The capacity of some of the reservoirs will be greater when finished than is here set down, in consequence of alterations; but the aggregate difference will not be very great.

The total water area of the fourteen service reservoirs will be 270 acres; the area of land, 360½ acres; the water capacity 1,580,650,000 gallons; and the gathering ground 5885 acres. The water area of the six compensation reservoirs will be 192 acres; the land area, 238 acres; the water capacity, 1,283,000,000 gallons; and the gathering ground, 12,020 acres. The aggregate water area of the twenty reservoirs will be 462 acres; the land area, 598½ acres; the water capacity, 2,863,650,000 gallons; and the gathering ground, 17,905 acres.

BRADFORD WATERWORKS.

Name.	Water area. Acres.	Total area. Acres.	Capacity in Gallons.	Level of Overflow above O.D.	Depth of Water.	Gathering ground. Acres.	Expended on Capital Account up to Dec. 31, 1872. £ s. d.
Service Reservoirs.							
High Level.							
*Horton Bank Reservoir,	14	36	160,000,000	905	60	—	56,659 11 0
†Stairs Reservoir,	14½	35	96,000,000	1230	30	460	—
Stubden Reservoir,	11	16	85,000,000	1028	55	900	45,381 0 0
†Shady Bank Reservoir,	14	29	72,000,000	1185	30	625	—
Brayshaw Reservoir,	13	22½	60,000,000	975	20	—	24,011 5 1
†Thornton Moor Reservoir,	43	—	250,000,000	1230	40	—	—
Intermediate Level.							
Upper Chellow Dean Reservoir,	8	17	50,000,000	691	44·7	—	402 16 11
Lower Chellow Dean Reservoir,	5½	6¾	28,000,000	640	32·2	—	—
Low Level.							
Barden Reservoir,	66	87	440,000,000	700	86	2,610	128,631 15 3
Chelker Reservoir,	56	66	250,000,000	722	36	1,290	17,588 4 0
Heaton Reservoir,	8¼	11½	31,000,000	523	33	—	8,174 5 11
†Bowling Reservoir,	8	16	28,000,000	490	20	—	—
†Bunkers Hill Reservoir,	8	16	28,000,000	485	20	—	—
Whetley Hill Reservoir,	1⅝	1¾	2,650,000	518	12	—	—
Compensation Reservoirs.							
High Level.							
*Leeming Reservoir,	18	25¼	119,500,000	835	49	510	8,170 3 10
*Leeshaw Reservoir,	20¼	32½	119,500,000	860	59	510	—
Doe Park Reservoir,	20	26	110,000,000	850	52·2	1,000	6,711 10 11
Intermediate Level.							
Hewenden Reservoir,	14	17	70,000,000	687	35·8	1,000	454 14 4
Low Level.							
Grimwith Reservoir,	95	107	634,000,000	877	66	7,000	47,576 11 4
Silsden Reservoir,	25	30	230,000,000	580	78	2,000	27,026 7 5
Totals,	462	598½	2,863,650,000	—	—	17,905	—

* In progress in 1873.   † Not commenced in 1873.

The small amounts spent on some of the older reservoirs are the expense incurred since they came into the hands of the Corporation. Barden reservoir has been almost entirely reconstructed by Mr. Gott, C.E., the original works having proved defective. Mr. Gott has also repaired Chelker reservoir, and has rendered it, as well as Doe Park reservoir, tight and strong.

Railway System of Bradford.—Soon after the introduction of railways Bradford was connected with the railway system. The first railway was the Leeds and Bradford line, which passes circuitously through the valley of the Aire, describing an irregular semi-oval of fourteen miles and a half. It is united to the "little North Western" at Shipley, from which place the latter line extends to Skipton, Colne, Settle, Lancaster, and Ingleton, and will soon be extended from Settle to Carlisle, forming a line into Scotland, by a new and beautiful route. The Leeds and Bradford line was completed in 1846, and is leased to the Midland Company, whence the name of its Bradford station, in Well Street, is the Midland Station. Second, a shorter route to Leeds, being only nine miles in length, proceeding from the Lancashire and Yorkshire Railway Station, near St. George's Hall. This direct line to Leeds was opened in 1854; and from the same centre branches extend to Halifax, Huddersfield, Dewsbury, Wakefield, Rochdale, and other important seats of industry. A new branch was making in 1873 from Shipley, round the hills to Idle, Eccleshill, and Laister Dyke, where it joins the Great Northern main line. The Bradford and Thornton Railway, for which parliamentary sanction had been obtained, was to start from the Lancashire and Yorkshire line at Bowling, passing through Horton and Clayton to Thornton, with a branch to Queensbury, 1000 feet above sea-level. Another branch would strike off at Horton in the direction of New Millers Dam, on Thornton Road. In connection with this line a scheme has been introduced into Parliament for continuing the Thornton line to Denholme, Cullingworth, and Keighley, and by a junction with the Halifax and Ovenden Railway facilitating communication, by a new route through the hills, between Halifax, Bradford, and Keighley. The bill had passed the House of Commons in May, 1873, and had to go up to the Lords. Another new line of some importance to Bradford is a short length from Shipley by Low Baildon and Esholt to Guiseley, to diminish the distance between Bradford and Ilkley, in Wharfedale, the latter being a favourite residence of the wealthy inhabitants of Bradford. This line had not been commenced in 1873. Should these various schemes be carried out, the borough will be encircled with a most convenient network of railways, but the rapid extension of the trade of Bradford has rendered the stations of the Midland, Great Northern, and Lancashire and Yorkshire Railways inadequate to meet the large and increasing traffic in passengers, goods, and minerals. Powers have, however, been obtained for improving the existing works on, or in connection with, all these lines.

Bradford made a Parliamentary Borough.—Bradford was empowered by the English Boroughs Reform Act of 1832 to return two representatives to the House of Commons, a number which has not been augmented. The town is also a court and polling-place for the election of members for the northern division of the West Riding. The following is a list of the members returned to Parliament by the borough since it obtained the franchise:—

Years.	Names.	Date of Election.
1832 to 1837	E. C. Lister, John Hardy.	December, 1832.
1837 to 1841	E. C. Lister, W. Busfield.	July and August, 1837.
1841 to 1847	John Hardy, W. Busfield.	June and July, 1841.
1847 to 1852	W. Busfield, Colonel P. Thompson.	August, 1847.
1852 to 1857	Robert Milligan, Henry W. Wickham.	July, 1852.
1857 to 1859	Henry W. Wickham, Major-gen. Thompson.	April, 1857.
1859 to 1865	Henry W. Wickham, Titus Salt, succeeded in February, 1861, by W. E. Forster.	May, 1859.
1865 to 1868	Henry W. Wickham, W. E. Forster. In October, 1867, Matthew Wm. Thompson succeeded Mr. Wickham.	July, 1865.
1868	Right Hon. W. E. Forster, H. W. Ripley.	November, 1868.
1869	Edward Miall.	March, 1869.

Bradford made a Municipal Borough.—In the year 1847 Bradford was made a municipal corporation by royal charter, with a commission of the peace, a mayor, fourteen aldermen, and forty-two town councillors. The area of the four townships comprised in the borough of Bradford is 6508 acres, 2 roods, 39 perches, namely:— Bradford, 1595 acres, 1 rood, 2 perches; Bowling, 1561 acres, 2 roods, 16 perches; Horton, 2033 acres, 39 perches; and Manningham, 1318 acres, 2 roods, 22 perches. There were at the latest return, in 1872, $56\frac{3}{10}$ths miles of paved and macadamized roads, and $79\frac{7}{10}$ths miles of flagged footways. The four wards of Bradford township return twenty-four of the councillors; Bowling and Little Horton return six each; while Manningham and Great Horton wards are represented each by three councillors. The parliamentary and municipal boundaries of the borough are identical, nor was any change made in these limits by the Reform Act of 1867. Power has been obtained in the Corporation Improvement Act, 1873, to incorporate the township of Bolton, which is to be made into a ward, and to be represented in the town council by one alderman and three councillors. The town council has sedulously employed the powers conferred by the Bradford Improvement Act of 1850 in improving and draining the streets and thoroughfares, and in supervising the erection of new buildings. The council is divided into several committees for the specific execution of the various objects of municipal administration. Under the authority of additional powers, obtained by the Corporation from time to time, vigorous steps have been taken to remodel and improve the centre of the borough and the principal thoroughfares leading therefrom. Much valuable work has been accomplished, but although the entire aspect of the centre of the town has been changed, a good deal remains to be done. The spirit and energy of the Corporation are such that the improvements begun will be steadily continued until the town is rendered more sightly, and the intricate network of narrow streets is pierced by broad and commodious thoroughfares. A large sum of money, upwards of £345,000, has been expended in these undertakings, and the work is still (1873) going on; but a considerable proportion of the cost has been recouped to the Corporation by sales of land left after the streets were formed. Powers were obtained by the Improvement Act of 1873 to borrow £300,000 for street and other improvements. The most important of these works is the formation of a new main artery, about three quarters of a mile long and twenty yards wide, starting from Sun Bridge, in the heart of the town, and proceeding in a westerly direction to Brick Lane. There are a series of other improvements projected in this Act, of almost equal magnitude. Amongst these are several streets in the Bradford valley, to unite one side of the town with the other, and a bridge to span the Midland Railway. The police force at the command of the Corporation consists of one head constable and 174 subordinate officers. The police station, with a depôt for the town engines, is in Swaine Street, but the police station and all other departments of business are to be removed to the town hall. A new fire-brigade station-house, with a free library above it, is to be built at the corner of Godwin Street and Aldermanbury. As the burial board, the town council have the cemetery at Scholemoor under their jurisdiction. The following are the names of the mayors of Bradford since the incorporation of the borough in the year 1847 :—

Robert Milligan, Esq.,	1847-48
Titus Salt, Esq.,	1848-49
Henry Forbes, Esq.,	1849-50
William Rand, Esq.,	1850-51
Samuel Smith, Esq.,	1851-52
" " "	1852-53
" " "	1853-54
William Murgatroyd, Esq.,	1854-55
" " "	1855-56
Henry Brown, Esq.,	1856-57
" " "	1857-58
" " "	1858-59
Isaac Wright, Esq.,	1859-60
Isaac Wright, Esq.,	1860-61
" " "	1861-62
Matthew Wm. Thompson, Esq.,	1862-63
Joseph Farrar, Esq.,	1863-64
Charles Semon, Esq.,	1864-65
John Venimore Godwin, Esq,	1865-66
William Brayshaw, Esq.,	1866-67
James Law, Esq.,	1867-68
Edward West, Esq.,	1868-69
Mark Dawson, Esq.,	1869-70
" " "	1870-71
Matthew Wm. Thompson, Esq.,	1871-72
" " " "	1872-73

Streets formed and Improvements made along the line of the Old Bradford Canal. — The capital of the new Canal Company is £35,000. The shares are mostly held by stone merchants and others interested in the development of this important branch of the Bradford trade. The canal is 2¾ miles long, and the proprietors are bound by penalty to keep the water clean, and not to suffer any "fetid or offensive water to flow or pass thence into the Leeds and Liverpool Canal." The company paid the small sum of £2900 — a mere acknowledgment — to the old company for that portion of the undertaking from below Northbrook Street to Shipley; but they were bound to re-open the canal. The aspect of this part of the borough, which was formerly covered with old and dilapidated buildings, has been completely changed. The Bradford Corporation has obtained powers to make the new Canal Road, eighteen yards wide, from Well Street, in the centre of the town, to Frizinghall, midway to Shipley. The total cost to the Bradford Corporation for the improvements adjacent to the canal will be between £30,000 and £40,000. Canal Road, which in 1873 was in progress, passes alongside the canal wharves. A row of stately warehouses has been raised on one side of the thoroughfare, and in a few years the street — one of the few level roads out of the town — will in all likelihood be entirely built up. On the west side of the valley the Midland Railway Company have determined to make a new thoroughfare, twenty yards wide, commencing at present at Salem Street, and proceeding to Bolton Lane, parallel with the Midland line, but which will no doubt eventually be continued to Kirkgate, in Bradford, and forward, down the valley, to Shipley. At the rate at which building operations were proceeding in 1873 there appears to be every probability that, within the next half century, the three miles of the valley between Bradford and Shipley will be covered with mills, manufactories, and houses. A railway station has been formed at Manningham, and the Midland company intend to open another at Frizinghall. The Bradford valley, which was originally picturesque, has lost nearly all its natural charms, and is becoming thickly populated; building operations extending down to Saltaire, in Airedale. Future developement will be much accelerated by the forming of the new roads mentioned above.

The New Town Hall of Bradford.—The public business of Bradford will shortly be carried on in the new Town Hall, which is nearly completed, and will be opened in a few months (1873). The building is a handsome erection, in the mediæval style. It stands on 2000 square yards of land, is constructed of beautifully-coloured stone, and will be ornamented on the exterior with thirty-seven stone statues of the kings and queens of England, placed in canopied niches. In the centre is a splendid tower, rising to a height of 220 feet, in which will be placed a clock and a peal of bells or carillons, to play a variety of tunes. The building is admirably adapted for conducting every department of public business. It is tastefully fitted up inside, and will cost, exclusive of land, about £100,000. Two small, but neat rooms, will be used as the council chamber and the borough court. The architects are Messrs. Lockwood and Mawson, of Bradford and London. The foundation stone of the hall was laid August 10, 1870, by Mr. Ald. Mark Dawson, mayor of Bradford.

Memorial Statues.—A bronze statue of Sir Robert Peel, Bart., by Mr. Behnes, of London, was erected in Peel Place, in 1855, by subscription, at a cost of about £4000. Mr. Jos. Brown, wool-stapler, Bradford, was one of the principal promoters. A memorial statue to Mr. Richard Oastler, styled the "Factory King," was reared in 1869, at a cost of £1500, as a testimonial of his exertions on behalf of the operatives during the agitation for the Ten Hours' Factory Bill. The memorial, which stands in Well Street, in front of the

Midland Railway Station, consists of a figure of Mr. Oastler and two factory children—boy and girl, attired in their working dresses. The figures are executed in bronze, and the group is placed on a red granite pedestal, with a base of grey granite. Mr. J. B. Philip, of London, was the artist. The prime movers in the erection of the statue were Mr. Matthew Balme, of Bradford, and Mr. Philip Grant, of Manchester, and the factory operatives of Yorkshire and Lancashire. The statue was uncovered by the earl of Shaftesbury, in the midst of a vast assemblage. In front of the town hall a memorial to Sir Titus Salt, Bart., of chaste design, was being erected by public subscription in 1873. The memorial will consist of an elaborate Gothic canopy, containing in the centre a marble figure of Sir Titus Salt, in a sitting attitude, by Mr. J. Adams-Acton, of London. The cost will be about £2500. The steps leading up to the statue will be flanked by figures of a couple of alpacas, emblematic of the new trade introduced into Bradford by the worthy baronet. At the other end of the town hall is to be placed a statue of S. C. Lister, Esq., a gentleman who, by his improvements in the wool-combing machine and his introduction of the silk and velvet manufacture, has rendered invaluable services to the town of Bradford. The statue, which is to be executed in white Sicilian marble, by Mr. M. Noble, of London, is also to be erected by public subscription, at a cost exceeding £2000. The Bradford corporation gave the sites for the Oastler, Salt, and Lister memorials.

The New Exchange of Bradford was begun in 1864, when Lord Palmerston, then prime minister, laid the foundation stone with the usual solemnities. The building was completed in 1867. The handsome and spacious interior is tastefully embellished with allegorical figures. The clock tower at the east end of the edifice is 150 feet high, its effect being enhanced by the turrets on the corners of the building, and by the statues of Bishop Blaize, the patron saint of woolcombers, and of King Edward VI., who granted a charter to the town. The circular medallions, placed between the windows on the ground floor, are not without interest. A news-room is provided for the subscribers. The Chamber of Commerce has a suite of rooms in the exchange. The cost of erecting the building was £40,000.

St. George's Hall.—From the mart of commerce to the hall of song will be no abrupt transition for music-loving Yorkshire men. Bradford became conspicuous among northern towns for its architecture, when the erection of St. George's Hall was completed in 1853. The foundation stone of the building had been laid in true masonic style in 1851, by the late earl of Zetland, grand-master of the order of freemasons. It is a handsome edifice, built of Yorkshire stone, with a lofty front, supported by Corinthian pilasters. The hall, more than fifty yards long and twenty-five yards broad, will contain upwards of four thousand persons. Saturday evening concerts for the people were tried for some short time by Mr. Angus Holden, J.P., with the view of drawing the operatives away from low singing rooms and public-houses, and were continued by Mr. W. Morgan with great success up to 1872, when the hall company themselves became caterers for the public. The Bradford Festival Choral Society, founded principally through the agency of Mr. Samuel Smith, J.P., has gained a high reputation for the excellent manner in which the choruses of the oratorios are sustained by the practical members of the society. There is another musical organization, known as the Old Choral Society, which has in connection with it an instrumental band. It was mainly through the persevering energy of Mr. S. Smith that Bradford possesses a music hall second to none in the kingdom, either for beauty of design, adaptability to the purpose intended, or comfort to the spectators. In 1873 the directors of the hall spent about £2000 in improving and embellishing the interior, and in remodelling the organ, originally built at the expense of Mr. S. Smith. The Bradford subscription concerts, promoted by a number of gentlemen with the view of affording to their townsmen the opportunity of hearing the finest vocal and instrumental music interpreted by the first musicians and vocalists that could be found, had been held in St. George's Hall for several years previous to 1873. The season of 1872-73 though financially not successful, was perhaps the best, in a musical point of view, that had been known. The concerts were to be continued. The name of Mr. H. Averdieck, a German merchant, may be alluded to as one of the most enthusiastic and liberal supporters of the subscription concerts and the Festival Choral Society. He was in 1873 one of the vice-presidents of the latter society, Mr. S. Smith being president. The subscription concerts would seem to have superseded the musical festivals, formerly held at Bradford with marked success. Messrs. Lockwood and Mawson were the architects of the hall, which cost about £30,000.

The Court-house.—The court-house, situated in Hall Ings, is a substantial building, with a portico of massive columns of the Ionic order. It was erected in 1834, at a cost of about £7000. Quarter and petty sessions for East Morley are held here, and it is the head-quarters of the police division of East Morley. Superintendent Ball had charge of the division in 1873.

The County Court for Bradford, which is held at the court-house in Manor Row, exercises jurisdiction over the following townships:—Allerton, Bradford, Bolton, Bowling, Calverley-cum-Farsley, Clayton, Cleckheaton, Drighlington, Eccleshill, Heaton, Horton, Hainsworth, Idle, Manningham, North Bierley, Pudsey, Shipley, Thornton, Tong, Wike, and Wilsden. Mr. W. T. S. Daniel, Q.C., was judge in 1873, and Mr. George Robinson, registrar.

Bradford and North Bierley Unions.—Bradford gives name to a poor-law union of four townships. To shelter the paupers of this large district a spacious well-arranged workhouse was erected, at Little Horton, in 1852, from designs by Messrs. Lockwood & Mawson, at a cost of about £7000. The building has since been enlarged, a new infirmary erected, and the place will hold 1000 inmates. The expenditure on land and buildings, up to 1873, was £27,700. The receipts of the union for the year ending Lady Day, 1873, inclusive of balance brought over, was £39,378 5s. 5d., and the expenditure for the same period was £34,459 4s. 1d., leaving a balance of £1582 6s. 4d. The paupers relieved in the workhouse, on the 1st January, 1873, were 480, and those relieved out of the house were 1373; total paupers in the union at this date, 1853. The number of vagrants relieved at the workhouse for the September quarter 1868, was 3381, while for the same quarter in 1872 they were only 144; a remarkable difference, which may be attributed to the prosperity of the district, and to the fact that the vagrants have to do a specified amount of labour on the workhouse farm for their temporary accommodation. Mr. John Darlington was clerk to the union in 1873, and was appointed in the year 1850. Another local division, to which Bradford gives name, is the superintendent registrar's district, covering an area of 41,622 acres. The population of this district, which in 1851 was 181,964, rose in 1861 to 196,463, and in 1871 to 257,706; of the latter 123,530 were males, and 134,176 females. On the 14th May, 1873, the assistant-overseers of the four townships of the union returned the annual value as follows:—Bradford, £321,052; Bowling, £63,842; Horton, £131,022;

Manningham, £93,603 10s.; total valuation, £609,519 10s. The increase on the previous year was about £25,000. The North Bierley Union—formerly included in the Bradford Union—comprising seventeen townships, is part of the Bradford superintendent registrar's district, and the population is comprised in the above figures. The workhouse, at Clayton, was built in 1856, and the total expenditure on the structure up to 1873 was £10,600. Accommodation is found for 326 inmates. The assessment of the union for 1873 was £301,405. The receipts for the year ending Lady Day, 1873, were £26,789 3s. 6d., inclusive of a balance brought over, and the expenditure to same date was £24,586 8s. 3d. leaving a balance in hand of £2202 15s. 3d. The paupers relieved in the workhouse on the 1st January, 1873, were 201, and those relieved out of the house numbered 2017; total paupers in the union at this date, 2218. For the half-year ending 1872, the number of vagrants relieved was upwards of 500. Mr. W. Lancaster, appointed clerk to the union in 1857, retained that office in 1873. The basis of values on which the county and police rates are levied, as confirmed at the West Riding Sessions on the 30th December, 1872, shows the following results as regards the East Morley division, which is co-extensive with the North Bierley Union:—Allerton, £10,178; Bolton, £5223; Calverley-cum-Farsley, £26,456; Clayton, £13,752; Cleckheaton, £32,968; Drighlington, £13,312; Eccleshill, £15,549; Heaton, £9154; Hunsworth, £8755; Idle, £34,394; North Bierley, £42,860; Pudsey, £36,028; Shipley, £42,170; Thornton, £23,183; Tong, £16,124; Wike, £12,323: total value of the division, £342,429. According to the same basis the valuation of the four townships forming the Bradford Union was—Bradford, £334,239; Bowling, £68,678; Horton, £136,787; Manningham, £84,754: total, £624,458. If the totals for the East Morley division and the Bradford Union are added together, it is found that within a radius of about five miles of the Bradford Exchange, the annual value of the property on which the above-named rates were levied, amounted to the very large sum of £966,887.

Position and Public Health of Bradford.—The soil of Bradford is dry, and the air salubrious. The annual mortality formerly did not exceed one in fifty, and modern civilization, while it has increased the wealth and population of the town, has not greatly increased the death-rate. The registrar-general now states that the average annual rate of mortality within the borough of Bradford was equal to 26·2 per 1000 of the mean population (126,024) during the ten years 1861-70. Of the twenty great cities and towns of the kingdom, arranged in the order of mortality, Bradford stood ninth in the average annual death-rate per 1000 for the years 1868-72. Portsmouth stood lowest with 21·9 per 1000; Bradford was 26·4, Leeds 27·6, and Liverpool had the highest, 31·3. The corporation has steadily directed its attention to sanitary improvement. The total number of deaths for the year ending September 28, 1872, was 3975, or 26·19 per 1000, taking the population of the borough at 151,720. The average weekly number of deaths was 76·44. For the quarter ending December 1872, the death-rate was 24·1 per 1000 persons, against 26·6 and 24·7 in the corresponding periods of 1870 and 1871. Four sweeping machines, forty-four men, fourteen boys, and fourteen horses and carts, were employed in cleansing the public streets; the roads were regularly watered in dry weather. In addition to the abattoirs of the Corporation, and those at Bolton Bridge, there were sixty-six slaughter-houses in the borough. As well-paved streets have something to do with the public health, it may be stated that the Corporation had purchased a stone-breaking machine for granite, and a steam road-roller for getting the macadamized roads rapidly into good condition. In 1873 the Bradford Corporation appointed Mr. H. Butterfield medical officer of health for the borough, at a salary of £500 per annum, subject to the approval of the Local Government Board, who pay half the salary. As against 6628 deaths registered in the Bradford district in 1872, there were of births 10,402, so that the increasing populousness of the town is progressive. Of marriages in the district, there were in the same year the goodly number of 2666.

Theatre-royal.—This building is situated in Manningham Lane, and supplanted an old wooden theatre that formerly stood in Duke Street. The theatre-royal belongs to a company, and was leased to Mr. C. Rice for seven years from July, 1872. The original lessee was the celebrated comedian, Mr. J. B. Buckstone. It is a roomy, comfortable place, and had in 1873 been enlarged and improved. The architects were Messrs. Andrews, Son, and Pepper. The building was opened in 1864. A large wooden building, capable of seating more than 3000 people, had been erected by Mr. Pullan, in Brunswick Place, and was used as a music hall.

The Manor and Market.—The manorial and the market rights, formerly held by Miss Rawson of Nidd Hall, were leased, so far as the market rights are concerned, on 13th December, 1865, to the Bradford Corporation for 999 years, at a rent of £5000 yearly. The fairs for horses, cattle, and sheep, on March 3, June 17 and 18, and December 9 and 10, were formerly held in the public streets; but the Corporation purchased a large tract of land adjacent to Leeds Road, where the wholesale markets and the fairs are now held. New abattoirs on the most approved principles have been constructed, and a range of warehouses and other conveniences were commenced in 1873 for the wholesale dealers in fish, fruit, vegetables, &c. The market is styled St. James'. Communicating with it will be a branch line from the Great Northern Railway, by means of which cattle and produce can be brought to the doors of the dealers and butchers. The total expenditure on the buildings will be about £23,000. The old uncovered market place being utterly inadequate to the requirements of Bradford, the manor hall and a range of other buildings, fronting to Kirkgate and Darley Street, were pulled down. On this site has been raised the first half of a beautiful, new, covered market. The market hall occupies the centre of the structure, and is approached from Kirkgate by a broad flight of stone steps. Round the interior are shops, and in the centre are grouped the stalls. The hall is well lighted and ventilated, and presents a very pleasing appearance. Underneath are vaults for storage. The exterior, of stone, is in the Italian style, three stories in height, the façades to Kirkgate and Darley Street being most effective. The grand entrance in Kirkgate is surmounted by a clock tower, and over the archway are carved representations of Flora and Pomona, the goddesses of flowers and fruit. There are shops fronting to Kirkgate and Darley Street, and over these are offices and the German Club, known as the Schiller-Verein. The entire structure will be 360 feet long by 200 feet wide. The portion opened in 1872 measures 200 feet by 125 feet, and its cost, including the exterior shops, was £28,000. The whole expenditure on the entire scheme is estimated at £50,000. Messrs. Lockwood and Mawson were the architects, and they had also charge of the erection of the abattoirs and the wholesale market premises. The Bradford butchers built abattoirs of their own at Bolton Bridge, just outside the borough; but these were bought up by the Bradford Corporation, in 1873, for £10,500. The total expenditure by the Corporation upon the markets up to December 31, 1872, was £70,775 19s. In connection with the markets the Corporation exercises jurisdiction over weights and measures and the testing of gas meters. It is a remarkable fact—worthy of record here, as showing the great increase in wealth and importance of the town—that the rights which Miss Rawson has leased to the Bradford Corporation, and for the use of which that lady and her heirs will receive such a handsome sum spread over 999 years, were conveyed by indentures dated 12th and 13th February, 1795, from John Marsden of Hornby castle, Lancashire, then lord of the manor, to Benjamin Rawson, Esq., of Bolton-in-the-Moors, for £2100.

The Mechanics' Institute.—The Mechanics' Institute was established in 1832. An attempt to form a useful society of this kind was made in 1825, but failed. Mr. Joseph Farrar, the secretary (now Mr. Ald. Farrar, J.P.), was principally instrumental in establishing the institute, and zealously laboured to promote its interests for many years. Dr. Steadman, principal of Horton Baptist College, was the first president of the Mechanics' Institute. His successor, the Rev. James Acworth, A.M., LL.D., had the opportunity, in 1839, of addressing the members in a new and handsome hall, erected at the junction of Well Street and Leeds Road. This commodious building contained a lecture-room, a library of 10,000 volumes, a reading-room, and an interesting collection of stuffed birds and other objects of natural history. It was sold in 1872, and is now converted into a warehouse. The foundation stone of a new Mechanics' Institute in Bridge Street, Bradford, was laid on Friday, January 29, 1870, by Lord Houghton, in the presence of a large body of gentlemen, among whom were the Rev. Dr. Campbell, the president of the Institute; Mr. Ald. M. Dawson, the mayor of Bradford; Right Hon. W. E. Forster, M.P., Mr. Edward Miall, M.P., Mr. Alfred Illingworth, M.P., Mr. H. W. Ripley, &c. The new building stands on a site 1000 yards in extent, purchased from the Bradford corporation at a cost of £12,500, and has frontages to Bridge Street, New Market Street, and Tyrrel Street. The structure is an excellent specimen of the Italian style, and was designed by Messrs. Andrews and Pepper, of Bradford. On the ground floor are a range of shops, and above these are the news-room and library, a lofty, well-lighted apartment, extending over the whole width of the building, and divided in the centre by a screen. Behind this room is the lecture-hall, which is chastely decorated, elegantly fitted up, and capable of seating 1500 persons. In the upper stories are the class-rooms and apartments for the science and art department, conveniently arranged and well lighted. The entire cost of this splendid People's College, as it has been termed, inclusive of land, was £35,839. The educational work of the institute has gone forward with energy in all its branches, and the results were on the whole satisfactory. The number of members in 1873 was 1845. The total receipts from all sources were £2061 17s. 5d., and the expenditure was £1948. The number of volumes in the library was 11,185, and the issues of the year were 52,531 volumes, being an increase of 8997. The lectures and readings, especially the scientific lectures, had been well attended. Of twenty-six students who were examined in connection with the science and art department at South Kensington, only one had failed to pass. The school of art had become an important branch of the institute. The debt was £4839 7s., beyond the amount of which interest on the other portion of the scheme was covered by the rental of shops. Mr. Charles Semon, of Broughton Hall, near Skipton, was president in 1873, and the vice-presidents were—Rev. Dr. Ryan (vicar of Bradford), Rev. J. R. Campbell, D.D., Rev. Dr. Fraser, Mr. Alderman Law, Mr. H. W. Ripley, Mr. James Wales, Mr. Sam Smith, and Mr. James Hanson; treasurer, Mr. C. Lund; honorary secretaries, Mr. J. T. Newboult and Mr. Thomas Clark.

The Bradford Grammar School.—The Bradford Grammar School was erected immediately after the Reformation. Extant is a decree of the Duchy of Lancaster Court, dated 1553, 7th Edward VI., showing that six or seven distinct plots of land "anciently belonged to the living and sustentation of a schoolmaster teaching grammar within the town of Bradford." This endowment was confirmed by Edward VI., and augmented by other gifts in the following century. In 1663 the trustees were incorporated by letters patent granted by Charles II., and a scheme of government was drawn out for the school. The old school-house was pulled down in 1818, and a new one erected at North Parade in 1820. Among the boys educated in the school, who attained celebrity, are enumerated Archbishop Sharp (1644–1713), Dr. Richardson, of Bierley Hall, the naturalist and antiquarian (1663–1741), and Abraham Sharp, the mathematician and assistant to Flamsteed (1651–1742). In

1871 the school was re-organized and placed on a new basis of management. The old masters were superannuated, and new ones appointed, and it was determined to replace the old building by a more commodious structure on the same site. A design was prepared by Messrs. Andrews and Pepper in the French Gothic style, and this work has been executed at a cost of upwards of £7000. The new building contains a large schoolroom for boys, many classrooms, and a master's house fronting to North Parade. A tower in the centre rises to a height of 110 feet, and there is a roomy playground in the rear of the building. Accommodation is found for 400 boys. Attached to the school are several valuable exhibitions, which have been increased by scholarships founded by the Right Hon. W. E. Forster, M.P., vice-president of the council, and by Mr. Henry Brown, of Bradford; the latter gentleman having given, in 1873, £6000 for this purpose. The new scheme for the management of this school, dated 12th August, 1871, and approved by an order in council, lays down that the general object of the foundation is to supply a liberal education for boys, and to promote the education of girls. The governing body to consist of not more than sixteen persons, nor less than thirteen, called governors. The *ex-officio* governors are—the vicar of Bradford, the mayor of Bradford, the chairman of the Bradford School Board, and the president of the Mechanics' Institute. Two representative governors are elected from the town council and two from the school board, and there are eight co-öptative governors. Religious opinions do not weigh in the election of governors. From the date of the scheme, or within three years, the governors have power to appropriate the annual sum of £200, and on the determination of the pensions to the late schoolmasters a further annual sum of £50, for the establishment and maintenance of a girls' school. The entrance fee for boys is not to exceed £1 in the junior, and £2 in the senior department; the tuition fees in the junior are not to be less than than £4, nor more than £10, nor less than £10, nor more than £20 in the senior department, and no extras of any kind to be allowed without the sanction of the governors. Boys are admitted into the junior department at eight years old, and may remain until they are fifteen; into the senior at thirteen, and may remain until they are nineteen. The school to be open to all boys of good character and of sufficient bodily health. No boy to be admitted without being examined by the head master, and found fit for admission.

In both departments the religious instruction is restricted to lessons in the Bible, but exemption from attendance at prayers or from any lesson on a religious subject may be claimed by written notice to the head master. The boys are to be examined every year. The governors have power to grant exhibitions tenable at the school itself, and entitling the holders to exemption from the payment of tuition fees, these exemptions to be the reward of merit only; and they have further power to confer other pecuniary emoluments. Three exhibitions, founded by Mr. H. Brown, are tenable at any institution of higher education; one of £60 per annum for three years will be offered for competition annually. One exhibition, to be held at the school itself, has been founded by Mr. Forster, M.P.; five by Mr. H. Brown; and others by the governors. There are three terms in the year. No entrance fee is charged, but 2s. 6d. has to be paid for registration. The tuition fee in the senior school is £5 6s. 8d. per term, and in the junior £3 6s. 8d. per term. The Rev. W. H. Keeling, M.A., was head master in 1873, and there are seven other masters. Mr. G. E. Mumford, solicitor, was the secretary. There were forty boys in the old school; but at the beginning of 1872, when the school was re-opened in the High School, Hallfield Road, there were 100 boys. The number had gone on increasing, and at the opening of the first term in 1873 the pupils numbered 172. The new buildings were to be opened in 1873.

Modern Establishments for Education.—The earnestness and activity of the desire for knowledge, secular and religious, among the people of Bradford, needs no stronger testimony than the following summary of educational establishments:—At Undercliffe is Airedale Independent College, founded at Idle in 1800, and removed to its present situation in 1834. The Church Literary Institute, intended to replace a small building in Albion Court, Kirkgate, has been erected in North Parade, at a cost of upwards of £7000; but the total expenditure on the entire scheme will be more than £13,000. This is a handsome structure, in the French Gothic style, designed by Messrs. Andrews and Pepper. The façade to North Parade is lofty and commanding in elevation. Two canopied niches in the centre of the institute are to be filled in with statuary. The interior of the building contains several fine, lofty, well-lighted, and tastefully-decorated rooms. There is a large gymnasium in the basement, the library is on the ground floor, and on the story above is the lecture-hall, to accommodate 500 persons, and forming one of the handsomest rooms in the town. In the rear are a large reading-room, class-rooms, and every convenience for effectually carrying on the work of the institute. The foundation stone was laid in 1871, by Earl Nelson, in the presence of a large assemblage of the local clergy and gentry. The mayor of Bradford (Mr. Ald. M. W. Thompson) contributed the liberal sum of £2000 to the building fund of the institute, and other churchmen have given liberally. The Bradford Female Educational Institute was established in November, 1857, for the education of the female factory workers of Bradford and its neighbourhood, by means of evening classes. The pupils are instructed in reading and writing, arithmetic, elementary geography, English grammar and history, plain sewing and dress-making. The operations of the institute were carried on by means of branches in the most populous parts of the town. The late Mr. S. C. Kell was a liberal supporter of the institution, and Mr. H. Brown was one of its most steadfast friends. Mr. J. H. Rawnsley had been manager from the commencement. The institute was the only one of its kind in the country; it had done much to instruct young women whose early education had been neglected, and was not without its influence in improving the homes of the members. The Rebecca Street Ragged Schools were built in 1865 by voluntary contributions, at a cost of £2754, for the education and welfare of destitute children, of whom about 200 are provided here with a daily dinner. Besides a School of Industry, many large day and Sunday schools are supported by subscription. Strenuous efforts were made, within twenty years previous to 1873, in the erection of schools. During that time a large sum of money had been expended by various Christian communions in providing day and Sunday schools in connection with their churches; so that now, in 1873, there is not a church in Bradford without its school, and attached to many of the dissenting places of worship are excellent day schools. Mr. H. W. Ripley has built a large school at Ripleyville, at his sole expense. An Industrial Reformatory School is established in Broomfields, where ninety children are accommodated. The inmates are taught various occupations, and in addition to being instructed in elementary knowledge, they are sent out to situations, and are boarded and lodged on the premises until they are of suitable age to leave the school. The Roman Catholics have not been behind their neighbours in providing schools.

In addition to the eight temporary board schools and the eight schools building for the board, forty-three other elementary schools were reported to the School Board by the Education Department of Government as efficient schools, situated within the school district of the borough of Bradford. These schools belong to the Church of England, Wesleyans, Independents, Wesleyan Reformers, Primitive Methodists, and Roman Catholics. In addition to the schools above enumerated, there are several superior private educational establishments where the children of the middle class receive instruction, as well as a number of minor schools which do not come within the category of the Educational Department.

The Bradford School Board.—The board was elected without a contest, November 30, 1870. The first meeting was held December 15, 1870, when Mr. M. W. Thompson (mayor of Bradford), was elected chairman, Mr. J. V. Godwin, J.P., vice-chairman, and the other members were—Rev. J. R. Campbell, D.D., Mr. W. Coates (postmaster of Bradford), Mr. E. P. Duggan, Mr. James Hanson, Mr. Angus Holden, J.P., Mr. Ald. Jas. Law, J.P., Very Rev. Canon Motler, Mr. Archibald Neill, Mr. Henry William Ripley, J.P., Rev. Vincent W. Ryan, D.D. (vicar of Bradford), Mr. Edward West, J.P., Mr. William Whitehead, and Mr. Ald. H. Mitchell, J.P. Premises were taken in Market Street, and the Rev. T. T. Waterman, B.A., was elected clerk; Mr. G. Ackroyd, Bradford Banking Company, treasurer; Mr. Ald. Jos. Dawson, solicitor. The first year was devoted to obtaining information as to the state of education in the borough, seeking and securing suitable sites, preparing plans, and negotiating loans for erection of schools. The returns obtained showed that on April, 2, 1871, there were 21,355 children in the borough for whom accommodation should be provided. The public accommodation for children in February, 1871, was—existing, 17,119; contemplated or in course of erection, 4296: total, 21,415. In the private schools there was accommodation for 2812 scholars. It was found that this accommodation was unevenly distributed, some districts being inadequately supplied when the existing schools were filled to the utmost of their capacity. Steps were taken to erect four others in places where they were most wanted; it was determined to borrow £20,000 from the Public Works Loan Commissioners to meet the cost, and an education committee was appointed to prepare a scheme of instruction. Various other measures were adopted, a form was prepared for the transfer of schools, and two precepts of £500 were issued, requiring the town council to pay those sums into the hands of the treasurer of the board. In 1872 measures were taken for the erection of more board schools, and to borrow money from the loan commissioners to pay for them. The board have since gone on in the course planned out, and decided to build eight handsome and capacious new school premises, with an aggregate capacity for 4800 scholars, at a total cost, inclusive of land, buildings, and fittings, of £116,400; to be met by loans from the commissioners, at $3\frac{1}{2}$ per cent. interest, to be repaid in fifty equal annual instalments. These school buildings, which are pretty evenly distributed about the borough, are in progress (1873), and they will all be erected with as little delay as possible. They are situated as follows:—Feversham Street, 800 scholars, cost £23,800; Bowling Back Lane, 500, £13,600; Ryan Street, 800, £18,000; Horton Bank, 220, £6200; Lilycroft, 500, £15,000; Whetley Lane, 500, £12,400; Dudley Hill, 480, £12,300; Barker-end, 500, £14,900. Architecturally, the Bradford Board schools, which have all been designed by local architects, will be commodious structures, provided with every modern convenience. To meet pressing necessities the board, early in 1873, opened several temporary schools, capable of accommodating 2170 children. The business had increased so much in 1873, that Mr. Ellis Ingham was appointed assistant-clerk. Since 1871 the other school accommodation in the borough has been increased, so that when the board schools are opened the town will be well supplied with educational appliances. Of the eight scholarships founded by Mr. Henry Brown, in connection with the Bradford Grammar School, three are eligible by boys educated at the Bradford Board schools, entitling them to admission to the grammar school, and the board school-boys have other advantages in respect to this endowment. Mr. Forster's endowment to the grammar school is open to all boys educated at elementary schools in Bradford.

Churches and Chapels.—The provision for religious worship is very large in Bradford, there being, according to the Bradford Corporation Year Book for 1873, no less than ninety-seven different edifices devoted to divine service. The religious denominations in the town are various, and are approximately represented by the number of their places of worship. There are twenty-six churches for members of the establishment, including preaching rooms (but three mission churches were opened in 1873, after the corporation book was issued), fifteen chapels for Wesleyans, nineteen for Primitive and other Methodists, eleven for Baptists, thirteen for Independents, five for Roman Catholics, one for Unitarians, one for Friends, one for Moravians, one for Plymouth Brethren, one for United Presbyterians, one for New Jerusalem, one for Latter-Day Saints, one for The Brethren, and one for Spiritualists. The parish church of St. Peter is a spacious building on the hill side, in the perpendicular style. It was erected about 1458, and has been restored, the south aisles having been rebuilt in 1832. Other alterations are of recent date; the old oak roof has been opened out to view, and the whole length of the church thrown open, with great advantage to the appearance of the interior. Most of the mural monuments have been removed into the tower. Chief among those in the chancel is Flaxman's beautiful personification of old age—an old man between his son and daughter—on a monument raised to the memory of Abraham Balme, a gentleman of Bradford. Five windows in stained glass add to the beauty of the restoration. Upwards of £6000 has been spent in this work, contributed by all shades of Christians. The mayor of Bradford (Ald. Thompson) gave a reredos, which cost £300. The living was in 1873 worth upwards of £1400 per annum, and is in the gift of the trustees of the late Rev. Charles Simeon. The old vicarage house was in Goodmansend. The vicar's residence now is in Horton Road. In 1671 there was a lectureship founded, of £40 a year, by Mr. Peter Sunderland, of Fairweather Green. Bierley Church was built in 1766, at the cost of R. Richardson, Esq., but it was not consecrated until 1824. It was enlarged, at the expense of Miss Currer, in 1828. The building is in the Grecian style, seats 900 persons, and has of late years been further improved. The other churches in Bradford are as follows: —Christ Church, situated at the top of Darley Street, was built in 1815, at a cost of £5400, which was raised by subscription; one anonymous subscriber, a lady, alone contributed £800. It was enlarged and repaired in 1826 and 1836. The register dates from 1837. The building is in the Gothic style, and contains 1300 sittings, of which 600 are free. On the 31st of October, 1836, the first stone of St. James' Church was laid in Manchester Road, by Mr. John Wood, of Bradford, who, with a liberality happily not unexampled, himself bore the entire cost, amounting to £14,000, of the structure, together with that of a parsonage house and schoolroom attached. The schoolhouse was subsequently considerably enlarged at Mr. Wood's expense. The church is an excellent specimen of the early English style, being surmounted by a handsome tower and spire, and contains 1100 sittings, of which 600 are free. St. John's Church, also in the Manchester Road, owes its existence to the liberality of two gentlemen, strangers to Bradford, and even to Yorkshire—Mr. Berthon, of Romsey, Hants, and Mr. Preston, of North Wales. About £4000 was expended on the erection, and the church was opened in 1840, with accommodation for 1150 worshippers. The patrons of the living are the two founders, in unison with the vicar of Bradford; but the situation being inconvenient, a large new church, to take its place, is now in course of erection (1873), in Little Horton Lane. The new edifice is in the geometrical decorated style, designed by Messrs. T. H. & F. Healey. It is built of stone outside, and coloured bricks and stone are used for the interior. The church is to have a lofty tower and peal of bells. The cost, inclusive of land, is estimated at £10,000, and accommodation is to be found for 750 worshippers. Mr. J. R. Cordingley, of Bradford, was to present eight bells, costing £700. St. John's Church, Bowling, which seats 980 persons, was built in 1840 at the expense of the proprietors of the Bowling Ironworks. St. Jude's Church, Lumb Lane, was erected in 1843 by subscription, cost £3000, and seats about 1000 persons. The congregation have opened a mission room in Golden Square, White Abbey, and intend to build a new church, schools, and house, in the district, at a cost of £13,000, towards which £2500 was raised early in 1873. St. Paul's Church, Manningham, designed in the early English style, by Messrs. Mallinson and Healey, was built at the expense of Mr. John Hollings, in 1848, at a cost of about £4000. It has since been twice enlarged, and is a handsome church, with a well-proportioned tower and spire. The church affords sittings for 1100 persons. Another church, St. Mark's, is to be built in Grosvenor Road, Manningham, designed in decorated Gothic by Messrs. Walford and Pollard, and is estimated to cost £7000. St. Andrew's Church, Lister Hills, was erected in 1853, from the plans of Messrs. Mallinson and Healey, and has since been enlarged. It seats 982 persons, and is one of the most flourishing of the Bradford churches. One of the best specimens of ecclesiastical architecture in the borough is the church of All Saints', Little Horton Green, the product of the ripened experience of the late Mr. Thomas Healey, who designed the building in the geometrical decorated Gothic; at his death the carrying out of his ideas was superintended by his son, Mr. Frank Healey. The church is composed of nave, side aisles, transepts, and chancel, and seats 1000 people. The tower and spire rise to a height of 200 feet, and the church is intended to have a peal of bells. It was built at the expense of Mr. F. S. Powell, M.P., of Horton Old Hall, cost about £20,000, and was consecrated in 1864. St. Luke's Church was built in 1862 on a piece of land in Chandos Street, Wakefield Road, which was given by the late Mr. Chas. Hardy, of Low Moor. The structure, which is in the decorated style, will accommodate about 750 persons, and cost £3000. In the same year rose St. Thomas' Church, Butterfield Place, built at a cost of £4000, on a piece of land given by Mr. F. S. Powell, M.P. It is capable of holding 700 persons, is endowed with £300 a year, and is in the gift of the bishop of the diocese. A neat little church in Leeds Road is dedicated to the Holy Trinity, and accommodates 650 persons. The living is in the gift of trustees. The other modern churches in the borough are— St. Matthew's, Wibsey Bank Foot; St. Mary's, Laister Dyke; St. Stephen's, Bowling; St. Michael's, Brick Lane; St. Philip's, Girlington Road; St. Stephen's School Chapel, Chapel Green; St. Augustine's School Chapel, Undercliffe, to be supplemented with a church, the site for which has been given by Mr. W. Garnett, J.P., Bradford. St. Chrysostom's Mission Church is in Bolton Road, and a site for a new church was given by Lieutenant-colonel Pollard, of Scarr Hill. Bolton School Church had been enlarged; it was proposed to build a church there. St. Bartholomew's Church, Ripleyville, intended as a memorial to the late Mr. Charles Hardy (who, in his lifetime, was a munificent contributor to the scheme for erecting ten new churches in Bradford), is an excellent example of early geometrical Gothic. The exterior is of stone, and the interior of coloured bricks and stone, the proportions of the edifice and its treatment being good. It is built on a site given by Mr. H. W. Ripley. The cost was £7000, and sittings are provided for 740 persons. The Hardy family were large contributors to the building fund. A new church is erecting at Great Horton in the early Gothic style, which is to cost a similar sum. It is to take the place of the old Bell Chapel, and will be a strong, substantial, stone edifice, with tower and peal of bells. The site was given by Mr. F. S. Powell, M.P., and the church will accommodate 800 persons. St. Barnabas' Church, Heaton, which may be said to belong to Bradford, is a neat structure, also in the early Gothic style, and has a tower and spire. With a few exceptions, the whole of the churches erected in recent years in Bradford have been designed and built under the superintendence of Messrs. Mallinson and Healey, or their successors, Messrs. T. H. & F. Healey. These gentlemen have had the advantage of the experience of a talented father, and they have shown, in the handsome churches that have come from their hands, that they have profited by the lessons they have learned. They have also designed most of the church schools. In the Ripon Diocesan Church Calendar for 1873, the number of churches in the borough of Bradford, to which districts had been assigned, was returned as nineteen. The aggregate population of the districts was stated to be 156,682, the total number of sittings was given as 13,814, and the aggregate annual value of the livings was £5583. The mission churches were not included in the returns. The greater portion of the Bradford churches, each with its school, have risen within the twenty years preceding 1873. The Bradford Church Building Society originated the movement in favour of church building; and although extraneous aid has not been wanting, the great bulk of the large sums expended of late years has been raised by the voluntary offerings of wealthy and liberal-hearted churchmen resident in the town and neighbourhood. Mr. John Rand was one of the most liberal contributors to the scheme of building ten churches, which had been nearly accomplished in 1873.

Nonconformist Chapels.—After the royal declaration of Charles II. in favour of freedom of worship in 1672, the Presbyterians built themselves a chapel, which in 1717 was replaced by another, in Chapel Lane. The cost of this humble structure was £340 3s. 5d.; but there was an antiquarian interest about it, the interior being fitted up with old oak wainscoting from Howley Hall, from which place also the ancient curiously wrought gateway was traditionally said to have come. The chapel has a valuable endowment bequeathed in 1724 by Jeremy Dixon, of Heaton Royds, yeoman. The old chapel was pulled down in 1868, and a new Gothic building erected on the site, from the designs of Messrs. Andrews & Pepper, at a cost of nearly £6000. It will seat 500 worshippers, and has a handsome appearance. In the rear of the chapel are Sunday schools. The Rev. J. G. Miall, of Salem Chapel, Bradford, in his "Congregationalism in Yorkshire," gives some reliable particulars of the origin of the Independents in Bradford. It is conjectured that Nonconformity was established about the year 1665, at Thornton, near Bradford, and that the first meetings were held in a place afterwards known as "Kipping House," situated in a lonely and retired valley. In 1672 the church at Kipping sent a member, George Wade, to be present at the formation of a Congregational church, Call Lane, Leeds. In 1766, when the Rev. John Whiteford was pastor, a new chapel was built. Rev. Joseph Cockin held the pastorate from 1778 to 1792, and was "the apostle and itinerant of his district." The chapel was subsequently enlarged, but in 1844 a new building and school-house were erected. The Rev. James Gregory became pastor in 1834, and held that position in 1873. About 1784 a chapel was built in Little Horton Lane, then in the outskirts of the town. Rev. Thomas Taylor followed in 1808. During his time and up to his death, in 1853, the congregation was very large, and the chapel and premises were enlarged. Rev. J. Glyde succeeded in 1836, but died, greatly lamented, in 1854. The Rev. J. R. Campbell, M.A., D.D., took charge of the pastorate in 1855, and was minister in 1873. The old structure, after being improved at various times, was at length, in 1862, superseded by a large new chapel, designed by Messrs. Lockwood & Mawson, in the Elizabethan style. This capacious edifice, together with the range of Sunday schools adjoining, cost upwards of £14,000. In 1836, owing to the increase of the congregation at Horton Lane Chapel, Salem Chapel, Manor Row, was built at a cost of about £7000. It was subsequently enlarged and improved, at a considerable expense. Preaching places at Spinkwell and Valley Road were attached to it. The Rev. J. G. Miall was pastor in 1873, having held the charge since the opening of the chapel, and was joined, in 1865, by Rev. J. Andrews as assistant. In 1843 a movement was originated at Salem Chapel, which had the effect of freeing multitudes of Independent chapels in the West Riding from debt, and "since then the former system of religious mendicancy, equally burdensome and disgraceful, has happily become obsolete." Airedale Independent College, for the training of Independent ministers, is the expansion of an academy founded for the same purpose, in 1756, at Heckmondwike. It was removed for a time to Northowram. The college was founded at Idle in 1800, and received £5000 three per cent. consols shortly afterwards from Mr. Edward Hanson; and in 1827 two estates at Fagley and Undercliffe, and £8000 in consols, from Mrs. Bacon, of Bradford. The present college at Undercliffe was erected by subscription in 1831, and is rather commanding in position. The place has, however, become objectionable for a college on several grounds. The constituents of Airedale College held a meeting in April, 1872, at which it was resolved to erect a new building in the neighbourhood of Bradford. The new college is to be on the non-resident principle, and will be open to lay students as well as to those who intend to enter the ministry. The endowments produced in 1872 about £500; but the total income of the college was £1300, and the expenditure about the same. The number of students that could be accommodated in the college was twenty-four, and in 1873 it was attended by eighteen. The Rev. D. Fraser, LL.D., was president in 1873; the Rev. Professor Shearer, classical and mathematical master; treasurer, Mr. Titus Salt, Milner Field; secretary, Rev. S. Dyson, Idle. Airedale College Chapel, in Park Street, Otley Road, was built by subscription in 1839, at a cost of £3000. The Independents also have chapels at Lumb Lane (Greenfield, proposed to be rebuilt); Lister Hills; Essex Street, Bowling; Cambridge Place; High Street, Great Horton; Thornton Lane; Wesley Place, Great Horton; Jer Lane, Horton Bank; Holme Lane; Cemetery Road, Lidget Green; and Valley Road. The Yorkshire Congregational Year Book for 1873 showed that in the Bradford district, which embraced a large area of country, there were forty-seven chapels, with sitting accommodation for 22,091 persons. In the borough of Bradford, included in the above returns, the aggregate number of sittings in the chapels was 7265. The Baptist church at Bradford was commenced in 1751 by some members of the churches at Rawden and Haworth. A few persons met at the house of Elizabeth Frankland, at Manningham, near Bradford. In the following year they invited Mr. Smith of Wainsgate, Mr. Hartley of Haworth, and Mr. Lord of Bacup, to preach once a quarter at Manningham. William Crabtree, a native of the township of Wadsworth, near Halifax, visited Bradford, and in November, 1753, received a call to the ministry, which he accepted. On the 4th December, 1753, the church at Bradford was formed, consisting of twenty-three members, and Mr. Crabtree was ordained. He was originally a shalloon weaver. The infant church met for some time in a private house; but this place becoming inconveniently crowded, they worshipped in "the Cock-pit," near the end of Thornton Road; the "good people exulting greatly that they had dispossessed Satan of a portion of his dominions." So poor were they that they could not afford to procure benches for their sanctuary, and "the old women wended their way thither with their stools under their arms." In those primitive days new members were baptized in the mill-goit at the bottom of Silsbridge Lane, then a pure stream, but now (1873) foul and discoloured from the refuse of manufactories. In 1755, £100 was raised, and a building capable of holding 400 or 500 people was erected at the top of Westgate, then the highest part of the town, and now the school-room of Westgate Chapel. In June, 1757, an association of Baptist churches was formed in Bradford, consisting of Wainsgate, Sunderland, Whitehaven, Haworth, Rawden, Bacup, Liverpool, and Bradford. On the 11th March, 1758, John Fawcett (a native of Lidget Green, near Bradford), afterwards the Rev. Dr. Fawcett, was baptized at Bradford. He was one of the most eminent ministers of his time. A chapel was erected at Farsley in 1777, and in March, 1780, thirty members were dismissed from Bradford to form a church at that place. In 1782 Westgate Chapel was erected, which then contained sittings for about 700 persons, but it has since been considerably enlarged. It now has sittings for 1400 persons, besides accommodation for the school children in the upper gallery. Mr. Crabtree laboured up to his eightieth year, preached twice in his eighty-ninth year, and died February 14, 1811, in his ninety-first year. He was succeeded by the Rev. W. Steadman, afterwards Dr. Steadman. This eloquent preacher was pastor of Westgate from 1805 to 1837, when he died, April 12, aged seventy-three. During his time the Baptist church increased from the year 1805 to 1825, when it reached the zenith of its prosperity. A baptistry was formed in Westgate Chapel about 1805, the chapel was enlarged in 1817 at a cost of £1000, and the Sunday school numbered 300 children. Dr. Steadman's name will always be honourably associated with the Baptist College, which he commenced in 1806 in Little Horton, as a private academy for the education of young men for the ministry. By means of gifts and bequests, both of books and money, it became in the course of a few years an important centre of education. In the year 1859 the college was removed to Rawden, where the teachers and students are housed in a handsome building, erected in the Tudor style, from the designs of Mr. H. J. Paull, Manchester.

The college stands in a commanding position, overlooking the valley of the Aire, and has a fine appearance. It is surrounded by beautifully laid-out grounds, and cost, inclusive of the estate on which it stands, £12,000. The revenue of the college, from endowments and other sources, is about £1500. Accommodation is provided for twenty-six students. Dr. Steadman was succeeded at Westgate Chapel by the Rev. H. Dowson, who laboured with great acceptance for many years until he resigned to become the principal of Bury Baptist College. Sion Chapel, Bridge Street, was erected in 1823, on a site given by Miss Ward. The Rev. Dr. Godwin, whose name is honoured and revered in Bradford, officiated as pastor for many years. He was followed by the Rev. Thomas Pottenger, who in his turn was succeeded by the Rev. J. P. Chown, the present able and esteemed pastor (1873). The chapel was enlarged to its utmost capacity, and it was decided to build a new one. A site was obtained in Harris Street, Leeds Road, and a large and beautiful edifice in the Italian style, designed by Messrs. Lockwood and Mawson, has been reared at a total outlay, for building and land, of nearly £16,000. The chapel has a handsome Corinthian portico, fronting Harris Street, and accommodation is provided for 1500 persons. In the rear of the chapel are large Sunday schools. The building is to be opened in 1873, and is styled Sion Jubilee Memorial Chapel and schools. Trinity Chapel, Little Horton Lane, rose in 1857, and contains 1000 sittings; the Sunday schools were subsequently enlarged. Hallfield Chapel and schools, a handsome pile of buildings in the Gothic style, were built in 1863, at a cost of £7000, in Manningham Lane; there are seats in the chapel for 1000 persons. There are also preaching places at Allerton Road (Lady Royd), New Leeds (Mulgrave Street), and Caledonia Street. The General Baptists have a chapel in Infirmary Street, and there are Baptist chapels in Tetley Street, Darfield Street, and Ripley Street, Manchester Road. The Baptist interest in Bradford is strong, and the people are active in well-doing. The rise of the Wesleyan Methodists of Bradford may be traced to the zealous and indefatigable preaching of John Wesley in the West Riding, of John Nelson, who suffered bonds and imprisonment from the bigots of his time, and of many other zealous and devoted men. The first Methodist chapel in the vicinity of Bradford was erected at Birstal in 1751, but it was not until 1756 that a "preaching place" was opened at Bradford. On June 17, 1744, John

Wesley first preached at Little Horton, and again visited Bradford and preached on the 24th January, 1746, and 25th April, 1747. Their first meeting-house was at the Cock-pit, which Mr. Crabtree and the Baptists vacated in 1755. It was not till 1766 that they had a chapel of their own building. It was called the Octagon, and stood in Great Horton Road. In 1769 Bradford became the head of a circuit, Halifax being then included; but in 1785 Halifax was separated from Bradford. In 1835 Bradford was divided into two circuits, Kirkgate and Eastbrook. Horton was constituted a circuit in 1842; Manningham became another in 1866, Low Moor in 1871, and in 1872, Greenhill (Bradford Moor) was made into a circuit. There are thus five circuits in Bradford. John Wesley preached last in Bradford, at five o'clock in the morning of May 2, 1788, at the Octagon, when there was a large congregation. Kirkgate Chapel was built in 1811, with 1400 sittings, and at a cost of £11,000; Eastbrook Chapel in 1825, with 1500 sittings, and a much handsomer exterior than that in Kirkgate. Its cost was upwards of £7000. White Abbey Chapel was built in 1838, and has been considerably enlarged; Centenary Chapel, Clayton Lane, in 1839. There are large chapels at Bradford Moor, Dudley Hill, Richmond Terrace, Undercliffe, Mount Street, Little Horton Lane (Annesley), Girlington, Great Horton, Prospect (Bowling), Carlisle Road (Manningham), and Heaton Road. A new chapel was building in 1873 in Otley Road, at a cost of £6400. Most of these chapels have roomy Sunday schools attached, and of late years the Wesleyans have spent a very large aggregate amount in the extension of chapel and school accommodation. A new chapel has been built at Frizinghall, just outside the borough. From the year 1744 to 1839, when the centenary of Methodism was celebrated, embracing a period of ninety-five years, the Wesleyans of Bradford had extended their numbers until, in the latter year, there were 3500 members, 4306 children in the schools, and at least 15,000 of the population directly or indirectly under its influence. In the thirty-five years up to 1839, upwards of £40,000 had been spent in the erection of chapels and schools. Up to the first half of 1873, the total number of sittings in the Wesleyan chapels built and building in the borough of Bradford was 13,000, and the chapels were all well attended. The number of Sunday scholars was between 8000 and 9000. From 1838 to 1873 no less a sum than

£80,000 had been spent in the borough of Bradford by the Wesleyans, in the building of chapels and schools. The Primitive Methodists are also prospering. They have places of worship at Carlisle Road, Manningham; at Daisy Hill; at Great Horton, Town-end; at Horton Bank; at Laister-dyke (Zion); at Manchester Road; at Sun Street (Philadelphia); at Rebecca Street; and at Park Lane. The Methodist New Connection have chapels at Horton Lane (Ebenezer), and Sticker Lane, and they opened a preaching place in Bowling Old Lane in 1873. The United Methodist Free Church people have built chapels at Bridge Street, Dudley Hill; Otley Road, Free Street (Mount Olive); Westgate, Holmes Street; and Swaine Green (Providence). The Wesleyan Reformers possess chapels at Bowling Old Lane (Muff Field), Peckover Street (Bethesda), and Abbey Street. The other dissenters, not capable of classification, who have places of worship, are—United Presbyterian, Infirmary Street; Moravians, Little Horton; New Jerusalem, Infirmary Street; Latter Day Saints, Kirkgate; and the Brethren, Salem Street. It does not come within the limits of this work to describe the operations of these bodies in detail; but it may be remarked that they all, more or less, have Sunday schools or other agencies by which the instruction of the young in religious knowledge is carefully attended to. The same may be said of the Roman Catholics, who celebrated public mass in Bradford, probably for the first time since the days of Queen Mary, in 1822, at the Roebuck Inn, Bradford, and who have now five chapels in the borough—St. Mary's, Stott Hill; St. Patrick's, Westgate; St. Ann's, Hardy Street; St. Joseph's, Grafton Street; and St. Peter's, Leeds Road. It is contemplated to build a large new chapel in connection with St. Mary's, and further extension is intended in respect to St. Patrick's. The Roman Catholics form a numerous portion of the population of Bradford; but the comparative poverty of the great mass of the people acts as a hindrance to the wish of the priests to extend the chapel and school accommodation for the members of their communion. The Society of Friends was established in Bradford as early as 1672; for in that year William Wright, clothier, gave an acre of land in Goodmansend, in trust for "the children of light, whom the people of the world commonly call Quakers," to use as a burial ground for them and their succeeding generations. Their meeting-house, which will accommodate 1400 persons, was built on the site of the old chapel in 1811, enlarged in 1825, and improved subsequently. A large Sunday school has been built adjoining the meeting-house.

Public Parks.—Bradford, like most of the manufacturing towns of England, has been liberally supplied with public parks for the pleasure and recreation of all classes, including those engaged in labour. Peel Park, containing an area of about fifty-six acres, was purchased and laid out by public subscription, at a cost of about £25,000. Sir Titus Salt, Bart., and Messrs. Milligan, Forbes, & Co. were each contributors of £1000. The park is on the north-east side of the town, and is situated in a beautiful valley, well wooded, and commanding extensive views to the west and north-west. One of the principal features of the park is a terrace 400 yards long and thirty feet wide. On the 7th November, 1863, this fine estate was conveyed to the Bradford Corporation, in trust for the people of Bradford. On the 28th October, 1870, the Corporation purchased Lister Park, Manningham, from Mr. S. C. Lister, for £40,000, with power to sell off not more than fourteen acres. The total area of the park was fifty-three acres, three roods, thirty-two poles, but it has, since the original purchase, been a little enlarged. This delightful domain, with its noble trees and extensive greensward, is not to be dismembered, the Corporation having decided not to sell any land in either of the parks. Land has been bought at Horton for a third park. An instalment of six acres out of forty which it is proposed to acquire, has come into the hands of the Corporation, and has been thrown open to the inhabitants as a recreation ground. A fourth park is to be purchased at Bowling, on the site known as Bowling Springs, not far from the ancient mansion of Bowling Hall. It is also proposed that Bradford Moor shall be acquired as a recreation ground. When all these schemes are matured, Bradford will have five places for outdoor recreation, within easy reach of the homes of the inhabitants, an advantage which few towns possess. Galas have been held for many years in Peel Park, at Whitsuntide and on other occasions, but the largest gatherings are at Whitsuntide, when business in Bradford is suspended for the holidays, and the proceeds of the galas are given to the charities. In 1873 upwards of 100,000 people paid for admission to the galas on Whit Monday and Tuesday, and a large sum was realized. Galas are also held in Lister Park, and a band, paid for by public subscription, played in the grounds on Saturday afternoons in the summer months of 1872, and was continued in 1873. No better indication of the prosperity of the town and districts can be afforded than the assemblages at these galas, where the people of both sexes are well dressed, displaying excellent taste in their attire, and their behaviour is highly commendable, such a thing as a complaint being very rarely heard. The good order observed in these vast assemblages no doubt arises, in a great measure, from the fact that intoxicating liquors are not allowed to be sold in the parks, either at galas or at other times.

Boundary Commissioners' Report on Bradford.—The position and limits of the parliamentary and municipal borough of Bradford, as described by the Boundary Commissioners of 1868, were as follows:—The large and flourishing borough of Bradford stands in a hilly country, very favourable for creating water-power, on the banks of a considerable brook which flows northward into the river Aire, at a distance of about two miles north of Bradford. Since the time when the Leeds and Liverpool Canal, which runs along the banks of the river Aire, was constructed, soon after the commencement of the reign of George III., Bradford has possessed the advantage of a cheap inland navigation, both to the eastern and western seas. The borough of Bradford in 1868 consisted of the several townships of Bradford, Manningham, and Bowling, and the township of Horton, including the hamlets of Great and Little Horton.

Free Library.—On the 5th March, 1868, an able report was prepared by a sub-committee of the general purposes committee of the Bradford Corporation, of which Mr. J. V. Godwin was chairman, setting forth what had been done in other towns as to the working of the Free Public Libraries Act, and stating that it was desirable that the Act should be adopted in Bradford "at as early a period as the ratepayers may deem expedient," and "that whenever the council shall be called upon by a decided expression of local public opinion, they should be prepared to do their part with alacrity and spirit." Nothing further was done that year, but subsequently the subject was warmly taken up. A town's meeting was convened, and Mr. J. V. Godwin moved a resolution in favour of adopting the Act, which was carried by a very large majority. The town council at once proceeded to make the necessary arrangements for establishing the library, and in 1872 the free library was opened in temporary premises in New Market Street. In 1873 it was proposed to erect a handsome building specially for the purpose at the corner of Godwin Street and Aldemanbury, over a new fire brigade station-house. The structure has been designed by Messrs. Andrews and Pepper, in the classical style, and is estimated to cost about £14,000. The library contains 14,000 volumes. There is a reading-room, supplied with the magazines and periodicals and the local newspapers, and a reference department. From the opening on 15th June, 1872, to 31st April, 1873, 27,544 volumes had been issued to be read on the premises. The lending department was opened on the 17th February, 1873, and from that time to 31st April in the same year, 25,130 volumes were issued to be read at home. In addition to the above, upwards of 130,000 persons had visited the library to peruse the current literature, &c., with which the tables in the reading room were regularly provided. Mr. Charles Virgo is librarian. The cost of purchasing books, fitting up the library, &c., to the end of 1872, was £1879 18s. 10d. The Bradford library, formed in 1774, is supported by subscription, and the books are stored in a commodious building devoted to the purpose in Darley Street. The number of volumes in the library in 1873 was 16,000.

Sewage Defæcation.—The Bradford Corporation, bound by an agreement in chancery to cleanse and purify the sewage flowing from the town into the river Aire, have had constructed, in the Bradford valley between Bolton and Frizinghall, a range of sewage defæcation works which it is expected will answer the desired purpose. The scheme is to be worked by the Peat Engineering Company, under an agreement with the Corporation. The process is simple, and is worked on the gravitation principle. The sewage matter flows from the main drain into subsiding tanks, and from thence passes into five filtering chambers; two filled with burned peat and clay, and three with charcoal. In its passage through these chambers the sewage is purified, and it flows thence into the Bradford beck on its way to the river Aire. The first section of the works was in operation in the early part of 1873, and appeared to be successful in cleansing the sewage. The whole scheme was expected to be worked during the year. The cost of these works, inclusive of land, &c., up to December, 1872, was £58,751. Adjoining the sewage works the Bradford beck was, in 1873, in course of being covered in at the joint expense of the Bradford Corporation and the Midland Railway Company. The cost of this important work to the Corporation was £19,906 13s. 9d., the Company paying sixty-two per cent. and the Corporation thirty-eight per cent. of the cost of the works.

Model Lodging Houses.—In the year 1865, during the mayoralty of Mr. Charles Semon, J.P., a German gentleman, a company was formed for the erection of model lodging houses, to give decent working people and wayfarers, who had to move about the country, the opportunity of securing clean lodgings at a moderate price. In 1866 a large building, costing £4000, was opened in Captain Street, Bolton Road, affording accommodation for 172 persons. The charges were 4d. and 6d. a night for single men, and 8d. for married couples. Mr. H. Gardner was appointed superintendent, and the scheme answered so well that a second house was built and opened in Wigan Street, in 1872, on the opposite side of the town. This building, which cost £5000, is exclusively devoted to single men, and has accommodation for 185. The charges are 4d. and 6d. a night. Mr. Gardner was given charge of the place, and Mr. G. Baldock was appointed to Captain Street. Begun in a philanthropic spirit, the lodging-houses have proved so useful and have been so largely appreciated, that the proprietors have derived a dividend from the undertaking.

Reading-rooms, the means of cooking their own food, and other conveniences are provided for the lodgers, many of whom remain for a lengthened period in the houses. Religious service is conducted on Sunday, and the lodgers are stated to behave well. Mr. Charles Semon, who has taken a lively interest in this provision for houseless wanderers, was chairman of the company. In 1873 there were thirty-six other registered lodging houses in Bradford (one to accommodate about 100 persons), and many houses that were not registered by the Corporation.

Baths and Washhouses.—The Bradford Corporation, in 1865, had the old waterworks offices in Thornton Road converted into baths and washhouses, by Messrs. Milnes and France, at a cost of £7500. The building was formally opened by the mayor (Mr. C. Semon) on July 22, 1865. There are first and second class swimming, slipper, vapour, and douche baths, and a beautifully fitted up Turkish bath. Swimming and slipper baths are also provided for females. There are ten compartments for washing, furnished with drying houses and other conveniences. The baths and washhouses have been extensively used, but these aids to cleanliness are required in other parts of the borough; the washing department being inadequate to meet the demand. In the first year of their formation the baths were used by 93,375 persons, and the receipts were £1436 16s. 7d. In 1872 there were 109,333 bathers, and the money earned was £1653 3s. 5d. Mr. John Howarth has been superintendent from the commencement. In 1873 the accommodation for bathers was enlarged.

Hospitals and Charitable Institutions.—The great increase of wealth in Bradford has been followed by liberal contributions to charitable objects, and the town now (1873) possesses many institutions for ameliorating the sufferings of the sick poor. Foremost amongst these is the Bradford Infirmary and Dispensary, begun in a small way in 1825; but in 1844 a large building in the Elizabethan style was erected between Westgate and Lumb Lane, from the designs of Mr. Walker Rawstorne, at a cost, inclusive of site and grounds, of upwards of £10,000. In 1864 the building was raised another story, by Messrs. Andrews and Delaunay, at an expenditure of £6578; and in 1873 a new dispensary was added by Messrs. Andrews and Pepper, the expenditure being upwards of £5200. An anonymous donation of £3000 was received towards the cost of the new dispensary. The outlay on the building, &c., although stated in the aggregate at £21,778, has been considerably more than this sum, as many minor additions have been made. The institution is liberally supported. Amongst the numerous list of benefactions is the princely legacy of £10,000 (less duty) bequeathed in 1863 by Mr. Abraham Musgrave, of Bramley. In 1872, 7976 patients were treated in the house, and 16,887 visits were paid by the dispensary surgeons to patients at their own homes. At December 31, 1872, the total money invested was £21,000, and there was a balance at the bank of £568 6s. The total income for 1872 was £5701 17s. 2d., the expenditure exceeding this sum by £6 0s. 7d. The average cost of a bed per annum, which, in 1869, was £36 2s. 5½d., rose in 1872 to £43 13s. 4½d.; but this does not include items of expense shared with the outpatients. In connection with the Infirmary is the Outhwaite Convalescent Fund, for sending patients who are recovering to Harrogate, Ilkley, Buxton, and Southport. Next in importance is the Bradford Fever Hospital. This institution owes it origin to Mr. Alfred Harris, of Sleningford Park, Ripon, formerly a partner in Harris' Old Bank, Bradford. Grateful for the prosperity of his life, Mr. Harris in 1867 offered £4398 15s. towards the foundation of a fever hospital. Sir Titus Salt, Bart., of Saltaire, seconded this handsome offer with the munificent sum of £5000; and "A Friend" giving £3000, other large donations flowed in, and the result was the erection of a building at Penny Oaks, Leeds Road, which is believed to be one of the most complete and efficient fever hospitals in the kingdom. The design was prepared by Messrs. Andrews and Pepper. The hospital is erected on the detached pavilion principle. The administration department and the wards are connected with each other by covered corridors of glass and wood. The wards are only one story in height, and attached to them are convalescent wards. No expense was spared to render the hospital as perfect for its purpose as possible. The building, picturesque in appearance, stands upon a hill in the centre of several acres of land, and the grounds are tastefully laid out and planted with trees. The memorial stone was laid on September 10, 1869, by Mr. Alfred Harris, and the hospital was opened 16th January, 1872. The total expenditure for land, building, furnishing, &c., up to December 31, 1872, was £24,269 3s. 7d. The Eye and Ear Hospital was established in 1857 by Mr. Edward Bronner, M.D., an eminent German oculist and aurist; and on March 29, 1864, the foundation stone of a new building was laid in Hallfield Road, by Sir Titus Salt, Bart. (then Mr. Salt), and was opened June 28, 1865, by the mayor (Mr. C. Semon). Mr. John Abbott, of Halifax, gave £1000, and an anonymous donor contributed a similar sum. The site, 1450 yards in extent, cost 3s. per yard. The hospital, one of the handsomest Gothic structures in Bradford, was designed by Messrs. Lockwood and Mawson, and was completed at a cost of £5500. It was to be enlarged in 1873 by the addition of two wards for infectious cases, at an estimated cost of £1200. The hospital does not confine its operations to Bradford, but receives patients from the surrounding towns and villages. The number of patients admitted in 1872 was 1443, and of these 240 were in-patients, who remained in the hospital 6364 days, or 26¼ days each, at a cost of only 11¼d. per day, or 25s. for each patient. Of the 1203 out-patients, 552 came from other towns, and of the 240 in-patients, 153 were from other places. The expenses for the year ending February, 1873, were £882 13s. 5d., and the income was £834 6s. 3d. The invested fund in that year amounted to £3000. The Nurses' Training Institution was opened in Eldon Place,

Bradford, in 1872, mainly through the instrumentality of Mr. C. Semon, J.P. Its object is to train up young women to become nurses in private families and in hospitals, there being great difficulty in Bradford, where employment for women in the mills is plentiful, to obtain good nurses. In 1873 there were eight trained nurses connected with the institution, and six probationers. The income from private nursing for ten months ending March 31, 1873, was £240 6s. 1d., and the total expenses had been £600, the funds required being raised by subscription. It was intended to commence district nursing amongst the sick poor as soon as a sufficient number of nurses had been trained and the funds would warrant. The Tradesmen's Benevolent Institution, originated in 1857 by the mayor (Mr. H. Brown), gives pensions to unfortunate tradesmen. In 1873 the number of pensioners was 37, of whom 10 were males, and 27 females. The males receive £24 yearly, and the females £18. The money invested in 1873 was £3400. In connection with this institution is the Tradesmen's Home at Manningham, a range of thirty houses, built from the designs of Messrs. Milnes and France in 1867. In the centre of the pile is a handsome chapel or reading-room elegantly furnished, and containing some fine stained glass windows. The foundation stone was laid by Sir Titus Salt, Bart., in September 1867, and the cost of the whole scheme was £14,000. The home stands in the midst of its own grounds. Like its kindred charity, it is for decayed tradespeople, male and female, who are each furnished with a house free. Mr. John Robinson has the credit of being the originator, and the home has been liberally supported by donations of 2000 guineas from Sir Titus Salt, Bart., 800 guineas from Mr. Henry Brown, 700 guineas from the late Mr. H. Harris, and large sums from other gentlemen. The Spinsters' Endowment Fund, for furnishing elderly maiden ladies with the means to qualify them for occupying the homes, was started, after the home was opened, by Mr. Thomas Buck, J.P., who gave £1080 for this purpose. Other donations have swelled the invested capital to £1470. The fund is managed by trustees, and in 1873 Mr. W. W. Harris was honorary secretary, the scheme being worked with very little cost. In 1873 six spinsters were on the fund, each receiving £18 per annum. The Bradford Association for improving the social condition of the blind, owes much to the late Mr. W. Lythall. It was begun in a small way, but in 1868 a large Gothic building was reared in North Parade, at a cost of £6590, from the designs of Messrs. Knowles and Wilcock, where the work of the institution is conducted. The institution is managed by ladies, Mrs. Gale and Miss Holloway being the honorary secretaries in 1873. A special donation of £2000 was given by a lady anonymously. In 1872, thirty-four men and eighteen women were constantly employed in the workshops, receiving regular wages. The mission woman had paid 495 visits to the blind in the town and neighbourhood in 1872, teaching them to read, administering religious consolation, and succouring the sick and aged blind. The amount received for goods in 1872 was £6552 19s. 9½d., and the surplus of assets, being the value of stock, &c., and inclusive of cash in bank and in hand, £930 18s. 4½d., was £5374 12s. 7½d. The Bradford Female Refuge was established in 1860, for reclaiming fallen women. The institution is in Arctic Parade, Great Horton. In 1872, fourteen women were received, and their earnings were £105 9s. 6d. The expenditure was £311 6s. 10d., and there was a balance in hand of £40 4s. 10d. A branch had been opened at Halifax. The refuge is doing a small but valuable work. The Bradford Female Orphanage for training up young girls as domestic servants, owes its establishment to Mrs. Lythall, a benevolent lady who has spent many years of her life in this good cause, and has contributed bountifully to the support of the orphanage. A building was erected in Shipley Road in 1870, at a cost of £3425 9s. 6d. Mrs. Lythall, Miss Crossley, and an anonymous donor, each gave £500. The number of orphans received is limited to twenty, but in 1872 there were twenty-seven. The receipts were £365 3s. and the expenditure £411 10s. 9d., leaving a balance of £46 7s. 9d. owing to the treasurer. In the year 1868, Mr. Briggs Priestley, of Bradford, established an orphan school at New Leeds, a poor district of the borough; and he also opened a free lending library, which in 1873 consisted of 1000 volumes, and had proved very useful; the issues being 150 to 180 per week. The object of the school was the reception of poor orphans, children without parents, or those of widows and widowers in destitute circumstances. The children are taught reading, writing, arithmetic, sewing, knitting, &c., and each child is provided with a dinner daily. The only condition enjoined on the parents or relatives is, that the children must be sent to school as clean and tidy as possible. Prizes are given to the children according to their merits, for regularity of attendance, progress, and general good behaviour. A teacher and a cook are engaged, who live on the premises. The cost of fitting up and furnishing the New Leeds School was £150. The number of scholars on the books in 1873 was 110, and the average attendance was ninety. Encouraged by the success of his first experiment, Mr. Priestley generously opened a second school on the same principle, in Pine Street, Bolton Road, in January, 1870, the expense of furnishing and fitting being £130. The number on the books in 1873 was ninety, and the attendance averaged seventy-six. The annual cost of this philanthropic scheme, entirely supported by Mr. Priestley, was £500 in 1872, and the whole of the advantages offered by the schools is supplied free of charge. The schools were ostensibly formed to enable poor widows to go out and earn their living, with the satisfaction of knowing that their children were well cared for during their absence from home. A small institution for the deaf and dumb exists in Bradford, and the Wesleyans originated the Benevolent or Strangers' Friend Society in 1813, which continues to distribute by its visitors weekly sums to the amount of £100 yearly.

Club Houses.—There are a large number of club-houses in Bradford, both for the wealthy merchants and manufacturers, and for the more humble operatives. The members of the Bradford Club have a large mansion, fitted up in a costly manner, in Manor Row. The Union Club have premises in Piece Hall Yard, which are to be largely extended and brought to the front of Kirkgate. The Germans have their *Schiller-Verein* in the New Market buildings. The Exchange Club is held in rooms in the Exchange buildings, and there are Anglo-French and Swiss Clubs.

The Stone and Building Trades.—An important branch of industry in the Bradford district is the stone trade. Rich in coal and iron, the district also yields some of the best stone in the kingdom. From the heights of Northowram, Queensbury, Denholme, Thornton, Allerton, Clayton, Heaton, Calverley, Pudsey, Bolton, and Idle, vast quantities of stone are brought down to Bradford, to be exported thence to all parts of the kingdom, especially to London, and even to such distant places as South America. Unfortunately no reliable statistics can be had as to the total quantity of stone quarried; but the aggregate amount must be very large, and the capital invested in these operations heavy. An approximate estimate, prepared by a gentleman conversant with the trade, gives the total value of the output of stone from the quarries in the Bradford district for the year 1872 at upwards of £350,000. Steam cranes are now generally used at the quarries, and the price of stone has risen considerably. From the Cliffe Wood quarries, near Bradford, a beautiful cream-coloured stone is obtained of fine texture, with which the front of the town hall at Bradford has been built, and the town hall at Manchester also is being erected. Stone and landings of almost any size and weight may be obtained, the only limit being the lifting power of the cranes. The flagstones quarried at Northowram are exceedingly hard and durable Machinery has been employed of late years to cut and polish stones and flags. Messrs. A. & A. R. Neill, of Bradford, have several of these machines in operation, which perform their work deftly and well. The stone is not only cut, chiselled, and polished, but it is also turned.

The Banks.—There are several large and handsome premises in Bradford devoted to banking purposes. The Bradford and East Morley Savings' Bank was commenced in 1818, and its operations are conducted in a building in Manor Row. The amount, including interest, deposited at the Bank for investment with government by 39,657 depositors since the opening of the bank in 1818, up to November 20, 1872, was £1,689,117 12s. 9d.; the repayments during the same period were £1,552,738 6s. 5d., leaving the balance due to depositors £136,379 6s. 4d. In April, 1870, a new investment fund was opened, by which the amount of deposits was not limited, interest was allowed at four per cent., and the funds invested in other than government security. From April, 1872, up to November 20, 1872, the total deposits in this manner by 2486 depositors, with interest, was £199,936 6s. 2d.; the repayments were £31,834 12s. 4d., leaving the balance due to depositors £168,101 13s. 10d. The total amount due to depositors in both departments was £304,481 0s. 2d., being an increase during the year of £51,263 0s. 6d. The combined capital of the bank in the two departments in May, 1873, was £323,246 5s. 7d., and the new scheme was working very well. The Old Bank, Limited, occupies a Gothic building at the corner of Cheapside and Market Street, erected from the designs of Mr. Waterhouse. The Bradford Banking Company have a classical edifice at the corner of Kirkgate and Darley Street, built from the plans of Messrs. Andrews & Delaunay. The Commercial Bank is housed in Old Market, in a French Gothic building, surmounted by a tower, designed by Messrs. Andrews & Pepper. The Bradford branch of the Yorkshire Banking Company was, in 1873, removed from the old premises in Market Street to a more commodious structure at the corner of Hustler Gate and Bank Street. This beautiful classical building was erected from the designs of Messrs. Lockwood & Mawson, and cost about £24,000. The Bradford District Bank is to find a home in a new building, in the Italian style, in course of construction in 1873, from the designs of Messrs. Milnes & France, at a cost, inclusive of land, of about £23,000. The space at our disposal does not allow of a detailed description of these handsome edifices, which form some of the principal architectural ornaments of the town, and have cost large sums of money, the banking rooms and other apartments being fitted up in a costly manner. There are branches of the Union Bank of Manchester, and the Leeds Exchange and Discount Bank. An approximate estimate of the business transacted by the seven last-named banks in the year 1872 shows that the aggregate amount was equal to the large sum of about £74,000,000. If to this be added the transactions of bankers in London, Manchester, Leeds, and Halifax, on account of Bradford traders, estimated at £24,000,000 for 1872, the product is the immense sum of £100,000,000 as the turn-over of the bankers in connection with the Bradford trade.

Chamber of Commerce of Bradford.—The trade of Bradford has received valuable aid, for many years, from the establishment of the "Chamber of Commerce for Bradford and the Worsted District," instituted in 1851. Mr. Jacob Behrens, one of the first of the German settlers who came to reside in Bradford, and who have done so much to advance the prosperity of their adopted town, has the credit of having originated the Bradford Chamber. The first annual meeting of the chamber was held on the 26th January, 1852, in the large room of the Bradford Exchange, Kirkgate. Mr. William Rand, president, occupied the chair, and amongst those present and who took part in the proceedings were the members for the borough (Colonel P. Thompson, M.P., and Mr. Robert Milligan, M.P.), Mr. W. E. Forster, Mr. Jacob Behrens, &c. Mr. John Darlington was appointed secretary, and was still acting in that capacity in 1873, having occupied that important position from the commencement. The number of members the first year was 189. The objects of the chamber are—to promote measures calculated to benefit and protect the mercantile and trading interests of the town and neighbourhood; to represent and express the sentiments of the trading classes of Bradford on commercial affairs; to collect statistics bearing upon the staple trade of the district; and to undertake the settlement, by arbitration or otherwise, of questions and disputes arising in the trade. All questions of party politics are strictly excluded. The business of the chamber is managed by a council of twenty-four members, who arrange themselves in committees, those for 1873 directing their attention to the questions of arbitration, law amendment, tariffs, wool supply, and postal and railway communication. The objects set forth at the foundation of the chamber have been steadily pursued, with great success. Mr. Cobden expressed himself greatly indebted to the Bradford Chamber for the successful working out of the first French tariff of 1860, which proved so advantageous to the Bradford trade; and the chamber was consulted on the changes proposed by M. Thiers in 1873. The Belgian tariff was also improved by the advice of the Bradford Chamber, and on many occasions matters affecting the well-being of the general trade of the country have been brought by it before the government in such a manner as to insure their recognition; one of the most recent being that of the trade with Yarkand and other little-known districts of Central Asia. At the meeting of the Social Science Association at Bradford, in 1859, a meeting of the representatives of chambers of commerce was held under the chairmanship of Mr. H. W. Ripley, president of the Bradford Chamber, when it was resolved, that, for the purpose of mutual co-operation and assistance, delegates from the chambers of commerce in the three kingdoms should meet annually in London. Meetings have since been held in the provinces; one was held in Bradford in 1870. The chamber secured the adequate representation of Bradford manufactures in the Exhibitions of 1851, in London; of 1855, in Paris; of 1862, in London; of 1867, in Paris; and at the Exhibition in London of 1871. Valuable reports were prepared on the Paris Exhibition of 1855 respecting wool, machinery, tops, warp, weft, and woven and dyed fabrics. These reports were drawn up by Messrs. Samuel Bottomley and Edward Waud, of Bradford, and Mr. J. W. Child of Halifax; Mr. John Darlington, the secretary, acting with those gentlemen. Similar reports were also prepared on the Paris Exhibition of 1867, by Messrs. J. V. Godwin, Alfred Illingworth, Charles Stead, and G. M. Waud. Three Bradford workmen were also sent to this exhibition, at the suggestion of the Society of Arts. Mr. John French reported on the machinery, and Messrs. George Spencer and Daniel Illingworth on the spinning and weaving of worsted goods. These reports were printed. No collective display of goods was sent to the Vienna Exhibition of 1873, but the trade of the town was represented there by articles sent by Bradford firms, the chamber lending its aid. In 1859 special attention was directed to the supply of wool, and in 1869 a revised report was issued by the chamber on colonial and foreign wool, which was sent to all foreign countries in which that article is grown. The report was accompanied by detailed descriptions of twenty-five sorts of wool, namely, those of Portugal, Iceland, Russia, Turkey, Transylvania, Wallachia, Belgium, Flanders, Holland, India and Persia, Egypt, Mogadore, Canada, California, Peru, River Plate, China, Port Phillip, Sydney, Adelaide, New Zealand, Cape of Good Hope, Natal. It also embraced alpaca, mohair, and China grass (*Urtica nivea*), which was described, and stated to be daily becoming more valuable. Great progress had been made in adapting it to textile purposes, and almost any quantity would find a ready market in this country. The Bradford Chamber had more than 300 members in 1873. The names of the gentlemen who have filled the office of president from the formation of the chamber were:—1852-54, Mr. William Rand; 1855, Mr. Samuel Smith; 1856-57, Sir Titus Salt, Bart. (then Mr. Titus Salt); 1858, and for ten succeeding years, up to 1867, Mr. H. W. Ripley; 1869-70, Mr. Jacob Behrens; 1871, Mr. J. V. Godwin; 1872, Mr. James Law; and 1873, Mr. Charles Stead (Sir Titus Salt, Bart., Sons, & Co.). The vice-presidents for 1873 were Messrs. A. Hoffmann and Joseph Oddy; auditor, Mr. W. H. Sachs; treasurer, Mr. H. W. Ripley. The *ex officio* members of the council are the members for the borough (the Right Hon. W. E. Forster, M.P., Mr. E. Miall, M.P.), and the mayor of Bradford (Alderman M. W. Thompson).

The Bonding Warehouses.—In 1860 bonding warehouses were opened at Bradford, and a custom-house was established. Business increased so rapidly that the Midland Railway Company soon built a large bonding warehouse in Commercial Street, Bradford, adjoining their station; and in 1873 they completed another large warehouse on the opposite side of the street, the two piles being joined together by a glass roof spanning the street. The

Bradford customs revenue for the year ending March 31, 1873, was £75,292, and for the corresponding period of the previous year, £62,100, showing an increase on the year of £13,192. The customs officers in charge in 1873 were—Mr. Francis Evans, collector and surveyor; Mr. Duncan M'Lellan, clerk; Mr. Alexander Gillanders, examining officer; Mr. James Middleton, locker.

The Volunteer Movement.—Bradford was in 1873 made the headquarters of the 10th Brigade Depot of the regular army, and the barracks at Bradford Moor, which have existed for many years, are to be largely extended. The depot consists of the 1st and 2nd battalions of the 14th Regiment of Foot (Buckinghamshire), Colonel F. G. Hibbert being the commanding officer; 4th West York Militia, Colonel-commandant Pollard; 5th Administrative Battalion of West Riding Rifle Volunteers, Hon. Colonel H. F. Beaumont; 29th West Riding Rifle Volunteers, Major John Wormald; and 34th West Riding Rifle Volunteers, Major Joseph Collins. In 1860 a volunteer artillery corps was formed. The first officer was Lieutenant W. Clarke, attested 3rd December, 1860, and the first adjutant was the late Captain Robson, appointed 4th January, 1861. In May of the same year the corps was increased to two batteries; a third was added in 1861, and the corps continued to increased up to May, 1863, when there were one major, five captains, five first and five second lieutenants, one adjutant, one surgeon, and 400 men of all ranks, in five batteries. In January, 1864, the corps was divided into two, styled the 2nd and 5th corps, of two and three batteries respectively. In 1864 Lieutenant-colonel G. Wood commanded, who was succeeded by Lieutenant-colonel W. M. Selwyn in 1866. In the same year the 6th and 7th corps were formed, and the whole was commanded by Lieut.-colonel Sir C. H. Firth. In 1871 the 8th corps (Halifax) was formed and joined the brigade, which in 1873 consisted of ten batteries, with a total, of all ranks, of 800 men. Lord F. C. Cavendish, M.P., was honorary colonel, Sir C. H. Firth, Knight, D.D., lieutenant-colonel, and Captain F. Page, adjutant. The brigade, whose headquarters were at Bradford, consisted of the 2nd corps (Bradford), 5th corps (Bowling), 6th corps (Heckmondwike), 7th corps (Batley), and 8th corps (Halifax), each of two batteries. The brigade has a battery of eight guns in Peel Park, Bradford. It has highly distinguished itself at the National Artillery competitions at Shoeburyness, and has twice won the Queen's Prize, the Prince of Wales' Prize, the prizes for repository drill and for highest average. It has also carried off the Lords' and Commons' Prize, the Elkington Prize, and the running target prize, no volunteer brigade in the service having excelled it. In 1873 means were taken to raise a new drill hall at Bowling, on land given by Mr. H. W. Ripley, father of Major Ripley, of the Bradford corps. The hall, which is to be a handsome, commodious building, is intended for the use of the 2nd and 5th corps. The 3rd West York Bradford Rifle Volunteers were formed in 1859, Captain S. C. Lister, the first commander, receiving his commission as captain, Sept. 22, 1859, and as lieutenant-colonel on Sept. 27, 1860. He resigned the command August 6, 1862, and was succeeded by Lieut.-colonel Hirst, who commanded in 1873, and who had been a captain in the corps from September 26, 1859. Captain Lepper was the first adjutant, and he has been succeeded in that post by Captain Neild. In 1873 the corps consisted of eight companies (seven at headquarters and one at Eccleshill). There was a very efficient staff, and seven captains, seven lieutenants, and six ensigns. Seventeen of the officers hold certificates of proficiency; the corps altogether is a smart, soldier-like body of men, and has been highly commended on every occasion by the inspecting officer. The handsome range of barracks in Manningham Lane were reared in 1861, at a cost of £3000. There is a spacious drill-room, armoury, gymnasium, orderly room, stores, non-commissioned officers' room, stable, house, &c., and an inclosed square for drill purposes. The corps holds a very high position for drill, being considered one of the best regiments in the county. The enrolled strength in 1873 was 600. The 39th (Saltaire) Rifle Volunteers is attached to the Bradford corps for drill, and musters ninety men of all ranks, under the command of Lieutenant Crowther and Ensign Delves. The corps was raised by Mr. Titus Salt, of Milner Field, in 1869, and does credit to Saltaire. The corps is drilled in the gymnasium at the Saltaire Institute. The Bradford corps, with the 39th attached, forms part of the 9th Depot Brigade, under the command of Colonel Collings, C.B., the headquarters being at Halifax.

Men of Note in Bradford.—Amongst men of distinguished talents and attainments born or who have settled in the town or parish of Bradford, we may mention Dr. Richardson, M.D., who was born at Bierley Hall, the residence of his ancestors, in the year 1663. He was educated at Bradford grammar school, which then stood very high as a seminary for education. Dr. Richardson, writing in the year 1718, speaks of it as the "renowned school of Bradford," and in after life he contributed to the school library, to which he considered himself greatly indebted. After receiving the best education which the universities of Oxford and Leyden, the latter then the great seat of medical knowledge, could impart, and after having taken the degree of Doctor of Physic at Oxford, he settled at his paternal seat of Bierley Hall, his ample estate rendering it unnecessary for him to practise physic as a profession. His whole life was spent in the pursuits of science, and more especially of botany and natural history. In 1712 he was admitted a fellow of the Royal Society, and during the greater part of his life lived on terms of the closest friendship with Sir Hans Sloane, Dr. Martin Lister, and John Ray, as well as with the antiquaries Hearne, Thoresby, and Drake. Dr. Richardson rendered an immense service to Yorkshire topography by purchasing Hopkinson's MSS. collected from the national records. He placed them at Bierley Hall, where they were always thrown open to men of letters with the utmost readiness, not only by himself, but by his descendants and representatives, including Miss Currer, whose kindness and hospitality are warmly acknowledged by Dr. T. D. Whitaker, and by Mr. James, the historian of Bradford. Amongst the memorials of his botanical pursuits was a beautiful cedar of Lebanon, in the grounds of Bierley Hall, which, notwithstanding the severity of the climate, in 1816 measured in circumference at the bottom twelve feet four inches, at the top of the solid trunk twelve feet nine inches, and in height, to the point where the stem begins to branch out, fourteen feet.* The tree was still alive in 1873. Another scholar of distinguished talents and attainments, was John Sharp, D.D., the son of a Bradford manufacturer and landowner, who was born at Bradford in the year 1644, and educated first at Bradford grammar school, and afterwards at the university of Cambridge. He was a friend of the not less celebrated Dr. Tillotson, born in the adjoining parish of Halifax, who attained the high position of archbishop of Canterbury in the same age in which Dr. Sharp attained the dignity of archbishop of York. He was raised to that dignity in his forty-seventh year. Another member of the same family, Abraham Sharp, the distinguished mathematician, was born at Little Horton, Bradford, in the year 1651. He also received his education at

* James' History of Bradford, p. 392.

Bradford grammar school, and ultimately settled in London, where he obtained the friendship of the great astronomer, Flamsteed. Abraham Sharp constructed and graduated most of the instruments used at the Royal Observatory. The great mural arch fixed at that place was made by his own hands, in fourteen months. According to the authority of the eminent engineer, John Smeaton, "Abraham Sharp was one of the best astronomical instrument-makers of his time." While at the observatory at Greenwich, he assisted Flamsteed "to model heaven and calculate the stars." The celebrated catalogue published by Flamsteed of 3000 stars, with their longitudes and magnitudes, their right ascensions and polar differences, owed much to the labours of Abraham Sharp. In his latter years he resided on his paternal estate at Little Horton, Bradford. He there built a square tower to his house, and fitted it up as an observatory. The telescopes which he made use of were of his own construction, and the lenses were ground and adjusted with his own hand. To every person intimately connected with Bradford this lonely tower possessed peculiar interest, and it was still standing in 1873. He had a workshop fitted up with a curious collection of tools, most of them made by himself. After he had settled at Horton, he still continued to assist Flamsteed. The elaborate tables in the second volume of the "Historia Cœlestis" were calculated by him. He also prepared drawings of all the constellations, which were sent to Amsterdam to be engraved by an eminent artist. During his long residence at Horton he maintained a scientific correspondence with Sir Isaac Newton, Flamsteed, Halley, Wallis, and other distinguished men of science. He died on the 18th of July, 1742, at the age of ninety-one years, and was interred in the parish church of Bradford with great solemnity.

The Rev. William Scoresby was vicar of Bradford from 1839 to 1847. He was the author of a valuable work on "The Arctic Regions," was in his earlier years one of the most accomplished of sea-captains, and afterwards a man of high scientific attainments, as well as an excellent clergyman. His observations, made during his numerous voyages, have added greatly to our knowledge of the natural history of those remote regions, especially in the departments of electricity and magnetism.

Bradford has not been of late years without many local men of note. The late Rev. Dr. Godwin was an eminent minister amongst the Baptists, and wrote some able controversial works. Dr. William Macturk, M.D., was a physician whose talents were sought far and wide round Bradford. The late Mr. John Wood, of Theddon Grange, of the firm of Wood and Walker, Bradford, rendered great services in connection with the Ten Hours' Factory Act, of which he was one of the foremost champions and most self-denying and liberal supporters. In 1873 Bradford had the honour of being represented by the Right Hon. W. E. Forster, M.P., vice-president of the Council. Before entering Parliament Mr. Forster had taken an active share in the promotion of every good work calculated to benefit society. The Right Hon. Gathorne Hardy, M.P., member for Oxford University, is a native of Bradford, and other members of the Hardy family are in Parliament. Mr. Alfred Illingworth, M.P. for Knaresborough, is also a native of Bradford.

Mr. John James, F.S.A., author of the "History of Bradford" and other valuable works, was born at West Witton, Wensleydale, January 22, 1811. By dint of perseverance he educated himself and became a clerk in the office of the late Mr. Ottiwell Tomlin, solicitor, Richmond. He was subsequently in the office of the late Mr. Tolson, solicitor, Bradford, and while with that gentleman he published his "History of Bradford" in 1842. His next work was the "Life of John Nicholson," the Airedale poet, which was followed by the "History of the Worsted Manufacture in England." He read a paper at the meeting of the British Association at Leeds, on the "Statistics of Trade in Yorkshire," and wrote an article on Yorkshire in the Encyclopædia Britannica. His "Continuation and Additions to the History of Bradford" was published in 1866. He removed from Bradford, died at Nether Edge, Sheffield, July 4, 1867, and was buried at West Witton. The author of this work is indebted to Mr. James for many facts contained in his excellent "History of Bradford," which shows him to have been a man of taste, judgment, and great literary industry.

Samuel Hailstone, Esq., F.L.S., of Horton Hall, was an eminent botanist and geologist. Born at Hoxton, near London, in 1768, the family settled at York, and at an early age he came to Bradford as an articled clerk to Mr. Hardy, solicitor, father of John Hardy, Esq., formerly M.P. for Bradford, and subsequently became a partner with Mr. Hardy. The study of botany and natural philosophy was the great pleasure of Mr. Hailstone's life.

He contributed to Dr. Whitaker's "History of Craven" a list of rare plants growing in that district, and botanists of later times gladly admit the value of Mr. Hailstone's untiring labours in this branch of natural history. He was also an excellent geologist, collected specimens of fossils, formed a large and well-selected library—rich in MSS. on the antiquities of Yorkshire—and had a large museum of geological remains and of antiquities. He was indefatigable in the promotion of the pursuits of science, contributed largely to the botanical and geological publications of the day, laboured in the formation of the Literary and Philosophical Society of Bradford in 1806, and at its resuscitation in 1823; and at length, as Mr. James states, "after passing a long and laborious life, without a blot on his memory, he sank to the grave with almost unperceived decay. His habits were simple and methodical. He rose early at all periods of his life. His intellect was ever quick and piercing, and, like his style in writing, clear and precise. He was very exact in all his work and actions. In politics and religion his views were liberal and philosophical." He married, in 1808, the daughter of Mr. T. Jones, surgeon, Bradford; died December 26, 1851; and rests by his wife at Boston Spa. He left two sons, the Rev. John Hailstone, and Edward Hailstone, Esq., F.S.A., late of Horton Hall, but now of Waterton Hall, near Wakefield, who has inherited his love of literature and science, and whose library is wonderfully rich, especially in local antiquities.

Colonel William Sykes, F.R.S., M.P., was born at Frizinghall, January 25, 1790, where his father, Samuel Sykes, Esq., a gentleman of considerable literary attainments, resided, and was cousin to the Rev. James Sykes, then vicar of Bradford. Colonel Sykes, in his early years, was educated at Bradford grammar school, and in 1804 entered the Bombay army. He served seventeen years in India with distinguished success, taking part in many of the great battles of that period. In 1820 he came to England for four years, married, and returned to India in 1824, staying until 1831, during which time his labours, as statistical reporter to the government, were most valuable. In 1840 he was appointed a director of the East India Company; in March, 1854, was elected Lord Rector of Marischal College and University, Aberdeen; in April, 1856, was chosen chairman of the East India Company; in March, 1857, was elected M.P. for the city of

Aberdeen; and in May, 1858, was president of the Royal Asiatic Society. He was the author of more than sixty papers on the ancient history, antiquities, statistics, &c., of India. He has often presided over the statistical section at the meetings of the British Association for the Advancement of Science, and rendered eminent services to the numerous literary and scientific societies over which he has presided or with which he has been connected. The King of Prussia conferred upon him the honour of commander of the first class of the Prussian Order of the Red Eagle, as an appreciation of his character as a public contributor to various branches of knowledge.

Mr. Thomas Rawson Taylor, eldest son of the Rev. T. Taylor, for some years minister of Horton Lane Chapel, was born at Ossett, near Wakefield. He came to Bradford with his father, 9th May, 1807. He was educated at Bradford grammar school, and by the Rev. Dr. Clunie, of Manchester, under whom he made great progress in classical learning. First placed in a bookseller's shop at Nottingham, he afterwards entered as a student at Airedale College, Bradford. He passed his probationary course with much success, and in October, 1829, became the minister of Howard Street Chapel, Sheffield. There he remained for five years, much esteemed by his congregation; but the fatal disease which ended his bright but brief career developed itself. He returned to Bradford, where he died March 7, 1835. He was a young man of great promise, gave indications of a fine poetic genius, and some of his printed poems clearly prove that had he lived he would have attained a high position as a poet. James Montgomery, of Sheffield, wrote of Mr. Taylor, "that nothing more natural, tender, or affecting can be quoted than some of his verses."

The Rev. Joshua Fawcett, M.A., second son of Mr Richard Fawcett, one of the first manufacturers of Bradford, was born there on the 9th May, 1809. He was first educated at Bradford grammar school, and proceeded to Trinity College, Cambridge, where he took the degree of M.A. in 1830. He became curate of Pannal, near Harrogate, and in 1832 was appointed incumbent of Wibsey, being inducted 17th February, 1833. He married in 1834 the third daughter of the Rev. L. Hird, and sister of H. W. Wickham, Esq., sometime M.P. for Bradford. Mr. Fawcett was a most amiable clergyman of distinguished ability, and adorned his profession. He was a writer of considerable talent, and much attached to antiquarian pursuits. He read a carefully prepared paper at the meeting of the Social Science Association in Bradford, in 1859, "On the rise and progress of the town of Bradford," and was an industrious lecturer on several subjects. During his time the church at Low Moor was rebuilt and the parsonage house erected. He was appointed domestic chaplain to Lord Radstock in 1854, chaplain to the bishop of Ripon in 1860, and honorary canon of Ripon Cathedral in the same year. He died suddenly, while returning home from visiting the sick, and was buried 28th December, 1864, in the graveyard of Holy Trinity Church, Low Moor. Mr. James writes, "A vast concourse of people assembled to do honour to his memory, nearly all the clergy of the neighbourhood being present, forty-eight in number. To pronounce his eulogy in full would be beyond my powers; but this much may be said, that in every relation of life, whether as a philanthropist, a man of letters, an unassuming, courteous gentleman, or a Christian pastor, he was beloved and admired by all who knew him." An exquisitely beautiful mural monument has been erected to his memory, in the church in which he officiated.

The Brontë family have become deservedly famous in the literary annals of the parish of Bradford. Charlotte Brontë, the most distinguished member of the family, was born April 21, 1816, at Thornton, near Bradford, where her father, the Rev. Patrick Brontë, was incumbent. The family removed about 1820 to Haworth, Mr. Brontë having been appointed incumbent of that place. Haworth is one of the most distant parts of Bradford parish, on the borders of Lancashire, is situated on the northern slope of a hill, and almost surrounded with wild moorlands. It is now a thriving place; but when the Brontës went to reside there it was lonely and desolate, and comparatively "out of the world." Mrs. Brontë died in September, 1821, and in September of 1824 Charlotte Brontë, being then but eight years of age, was sent to school at Cowan Bridge, near Kirkby Lonsdale, along with her sisters, Maria, Elizabeth, and Emily. In 1825 a fever broke out at the school. Maria and Elizabeth died, and Charlotte and her sister Emily returned home. The children amused themselves and relieved the tedium of life at Haworth by writing tales, magazines, and plays, the germs of future excellence. In January, 1831, Charlotte went to school at Roehead, near Heckmondwike, and in 1835 became a teacher at that place. She afterwards, in 1838, held a situation as governess at Bradford. In 1842 Charlotte and Emily went to a boarding school at Brussels. Emily returned to Haworth, and Charlotte took at Brussels a situation as teacher. She left that city in 1843, and in 1846 the three sisters published a volume of poems, some of them of great merit. In July, 1847, Charlotte Brontë's celebrated work, "Jane Eyre," was published, and the family at once became famous. Charlotte visited London, and was introduced to many of the leading celebrities of the day. "Shirley" followed in October, 1849, and proved, like its predecessor, a great success. "Villette" was produced in 1853; and she also wrote "The Professor." On the 29th of June, 1854, Charlotte Brontë was married to the Rev. A. B. Nicholls, B.A., her father's curate. Their union, though happy, was of short duration. Mrs. Nicholls took cold during a walk on the moors, and on March 31, 1855, she died in her thirty-ninth year, and was buried in Haworth church. Patrick Branwell Brontë, younger brother of Charlotte, was a young man of some ability, and had a taste for painting, producing some creditable specimens. His career was unfortunate. He died September 24, 1848, aged thirty-one. Emily Jane Brontë, born at Thornton in 1818, had carefully trained herself in poetic composition, and her poems show that she possessed a powerful intellect. In 1846 she produced the tale of "Wuthering Heights," but the work was not very successful. The critics treated it harshly, and this preyed upon her spirits. She died December 19, 1848, and lies in Haworth church. Anne Brontë, the youngest of the family, was born at Thornton. About 1846 she wrote a tale, "Agnes Grey," and afterwards the "Tenant of Wildfell Hall;" but neither of these works, which, like Emily's, show great literary ability, was successful. She died on the 24th of May, 1849, in her twenty-ninth year, at Scarborough, where she had gone for her health. The Rev. Patrick Brontë has since passed away, and thus not one member of this remarkable family is left.

The Cemeteries.—Bradford has three cemeteries, one at Undercliffe, on the east side of the borough, the second at Scholemoor, to the west, and the third at Leeds Road. The Undercliffe cemetery belongs to a private company, and was beautifully laid out by Mr. W. Gay in the year 1852. The total amount expended on the cemetery freehold estate account up to December 31, 1872, was £17,498 10s., and it covers twenty-six acres. There are two chapels, registrar's house, and entrance lodges. The place was fast filling up, and attempts were made in 1872 to extend the grounds to a plot of land on the opposite side of Otley Road, sixteen acres in extent; but the opposition of the landowners and others in the neighbourhood defeated the new scheme. Scholemoor cemetery, which occupies a site in the vicinity of Great Horton, and is owned by the Bradford Corporation, was opened in 1860. The grounds are laid out in a tasteful manner, and comprise nineteen and a half acres. The expenditure on the cemetery up to December 31, 1872, was £11,271 10s. 8d. Mr. James Seaton was registrar in 1873. There are two large chapels, built of stone from the plans of Messrs. Milnes and France, and a registrar's house. The Roman Catholics have a small cemetery in Leeds Road, to which is attached the registrar's house and a school-chapel. It was proposed to enlarge this place in 1873.

The Aspect of Bradford in 1873.—Those who knew Bradford twenty years previously would hardly recognize it in 1873, the changes in the intervening period having been great and numerous. The old, narrow, crooked thoroughfares have given place to wide streets, and although Bradford, from its position in the hollow of a basin with hills rising on almost every side, may never become what can be considered a commanding town, it has, nevertheless, been immensely improved. No new street is allowed by the corporation to be laid out less than fourteen yards wide. Eighteen and twenty yards is the width prescribed for the principal thoroughfares leading out of the town, which are to be widened to this extent as occasion offers. As the streets have been widened, public and private enterprise has reared handsome structures to face them. The merchants led the way with their magnificent ranges of warehouses, the bankers followed the example, and tradesmen have not been behind in building retail premises of colossal size. The style of the public institutions, churches, chapels, and schools, shows that that a similar spirit actuates their builders; and it is a rare thing to see a structure of any kind erected without some regard to architectural pretension, though not always to good taste. The residences of the merchants and manufacturers display similar characteristics. The buildings of this class erected in modern times in Horton and Manningham will bear comparison with similar buildings in any town in the kingdom. The Wellington and Oak Mount estates at Manningham, consisting of villas, semi and detached, terraces, and streets of houses, comprise some as good residental property as can be found anywhere. These residences, as well as all the other erections in the town and neighbourhood, are built externally of stone.

The cottages of the operatives were formerly constructed on the back-to-back principle, allowing no free circulation of air, and generally consisting of two large apartments, a living-room and a bedchamber. After a fierce struggle with property-owners, a new code of bye-laws for building was passed by the corporation; but although the principle of back-to-back houses was not entirely done away with, the new regulations, which are stringently carried out, specified that cottage houses should be built in blocks of four, with a wide passage leading from the street to the back houses. The streets of the town, formerly covered with Yorkshire setts, are now being gradually paved with granite, set in hot pitch, and they have been levelled and straightened to assume a more sightly aspect. The dense black pall of smoke which formerly rested over the town has been somewhat dissipated—though it is still bad enough—by the vigorous action of the corporation, through the smoke committee of the town council. The borough is now well lighted with gas, and the appearance of the hill-sides at night time, as seen from any of the adjacent heights, is most striking; myriads of lights dotting the country side for many miles to the boundaries of the borough, and spreading out in all directions from a mile and a half to three miles from the Bradford town hall. The number of new public lamps erected in 1872 was 268, making the total in the borough up to that time 2817. Hackney carriages had increased from 85 in 1862, to 135 in 1872, and 267 drivers' licenses were granted in the latter year. Omnibuses formerly had no existence in the town, but in 1872 licenses were obtained for sixty-two vehicles to ply for hire under this designation. The hackney carriage committee of the corporation exercises a careful supervision over all kind of licensed vehicles, and the result is that all the hackney carriages and omnibuses are kept in excellent order, and the horses are generally in good condition.

In 1873 land and property in Bradford of all kinds had risen considerably in value. Shop property in the centre of the town had more than doubled its value in twenty years, warehouses and mills had risen in price — warehouses especially had gone up, in some instances, fifty per cent.—and residences of all kinds were much higher rented. Land on the outskirts of the borough, which could have been purchased twenty years ago at 1s. 6d. and 2s. a yard, was fetching in 1873 from 5s. to 10s. and in good situations 12s. 6d. a yard. In the town, land which was sold at 10s. a yard thirty years ago now brings £10 and upwards. As much as £23, £24, and £28 a yard has been given for choice situations. In one instance, when the Boar's Head Hotel, at the corner of Cheapside and Market Street, was sold, it realized, with the license attached, £32 a yard. It was then, in the opinion of an eminent valuer, cheap at the price. In 1857 and 1863, when trade was at a low ebb, when many houses were empty, and when, as in 1857, thousands of the operatives were absolutely in a state of want, property of all descriptions sunk rapidly in value. There was one district, known as New Leeds, where whole rows of houses—certainly not the most eligible property—were tenantless; but in 1873 these houses were all occupied, and the tenants were paying good rents. In 1857-58 cottage houses in Bedford Street let at 2s. a week, but in 1873 the tenants had to pay 3s. 6d. a week and upwards. In another instance, a house which had cost £220 to build was sold in 1872 for £530. In 1863 fifty houses were purchased in Bolton Road at £35 each. The owners would not sell them in 1873 for less than three times that amount, and some of the tenants were paying 4s. a week. These are but samples of what was going on in other parts of the borough. Buildings of every description were being erected at a rapid rate, especially the better classes of houses and cottages. The following table gives some interesting particulars of the number of plans approved by the corporation for the six years ending October 30, 1872 :—

Year.	Dwelling Houses.	Warehouses, Mills, &c.	Churches, Chapels, &c.	Public Buildings	Sundry Buildings.	New Streets.	Plans Deposited.	Plans Approved.
1867	758	38	4	1	226	17	401	362
1868	1428	31	0	3	189	42	556	467
1869	1708	33	3	4	149	54	476	438
1870	1808	75	6	5	198	46	390	348
1871	1769	125	21	4	134	41	512	444
1872	1926	91	15	1	143	76	523	478
Totals,	9397	393	49	18	1039	276	2858	2537

In the plans of houses approved in 1872 the number of rooms ranged from three to eighteen. There was only one with the latter number, but there were 72 houses with three rooms each, 1419 with four, 99 with five, 135 with six, 59 with seven, 53 with eight, and 28 with twelve rooms each. It will, therefore, be seen that although the great proportion of houses approved may be styled cottages, yet the plans of many good houses were passed.

Bradford and District Tramways.—In 1872 a scheme was launched to provide Bradford with tramways along the principal streets. Owing to the hilly nature of the town and the comparative narrowness of some of the streets, there was a difficulty in devising a scheme to meet the wants of the borough in this respect. The promoters of "The Bradford and District Tramway Act, 1873," however, have overcome the difficulty. The company propose to make the space between the rails three feet nine inches wide, and the cars are to be light and handy. Thornton Road was the only level thoroughfare out of the borough in 1872, the other roads being more or less hilly. The scheme comprises lines to Saltaire, Thornton, Wibsey, Bradford Moor, and Bolton, and no doubt is entertained that the increased facility of communication which these lines will afford will render the scheme advantageous to the borough. The promoters applied to Parliament in the session of 1873 for powers to make the tramways. The Bradford Corporation, under the conviction that the tramways ought to be tried, entered into an agreement with the promoters, on certain terms, conditions, and stipulations, to be incorporated in the bill, for the protection of the interests of the Bradford ratepayers. The corporation gave their assent to the bill on condition that the plans, &c., should be approved by the borough surveyor, Mr. Gott, C.E.; that the tramways should be commenced within six months of the passing of the Act, and should be completed within two years, except the corporation consented to the postponement of any part of the undertaking—the corporation to be at liberty to construct any tramway abandoned or delayed; that the gauge or width of the carriages should not be altered without the consent of the corporation; that, while making the tramways, subject to the approval of the borough surveyor, the street traffic should not be unnecessarily interrupted; that the space between the rails, and for eighteen inches on either side, should be laid with granite setts, and be maintained by the company on a level with the streets; that passing places for the cars should be laid down as the corporation considered necessary, and that the corporation should have power to regulate the traffic as with other vehicles, to prescribe whether second lines should be laid, and in case the levels of the streets were altered, the company to conform to such level, pay their own costs of alteration, and afford facility for other necessary work of the corporation in the streets without any claim for damages. If the company fail to lay down any work as required by the agreement, and neglect to keep their portion of the roads in repair, they are to forfeit £5 a day while the neglect continues, the corporation having authority to do the work after giving notice, charge the company with the cost, and not be answerable for any loss or damage. If the corporation, within five years from the completion of the tramways, think they ought to be discontinued, the company are to remove them after three months' notice, and make good the streets to the satisfaction of the borough surveyor; failing to do this, the corporation to have authority to remove the tramways, sell the material, and hand the residue of expenses to the company. For the first three years after the tramways are opened the company are to pay £10 per acre for each street mile of tramway, and in proportion for a less distance; after that time £60 per annum for the same distance, and the like proportion for any part of a mile; the agreement to be in force for twenty-one years, the corporation to have power to purchase in the meantime, but at the expiration of twenty-one years the paving to belong to the corporation and the rails to the company, the latter to pay all the costs of the agreement, and after the passing of the Act, deposit £5000 to indemnify the corporation against loss. The agreement, however, was made dependent on the condition that the bill should pass in the parliamentary session of 1873. The entire length of the projected tramways is fourteen miles.

The Ripley Convalescent Home.—In 1873 Mr. H. W. Ripley, of Bradford, who had intimated his intention to give £10,000 towards the cost of a convalescent home for the town, purchased an estate of twenty acres at Rawden, beautifully situated, where he intends to have the home erected at his sole expense, paying as much more than £10,000 as may be required. When finished it will be handed over to trustees for the benefit of the people of Bradford. A design for the home was prepared by Messrs. Andrews and Pepper, of Bradford. The style is a satisfactory attempt to engraft upon Gothic the domestic characteristics of Yorkshire architecture of the sixteenth century, and a picturesque pile is the result, with mullioned and transomed windows and gables. The building will be 300 feet long, and the front to the south will consist of two pavilions at either end, joined in the centre with a winter garden, thirty-four feet by forty-five feet. One pavilion will be for males, and the other for females. The dining-hall, thirty-six feet square, is to be in the rear of the conservatory or winter garden. The pavilions will be two stories in height, and the north front, in which will be the entrance hall and suites of rooms, is to be of similar height. Ample provision is made in light airy apartments for the inmates and the administrative department, and conveniences of all kinds are arranged with no sparing hand. Along the south front will be a fine wide terrace, divided for the males and females, and accessible from the winter garden. The home is to accommodate about sixty-four inmates. The idea is not to keep many servants—that the female inmates should do a portion of the household work, and the males employ themselves in any light jobs that they may be considered capable of undertaking; the object being to give them a little of something to occupy their minds. The land around will be laid out and part of it farmed, and the little community will be so arranged as to really constitute a home. The works were to be prosecuted with the utmost practicable despatch. The home will be situated just above Mr. Ripley's beautiful estate of Acacia, overlooking Airedale, where he has built a mansion.

The Rate of Wages and Palaries in the Worsted Trade.—The author is indebted to the kindness of gentlemen practically engaged in the trade for the subjoined valuable table as to the rate of wages ruling in the worsted trade from 1836 to 1840, and the comparative rate in 1873. In the case of the warehouses no comparative rate is given, but the advance in that department in the intervening period from 1840 to 1873 will be somewhere about ten per cent. In some instances, such as pressers and weavers, the payment is by piece-work. The weavers formerly had charge of one loom, but now they have to "mind" two looms, and both the length of the piece and the speed of the loom have been increased. A piece of stuff goods was formerly woven thirty yards long, but now the length is from fifty to fifty-five yards. The hand wool-combers were paid by the quantity of wool combed. They were once a numerous body in Bradford, before the introduction of the combing machine; but that machine, which has proved of such immense value to the worsted trade—which, in fact, could not be carried on without it—annihilated the hand wool-combers. Unfortunately for the men who have to attend to the combing-machine, it does its work so well that an unskilled man can soon get a knowledge of it, and hence the machine wool-combers are about the worst-paid class in the worsted trade. The hand wool-comber, when he would work, could make from 20*s.* to 30*s.* weekly, or with the assistance of his wife and other members of his family might perhaps earn more. The occupation was most unwholesome. The wool was combed at home, generally in the bedchamber, the bed being rolled up in one corner out of the way. What with the fumes emitted from charcoal fires that had to be kept up to heat the steel combs, and the smell of burnt oil used in the process, the house of the wool-comber was neither an agreeable nor healthful place of abode, and the combers bore a bad reputation for their dissolute habits. There were, doubtless, bright exceptions. Badly paid, however, as the machine wool-comber is, if he has a family, the united earnings in the mill will now be large. There are families in Bradford, where the sons and daughters are steady and unmarried, whose united income will not fall much short of £5 a-week, and they are never troubled with an income-tax collector. The hand wool-comber, in the old time, could turn out weekly from 80 lbs. to 100 lbs. of long English wool. A combing machine, on the contrary, attended by two men and four or five women, will in the same time comb about 4000 lbs. of the same kind of wool. But, while the machine wool-comber receives only a moderate remuneration, wool-combing is for the employers one of the most prosperous departments of the trade. The rates given in the table are the lowest and highest paid, the minimum being paid to learners, and the maximum is the reward of talent and experience in the several departments. Exception may possibly be taken to some of the highest averages, but they are wages and salaries that were actually paid in Bradford in 1873, and in rare instances they were even exceeded, especially in the case of heads of departments and managers noted for superior efficiency. The following is the table of wages and salaries:—

RATE OF WAGES AND SALARIES IN BRADFORD.

People Employed.	1836 to 1840. Twelve Hours Daily—Average per Week.		1873. Ten Hours Daily—Average per Week.	
	s.	s. d.	s. d.	s. d.
WORSTED FACTORIES.				
Wool-combers by hand,	20 to	30 0	—	—
Machine wool-combers (men),	—	—	12 0 to	18 0
" " " (women),	—	—	10 0 "	13 0
Children, age 8 to 13, half-timers, spinners,	1 "	2 6	1 6 "	4 6
Spinners above 13, full-timers,	3 "	7 0	5 0 "	10 6
Preparing room hands (females), full-timers,	7 "	9 0	9 6 "	13 0
Overlookers' assistants (males) in spinning mills,	7 "	9 0	9 0 "	15 0
Spinning overlookers,	15 "	24 0	24 0 "	40 0
Preparing overlookers,	24 "	30 0	30 0 "	60 0
Packers in warehouse in connection with mills,	12 "	15 0	15 0 "	24 0
Wool-sorters,	20 "	30 0	20 0 "	30 0
Warp-dressers,	30 "	40 0	30 0 "	40 0
Female weavers above 16 years old (men generally rather more than women),	12 "	16 0	14 0 "	20 0
Weaving overlookers,	15 "	26 0	20 0 "	60 0
Enginemen,	21 "	30 0	26 0 "	50 0
Stokers,	12 "	16 0	18 0 "	24 0
Book-keepers in mills,	—	—	20 0 "	100 0
Market-men, wool-buyers, &c.,	30 "	50 0	40 0 "	100 0
DYEING AND FINISHING.				
Boys under 18,	9 "	15 0	12 0 "	16 0
Dyers,	14 "	16 0	20 0 "	22 0
Pressers and finishers,	24 "	30 0	40 0 "	50 0
Pattern dyers,	60 "	100 0	60 0 "	140 0
Managers,			£150 to £300 and upwards per annum.	
MACHINE SHOPS.				
Boys,	3 "	4 0	6 0 "	10 0
Young Men,	7 "	10 0	12 0 "	18 0
Journeymen,	18 "	22 0	24 0 "	34 0
Foremen,	26 "	30 0	35 0 "	40 0
Managers,			50 0 "	80 0

Persons Employed.	1873.
BANKS:—	
Junior clerks—youths,	£20 to £30 per annum.
Clerks,	£150 to £200 "
Cashiers,	£200, £500, to £700 per annum.
Managers,	£600, £1000, to £1500 "

RATE OF WAGES AND SALARIES.—*Continued.*

Persons Employed.	1873.
STUFF WAREHOUSES, home trade :—	
Apprentice boys,	2s. and 5s. to 10s. per week.
Junior clerks,	5s. to 15s. "
Makers up, packers, &c., under twenty-one,	8s. to 18s. "
Do. adults,	20s. to 28s. and 30s. "
Clerks,	£50 to £300 per annum.
Managers,	£200 to £600 "
Travellers,	£200 to £600
STUFF WAREHOUSES, foreign trade (in office) :—	
Boys,	5s. to 8s. and 10s. per week.
Junior clerks,	15s. to 30s. "
Clerks and junior buyers,	£80 to £200 per annum.
Head buyers and managers,	£300 to £1500 " [turnover.
Agents abroad instead of travellers,	½ and 1 per cent. to 2 per. cent. on
Boys (in warehouse),	5s. to 10s. per week.
Table-siders,	10s. to 18s. "
Makers up and packers,	20s. to 30s. "
Foremen,	32s. to 40s. "
Pattern men,	28s. to 50s. "

Rapid Progress of Population at Bradford in the Present Century.—How rapidly the town has increased in population during the present century may be seen from the following figures:—

Years.	Inhabitants.
1801,	13,264
1831,	43,527
1841,	66,508
1851,	103,778
1861,	106,218
1871,	145,815
1873,	156,005, as estimated.

The number of inhabited houses in 1832 was 6224, and in 1861, 22,518. Of 22,796 male occupiers in 1866, as many as 16,626 were at a rental below £10, and the number of "ten pound" electors on the register was 5189. The change wrought in the constituency by the Reform Act of 1867 was manifest at the election which ensued in 1868, when more than 18,000 electors voted. In 1871 the number of inhabited houses was 29,413; uninhabited 782; building 578. In 1849 the burgesses numbered 4741; in 1859, 15,333; in 1869 they had increased to 24,775; and in 1872 to 27,774. In 1849 the parliamentary electors were 2117; in 1859 there were 3770; but in 1868-69 they rose to 21,518; and in

1872 are stated to number 21,121. The property assessable to the poor rates in Bradford in 1852 was £213,674 18s.; in 1862 it was £294,022; in 1872 it had reached £580,689 10s.

Local Press of Bradford.—Bradford has four daily newspapers. The *Observer* and the *Chronicle* are morning papers, published at a penny; the *Telegraph* and the *Mail* are evening papers, published at a halfpenny. There is also a small weekly newspaper the *Bradford Advertiser.* Previous to July, 1868, there was no daily paper published in Bradford.

Meeting of the Yorkshire Union of Mechanics' Institutes at Saltaire, 1873.—The thirty-sixth annual meeting of this institution was held at Saltaire, near Bradford, on the 4th of June, 1873, and was attended by Lord Lyttleton, Lord F. Cavendish, M.P., Sir A. Fairbairn, Mr. F. S. Powell, M.P., Mr. Isaac Holden, Mr. Stuart, of Cambridge, the mayors of Bradford and Leeds, and other friends of education; Mr. Baines, M.P., the president, occupying the chair. Sir Titus Salt, Bart., the founder and owner of Saltaire, was present, and met with a most cordial reception from the 250 or 300 delegates of the Yorkshire Mechanics' Institutes present on that occasion. The morning sitting of the conference lasted three hours and a half, after which the delegates were conducted through the various institutions in Saltaire, which are all supported by Sir Titus Salt's munificence—namely, the schools, the alms-houses, the infirmary, the working men's large dining hall, the recreation ground, and the extensive mill in which the alpaca and mohair manufacture is carried on. The business of the day was transacted in the Mechanics' Institute, a building noble in its exterior, and perfectly commodious and handsomely fitted up in its interior. Mr. Baines, in opening the proceedings, said that without unduly magnifying the importance of this Union, he must say that every year it was growing more necessary, great industries continually becoming less dependent on mere manual exertion and more dependent on art and science. The first object of this Union was to give the working class that power which knowledge alone could impart, and they threw their doors wide open to the humblest, and inscribed above them "Come, and welcome."

At the annual meeting held in the lecture hall in the evening, Lord Lyttleton in the chair, his lordship said that his reading of the reports of this Union for the year 1871 and 1872 had shown him great results, such as often moved the admiration of the people coming south of the Trent. Such figures as 109 institutes in connection with this Union, numbering 30,000 members, and an issue of books amounting to all but 350,000 a year, undoubtedly spoke of a very active and stirring state of things. These figures, they must hope, represented some tangible amount of good, and indicated that there was not one person connected with the institute who was not thereby raised in the scale of existence.

The Bradford Philosophical Society.—The present year (1873) will be rendered memorable in Bradford by the visit of the British Association for the Promotion of Science to this great seat of the arts of life; and confident hopes are entertained that the visit will have a lasting influence in increasing the progress of scientific knowledge in the district, as similar visits of that important truth-diffusing institution have done in other places. A hundred years ago, about the year 1766, a Philosophical Society was established at Bradford, chiefly by the influence of Dr. Priestley, then residing at Warrington; but after a brief existence the society was dissolved. A similar society was again formed in 1823, through the exertions of Mr. Samuel Hailstone. Money was subscribed towards the erection of a hall, and the purchase of a library, apparatus, &c., but, as Mr. James remarks, "The (then) vicar of Bradford having preached a sermon in which he enlarged on the irreligious tendency of a philosophizing spirit, several of the subscribers took fright and withdrew their subscriptions, and thus a society so auspiciously formed was broken up." In 1839 these scruples were overcome, owing to the energy of Mr. William Sharp, F.R.S., and a Philosophical Society was once more established, one of the objects of which was "the formation of a local museum, or a collection of the natural productions of the district within fifteen miles of Bradford." In the first year 174 ordinary and fourteen honorary members were elected. This society was resuscitated in 1865, the president being Lord Rosse, and the vice-presidents—Mr. J. Behrens, Rev. Dr. Burnet, Mr. H. W. Ripley, and Mr. M. W. Thompson. The first report of the council in 1866 stated that "an auspicious commencement was made with a roll of 282 members and sixty-two associates, of whom sixteen became life members, at a composition of fifty guineas, and two at the lower scale of twenty guineas; the remaining list comprising forty-five members, subscribing three guineas annually, fifty-one subscribing two guineas, and 168 one guinea." Lectures and papers were delivered by the most eminent men of science in the country. A museum was formed, in which the old town-horn of Bradford was deposited as a gift by Sir Titus Salt, Bart.; the geological collection formed by Mr. Richardson, of Northowram, was purchased; the mineralogical collection of the late Mr. Dawson, of Royds Hall, was deposited with the society; and the museum was enriched with other valuable presents. A house was taken in Manor Row, and the foundation of a scientific library was laid; a complete set of the Philosophical Transactions from its commencement in the year 1660, the annual Reports of the British Association, as well as a number of other books, were presented by the family of Mr. Dawson. The society also purchased a number of valuable works, and the reading room was kept open two evenings in each week. The premises being too small for all the objects of the society, the design of erecting a suitable lecture hall and museum was entertained. At the last annual meeting of the society, February 28, 1873, Mr. H. W. Ripley was elected president; the vice-presidents were Rev. Dr. Campbell, Mr. Titus Salt (Milner Field), Rev. Dr. Ryan, and Mr. M. W. Thompson. The advisability of erecting a building was again urged, and steps were being taken, in co-operation with the School of Art, to rear a joint structure that would be adequate for the efficient management of both institutions. The society was stated to possess an excellent museum, a scientific library of nearly 1000 volumes, a collection of philosophical instruments, &c. In conjunction with the Bradford Corporation and the committee of the Mechanics' Institute, the British Association has been induced to hold its meeting in Bradford in the autumn of 1873, which it was thought would be of considerable benefit, tending to stimulate and promote a more extended taste for philosophical research in the town. Mr. H. W. Ripley promised to head the subscription list for a new building with £1000, and it is thought that for about £10,000 an excellent structure might be erected. The Society of Arts was held in 1873 in the High School, Hallfield Road, tenanted temporarily by the boys of the Grammar School; and when they vacated the place in 1873, it was considered that the site would be an admirable place for the proposed building of the Philosophical Society. The number of members of the society in 1873 was 227, and of associates, principally ladies, 100; total, 327. The receipts for 1872 were £413 7s. 7d., and the expenditure £882 6s. 11d., including a deficiency brought over from 1871 of

£377 6s. 9d., leaving the deficiency in 1872, £468 19s. 4d. Every other society has succeeded well in Bradford, and this is specially deserving of success.

Bradford Art Treasures and Industrial Exhibition at the Mechanics' Institute.—With a view to clear away a debt of £5000 on the new building of the Mechanics' Institute at Bowling Green, an Art Treasures and Industrial Exhibition was opened in the institute on the 16th of July, 1873. The exhibition comprised an extensive and valuable collection of oil paintings, water-colour drawings, engravings, statuary, carving, bronzes, porcelain, pottery, selections from the South Kensington and India Museums, ancient armour from the Tower of London, and other antiquities. The machinery in motion included combing, spinning, weaving, printing, lithography, envelope-folding, card-making, glass-blowing, and other interesting arts and manufactures. In addition to these there were musical instruments, stained glass, mechanical models, electric and other scientific apparatus. The whole of the building, with the exception of the library, was devoted to the purposes of the exhibition. In addition to these varied attractions, concerts were given in the lecture hall. Underneath this hall, in a large unused room in the basement, Mr. John Parker, of Bowling, constructed an extensive grotto, with mimic waterfall and lake. Mr. Parker displayed considerable taste and ingenuity in the work, and produced a surprising effect in the circumscribed area on which he had to operate. The committee were liberally supported by the owners of works of art, and they could have obtained double the number of pictures that they required. The large class-rooms and other well-lighted apartments in the upper part of the building were found admirably adapted, not only for hanging paintings and water-colour drawings, but for the efficient display of other works of art generously lent to the committee. There was every prospect that the exhibition would prove as successful in a pecuniary point of view, as it was undoubtedly rich in the choicest productions of painters and artists in the higher departments of industry. The exhibition was opened under the auspices of a distinguished array of patrons.

APPENDIX.

CHURCHES AND CHAPELS IN BRADFORD.

Religious Denomination.	1851. Population, 103,778.		1871. Population, 145,827.		Increase between 1851 and 1872.	
	No. of Places of Worship.	No. of Sittings.	No. of Pl. of Worship, 1872.	No. of Sittings, 1872.	No. of Places of Worship.	No. of Sittings.
Church of England (a),	12	10,026	22	15,332	10	5,306
Presbyterians,	1	639	1	639	—	—
Congregationalists (b),	6	3,568	13	7,548	7	3,980
Baptists (c),	5	3,425	10	6,640	5	3,215
Society of Friends,	1	1,000	1	1,000	—	—
Unitarians,	1	490	1	490	—	—
Wesleyan Methodists,	12*	7,070	12	11,800	-	4,730
United Methodists,	3	1,440	5	3,050	2	1,610
New Connection,	1	773	1	1,000	—	227
Primitive Methodists,	5	1,980	10	3,781	5	1,801
Wesleyan Reformers,	3	810	4	2,100	1	1,290
Moravians (d),	1	286	1	286	—	—
Roman Catholics,	1	380	5	1,410	4	1,030
All others,	2	500†	4	250	2	dec. 250
Total,	54	32,387	90	55,326	36	22,939

* We are informed that this number was incorrect, there being only seven Wesleyan chapels in 1851.
† Allowance (100) for a defective return.

(a) Including three mission stations (430).
(b) Including five mission stations (880).
(c) Including two mission stations (600). Also large new chapel in course of erection.
(d) One very small mission room.

Coal Mines of the Bradford District.—The mineral statistics of the United Kingdom for the year 1871, published in 1872, give the number of collieries in the Bradford district, at forty-nine. The following are their names as furnished by Mr. Frank N. Wardell, colliery inspector for Yorkshire for the year 1871 :—

COLLIERIES IN THE BRADFORD DISTRICT.

Allerton (2), Aycliffe Hill (Horton), Bolton Wood, Booth Holme Field (Tong), Bowling (4), Bradford, Broom Hall, Bunkers Hill, Cleckheaton (2), Clifton, Cotton Hole (North Bierley), Culter Height, Dog Lane, Eccleshill, Haycliffe Uilt (Horton), Heaton, Heaton (Shipley), Holme Bank, Hunsworth, Laister Dyke, Little Horton, North Bierley (2), North Cliff, Red Hill (Tong), Rockwell, Scholes, Seventeens (Clifton), Shelf (2), Shipley, Shipley Moor, Smeddles (Bowling), Thornton, Thornton Road (2), Tong Street, Tong (3), Wibsey, Wibsey Bank Foot, Wike, Wroe.

The Bradford district in 1869 yielded 1,799,500 tons of coal.

DATES OF THE PRINCIPAL EVENTS CONNECTED WITH THE HISTORY OF THE BOROUGH OF BRADFORD.

A.D. 284 to 337.—Roman remains of this age found in iron mines near Bradford.—Roman roads in neighbourhood of Bradford.—Yorkshire: Past and Present, vol. ii. p. 243.

A.D. 600 to 800.—Anglian origin of the name of Bradford and of the names of the surrounding townships.—Vol. ii. p. 243.

1066.—Gamel, a Danish chief, lord of Bradford before the Norman Conquest.—Vol. ii. p. 244.

1084–86 —Account in Domesday Book of manor of Bradford and its six berewicks or subordinate manors, supposed to be Great and Little Horton, Manningham, Stanbury, Hayworth, and Oxenhope.—Vol. ii. p. 244.

1084–86.—Value of Bradford at time of Domesday Survey.—Vol. ii. p. 244.

1084–86.—Bradford granted by William the Conqueror to Ilbert de Laci, one of his Norman followers.—Vol. ii. p. 245.

Bradford in the hands of the De Lacis, earls of Lincoln from 1080 to 1311 —Vol. ii. p. 245.

About 1086.—Castle or manor-house of Bradford built by the De Lacis.—Vol. ii. p. 246.

1216–72.—Bradford as described in " Testa de Nevill."—Vol. ii. p. 248.

1246, 30th Henry III.—Bradford paid tax or tallage to the crown, equal to £40 of present money.—Vol. ii. p. 247.

1256, 40th Henry III.—Grant of market to Bradford.—Vol. ii. p. 247.

1273.—Inquiry into royal rights at Bradford, and into those of the De Lacis, lords of the manor.—Vol. ii. p. 247.

1291.—Valuation of the rectory, vicarage, and tithes of Bradford, in the time of Pope Nicholas.—Vol. ii. p. 249.

1294.—Charter of King Edward 1. for holding a market and a fair at Bradford.—Vol. ii. p. 249.

1311, 5th Edward II.—Inquiry into the value of Bradford on the death of Henry de Laci, the last earl of Lincoln.—Vol. ii. p. 251.

1311.—Lordship of Bradford in the hands of the Plantagenets, earls and dukes of Lancaster.—Vol. ii. p. 253.

1361.—Bradford in the hands of John of Gaunt, duke of Lancaster.—Vol. ii. p. 255.—Grant of land to John Northrop, of Manningham, Bradford, by John of Gaunt, held by blowing one blast of a horn on St. Martin's day.—Vol. ii. p. 256.

1365.—Extensive privileges to John of Gaunt and his tenants at Bradford granted by Edward III., which continued in force to the year 1690.—Vol. ii. p. 258.

1399, 1400 to 1482.—Bradford in the hands of the Plantagenet kings.—Vol. ii. p. 259.

1485.—Bradford in the time of the Tudors.—Vol. ii. p. 259.

1536.—Leland's account of Bradford in the reign of Henry VIII.—Vol. ii. p. 261.

1639.—Baptisms at Bradford this year, 209 ; marriages, 61 ; deaths, 183.

1642-45.—Bradford in the great civil war.—Vol. ii. p. 262.

1643.—The parliamentary general, Sir Thomas Fairfax, assembles his army at Bradford.—Vol. ii. p. 262.

1645.—Progress of Bradford from the close of the great civil war, 1644, to the accession of King George III., 1760.—Vol. ii. p. 268.

1665-66.—Plague raged at Bradford.

1690.—Trial as to the right of people of Bradford to be free from tolls throughout England, under Edward III.'s charter to John of Gaunt.—Inhabitants of Bradford free from tolls to this date.

1700.—Plan of Bradford, belonging to Mr. Edward Hailstone, showing the town to consist chiefly of half a dozen streets, forming a sort of cross, with three brooks running through them; the brooks and two bridges very clearly traced. Also a few houses in Goodman's End and Baker End.—James' "Bradford."

1727.—Daniel de Foe's account of Bradford at this time.—Vol. ii. p. 269.

1738.—Great number of persons receiving parish relief at Bradford.

1743.—Henry Marsden, of Wennington Hall, lord of manor of Bradford.

1744.—Water Company established at Bradford.

1768.—Bridge at Broadstones, Bradford, swept away in a great flood.

1773.—Introduction of water carriage at Bradford by the making of the Lancashire and Yorkshire or Leeds and Liverpool Canal, running within three miles of Bradford.—Vol. ii. p. 271.

1774.—Making of the Bradford Canal to join the Leeds and Liverpool Canal.—Vol. ii. p. 273.

1774 to 1800.—Progress of Bradford from the making of the canal to the end of the eighteenth century.—Vol. ii. p. 274.

1783.—Riotous mob in Bradford.

1789.—The Bowling and Low Moor and Bierley Iron Works constructed in the neighbourhood of Bradford.—Vol. ii. p. 276.

1790.—Water-works company incorporated by Act of Parliament.

1793.—Introduction of steam-power into Bradford.—Vol. ii. p. 275.

1793.—Court of Requests at Bradford.

1794.—Volunteer regiment raised, commanded by Colonel Busfield.

1798.—Flaxman, monument to Abraham Balme, a gentleman of Bradford.

1801.—Bradford at the commencement of the nineteenth century.—Vol. ii. p. 277.

1803.—Bill obtained for lighting and cleansing the town of Bradford.—Vol. ii. p. 277.

1819.—Steam-engines employed in mill-work in Bradford and its immediate neighbourhood, 492 horse-power.

1822.—Bill for lighting town with gas.—Vol. ii. p. 277.

1823.—The first Edward Baines' description of Bradford fifty years ago (1823).—Vol. ii. p. 278.

1825.—Procession of Bishop Blaize, the patron of wool-combers.—Great turn-out of the wool-combers.

1830.—Steam-engines, 1047 horse-power.

1831.—History of the Worsted Trade of Bradford.—Vol. i. pp. 673–696.
1831.—Manufactures of Bradford.—Vol. ii. p. 278.
1831.—The steam-power of Bradford.—Vol. ii. p. 279.
1831.—Value of trade of Bradford.—Vol. ii. p. 280.
1832.—Bradford made a parliamentary borough.—Vol. ii. p. 286.
1832.—List of members returned to Parliament by the borough of Bradford from 1832 to 1873.—Vol. ii. p. 286.
1834.—Court house of Bradford built.—Vol. ii. p. 292.
1834.—Bradford and North Bierley Unions.—Vol. ii. p. 292.
1837.—Destructive flood in brooks at Bradford.
1842–73.—Progress of the Water-works of Bradford.—Vol. ii. p. 282.
1846.—The railway system of Bradford from 1846 to 1873.—Vol. ii. p. 285.
1847.—Bradford made a municipal borough, and great works carried out by the Corporation.—Vol. ii. p. 286.
1847.—List of mayors of Bradford from 1847 to 1872.—Vol. ii. p. 288.
1851.—St. George's Hall, Bradford; foundation stone laid by the earl of Zetland.—Vol. ii. p. 291.
1851.—Petty Sessions and County Court of Bradford.
1852.—Bradford Poor Law Union Workhouse at Little Horton.
1853.—St. George's Hall, Bradford, completed.
1854.—Direct line of Railway to Leeds completed.
1861.—Number of inhabited houses, 22,518.
1863.—Manor and market of Bradford.—Vol. ii. p. 285.
1864.—Lord Palmerston laid foundation-stone of New Exchange.
1864–65.—Philosophical Society formed this year.
1865.—Model lodging houses, baths, and wash houses, the hospitals and charitable institutions, the club houses and banks of Bradford.—Vol. ii. pp. 316 to 322.
1865.—Chamber of Commerce at Bradford.—Vol. ii. p. 323.
1865.—The Volunteer movement in Bradford.—Vol. ii. p. 326.
1865.—Men and women of note born in, or connected with, Bradford.—Vol. ii. pp. 327 to 334.
1865.—The cemeteries of Bradford.—Vol. ii. p. 334.
1865.—Aspect of Bradford in 1873.—Vol. ii. p. 335.
1867.—The New Exchange of Bradford completed.—Vol. ii. p. 290.
1867.—The parliamentary and municipal boundaries of the borough identical, and no change made in the limits by the Reform Act of 1869.—Vol. ii. p. 287.
1867.—Area of borough of Bradford, 6508 acres, 2 roods, 39 perches; namely—Bradford, 1595 acres, 1 rood, 2 perches; Bowling, 1561 acres, 2 roods, 16 perches; Horton, 2033 acres, 39 perches; and Manningham, 1380 acres, 2 roods, 22 perches.—Vol. ii. p. 286.
1868.—Boundary Commissioners' report on Bradford.—Vol. ii. p. 314.
1868.—Free Library of Bradford.—Vol. ii. p. 314.
1868.—Sewage defæcation at Bradford.—Vol. ii. p. 315.
1870.—Foundation stone of new Mechanics' Institute at Bradford laid by Lord Houghton.

1870.—The Bradford School Board and its operations.—Vol. ii. p. 301.
1870.—Churches and chapels in Bradford.—Vol. ii. pp. 302 to 313.
1870.—Public parks of Bradford : their extent and beauty.—Vol. ii. p. 313.
1871.—The Bradford Grammar School reorganized.—Vol. ii. p. 297.
1871.—Modern establishments for education in Bradford.—Vol. ii. p. 299.
1871.—Population of Bradford, 145,827.
1872.—People's College founded at Bradford.
1872.—Bradford and district tramways.—Vol. ii. p. 338.
1872.—The Ripley Convalescent Home.—Vol. ii. p. 339.
1872.—The rate of Wages and salaries in the worsted trade.—Vol. ii. p. 342.
1872.—Rapid progress of population of Bradford in the present century.—Vol. ii. p. 343.
1873.—The new town hall of Bradford opened in 1873.—Vol. ii. p. 289.
1873.—Local Press of Bradford.—Vol. ii. p. 344.
1873.—Meeting of the Yorkshire Union of Mechanics' Institutes at Saltaire.—Vol. ii. p. 344.
1873.—The Bradford Philosophical Society, and the Meeting of the British Association at Bradford.—Vol. ii, p. 345.
1873.—Bradford Art Treasures and Industrial Exhibition at the Mechanics' Institute.—Vol. ii. p. 347.
1873.—Appendix.—Churches and Chapels at Bradford.—Vol. ii. p. 348.
1873.—Coal Mines of the Bradford District.—Vol. ii. p. 348.

www.ingramcontent.com/pod-product-compliance
Lightning Source LLC
Chambersburg PA
CBHW020318240426
43673CB00039B/852